MERGERS AND ACQUISITIONS IN PRACTICE

The growth in mergers and acquisitions (M&A) activity around the world masks a high rate of failure. M&A can provide companies with many benefits, but in the optimism and excitement of the deal many of the challenges are often overlooked. This comprehensive collection, bringing together an international team of contributors, moves beyond the theory to focus on the practical elements of mergers and acquisitions.

This hands-on, step-by-step volume provides strategies, frameworks, guidelines, and ample examples for managing and optimizing M&A performance, including:

- ways to analyze different types of synergy;
- understanding and analyzing cultural difference along corporate and national cultural dimensions, using measurement tools;
- using negotiation, due diligence, and planning to analyze the above factors; making use of this data during negotiation, screening, planning, agreement, and when deciding on post-merger integration approaches.

Students, researchers, and managers will find this text a vital resource when it comes to understanding this key facet of the international business world.

Shlomo Y. Tarba is Associate Professor in Business Strategy and Head of the Department of Strategy and International Business at Birmingham Business School, University of Birmingham, UK.

Sir Cary L. Cooper is the 50th Anniversary Professor of Organizational Psychology and Health at Manchester Business School, University of Manchester, UK, and President of the CIPD.

Riikka M. Sarala is Associate Professor of Management at the University of North Carolina at Greensboro, USA.

Mohammad F. Ahammad is Reader in Strategy and International Business at Sheffield Business School, Sheffield Hallam University, UK.

MERGERS AND ACQUISITIONS IN PRACTICE

Edited by Shlomo Y. Tarba, Sir Cary L. Cooper, Riikka M. Sarala, and Mohammad F. Ahammad

LONDON AND NEW YORK

First published 2017 by Routledge

2 Park Square, Milton Park, Abingdon, Oxon OX14 4RN
605 Third Avenue, New York, NY 10017

Routledge is an imprint of the Taylor & Francis Group, an informa business

First issued in paperback 2021

Publisher's Note

The publisher has gone to great lengths to ensure the quality of this reprint but points out that some imperfections in the original copies may be apparent.

British Library Cataloguing in Publication Data
A catalogue record for this book is available from the British Library

Library of Congress Cataloging in Publication Data
A catalog record for this book has been requested

ISBN: 978-1-138-78778-0 (hbk)
ISBN: 978-0-367-25383-7 (pbk)

Typeset in Bembo
by Keystroke, Neville Lodge, Tettenhall, Wolverhampton

CONTENTS

FIGURES

TABLES

CONTRIBUTORS

Timo Aarrevaara is a Professor of Public Management at the University of Lapland, and has professional experience in public administration as well as in research and teaching. Aarrevaara has participated in and conducted several evaluating and auditing projects, and acted as the principal investigator of a number of projects in higher education, including "The changing academic profession survey in Finland" (CAP), "The changing academic profession: the impact of globalisation, diversification and institutional reorganisation on academic work and employment conditions in Finland" (EUROAC-FIN), and Public Engagement Innovations for Horizon 2020 (PE2020, pilot initiatives). Professor Aarrevaara has strong international higher education research links, and is a co-editor of Springer's *The Changing Academy* Series and author or co-author of several papers and book chapters.

Mohammad F. Ahammad is a Reader (Associate Professor) in Strategy and International Business at Sheffield Hallam University, UK. Previously he was a Senior Lecturer at Nottingham Trent University, UK. Professor Ahammad is a researcher in the field of global strategy, international business, and human resource management. He holds a Ph.D. degree from the University of Sheffield. He has published his research studies in *Human Resource Management* (US, Wiley), *International Journal of Human Resource Management*, *International Business Review*, *International Marketing Review*, *International Studies of Management & Organization*, *European Journal of International Management*, and others. Professor Ahammad has served as a guest editor for special issues at the *International Journal of Human Resource Management*, *Human Resource Management Review*, *International Studies of Management & Organizations*, and *Thunderbird International Business Review*. His current projects include: strategic agility, organizational ambidexterity, pre-acquisition evaluation, negotiations, post-acquisition integration issues, and cross-border acquisition performance.

Ruth Alas, Estonian Business School, Tallinn, Estonia.

Tiiu Allikmäe, Estonian Business School, Tallinn, Estonia.

Florian Bauer is a Professor in the Department of Strategic Management, Marketing and Tourism, University of Innsbruck, and Department of Management and Law, MCI Management Centre, Innsbruck, Austria.

Agyenim Boateng is Professor of Finance and Banking in the Department of Finance, Accounting, and Risk at Glasgow Caledonian University, UK.

Fang Lee Cooke, Monash University, Australia.

Sir Cary L. Cooper is 50th Anniversary Professor of Organizational Psychology and Health, Manchester Business School, University of Manchester, UK. Professor Cooper is the author/editor of over 140 books on occupational stress, industrial and organizational psychology, and over 500 scholarly articles. He is currently founding editor of the *Journal of Organizational Behavior*, editor-in-chief of the *Blackwell Encyclopedia of Management* and co-editor-in-chief of the *Journal of Organizational Effectiveness: People and Performance*. He served as a guest editor for special issues at the *Journal of Management Studies, Human Resource Management, International Journal of Human Resource Management*, and others. Professor Cooper's work has been published in such journals as *Academy of Management Journal, Journal of Management, Academy of Management Executive, Personnel Psychology, Journal of Management Studies, Human Resource Management, Human Relations, British Journal of Management, Management Learning, Management International Review*, and others. He is an Honorary Fellow of the British Psychological Society and former Chair of the Academy of Social Sciences. Professor Cooper is President of the British Academy of Management, one of the first UK-based Fellows of the (American) Academy of Management, and President of the CIPD. In 2001, he was awarded a CBE in the Queen's Birthday Honours List. In June 2014, he was awarded a knighthood for services to social science.

Christoph Dörrenbächer, Berlin School of Economics and Law, Germany.

Tiit Elenurm, Estonian Business School, Tallinn, Estonia.

Fabian Jintae Froese, University of Goettingen, Germany.

Lars Geschwind is Associate Professor in Engineering Education Policy and Management, Research Leader and Director of Doctoral Studies at the School of Education and Communication in Engineering Science, KTH Royal Institute of Technology, Stockholm. He holds a PhD in History from Uppsala University and is affiliated to the Research Unit for Studies in Educational Policy and Educational

Philosophy (STEP) at the same university. His main research interests are higher education policy, institutional governance, academic leadership, and management and academic work. He is currently leading a number of projects focusing on change processes in higher education institutions, including e.g. governance and steering, quality assurance, academic careers, and partnership with industry. Most studies include a comparative component and a historical perspective. He has recently published and co-edited a book (Springer 2016) and a peer-reviewed journal (*European Journal of Higher Education*) on the topic mergers in higher education.

Steffen Robert Giessner, Department of Organization and Personnel Management, Rotterdam School of Management, Erasmus University, the Netherlands.

Keith W. Glaister is Professor of International Business at Warwick Business School, University of Warwick, UK.

Paulina Junni, Department of Strategy and Logistics, BI Norwegian Business School, Oslo, Norway.

David Kroon, VU University, Amsterdam, the Netherlands.

Ian P. L. Kwan, School of Economics and Business Administration, University of Navarra, Spain.

George Lordofos is Principal Lecturer and Head in the School of Strategy, Leeds Business School, Leeds Metropolitan University, UK.

Anna Lupina-Wegener, University of Applied Sciences and Arts, Western Switzerland, Switzerland.

Kurt Matzler, Professor, Faculty of Economics and Management, Free University of Bozen-Bolzano, Italy.

Luiz Montanheiro, Management School, University of Sheffield, UK.

Laila Nordstrand Berg has a PhD in Public Policy and Administration. She is working as a researcher and project coordinator at the University of Agder, Norway, where she is participating in projects comparing health and higher education in different countries. Laila's interests are related to the intersection between public policy and administration, organizational studies, reforms, and management in the sectors.

Rómulo Pinheiro is Professor of Public Policy and Administration and Head of the Research Group in Governance and Leadership in the Public Sector (GOLEP) at the University of Agder, Norway. He is also a Senior Researcher and Project Leader at Agderforskning, and a Visiting Professor at the University of Tampere,

Finland. Rómulo's research interests are located at the intersection of the fields of public policy and administration, organizational studies, regional science and innovation studies, and higher education studies. He has published extensively on the changing nature of higher education systems and institutions, including being a guest editor for several special issues (*European Journal of Higher Education, Public Administration Review, Science and Public Policy, Tertiary Education and Management*). He has also co-edited a number of volumes on topics such as higher education and regional development (Routledge, 2012), mergers in higher education (Springer, 2016), higher education in the BRICS countries (Springer, 2015), and comparing the fields of health care and higher education (Emerald, 2016).

Riikka M. Sarala is an Associate Professor of International Business at the University of North Carolina, Greensboro, USA. She completed her Ph.D. degree at Hanken School of Economics, Helsinki, Finland. In addition, she completed part of her Ph.D. studies at Columbia University, New York City, USA, and at EM Lyon, France. Her research focuses on how organizations increase their flexibility through mergers and acquisitions, knowledge transfer, ambidexterity, and HR practices. She has published articles in the *Journal of Management, Strategic Management Journal, Journal of Management Studies, Journal of International Business Studies, Academy of Management Learning and Education, Academy of Management Perspectives, British Journal of Management*, and others. She is an associate editor of the *Journal of Management Studies* and a member of the editorial board of the *British Journal of Management.* Professor Sarala has received several awards, including the Academy of Management Global Forum Best Symposium Award, Strategic Management Society Runner-up Award for Best Student, and Bryan School Research Excellence Award. She has served as a guest editor for special issues at the *Journal of Management Studies, Group and Organization Management*, and *Human Resource Management Review.*

Marina Schmitz, University of Goettingen, Germany.

Lars Schweizer, UBS-Endowed Chair for Strategic Management, Goethe-University, Frankfurt, Germany.

Elizabeth Solberg, Department of Leadership and Organizational Behavior, BI Norwegian Business School, Oslo, Norway.

Andreas Strobl is Assistant Professor in the Department of Strategic Management, Marketing, and Tourism, University of Innsbruck, Austria.

Shlomo Y. Tarba is an Associate Professor (Reader) in Business Strategy and Head of the Department of Strategy and International Business at the Business School, University of Birmingham, UK, and a Visiting Professor at Recanati Business School, Tel-Aviv University, Israel. He received his Ph.D. degree in Strategic Management from Ben-Gurion University and Master's in Biotechnology degree at the Hebrew University of Jerusalem, Israel. His research interests include strategic agility, organizational ambidexterity and innovation, and mergers and acquisitions. Professor Tarba is a member of the editorial boards of the *Journal of Management Studies*, *British Journal of Management*, *Human Resource Management* (US, Wiley), and *Journal of World Business*. He has served as a guest editor for special issues at the *Journal of Organizational Behavior* (US, Wiley), *Human Resource Management* (US, Wiley), and *Management International Review*. His research papers have been published or are forthcoming in such journals as the *Journal of Management* (SAGE), *Academy of Management Perspectives*, *California Management Review*, *British Journal of Management*, *Human Resource Management*, *Management International Review*, *International Business Review*, *International Journal of Human Resource Management*, *Human Resource Management Review*, *International Studies of Management and Organization*, *Thunderbird International Business Review*, and others. One of his papers was selected for and published in the *Best Paper Proceedings of the Academy of Management* (USA) in 2006. Professor Tarba's two recent co-authored books are *A Comprehensive Guide to Mergers and Acquisitions: Managing the Critical Success Factors across Every Stage of the M&A Process* (Pearson and Financial Times Press, 2014) and *Mergers, Acquisitions, and Strategic Alliances: Understanding the Process* (Palgrave Macmillan, 2011). His consulting experience includes biotechnological and telecom companies, as well as such industry associations as the Israeli Rubber and Plastic Industry Association and the US–Israel Chamber of Commerce.

Dag Olaf Torjesen is Associate Professor at the University of Agder, Norway. He is an expert on the health care sector and has published and consulted widely in the area, including comparative studies within the Nordic regions.

Rolf van Dick, Goethe-University, Frankfurt, Germany.

Riina Varts, Estonian Business School, Tallinn, Estonia.

Winno V. Wangenheim, WHU–Otto Beisheim School of Management, Germany.

Natalie Witzmann, Edinburgh Napier University, UK.

Sut I Wong, Department of Communication and Culture, BI Norwegian Business School, Oslo, Norway.

1

MERGERS AND ACQUISITIONS IN PRACTICE

A state-of-art and future directions

Shlomo Y. Tarba, Sir Cary L. Cooper, Riikka M. Sarala, and Mohammad F. Ahammad

The frequency and scale of cross-border and domestic mergers and acquisitions have significantly increased during the past two decades in spite of continuous reports on their high failure rates (e.g., Cartwright and Cooper, 1996, 2000; Gomes, Weber, Brown, and Tarba, 2011; Junni, Sarala, Tarba, and Weber, 2015; Zhang, Ahammad, Tarba, Cooper, Glaister, and Wang, 2015). Surprisingly, research studies conducted in different research streams (business strategy, finance, accounting, organizational behavior, and human resource management) have generally failed to step into each other's turf, hence missing the opportunities for cross-fertilization (Weber and Tarba, 2010; Weber, Tarba, and Reichel, 2009).

Several studies (Sarala, Junni, Cooper, and Tarba, Forthcoming; Weber and Tarba, 2014; Weber, Tarba, and Reichel, 2011; Gomes, Angwin, Weber, and Tarba, 2013) point out that most of the existing research on global mergers and acquisitions has not been systematic or linked to any comprehensive theory. Furthermore, rarely have models been proposed that were applicable across different organizations, as well as various national, cultural, and industry settings.

In our edited book we have compiled a diversity of chapters that deal with an M&A process highlighting the degree of organizational change and its resultant outcomes.

The chapter by Boateng, Lordofos, and Glaister considers the motives for cross-border M&As utilizing pre-merger press announcements and 44 post-merger interviews based on a sample of 22 companies from 8 European countries. Their findings suggest that there are no differences between the secondary data sources reporting the motives for M&As prior to the deal and the primary, first-hand data gathered from interviews with senior managers after the merger deal.

The next chapter by Ahammad, Tarba, Glaister, Kwan, Sarala, and Montanheiro, which explores the strategic motivation for cross-border mergers and acquisitions (CBM&As) for a sample of UK firms acquiring North American and European firms, lends support to the theories of strategic positioning and the resource-based view. The highest-ranked strategic motives for CBM&As are enabling presence in new markets, enabling faster entry to market, facilitating international expansion, gaining new capabilities and obtaining strategic assets.

The following chapter by Pinheiro, Aarrevaara, Nordstrand Berg, Geschwind, and Torjesen addresses the following question: 'What can be learnt from public sector mergers that could assist in the planning and execution of successful strategic mergers more broadly?' Undertaking a comprehensive literature review across two sectors of the economy – health and higher education – the authors investigate merger dynamics involving public hospitals and universities, and point to the existing gaps in the rationale for merging, the merger process, and the tangible effects.

Froese, Schmitz, and Wangenheim emphasize that despite the increasing importance of Chinese M&As, little research exists on the outward M&As of Chinese and other emerging market multinational enterprises (EM MNEs). To fill this void, their chapter is aimed at increasing our understanding of the cross-border M&As of Chinese MNEs into industrialized countries by investigating both the pre-M&A and post-M&A integration phase. The case of the Sany and Putzmeister acquisition, one of the most well-known Chinese M&A acquisitions in Germany, is used in order to illustrate their model.

The next chapter by Schweizer deals with the integration of an acquired, small biotechnology firm by a large pharmaceutical company. Based on the in-depth examination of organizational integration activities of German-based Merck's acquisition of Boston-based Lexigen Pharmaceuticals, this chapter concludes by developing a practical post-acquisition integration framework.

The chapter by Cooke examines a number of specific human resource management (HRM) problems and challenges encountered in domestic and cross-border M&As. Drawing on empirical examples of extant studies on M&As in different organizational, industrial, national, and international contexts, it illustrates the complexity and difficulties M&A partners may experience, outlines some of the key HR activities throughout the M&A process, and, in doing so, reveals the dynamics of political, institutional, cultural, and psychological factors at play in post-M&A integration.

The following chapter by Humborstad, Solberg, Junni, and Giessner systematically reviews four relevant theoretical landscapes addressing human resource issues in M&As in an effort to provide a more comprehensive picture of the role that HRM plays in facilitating the M&A process and explain how its implementation can contribute to M&A success. Conditions under which HRM should be most effective in facilitating positive M&A outcomes are also addressed.

In the next chapter Kroon presents a study of two recently merged dairy firms in the Netherlands in order to illustrate the importance of employee communication and perceived organizational cultural differences as determinants of employees' identification with the post-merger organization. Specifically, he shows that a perceived communication climate mediates the relation between merger communication and post-merger identification, and merger communication moderates the relation between cultural differences and post-merger identification.

Building on literature on multiple identities and identity complexity, the chapter by Lupina-Wegener and van Dick reveals that constructing a shared identity is crucial to the success of mergers and acquisitions, and has been typically conceptualized as both *content* – i.e. the perception of a common in-group identity – and *process* – i.e. the degree of identification with the new organization. Moreover, it extends current operationalization of a shared identity in M&As by introducing a more nuanced concept of multiple shared identities (MSI) that accounts for multiple group memberships that are shared by organizational members.

The following chapter by Witzmann and Dörrenbächer attempts to clarify whether cultural due diligence (CDD) is a necessary prerequisite for successful post-merger integration (PMI). It concludes that the CDD process creates considerable value for the subsequent PMI as it facilitates a fast and smooth cultural integration and as such accelerates the operative integration of M&As.

Alas, Elenurm, Allikmäe, and Varts examine the Estonian Hansabank's acquisition of the Lithuanian Lietuvos Taupomasis Bankas. They explore whether activities of the personnel department, such as staffing the new structure and top management team development, were key success factors that helped to improve the management of the Lithuanian bank and achieve the desired organizational culture. By doing so, they enhance our understanding of the role of human resource management in change management processes resulting from cross-border acquisitions in transition economies.

Bauer, Strobl, and Matzler review the studies that indicate positive, negative, U-shaped, inverted U-shaped, and non-significant relationships between acquisition experience and performance. Drawing a more fine-grained and nuanced perspective on acquisition experience, their chapter investigates why, when, and how acquisition experience can have beneficial or detrimental effects.

The final chapter by Kwan presents a comprehensive review of relevant theories and methods from the strategy literature on organizational learning (market-based view, resource-based view, knowledge-based view, and transaction-cost approach) and the finance literature on valuation (the discounted cash flow, real options, and event study methods), applying them to the strategic alliances and thus deepening our understanding of these important and complex business transactions.

We hope that the chapters in this book, taken together, will encourage further research on mergers and acquisitions, and provide important insights to both scholars and executives.

References

Cartwright, S. and Cooper, C. L. (1996). *Managing Mergers, Acquisitions, and Strategic Alliances: Integrating People and Cultures*. Butterworth-Heinemann, Oxford and Boston, MA.

Cartwright, S. and Cooper, C. L. (2000). *HR Know-How in Mergers and Acquisitions*. Chartered Institute of Personnel and Development, London.

Gomes, E., Angwin, D., Weber, Y., and Tarba, S. Y. (2013). Critical success factors through the mergers and acquisitions process: revealing pre- and post-M&A connections for improved performance. *Thunderbird International Business Review*, 55, 13–36.

Gomes, E., Weber, Y., Brown, C., and Tarba, S. Y. (2011). *Mergers, Acquisitions and Strategic Alliances: Understanding the Process*. Palgrave Macmillan, London and New York.

Junni, P., Sarala, R., Tarba, S. Y., and Weber, Y. (2015). Strategic agility in acquisitions. *British Journal of Management*, 26, 596–616.

Sarala, R. M., Junni, P., Cooper, C. L., and Tarba, S. (forthcoming). A socio-cultural perspective on knowledge transfer in mergers and acquisitions. *Journal of Management*.

Weber, Y. and Tarba, S. Y. (2010). Human resource practices and performance of mergers and acquisitions in Israel. *Human Resource Management Review*, 20, 203–211.

Weber, Y. and Tarba, S. Y. (2014). Strategic agility: a state-of-art. *California Management Review*, 56, 3, 1–8.

Weber, Y., Tarba, S. Y., and Reichel, A. (2009). International mergers and acquisitions performance revisited: the role of cultural distance and post-acquisition integration approach. In C. Cooper and S. Finkelstein (Eds.) *Advances in Mergers and Acquisitions*, Vol. 8, Emerald Publishing, Bingley.

Weber, Y., Tarba, S. Y., and Reichel, A. (2011). International mergers and acquisitions performance: acquirer nationality and integration approaches. *International Studies of Management and Organization*, 41, 3, 9–24.

Zhang, J., Ahammad, M. F., Tarba, S., Cooper, C. L., Glaister, K. W., and Wang, J. (2015). The effect of leadership style on talent retention during merger and acquisition integration: evidence from China. *International Journal of Human Resource Management*, 26, 1021–1050.

2

MOTIVES FOR EUROPEAN MERGERS AND ACQUISITIONS

Analysis of pre-merger press announcements and post-merger interviews

Agyenim Boateng, George Lordofos, and Keith W. Glaister

The motivation for mergers and acquisitions (M&As) has been a topic of immense interest to academics and practitioners over the past two decades. This interest stems from the various empirical findings which suggest that more than two-thirds of all M&A deals are financial failures when measured in terms of their ability to deliver profitability (Ravenscraft and Scherer, 1987; Tetenbaum, 1999; Hudson and Barnfield, 2001). In a more board context, prior studies suggest that the ability of M&As to create value for acquiring shareholders has been mixed. One stream of research has reported significant positive returns for acquirers (see, Kang, 1993; Markides and Ittner, 1994; Kiymaz, 2003). Other studies have found negative and insignificant bidders' returns (Eun, Kolodny and Scheraga, 1996; Datta and Puia, 1995; Aw and Chatterjee, 2004). Studies such as those by Erez-Rein et al. (2004) and Carleton (1997) have noted that M&As, generally fail to meet their anticipated goals. Despite the apparent failure of many M&As, we continue to see a rising trend in this activity. For example, UNCTAD (2006) reported that over 80 percent of world foreign direct investments (FDI) are carried out via cross-border M&As.

The above empirical evidence raises the question as to why companies persist with M&A transactions, given the solid evidence of their relative failure. The paradox of whether M&As create value for the acquiring firms is central to the study of M&As. Yet a number of the studies that have attempted to examine the motives for M&As by surveying senior managers have encountered some methodological criticism. It is argued that studies that rely on an *ex post* assessment of senior managers' opinions are flawed due to self-justification or social desirability bias. The latter, defined as a tendency of the respondent to present him/herself in a favorable light (Nunnally, 1978), has been recognized as a major problem that can adversely affect the validity of studies in social science disciplines (see Neeley and Cronley, 2004; Fisher, 1993; Bruner, 2002). Researchers such as Fisher (2000) and Mick (1996) have called for increased attention to social desirability bias in design, measure construction, and analysis.

Given the high rate of failure for M&As to meet their anticipated goals, it is important to ask why a chief executive officer (CEO) should give correct answers to questions concerning the motives for M&A when the M&A has failed to deliver the anticipated outcomes of the M&A transaction. The main focus of this study is to shed light on the above question by examining the effects of social desirability bias by carrying out correlational analysis on the pre-merger and post-merger motivation for M&A in eight European countries. We do so by examining senior managers' opinions regarding the motives for the M&A post-M&A and compare these responses with data collected from secondary sources (press reports) at the time of the M&A announcement. We undertake this procedure in order to shed light on the reliability of data provided by senior managers through interviews after the M&A.

This chapter contributes to the literature in two important ways. First, the study adds to the discussion of the effects of social desirability bias in M&A research by comparing the differences between motives given in interviews with senior managers and motives identified in press reports published at the time of the M&A announcement. Such triangulation linking data on motivation prior to and following the M&A has been reported only rarely in the finance and strategic management literature. Second, this approach provides a potentially fruitful way of shedding light on the reliability of studies that use managers' *ex post* assessments of M&As, which are common in strategic management and marketing research.

The rest of the chapter is organized into four sections. The first of these briefly reviews the relevant literature and develops the hypothesis of the study. The next sets out the research method and sample characteristics. Then we present the findings and discussion. Finally, we discuss the implications for management and present our conclusions.

Literature review and hypothesis development

Literature review

Self-report questionnaires are commonly used in social science research for a number of reasons, including convenience, ease of use, and low cost. They are often also an effective way of measuring unobservable attributes, such as values, preferences, intentions, perceptions, and opinions about particular issues (Ganster, Hennessey and Luthans, 1983; De Jong, Pieters and Fox, 2010; Kim and Kim, 2016). In attempting to identify the motives for M&As, researchers commonly ask respondents to complete questionnaires containing questions with Likert-scale type responses. However, answers to questions on motives for acquisitions with Likert-scale type responses are often susceptible to social desirability bias due to the respondents' tendency to answer in a more socially acceptable way (Fisher, 1993; Neeley and Cronley, 2004).

Prior literature suggests that social desirability bias may take two forms: self-deceptive enhancement and impression management (Zerbe and Paulhus, 1987; Paulhus, 1984, 1991). Self-deceptive enhancement refers to the tendency to describe oneself in an inflated – albeit honestly held – manner and to see oneself in a positive, overconfident light. This type of bias is driven by the desire to see oneself as competent and self-reliant, to protect self-beliefs, and to hold off anxiety and depression (Kim and Kim, 2016). Paulhus (1986) argues that because of optimism and positivistic bias, the self-deceiver is more likely to say good things about him/herself, and report inflated or overconfident views of his/her skills and capabilities.

In comparison, impression management describes respondents' attempts to distort their self-reported actions in a positive manner to maintain a favorable image (Paulhus, 1984). Impression management is associated with the desire to portray oneself in a socially conventional way (Paulhus, 1991). Respondents act in this way to save face and maintain social approval (Lalwani, Shavitt and Johnson, 2006).

The distortion occurs through both self-deception and impression management (Barrick and Mount, 1996).

Nyaw and Ng (1994) and Paulhus (1991) point out that when research does not control for social desirability bias, the validity of findings may be questioned. Social desirability bias poses a major threat to construct validity, making it unclear whether measures actually represent their intended constructs (Cote and Buckley, 1987). In short, construct invalidity directly leads to inferential problems, depending on the validity of other measures. Supporting the above line of thinking, Ganster, Hennessey and Luthans (1983) argue that social desirability bias may understate the relationship between two or more variables (suppressor effect), provide an inflated correlation between independent and dependent variables (spurious effect), or moderate the relationship between those variables (moderator effect). Fisher (1993) notes that research that does not recognize and compensate for social desirability bias may lead to unwarranted theoretical or practical conclusions.

It is pertinent to point out that social desirability bias has been found in virtually all types of self-reporting measures and across the social science literature (Zerbe and Paulhus, 1987), and M&A studies are no exception (see Bruner, 2002).

The literature suggests that attempts to check for social desirability bias after the data have been collected include social desirability response (SDR) scales, such as the Marlowe–Crowne Social Desirability Scale (MCSDS)[1] and the Balanced Inventory of Desirable Responding (BIDR),[2] applied mostly in marketing (see Mick, 1996; Podsakoff et al., 2003; Steenkamp, De Jong and Baumgartner, 2010). However, the use of SDR scales has been challenged (Paulhus, 2002; Smith and Ellingson, 2002). Scholars point to the difficulty of separating valid personality content in the SDR measures from the bias they are meant to measure. Other researchers, such as Aguinis, Pierce and Quigley (1993), Fisher (1993), Hill, Dill and Davenport (1988), Jones and Sigall (1971), Roese and Jamieson (1993); Tourangeau and Smith (1996), suggest the use of indirect questioning and bogus pipeline techniques[3] to prevent SDR from biasing the measures in the first place. While such approaches may partially alleviate SDR, the effectiveness of these techniques is limited because they may introduce other biases (indirect questions), and their implementation may be expensive and prone to ethical issues (bogus pipeline) (Tourangeau, Rips and Rasinski, 2000).

Hypothesis development

A number of studies have been conducted on the motivation for M&As by examining *ex post* assessments of senior managers' opinions regarding the motives for M&As (see Walter and Barney, 1990; Mukherjee, Kiymaz and Baker, 2004). These studies have relied solely on senior managers' opinions after the M&A has taken place. As far as we are aware, no published study has identified motives at the time of the M&A announcement and compared them with the rationales given post-merger, using both secondary and primary data sources. Comparing the motives given for M&As from data sources (press reports) available at the time of the announcement with motives given in post-merger interviews with senior managers provides a way of assessing the reliability of primary data obtained from managers post-M&A.

It is argued that studies relying on senior managers' opinions obtained after the merger or acquisition has occurred may be flawed (Walter and Barney, 1990). Reasons given by researchers such as Goldberg (1983) suggest that managers may not provide accurate responses because of self-justification or social desirability. Another argument put forward by critics is that, due to memory decay, managers may have forgotten the real motives for the M&As and may therefore give inaccurate information (Bruner, 2002). Moreover, managers who are aware of the motives at the time of the deal may have left the company and so responses provided by current managers with limited information may be misleading or inaccurate. Such problems impair the credibility of the data collected from senior managers after the M&As have taken place.

Despite these potential problems, it may also be maintained that senior managers are responsible officials and are best placed to answer strategic questions related to M&As. Mergers and acquisitions are important strategic decisions and therefore the motives for engaging in them are likely to persist in the memories of those responsible for making those decisions. Glaister and Buckley (1996) make this argument in connection with the motives for the formation of international joint ventures. Moreover, official company minutes and records would be kept on the discussions and deliberations of senior executives relating to such crucial investment decisions. This means that if the senior managers who were responsible for taking the M&A decision have left the company, current managers should have records on which to base their answers.

In light of this discussion, we propose the following hypothesis:

> *There will be no difference between the motives given by senior managers for the M&A published in press reports at the time of the deal announcement and the motives provided by senior managers for the same M&A obtained by direct data collection some time after the M&A has been completed.*

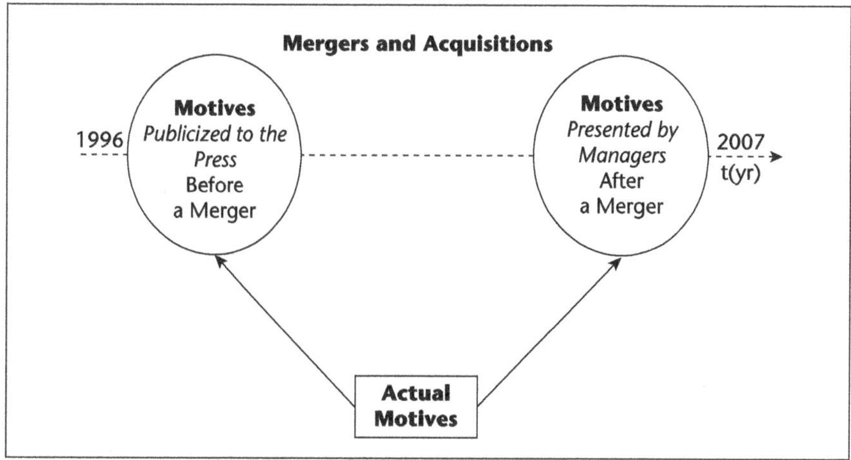

FIGURE 2.1 Conceptual model

The conceptual model shown in Figure 2.1 illustrates the hypothesis that motives identified at the pre-M&A and post-M&A stages will be identical, irrespective of the time gap between the announcement of the M&A and the collection of data in interviews.

Research method

This study involves M&As from eight European countries which were initiated and completed over the period 1996–2007. The sampling frame for the study was derived from published reports of M&As in *Chemical Market Reporter* (6/3/2000, 19/8/2002, 23/2/2004), *Chemical Engineering News* (16/12/2002), the *Financial Times*, and *Hoover's Online*. Two techniques were employed to collect the data: namely, secondary sources and interviews. First, from the press reports, we selected 22 benchmark companies that provided a good cross-section from the sampling frame. Data were collected in respect of the motives for 22 M&As which occurred in different time periods in 8 European countries from the press announcements in the *Financial Times*, *Chemical Market Reporter*, company press releases, and reports made at the time of the M&A announcement.

In the second phase of the data collection process, we used a multiple interview approach involving two senior officials of each of the 22 M&As. The design of the questions for the interviews was based on the aims of the study and literature review. The questionnaire for the interviews was divided into two main parts: the first part was concerned with the company's background (e.g. products, markets, and size); the second part contained questions on the motives for the company's decision to engage in the M&A. To encourage the respondents to disclose an accurate set of motives for the M&A, we assured them of confidentiality, told them that the information provided would be used only for academic purposes, and explained that the names of the managers would not be disclosed when the results were published.

Between 2000 and 2008, 44 open and semi-structured interviews, 95 percent by telephone and 5 percent personal, were conducted to elicit data from the senior managers of the same 22 benchmark companies in the 8 European countries.

Sample

The characteristics of the sample are summarized in Table 2.1. The respondents were key decision-makers involved in the M&As. An examination of the job titles of the respondents revealed: 15.6 percent were senior managers in charge of mergers and acquisitions; 25 percent were finance directors; 31.2 percent were managing directors; 18.8 percent were others, including R&D managers, vice-president, chief technology officer, and vice-chairman; and 9.4 percent were corporate communication directors. It is likely that these respondents were not only familiar with the acquisition strategy but were involved in strategic decision-making relating to the M&As of their respective companies. We carried out the interviews with the 44 respondents (2 from each of the 22 M&As) between 2000 and 2008 with respect to M&As that occurred between 1996 and 2007. Each interview lasted between 30 and 45 minutes and was recorded, allowing the researchers to pay more attention to the respondents and to ask supplementary questions in light of their answers.

Analysis

All the interviews and the secondary data from the press announcements were analysed by building categories. We applied the rules of 'pattern matching' and comparative methods to draw conclusions (Yin, 1994; Miles and Huberman, 1994). To derive further in-depth inferences, the complex relationships among the variables were studied for each M&A, using the content-analysis and explanation-building modes of analysis. The individual motives were classified and awarded scores

TABLE 2.1 Characteristics of the sample

Country of acquirer	*Number*	*%*	*Acquirer turnover in $billion*	*Number*	*%*
United Kingdom	6	27.4	5–15	11	50.0
Switzerland	5	22.7	Over 15–25	3	13.60
Netherlands	3	13.6	Over 25–35	4	18.20
Germany	2	9.1	Over 35	4	18.20
France	2	9.1			
Belgium	2	9.1			
Sweden	1	4.5			
Spain	1	4.5			
Total	22	100	Total	22	100

depending on the emphasis given to them for the M&A formation at the time of announcement and during the interviews. The assigned scores were:

- 1 = not mentioned;
- 2 = important;
- 3 = very important.

A two sample t-test was implemented to test for differences in means of the importance of the motives for the M&As between the two data sources.

Findings

Motivation for M&As: secondary data and primary data compared

The analysis of the differences between secondary data (press) and primary data (post-merger interviews) is shown in Table 2.2. The rank order of the motivation for M&A formation based on the mean measure of the importance of 14 motives is also shown Table 2.2. For the full set of motives for mergers and acquisitions from secondary data, the median measure is exceeded by seven motives: speed of expansion (2.43); acquire strategic asset (2.00); reduce riskiness of the firm (1.94);

TABLE 2.2 Motives for M&As in European firms: secondary data versus primary data

Motivation	*Data source*	*Rank*	*Mean*	*SD*	*t-value*
Revenue/profit enhancement	Secondary	6	1.62	0.50	
	Primary	5	1.81	0.40	–1.17
Managerial synergy	Secondary	7	1.50	0.52	
	Primary	11	1.26	0.25	1.05
Reducing the riskiness of the firm	Secondary	3	1.94	0.25	
	Primary	6	1.72	0.50	1.24
Operating synergy	Secondary	5	1.63	0.50	
	Primary	4	1.83	0.40	–1.68
Access to R&D capabilities	Secondary	12	1.25	0.45	
	Primary	8	1.56	0.51	1.84*
Acquire strategic asset	Secondary	2	2.00	0.00	
	Primary	2	2.06	1.06	–0.84
Taking advantage of good location	Secondary	10	1.38	0.50	
	Primary	12	1.31	0.48	0.36
Access to channels of distribution	Secondary	8	1.45	0.44	
	Primary	7	1.69	0.48	–1.67
Increasing market share/power	Secondary	9	1.44	0.51	
	Primary	10	1.38	0.51	0.79
Speed of expansion	Secondary	1	2.43	1.51	
	Primary	1	2.83	1.18	–1.71

(continued)

TABLE 2.2 Motives for M&As in European firms: secondary data versus primary data *(continued)*

Motivation	*Data source*	*Rank*	*Mean*	*SD*	*t-value*
Enhance prestige and job security	Secondary	14	1.00	0.00	
	Primary	13	1.15	0.42	–0.91
Accelerate growth/increase size	Secondary	4	1.81	0.40	
	Primary	3	1.87	0.34	–0.47
Circumvent trade barrier	Secondary	13	1.19	0.40	
	Primary	14	1.06	0.25	1.05
Product portfolio extension	Secondary	11	1.31	0.40	
	Primary	9	1.44	0.51	0.71

Notes: The individual motives were collected from secondary sources at the time of merger announcement and compared with those obtained from primary sources through interviews after the acquisitions.
* $p < 0.10$.

accelerate growth/increase size (1.81); operating synergy (1.63); revenue/profit enhancement (1.62); and managerial synergy (1.50). For the primary data, the median measure is exceeded by eight motives: speed of expansion (2.83); acquire strategic asset (2.06); accelerate growth/increase size (1.87); operating synergy (1.83); revenue/profit enhancement (1.81); reduce riskiness of the firm (1.72); access to channels of distribution (1.69); and access to R&D capabilities (1.56). Both data sources indicate that 'faster entry into new market' and acquiring strategic assets are the highest-ranked motives.

The t-test results indicate that there is only one significant difference ($p < 0.10$) between the mean scores of the motives announced in the press prior to the merger deals and the information provided by senior managers in interviews after the deals. This renders strong support to our hypothesis. Moreover, this finding provides strong justification for relying on information provided by senior managers during interviews regarding the motives for mergers and acquisitions.

Conclusions and implications

The past four decades have witnessed an increasing volume of cross-border M&A activity. Commensurate with the rising volume of M&As has been the number of studies attempting to explain why M&As take place against a backdrop of prior studies that suggest the failure rate of M&As ranges between 46 and 82 percent (see Kitching, 1967; Jensen and Ruback, 1983; Hunt, 1990; Jarrell and Poulsen, 1984). Most prior studies have investigated the motives for M&As using data based on the opinions of senior managers (see Walter and Barney, 1990; Ingham, Kran and Lovestam, 1992; Brouthers, Hastenburg and Van den Ven, 1998; Boateng and Bjortuft, 2003). In contrast, this study uses data collected from secondary sources (press reports) at the time of merger announcements and then compares them with data based on the opinions of senior managers interviewed after the M&A deals.

Such triangulation is rarely tested empirically in the finance and strategic management literature. We find that, with the exception of one motive, there are no significant differences between the means of the motives from each data source. This finding, therefore, renders support for our hypothesis.

The conclusion to be drawn is that primary data based on the *ex post* assessment of the opinions of senior managers are valid and reliable. This is contrary to the views of some critics who have claimed that studies using data from such sources are flawed. The implications of this research are that studies relying on *ex post* assessment of senior managers' opinions relating to the motives for M&A formation are sound and that such studies are unlikely to suffer from social desirability bias.

Notes

1 MCSDS, the most commonly used social desirability bias assessment, conceptualizes social desirability bias as an individual's need for approval.
2 BIDR measures social desirability bias in two separate constructs: impression management and self-deception.
3 Bogus Pipeline techniques comprise a set of procedures that lead respondents to believe that researchers have a powerful, sophisticated, and practically infallible lie detector to help reduce the social desirability component of traditional self-report measures in social psychological research (Jones and Sigall, 1971; Aguinis and Handelsman, 1997).

References

Aguinis, H. and Handelsman, M. M. (1997). Ethical issues in the use of the Bogus Pipeline, *Journal of Applied Social Psychology*, 27 (7), 557–573.

Aguinis, H. and Henle, C. A. (2001). Empirical assessment of the ethics of the Bogus Pipeline, *Journal of Applied Social Psychology*, 31 (2), 352–375.

Aguinis, H., Pierce, C. A. and Quigley, B. M. (1993). Conditions under which a Bogus Pipeline procedure enhances the validity of self-reported cigarette smoking: a meta-analytic review, *Journal of Applied Social Psychology*, 23, 352–373.

Aw, M. and Chatterjee, R. (2004). The performance of UK firms acquiring large cross-border and domestic takeover targets, *Applied Financial Economics*, 14, 337–349.

Barrick, M. R. and Mount, M. K. (1996). Effects of impression management and self deception on the predictive validity of personality constructs, *Journal of Applied Psychology*, 81, 261–272.

Boateng, A. and Bjortuft, V. (2003). An analysis of motives for mergers and acquisitions: evidence from Norway, paper deliver at the BAM Conference, Harrogate, UK.

Brouthers, K., Hastenburg P. V. and Van den Van, J. (1998). If most mergers fail why are they so popular?, *Long Range* Planning, 31(3), 347–358.

Bruner, R. F. (2002). Does M&A pay? A survey of evidence for the decision- maker, *Journal of Applied Finance*, Spring/Summer, 48–68.

Carleton, R. J. (1997). Cultural due diligence, *Training*, 34, 67–80.

Cote, J. A. and Buckley, M. R. (1987). Estimating trait, method, and error variance: generalizing across 70 construct validation studies. *Journal of Marketing Research*, 24, 315–318.

Datta, D. K. and Puia, G. (1995). Cross-border acquisitions: an examination of the influence of relatedness and cultural fit on shareholder value creation in US acquiring firms, *Management International Review* 35 (4), 337–359.

De Jong, M. J., Pieters, R. and Fox, J.-P. (2010). Reducing social desirability bias through item randomized response: an application to measure underreported desires, *Journal of Marketing Research*, 47, 14–27.

Erez-Rein, N., Erez, M. and Maital, S. (2004). Mind the gap: key success factors in cross-border acquisitions, in A. L. Pablo and M. Javidan (eds.), *Mergers and Acquisitions: Creating Integrative Knowledge*, Oxford: Blackwell Publishing.

Eun, C. S., Kolodny, R. and Scheraga, C. (1996). Cross-border acquisitions and shareholder wealth: tests of the synergy and internalization hypotheses, *Journal of Banking and Finance*, 20, 1559–1582.

Fisher, R. J. (1993). Social desirability bias and validity of indirect questioning, *Journal of Consumer Research*, 20, 303–315.

Fisher, R. J. (2000). The future of social desirability bias, *Psychology and Marketing*, 17 (2), 73–77.

Ganster, D. C., Hennessey, H. W. and Luthans, F. (1983). Social desirability response effects: three alternative models, *Academy of Management Journal*, 26, 321–331.

Glaister, K.W and Buckley, P. J. (1996). Strategic motives for international alliance formation, *Journal of Management Studies*, 33 (3), 301–332.

Goldberg, W. H. (1983). *Mergers: Motives, Modes, Methods*, Aldershot: Gower.

Hill, P. C., Dill, C. A. and Davenport, E. C. (1988). A reexamination of the Bogus Pipeline, *Educational and Psychological Measurement*, 48 (3), 587–601.

Hudson, J. and Barnfield, E. (2001). Mergers and acquisitions requires social dialogue, *Strategic Communications Management*, 5, 207–239.

Hunt, J. (1990). Changing pattern of acquisition behaviour in takeovers and consequencies for acquisition process, *Strategic Management Journal*, 11, 66–71.

Ingham H., Kran I. and Lovestam, A. (1992). Mergers and profitability: a managerial success story, *Journal of Management Studies*, 29 (2), 195–209.

Jarrell, G. A. and Poulsen, A. B. (1994). The returns to acquiring firms in tender offers: evidence from three decades, in P. Gaughan (ed.), *Readings in mergers and acquisitions*, Oxford: Basil Blackwell.

Jensen, M. C. and Ruback, R. S. (1983). The market for corporate control: the scientific evidence, *Journal of Financial Economics*, 11, 5–50.

Jones, E. E. and Sigall, H. (1971). The Bogus Pipeline: a new paradigm for measuring affect and attitude, *Psychological Bulletin*, 76, 349–364.

Kang, J. K. (1993). The international market for corporate control: mergers and acquisitions of US firms by Japanese firms, *Journal of Financial Economics*, 34, 345–371.

Kim, S. H. and Kim, S. (2016). National culture and social desirability bias in measuring public service motivation, *Administration and Society*, 48 (4), 444–476.

Kitching, J. (1967). Why do mergers miscarry?, *Harvard Business Review*, November–December, 84–101.

Kiymaz, H. (2003). Wealth effect for US acquirers from foreign direct investments, *Journal of Business Strategies*, 20 (1), 7–21.

Lalwani, A. K., Shavitt, S. and Johnson, T. (2006). What is the relation between cultural orientation and socially desirable responding?, *Journal of Personality and Social Psychology*, 90, 165–178.

Lalwani, A. K., Shrum, L. J. and Chiu, C.-Y. (2009). Motivated response styles: the role of cultural values, regulatory focus, and self-consciousness in socially desirable responding, *Journal of Personality and Social Psychology*, 96, 870–882.

Markides, C. and Ittner, C. D. (1994). Shareholders benefit from corporate international diversification: evidence from US international acquisitions, *Journal of International Business Studies*, 25 (2), 343–366.

Mick, D. G. (1996). Are studies of dark side variables confounded by socially desirable responding? The case of materialism, *Journal of Consumer Research*, 23, 106–119.

Miles, M. and Huberman, A. (1994). *A Qualitative Data Analysis*, Thousand Oaks, CA: Sage

Mukherjee T. K., Kiymaz H. and Baker K. H. (2004). Merger motives and target valuation: a survey of evidence from CFOs, *Journal of Applied Finance*, 14 (2), 7–24.

Neeley, S. M. and Cronley, M. L. (2004). When research participants don't tell it like it is: pinpointing the effects of social desirability bias using self vs. indirect-questioning, *Advances in Consumer Research*, 31, 432–433.

Nunnally, J. C. (1978). *Psychometric Theory*, New York: McGraw-Hill.

Nyaw, M.-K. and Ng, I. (1994). A comparative analysis of ethical beliefs: a four country study, *Journal of Business Ethics*, 13, 543–555.

Paulhus, D. L. (1984). Two-component models of socially desirable responding, *Journal of Personality and Social Psychology*, 46, 598–609.

Paulhus, D. L. (1986). Self-deception and impression management in test responses, in A. Angleitner and J. S. Wiggins (eds.), *Personality Assessment via Questionnaire*, New York: Springer.

Paulhus, D. L. (1991). Measurement and control of response bias, in J. P. Robinson, P. Shaver and L. S. Wrightsman (eds.), *Measures of Personality and Social Psychological Attitudes*, San Diego, CA: Academic Press.

Paulhus, D. L. (2002). Social desirability responding: the evolution of a construct, in H. I. Braun, D. N. Jackson and D. E. Wiley (eds.), *The Role of Constructs in Psychological and Educational Measurement*, London: Lawrence Erlbaum Associates.

Podsakoff, P. M., MacKenzie, S. B., Lee, J. Y. and Podsakoff, N. P. (2003). Common method biases in behavioral research: a critical review of the literature and recommended remedies, *Journal of Applied Psychology*, 88, 879–903.

Ravenscraft, D. J. and Scherer, F. M. (1987). *Mergers, Sell-offs and Economic Efficiency*, Washington, DC: The Brookings Institution.

Roese, N. J. and Jamieson, D. W. (1993). Twenty years of Bogus Pipeline research: a critical review and meta-analysis, *Psychological Bulletin*, 114 (2), 363–375.

Smith, D. B. and Ellingson, J. E. (2002). Substance versus style: a new look at social desirability in motivating contexts, *Journal of Applied Psychology*, 87, 211–219.

Steenkamp, J.-B. E. M., de Jong, M. G. and Baumgartner, H. (2010). Socially desirable response tendencies in survey research, *Journal of Marketing Research*, 47 (2), 199–214.

Sudman, S. and Bradburn, N. M. (1974). *Response Effects in Surveys: A Review and Synthesis*, Chicago: Aldine.

Tetenbaum, T. J. (1999). Beating the odds of mergers and acquisition failure: seven key practices that improve the chance for expected integration and synergies, *Organizational Dynamics*, Autumn, 22–35.

Tourangeau, R., Rips, L. J. and Rasinski, K. (2000). *The Psychology of Survey Response*, Cambridge: Cambridge University Press.

Tourangeau, R. and Smith, T. W. (1996). Asking sensitive questions: the impact of data collection mode, question format, and question context, *Public Opinion Quarterly*, 60 (2), 275–304.

UNCTAD (2006). *World Investment Report: FDI from Developing and Transitional Economies: Implications for Development*, New York and Geneva: United Nations.

Walter, G. A. and Barney, J. B. (1990). Management objectives in mergers and acquisitions, *Strategic Management Journal*, 11, 79–86.

Yin, R. K. (1994). *Case Study Research: Design and Methods*, London: Sage.

Zerbe, W. J. and Paulhus, D. L. (1987). Socially desirable responding in organizational behavior: a reconception, *Journal of Management Review*, 12, 250–264.

3

MOTIVES FOR CROSS-BORDER MERGERS AND ACQUISITIONS

Perspective of UK firms

Mohammad F. Ahammad, Shlomo Y. Tarba, Keith W. Glaister, Ian P. L. Kwan, Riikka M. Sarala, and Luiz Montanheiro

Introduction

Cross-border mergers and acquisitions (CBM&As) have become the dominant means of internationalisation, accounting for approximately 60 pre cent of all foreign direct investment inflows (Hopkins, 1999). Consistent with this, cross-border acquisitions now represent over 25 per cent of all global M&A transactions, a considerable rise from the 15 per cent of ten years ago (Schoenberg and Seow, 2005). According to Thomson Reuters, firms invested almost $3,500 billion in M&As in 2014 – a significant increase since 2008 (Forbes, 2015). Cross-border M&A activity by UK firms was volatile between 2008 and 2013. During 2008 and 2009 the number of acquisitions made abroad by UK companies fell by 60 per cent, from 298 acquisitions reported during 2008 down to 118 transactions reported at the end of 2009. At the end of 2013, the number of outward acquisitions decreased by 59 per cent, falling from 112 acquisitions reported during 2012 to 50 acquisitions at the end of 2013 (ONS, 2014).

Yet, in parallel with this rise in activity, there has been increasing recognition of the poor performance of many cross-border M&As (Gomes *et al.*, 2011). For example, Rostand (1994) reports that 45 per cent of such acquisitions fail to meet their initial strategic objectives, while Datta and Puia (1995) find that on average cross-border acquisitions destroy value for acquiring firm shareholders. A study by KPMG found that only 17 per cent of cross-border acquisitions created shareholder value, while 53 per cent destroyed it (*The Economist*, 1999). Moreover, cross-border M&As are widely perceived as higher risk compared to their domestic counterparts. Aw and Chatterjee's (2004) data on two-year post-acquisition shareholder returns confirm this, reporting that cumulative abnormal returns for acquiring firms were significantly more negative for European cross-border targets than in the case of domestic UK targets. Other researchers remain pessimistic over the success potential of cross-border acquisitions (e.g. Moeller and Schlingemann, 2005). Furthermore, there is no corroborative evidence that M&A strategy has a significant positive impact on the financial performance of the acquiring company since the findings of the research studies are often inconsistent, mixed, and even contradictory (Gomes *et al.*, 2013; Haleblian *et al.*, 2009; Papadakis and Thanos, 2010; Weber *et al.*, 2014).

An examination of CBM&As performance studies (see Eun *et al.*, 1996; Danbolt, 2004) reveals that target firms are clear winners. This may justify the reasons for target firms to engage in cross-border deals. But as the empirical literature suggests the bidding firms in cross-border deals do not always win, it is difficult to conclude that the huge growth of cross-border M&A activity has been for financial benefit only. Therefore, it has become an empirical necessity to discover what motivates the bidding firms to acquire foreign targets.

This study examines the reasons why firms engage in cross-border acquisitions or international acquisitions (the two terms will be used interchangeably). Specifically, the objectives of this study are:

a. To identify the relative importance of factors motivating the decision to acquire foreign target firms by UK acquiring firms.
b. To provide a parsimonious set of factors influencing CBM&As for the sample.
c. To test hypotheses on the way in which the relative importance of factors motivating CBM&As may vary with the sample characteristics.

The rest of the chapter is set out as follows. The next section reviews the literature relating to motives for CBM&As. The third section develops the hypothesis of the study. The findings and discussion are in the fourth section. A summary and conclusions are provided in the final section.

Literature review

Most of the prior literature describes M&As as ways predominantly to achieve additional market share or synergies (Walter and Barney, 1990; Schmitz and Sliwka, 2001). Such motives indicate that M&As are means to realise the strategies of the acquiring or merging parties. Discussing M&A motives from other perspectives adds additional dimensions to the picture: agency theory (Kesner *et al.*, 1994), hubris (Weston and Weaver, 2001; Berkovich and Narayanan, 1993; Roll, 1986; Seth *et al.*, 2000) and empire building (Trautwein, 1990) indicate the existence of more than one motive for M&As. Hitt *et al.* (2001), Calipha *et al.* (2010) and Gomes *et al.* (2011) also suggest multiple motives for firms to complete CBM&As.

Several of the same motives are identified by various authors, while some of them overlap. The main motives discussed in the literature include the following.

Facilitate faster entry into foreign market

As compared to internally generated product developments and new business, acquisitions allow the firm to enter a new market more rapidly. It is argued that in general it is expensive, difficult and time-consuming to build up a global organisation and a competitive presence due to issues such as differences in culture, liability of foreignness, different business practices and institutional constraints. Cross-border M&As offer significant time saving in this respect. For example, cross-border M&As allow immediate access to a local network of suppliers, marketing channels, clients and other skills.

Martin *et al.* (1998) have suggested that CBM&As can be used to access new markets as well as expand the market for a firm's current goods. Similar conclusions have been drawn by Datta and Puia (1995) who state that CBM&A activity provides the opportunity for instant access to a market with established sales volume. UNCTAD (2000) also indicates that cross-border mergers provide the fastest means for international expansion compared to greenfield investment or joint ventures.

Research on entry mode choice also suggests that acquisition is more appropriate for a faster entry into a new market compared to greenfield investment (Shimizu *et al.*, 2004). If the investor has a short amount of time to penetrate the foreign market, the only available choice will be acquiring an existing firm. In fact, greenfield entries require a much slower and more moderated approach. Hennart and Park (1993) found that the timing of the investment influenced the mode of entry choice. Specifically, if the target market has a high growth rate, the choice of an acquisition allows the investor to penetrate it more quickly.

Uddin and Boateng (2011) examined the growth of CBM&As over recent decades and highlighted that prior studies referring to cross-border M&A activities as an entry mode of FDI have focused on industry and firm level-related factors. Therefore, Uddin and Boateng investigated the role of macroeconomic influences on CBM&A activities in the UK over the 1987–2006 period and found that GDP, exchange rate, interest rate and share price have all had significant impact on the level of outward UK CBM&As, thus contributing to our understanding of the effects of macroeconomic variables.

Increase market power

Market power exists when the firm can sell its products above the existing competitive market prices or when its manufacturing, distribution and service costs are lower than those of competitors. Market power is a product of the firm's size, the degree of sustainability of its current competitive advantage, and its ability to make decisions today that will yield new competitive advantages tomorrow (Hitt *et al.*, 2001).

Cross-border acquisitions are used to increase market power when the firm acquires: (a) a company competing in the same industry and often in the same segments of the primary industry; (b) a supplier or distributor; or (c) a business in a highly related industry (Hitt *et al.*, 2001). If a company operates within a concentrated market where there are fewer competitors, merging via horizontal integration could provide the company with even more market power. Having more market power also means having the ability to impact and/or control prices. Through vertical acquisitions, firms seek to control additional parts of the value-added chain. Acquiring either a supplier or a distributor or an organisation that already controls more parts of the value chain than the acquiring firm can result in additional market power. Market power can also be gained when the firm acquires a company competing in an industry that is highly related.

Cui *et al.* (2014), using a sample of 154 Chinese firms, found that firms' strategic assets seeking managerial intent to catch up with world-leading economies by acquiring strategic assets abroad has been influenced by their exposure to foreign competition, their governance structure and relevant financial and managerial capabilities. Nicholson and Salaber (2013), for their part, explored the value creation of cross-border acquisitions in emerging markets and its impact on shareholder wealth creation, and concluded that Chinese investors gain from the cross-border expansion of manufacturing companies, and that location also affects the performance of cross-border acquisitions, with acquisitions into developed countries generating higher returns for shareholders.

Access to and acquisition of new resources and technology

A number of studies have examined the motivation for cross-border M&As from the resource-based and organisational learning perspectives (Barkema and Vermeulen, 1998; Madhok, 1997; Vermeulen and Barkema, 2001). These studies suggest that cross-border M&As are motivated by an opportunity to acquire new capabilities and learn new knowledge. Today's products rely on so many different critical technologies that most companies can no longer maintain cutting-edge sophistication in all of them (Ohmae, 1989).

Tapping external sources of know-how becomes imperative. Acquisition of an existing foreign business allows the acquirer to obtain resources such as patent-protected technology, superior managerial and marketing skills, and special government regulation that creates barriers to entry for other firms. Shimizu *et al.* (2004) endorse this by suggesting that firms may engage in M&As to exploit intangible assets. This line of reasoning is consistent with Caves (1990), who argues that acquisition of a foreign competitor enables the acquirer to bring under its control a more diverse stock of specific assets, which enables it to seize more opportunities.

Deng (2009), drawing on a multiple-case study of three leading Chinese firms – TCL, BOE and Lenovo – stressed the strategic assets resource-driven motivation behind Chinese cross-border M&A in order to retain their competitive advantages. In the same vein Rui and Yip (2008) utilised a strategic intent perspective (SIP) in order to analyse the foreign acquisitions pursued by Chinese firms, and suggested that acquiring firms from China strategically use cross-border acquisitions to obtain strategic capabilities that help them to to offset their competitive disadvantages and leverage their unique ownership advantages, while making use of institutional incentives and minimising institutional constraints. Extending this logic, Buckley *et al.* (2014) developed and tested a framework of the resource- and context-specificity of prior experience in acquisitions conducted by multinational companies from emerging countries (EMNCs) that acquire companies in developed countries. They found that acquisitions made by EMNCs often enhance the performance of target firms in the developed economies, and the role of EMNCs' idiosyncratic resources (such as access to new markets and cheap production facilities) and investment experience in enhancing the performance of target firms differs across acquisition contexts. Specifically, they indicated that while certain types of resources and investment experience might be beneficial, due to facilitating resource redeployment and the exploitation of complementarities, some other types of experience may have a detrimental impact on the performance of the incumbent target companies.

Kohli and Mann (2012) assessed the acquiring company announcement gains, and determinants thereof, in both domestic and cross-border acquisitions pursued in India. Specifically, their sample consisted of 268 acquisitions comprising of 202 cross-border and 66 domestic deals. Interestingly, this study found that cross-border acquisitions have created significantly higher wealth gains than the domestic deals. Furthermore, Kohli and Mann concluded that cross-border acquisitions involving both an acquiring company and a target company in the technology intensive sector provide opportunities for the acquiring company to combine and judiciously utilise intangible resources of both companies on a broader scale across new geographies and as a result create superior wealth gains.

Zheng *et al.* (2016), drawing on multiple cases of cross-border mergers and acquisitions by Chinese multinational enterprises (CMNEs), investigate their search for strategic assets in developed economies. Their study reveals that CMNEs possess firm-specific assets that give them competitive advantages at home and seek complementary strategic assets in similar domains, but at a more advanced level. Moreover, the focal CMNEs utilised the partnering approach that facilitated the securing of the aforementioned strategic assets through no or limited integration, namely granting autonomy to the target firm's management team and retaining talents.

Park and Ghauri (2011) investigated whether foreign acquiring firms contribute towards enhancing technological capabilities of local firms in foreign markets, and found that mere exposure to favourable learning environments is insufficient to develop an effective absorptive capacity, and that intensity of effort is a critical component functioning as a facilitator towards the extent of learning. In addition, their findings indicate that existing knowledge can be improved when the combining entities share similar business backgrounds, and finally that collaborative support from knowledge transferers serves as a significant catalyst leveraging a specific learning capability.

Almor *et al.* (2014), based on an empirical study of Israeli knowledge-intensive companies between 2000 and 2009, found that maturing, technology-based, born-global companies can increase their chances of survival by acquiring other firms. Although such acquisitions do not increase profits, they allow born-global firms to continue increasing their sales and to expand and upgrade their product lines, which in turn increases their chances of remaining independent. It is worth highlighting that although the majority of aforementioned born-global companies can continue operations if they survive the first decade, they are not highly successful in terms of growth or enhancing shareholder wealth. Therefore, Almor *et al.* recommend that maturing, technology-based, born-global companies should be more aggressive in pursuing their M&A strategies if they wish to be successful.

Diversification

Diversification is a well-documented strategy for firm expansion and has been suggested as one of the dominant reasons for cross-border M&As. Sudarsanam (1995) notes that diversification is generally defined as enabling the company to sell new products in new markets. This implies that the target company in an acquisition operates in a business that is unrelated to that of the buyer firm.

It is argued that international acquisitions not only provide access to important resources but also allow firms an opportunity to reduce the costs and risks of entering into new foreign markets. Seth (1990) reported that geographical market diversification is a source of value in cross-border acquisitions. This is because the sources of value, such as those associated with exchange rate differences, market power conferred by international scope and ability to arbitrage tax regimes, are unique to international mergers. Moreover, as economic activities in different countries are less than perfectly correlated, portfolio diversification across boundaries should reduce earnings volatility and improve investors' risk–return opportunities.

Improved management

Sirower (1997) notes that managers try to maximise shareholder value either by replacing inefficient management in the target firm or by seeking synergies through the combination of the two firms. Gaughan (1991) claims that some M&As are motivated by a belief that the acquiring firm's management can better manage the target's resources. The acquirer may feel that its management skills are such that the value of the target would rise under its control.

The improved management argument may have particular validity in the case of large companies making offers for smaller companies. The smaller companies, often led by entrepreneurs, may offer a unique product or service that has sold well and facilitated the rapid growth of the target. As the target grows, however, it requires a very different set of management skills than were necessary when it was a smaller business. The growing enterprise may find that it needs to oversee a much larger distribution network and may have to adopt a very different marketing philosophy. Many of the decisions that a larger firm has to make require a vastly different set of managerial skills than those that resulted in the dramatic growth of the smaller company. The lack of managerial expertise may be a stumbling block in the growing company and may limit its ability to compete in the broader market place. These managerial resources are an asset which the larger firm can offer the target (Gaughan, 1991).

Synergy

Bradley *et al.* (1988) and Trautwein (1990) argue that firms engage in M&As in order to achieve synergies. Synergies stem from combining operations and activities such as marketing, research and development, procurement and other cost components, which were hitherto performed by the separate firms. It is argued that by combining operations and activities, M&As can increase a firm's capacity and opportunity to reduce costs through economies of large-scale production, pooling resources to produce a superior product and generate long-run profitability. Interestingly, in the particular context of declining industries, Anand and Singh (1997) found that assets in the aforementioned industries are redeployed more effectively through market mechanisms than within the firm through the acquisition of complementary assets, and consolidation-oriented acquisitions outperform diversification-oriented acquisitions in the decline phase of their industries in terms of both *ex ante* (stock-market-based) and *ex post* (operating) performance measures.

In the specific context of cross-border M&As, the literature on corporate foreign investment describes various means by which cross-border M&As may create value. Acquiring an existing foreign facility provides a means for the rapid exploitation of the potential for synergistic gain compared with *de novo* entry. Porter (1987) suggests that one source of operating synergy comes from the potential to transfer valuable intangible assets, such as skills, between the combining firms. If a firm has know-how that can be used in markets where the sale or lease of such knowledge is inherently "inefficient," then the firm will tend to exploit it through its own organisation. Although different versions are developed by various scholars (e.g. Williamson, 1975; Rugman, 1982), all assume that transacting in the international market entails substantial costs which will reduce the value of proprietary information. Faced with this cost, a firm will be likely to internalise the transaction and use the proprietary information within its expanded organisation. Gains may also be realised form "reverse internalisation": firms acquire skills and resources from cross-border M&As that are expected to be valuable in their home markets. A related source of synergistic gains in cross-border acquisitions focuses on market development opportunities. In order to utilise their "excess" resources for long-run profitability efficiently, firms will invest abroad when growth at home is limited or restricted and in the presence of trade barriers which restrict exports. In addition, devising and implementing the tailor-made post-acquisition integration approach was found to be critical for potential synergy realisation in cross-border M&As (Almor *et al.*, 2009; Weber and Tarba, 2011; Weber, Tarba and Reichel, 2009, 2011; Weber, Tarba and Rozen Bachar, 2011, 2012).

Managerial motive

The managerialism hypothesis suggests that managers embark on M&As in order to maximise their own utility at the expense of their firm's shareholders (Seth *et al.*, 2000). Managers can have private or personal reasons for their behaviour and make investments which from an economic point of view may seem irrational, but for the individual can be of high value. The empire-building theory maintains that management want firm growth for personal reasons, and acquisitions provide this growth. An important aspect of this is the wage explanation, whereby the salary paid to managers is a function of the size of the company (Mueller, 1969). Motives like power and prestige are also stressed (Ravenscraft and Scherer, 1987): for instance, managers in large companies have an easier route to senior positions in committees and on boards of directors (Pfeffer and Salancik, 1978).

While managerialism has been proposed as a motive for domestic M&As, it may also be relevant for cross-border M&As if managers have the incentive and the discretion to engage in M&As aimed at empire building (Seth *et al.*, 2000). In an integrated capital market, firm-level diversification activities to reduce risk are generally considered non-value maximising as individual shareholders may duplicate the benefit from such activities at lower cost. However, managers may still seek to stabilise the firm's earnings stream by acquiring foreign (rather than domestic) firms, given low correlations between earnings in different countries. Foreign acquisitions may be more satisfactory vehicles for risk reduction than domestic acquisitions; and, in the absence of strong governance mechanisms to control managerial discretion, managers may overpay for these acquisitions.

Hypotheses

The literature gives little indication of what to expect in terms of the relative importance of a set of motivating factors for international acquisition. It may be conjectured, however, that the relative importance of the motives would vary with the underlying key characteristics of the sample. For the purposes of this study, these characteristics are identified as regional origin of the target firm, sector of operation and pre-acquisition performance of the target firm.

Regional origin of the target firm

There is no prior literature that provides an extensive examination of the strategic motives of international acquisition according to the choice of nationality of the foreign firm. Foreign firm choice will presumably hinge on the tasks to be accomplished by the acquisition and the particular characteristics required from a target. To the extent that UK firms believe that targets in particular foreign nations can provide certain requirements of the acquisition – for example, access to specific markets or types of technology – these targets will be chosen in preference to potential targets in different places when the acquisition is made. The fundamental motive for the acquisition may then be expected to vary according to the nationality of the foreign target. This leads to Hypothesis 1:

> *The relative importance of strategic motives for CBM&As will vary with the regional origin of the target firm.*

Industry of operation

The motives for carrying out M&As from the acquiring firm's perspective tend to be different across various industries (see Walter and Barney, 1990; Brouthers *et al.*, 1998). Kreitl and Oberndorfer (2004) argued that motives vary across industry and time, and found that more emphasis was placed on certain motives in engineering consulting firms than in other manufacturing sectors. Several of the strategic motives appear to lend themselves more readily to acquisitions in the manufacturing sector – for example, product rationalisation and economies of scale, and transfer of complementary technology/exchange of patents – than they do to acquisitions in the service sector, where risk sharing, shaping competition and the use of acquisition to facilitate international expansion appear to be more relevant. To the extent that this is the case, it would be expected that strategic motivation would vary with the industry sector of the acquisition, which is reflected in Hypothesis 2:

> *The relative importance of strategic motives for CBM&As will vary with the industry of the target firm.*

Pre-acquisition performance of the target firm

An acquiring company can correct an efficiency problem in the target firm, which will increase the target's value and create synergistic gains. To detect a situation in which the target's inefficiencies can be improved, the target's performance prior to the acquisition is examined for inefficient management. According to Servaes (1991) the largest synergistic gains are possible when an efficient firm acquires an inefficient firm. Therefore, an acquirer may be motivated to acquire a poorly performing foreign firm with a view to turning it around, for example by replacing inefficient management. On the other hand, an acquirer may be motivated to acquire a profitable foreign firm in order to realise synergic benefits, such as economies of scale or cost reduction. The fundamental motive for the international acquisition may then be expected to vary according to the pre-acquisition performance of the target firm, which leads to Hypothesis 3:

> *The relative importance of the strategic motives for CBM&As will vary according to the pre-acquisition performance of the target firm.*

Methodology

The data were gathered via a cross-sectional survey using a questionnaire on a sample of UK firms acquiring North American and European firms during the five-year period from 2000 to 2004, inclusive. The development of the questionnaire was guided by a review of previous mergers and acquisitions research (e.g. Seth *et al.*, 2000; Walter and Barney, 1990).

A list of potential sample firms was generated from the Mergers and Acquisitions Database of the Thomson One Banker. This database provides comprehensive secondary information about mergers and acquisitions, including cross-border deals. The sample includes those deals in which the acquirer bought a 100 per cent equity stake in the acquired company. Based on the results of the website search and telephone conversations, a list of key informants and potential survey participants was assembled. This procedure produced a sample of 798 firms. After an initial attempt to contact executives all 798 UK firms, 207 were deleted because they had a policy of not participating in survey research, or the executives indicated that they did not have the time or the capacity to take part in the study. Accordingly, the final sampling frame of international acquirers was 591.

In April 2007, 591 questionnaires with covering letters and return envelopes were posted to the executives of the potential survey participants. To provide motivation for accurate responses, the respondents were guaranteed anonymity and promised a summary report of the research findings, if requested. After three reminders (by means of telephone, email or follow-up letter), 69 questionnaires were returned, of which 65 were fully completed and usable; effectively a response rate of 11 per cent. Given the well-documented difficulties of obtaining questionnaire responses from executives (Harzing, 1997) and decreasing response rates from executives (Cycyota and Harrison, 2002), a response rate of 11 per cent can be considered satisfactory. It is similar to that reported in other academic studies of executives. For instance, Graham and Harvey (2001) achieved a response rate of nearly 9 per cent from CFOs, and Mukherjee *et al.* (2004) obtained an 11.8 per cent response rate in a survey mailed to 636 CFOs who were involved in acquisitions management.

All of the respondents had been directly involved in managing the CBA process. An examination of their job titles revealed that 12 chief executive officers, 16 finance directors or chief financial officers, 23 business development directors, 8 managing directors and 6 executive directors. The sample represents acquisition activity in two continents: North America and Europe. In North America, the acquired firms are from the USA and Canada (21 and 9, respectively). Europe is represented by 35 acquisitions.

In order to assess potential retrospective bias, responses concerning acquisitions made in 2004 were compared to acquisitions made in 2000. A number of variables were included in this test, such as prior performance, acquisition experience and relative size. The t-tests for mean differences were calculated and evinced no statistically significant differences. These findings suggest that retrospective bias does not influence the study.

The possibility of non-response bias was checked by means of two procedures. The first of these was a test to compare early and late respondents along a number of key description variables. Differences between the two groups were not statistically significant, suggesting that non-response bias was not a major problem. Second, respondent and non-respondent firms were compared with respect to their relative size and primary sector of operation. The t-tests of mean difference were insignificant, confirming no systematic bias between the responding firms and the non-responding firms.

Findings and discussion

Relative importance of the strategic motives

The rank order of the twenty strategic motives for international acquisition by UK companies, based on the mean measure of importance, is shown in Table 3.1. The median measure is exceeded by nine acquisition motives, of which "to enable presence in new market" (3.55), "to enable faster entry to market" (3.54), "to facilitate international expansion" (3.52), "gain new capabilities" (3.42), "gain strategic assets" (3.26) and "increase market power" (3.09) constitute the six with the highest degrees of importance. It is clear from the table that the managers perceived their motives for international expansion to be strongly influenced by growth-oriented factors. The highest-ranked strategic motives are concerned with relative competitive positions in new markets.

Considering the motives in terms of their underlying theoretical explanations, it is apparent that, for this sample, the main strategic motives are underpinned by the theories of strategic positioning and the resource-based view (RBV). The first three ranked motives are concerned with improving the firm's competitive position

TABLE 3.1 Relative importance of strategic motives for international acquisition by UK companies

Rank	*Motivation*	*Mean*	*Standard deviation*
1	To enable presence in new markets	3.55	1.392
2	To enable faster entry to market	3.54	1.668
3	To facilitate international expansion	3.52	1.511
4	Gain new capabilities	3.42	1.223
5	Gain strategic assets	3.26	1.350
6=	Increase market power	3.09	1.444
6=	Gain efficiency through synergies	3.09	1.400
8=	Acquire complementary resources	3.08	1.315
8=	Increase market share	3.08	1.461
10	Enable product diversification	2.86	1.488
11	Obtain non-manufacturing scale economies	2.31	1.198
12	Obtain economies of large-scale production	2.17	1.269
13	To reduce risk of the business	1.95	1.067
14	Cost reduction	1.92	1.136
15	Elimination or reduction of competition	1.66	1.020
16	Enable the overcoming of regulatory restrictions	1.63	1.098
17	Turn around failing acquired firm	1.62	1.041
18=	Redeploy assets to the acquisition	1.54	0.772
18=	Replace inefficient management of acquired firm	1.54	0.867
20	Tax reasons (savings)	1.32	0.773

Notes: N = 65; the mean is the average on a scale of 1 (no importance) to 5 (very important); = indicates motives that have the same rank in terms of mean value.

through the use of acquisitions that may be characterised as most importantly allowing the UK firms to enter new foreign markets at speed and/or consolidating existing market positions.

The leading set of motives also lends support to the RBV of acquisitions, particularly when it is recognised that the acquisition takes place because the acquirer lacks the necessary capabilities or assets required for remaining competitive in the foreign market. Where one firm wishes to acquire a capability that it does not have but is possessed by a target firm (such as tangible resources – for example, capital, machinery and land – and intangible resources – for example, capabilities, organisational culture and know-how), then an acquisition may facilitate obtaining these capabilities.

The most important acquisition motive for the surveyed firms was to enable presence in new markets. Thus, expanding the acquiring firm's market portfolio to reach new markets was obviously a top priority for the surveyed firms. The importance of presence in new markets supports Ingham *et al.*'s (1992) study of British firms where the penetration of new geographic markets ranked second.

Enabling faster entry to market was highly ranked. International mergers and acquisitions are the fastest means for firms to expand their production and markets internationally (Chen and Findlay, 2003). When time is crucial, acquiring an existing firm in a new market with an established distribution system is far preferable to developing a new local distribution and marketing network. For a latecomer to a market or a new field of technology, international M&As can provide a way to catch up rapidly. With the acceleration of globalisation, and enhanced competition, there are increasing pressures for UK firms to respond quickly to opportunities in the fast-changing global economic environment. Thus, for UK companies seeking to compete in nations outside their home base, acquiring a firm is a much faster way to reach this objective when compared with the time required to establish a new facility and new relationships with stakeholders in a different country.

The third-ranked motive was to facilitate international expansion. The desire to expand from the national domestic market is not surprising as the search for new markets and market power is a constant concern for firms in an increasingly competitive environment. In conditions of rapid change and high innovation costs, expansion through external means has become an absolute necessity (Child *et al.*, 2001). A company can expand through greenfield or through mergers and acquisitions. When expanding abroad via direct investment, firms face greater risks than local firms due to their lack of familiarity with the host market. Thus, the firm often prefers the lower risk of acquisition once a foreign firm is thought suitable for the purpose of international expansion (Caves, 1996).

Another important motive for cross-border M&As for UK acquiring firms is to acquire strategic assets and capabilities, which encompass technology, R&D and management know-how. This finding is consistent with Granstrand and Sjolander (1990), who suggest that firms with low skills may enter foreign markets via M&As that allow the firms to obtain new technological resources and other strategic assets. Caves (1990) endorses this by suggesting that foreign acquisitions may be motivated by the quest to bring a more diverse collection of specific assets under the acquirer's control and to enable more opportunities to be seized. This explanation is also in line with the views of Hill *et al.* (1990), who point out that foreign acquisition by MNCs may be motivated by strategic objectives. Bresman *et al.* (1999) also suggest that cross-border M&A is an effective way to expand the knowledge base of a firm.

The ranking of the motives revealed that British CBM&As are not driven by diversification motives (rank 10 and 13) or by the desire to reduce costs (rank 11 and 14). Firms usually pursue diversification in order reduce earnings volatility and improve investors' risk–return opportunities. However, one of the disadvantages of acquisitions that are motivated by diversification is the tendency to stretch the acquiring company's management (Gaughan, 1991). The ability to manage a firm successfully in one industry does not necessarily translate to other businesses. Moreover, the acquiring company is providing a service (i.e. diversification) to stockholders that they can accomplish better themselves (Levy and Sarnat, 1970). For instance, a steel company that has a typical pattern of cyclical sales may consider acquiring a pharmaceutical company that exhibits a recession-resistant sales pattern. Financial theory states that the managers of the steel company are doing their stockholders a disservice through acquisition of the pharmaceutical company. If stockholders in the steel company wanted to be stockholders in a pharmaceutical firm, they could easily adjust their portfolios to add shares of such a firm. Stockholders can accomplish such a transaction in a far less costly manner than through a corporate acquisition.

The lowest-ranked international acquisition motives (rank 15 to 20) include "enable overcoming of regulatory restrictions" (1.63), "turn around failing acquired firm" (1.62), "redeploy assets to the acquisition" (1.54), "replace inefficient management" (1.54) and "tax reasons" (1.32). Overcoming regulatory restrictions appears not to be an important motivation for British international acquisitions. This is not surprising as most of the regulatory restrictions were removed before 2000 (all of the acquisitions in the sample were completed in the 2000 to 2004 period). Regulatory reform and deregulation in the 1990s in industries such as telecommunications (the WTO agreement on basic telecommunications services came into effect in 1998), electricity and finance played a significant role in the remarkable increases in M&As in both developed and developing countries (UNCTAD, 2000). The promotion of regional integration in the 1990s, as in Europe and North America, provided opportunities for expansion through cross-border M&As. Thus, regulatory restrictions are now less important factors for making an acquisition overseas. "Tax reasons (savings)" is ranked lowest, indicating that British CBM&As are rarely driven by this motive. Weston *et al.* (2001) suggest that the synergies resulting from tax savings are insufficient to motivate an acquisition, which seems to be supported by this study.

Factor analysis of strategic motives

Due to potential conceptual and statistical overlap, an attempt was made to identify a parsimonious set of variables to determine the underlying dimensions governing the full set of twenty strategic motives. Exploratory factor analysis (EFA) using varimax rotation was used to extract the underlying factors. The EFA initially produced seven factors for the twenty strategic motives. A content analysis (Cavusgil and Zou, 1994; Deshpande, 1982) was conducted to remove items that had inconsistent substantive meanings with the factor or that had low factor loadings from further analysis. This purification process resulted in the elimination of three motives: "enable the overcoming of regulatory restrictions," "tax reasons (savings)" and "to reduce risk of the business." The remaining seventeen motives were again factor analysed and produced six non-overlapping factors, as shown in Table 3.2. Six factors explained a total of 71.50 per cent of the observed variance (with Cronbach's α ranging from 0.54 to 078). The remainder of this section discusses the interpretation of each of these factors.

TABLE 3.2 Factor analysis of strategic motives for CBM&As

Factors	*Factor loads*	*Eigenvalue*	*Percentage variance explained*	*Cumulative percentage*	*Cronbach's α*
Factor 1: Synergies		3.61	21.27	21.27	0.78
Obtain economies of large-scale production	.858				
Obtain non-manufacturing scale economies	.773				
Gain efficiency through synergies	.773				
Cost reduction	.493				
Factor 2: Market development		2.77	16.29	37.57	0.68
To facilitate international expansion	.774				
To enable presence in new markets	.773				
To enable faster entry to market	.697				
Factor 3: Target improvement		1.84	10.84	48.41	0.62
Turn around failing acquired firm	.841				
Replace inefficient management of acquired firm	.768				
Redeploy assets to the acquisition	.489				
Factor 4: Market power		1.42	8.40	56.81	0.68
Increase market power	.813				
Increase market share	.681				
Elimination or reduction of competition	.574				

(continued)

TABLE 3.2 Factor analysis of strategic motives for CBM&As *(continued)*

Factors	*Factor loads*	*Eigenvalue*	*Percentage variance explained*	*Cumulative percentage*	*Cronbach's α*
Factor 5: Acquiring strategic resources		1.30	7.66	64.48	0.54
Acquire complementary resources	.698				
Gain strategic assets	.671				
Gain new capabilities	.663				
Factor 6: Product diversification		1.19	7.02	71.50	N/A
Enable product diversification	.882				

Notes: Principal component factor analysis with varimax rotation; K-M-O measure of sampling adequacy = 0.649; Bartlett's test of sphericity = 379.071; $p < 0.000$.

Factor 1: Synergies. The first factor had high positive loadings on the following four strategic motives: obtain economies of large-scale production; obtain non-manufacturing scale economies; gain efficiency through synergies; and cost reduction. This first factor was, therefore, interpreted to be a motive related to synergies.

Factor 2: Market development. This factor had high positive loading on three strategic motives: to facilitate international expansion; to enable presence in new markets; and to enable faster entry to market. It was interpreted that this second factor reflects market development.

Factor 3: Target improvement. This factor had high positive loading on three strategic motives: turn around failing acquired firm; replace inefficient management of acquired firm; and redeploy assets to the acquisition. This factor was interpreted as a motive to improve the target.

Factor 4: Market power. The fourth factor had high positive loading on three strategic motives: increase market power; increase market share; and elimination or reduction of competition. Therefore, this factor was interpreted as a motive related to market power.

Factor 5: Acquiring strategic resources. This factor had high factor loading on three strategic motives: acquiring complementary resources; gain strategic assets; and gain new capabilities. This factor was interpreted as a motive to acquire strategic resources.

Factor 6: Product diversification. This factor had high factor loading on one strategic motive: enable product diversification. This factor was interpreted as a motive for product diversification.

Strategic motivation and sample characteristics

To investigate the underlying nature and pattern of the strategic motivation for this sample of international acquisitions further, the analysis was developed by considering the strategic motives in terms of the characteristics of the sample. For each of the relevant characteristics of the sample under consideration, Tables 3.3 to 3.5 report the means and standard deviations of the five factors and the individual strategic motives comprising each factor, the rank order of the individual strategic motives, and the appropriate test statistic for comparing differences in mean scores.

Strategic motives and origin of the target firm

The rank order of strategic motivation according to the geographical region of the acquisition, North America or Europe, is shown in Table 3.3. Some of the motives have a similar rank; however, there are several differences in rank order according to the location of the acquisition. The joint highest-ranked motive for North American acquisitions is to gain new capabilities, while for European acquisitions

TABLE 3.3 Strategic motives for international acquisitions: origin of the target firm

Factors	*Group*	*Rank*	*Mean*	*SD*	*T-value*
Factor 1: Synergies	North America		2.21	0.93	–1.13
	Europe		2.49	1.00	
Obtain economies of large-scale production	North America	13=	1.82	1.15	–1.99**
	Europe	11	2.43	1.30	
Obtain non-manufacturing scale economies	North America	11	2.32	1.15	0.08
	Europe	12	2.30	1.24	
Gain efficiency through synergies	North America	9	2.89	1.42	–.99
	Europe	6=	3.24	1.38	
Cost reduction	North America	13=	1.82	1.15	–0.62
	Europe	13	2.00	1.13	
Factor 2: Market development	North America		3.51	1.17	–0.15
	Europe		3.55	1.22	
To facilitate international expansion	North America	3	3.46	1.52	–0.27
	Europe	2	3.57	1.51	
To enable presence in new markets	North America	4	3.43	1.37	–0.63
	Europe	1	3.65	1.41	
To enable faster entry to market	North America	1=	3.64	1.74	0.43
	Europe	4	3.46	1.62	
Factor 3: Target improvement	North America		1.71	0.77	1.56
	Europe		1.45	0.57	
Turn around failing acquired firm	North America	15	1.79	1.13	1.12
	Europe	16	1.49	0.96	
Replace inefficient management of acquired firm	North America	12	1.89	0.95	2.91**
	Europe	17	1.27	0.69	

(continued)

TABLE 3.3 Strategic motives for international acquisitions: origin of the target firm *(continued)*

Factors	*Group*	*Rank*	*Mean*	*SD*	*T-value*
Redeploy assets to the acquisition	North America	17	1.46	0.74	–0.67
	Europe	15	1.59	0.79	
Factor 4: Market power	North America		2.51	1.09	–0.66
	Europe		2.68	1.00	
Increase market power	North America	6	3.07	1.51	–0.10
	Europe	9	3.11	1.41	
Increase market share	North America	10	2.75	1.48	−1.57
	Europe	5	3.32	1.41	
Elimination or reduction of competition	North America	16	1.71	0.89	0.37
	Europe	14	1.62	1.11	
Factor 5: Acquiring strategic resources	North America		3.17	1.05	–0.54
	Europe		3.30	0.84	
Acquire complementary resources	North America	8	2.93	1.51	–0.76
	Europe	8	3.19	1.15	
Gain strategic assets	North America	7	2.96	1.45	−1.52
	Europe	3	3.49	1.23	
Gain new capabilities	North America	1=	3.64	1.22	1.31
	Europe	6=	3.24	1.21	
Factor 6: Product diversification	North America				
	Europe				
Enable product diversification	North America	5	3.21	1.61	1.64
	Europe	10	2.59	1.34	

Notes: The mean for the factors is the mean of the factor scores; the mean for the individual motives is the average on a scale of 1 (no importance) to 5 (very important); * $p < 0.1$; ** $p < 0.05$; *** $p < 0.01$.

this motive is ranked only sixth. UK firms appear to believe that North American firms provide access to specific capabilities more readily than do European firms. Acquisition of new capabilities appears to be an essential step, because today's products rely on so many different critical technologies that most companies can no longer maintain cutting-edge sophistication in all of them (Ohmae, 1989). In this respect it appears that North American firms have developed these capabilities more than European firms.

The highest-ranked motive for European acquisitions is to enable presence in new markets, whereas for North American acquisitions this motive is ranked only fourth. It appears that it is more of a priority for UK firms to gain a presence in Europe than in North America. The desire to access the European market tends to support the survey findings ofJansson *et al.* (1994), in which "nearness and potential of the single market" was identified as the main reason for cross-border M&As in Europe by UK manufacturing firms.

Similar variations exist in the case of other motives, such as increase market share, enable product diversification, and replace inefficient management of acquired firm.

For acquisitions in Europe, the motive to increase market share is ranked fifth; in contrast, the same motive is ranked tenth for North American acquisitions. It appears that for UK firms it is relatively more important to increase market share in the European market than in North America. This finding supports a survey reported by KPMG Management Consulting (1998), where increasing market share was identified as one of the most important motives for M&As in Europe by UK firms.

For North American acquisition, the motive to enable product diversification is ranked fifth, whereas this motive is ranked tenth for European acquisition. It appears that it is more of a priority for UK firms to enable product diversification in North America than in Europe. To remain competitive in the North American market, UK firms may have acquired firms that enable product diversification.

The motive to replace inefficient management of the acquired firm is ranked twelveth for North American acquisitions and seventeenth for European acquisitions. It appears that for UK firms it is relatively more important to replace inefficient management in North American acquired firms than in European acquired firms. The management of UK firms may believe that they can better manage the North American firms' resources.

Despite the variations in ranking, Table 3.3 indicates a lack of support for Hypothesis 1, in that the relative importance of the strategic motives does not vary significantly between the origins of the target firm. None of the factors has mean scores that are statistically different. With regard to individual motives, only the relative importance of two – obtain economies of large-scale production ($p < 0.05$) and replace inefficient management of acquired firm ($p < 0.05$) – are found to vary significantly between region of target firm. The mean score for the obtain economies of large-scale production motive is higher for acquisitions in Europe than those in North America. In the case of replace inefficient management of the acquired firm, the mean score is higher for North American than European Union acquisitions.

In general, then, similar motives are driving CBM&As in the EU and North America, with little significant variation in terms of the relative importance of the motives.

Strategic motives and sector of acquisition

To facilitate the statistical testing of the strategic motives, the industry of the acquisition was categorised in the conventional way by distinguishing between manufacturing and service sectors. The strategic motivation for international acquisitions by sector of operation is shown in Table 3.4.

The rank order of the strategic motives has a degree of similarity for the two sectors; however, there are some differences. For instance, the highest-ranked motive for acquisitions in the manufacturing sector is to gain strategic assets, while this motive is ranked only tenth in the service sector. It appears that it is more of a priority for UK firms to gain strategic assets in the manufacturing sector than in service sector. This suggests that UK firms lack the necessary strategic assets to

TABLE 3.4 Strategic motives for international acquisitions: sector of acquisition

Factors	*Group*	*Rank*	*Mean*	*SD*	*T-value*
Factor 1: Synergies	Manufacturing		2.35	1.00	–0.17
	Service		2.39	0.96	
Obtain economies of large-scale production	Manufacturing	12	2.17	1.32	–0.01
	Service	12	2.17	1.22	
Obtain non-manufacturing scale economies	Manufacturing	11	2.28	1.18	–0.22
	Service	11	2.34	1.23	
Gain efficiency through synergies	Manufacturing	6	3.03	1.46	–0.41
	Service	9	3.17	1.33	
Cost reduction	Manufacturing	13	1.94	1.21	0.16
	Service	13	1.90	1.04	
Factor 2: Market development	Manufacturing		3.42	1.30	–0.84
	Service		3.67	1.04	
To facilitate international expansion	Manufacturing	3	3.47	1.55	–0.30
	Service	5	3.59	1.47	
To enable presence in new markets	Manufacturing	2	3.50	1.48	–0.34
	Service	4	3.62	1.29	
To enable faster entry to market	Manufacturing	4	3.31	1.75	–1.27
	Service	1	3.83	1.53	
Factor 3: Target improvement	Manufacturing		1.50	0.58	–0.82
	Service		1.64	0.78	
Turn around failing acquired firm	Manufacturing	16	1.53	1.02	–0.75
	Service	15=	1.72	1.06	
Replace inefficient management of acquired firm	Manufacturing	17	1.39	0.76	–1.52
	Service	15=	1.72	0.96	
Redeploy assets to the acquisition	Manufacturing	14	1.58	0.73	0.51
	Service	17	1.48	0.82	
Factor 4: Market power	Manufacturing		2.30	1.01	–2.79***
	Service		2.98	0.95	
Increase market power	Manufacturing	9	2.64	1.43	–3.03***
	Service	3	3.66	1.26	
Increase market share	Manufacturing	8	2.72	1.46	–2.26***
	Service	6	3.52	1.35	
Elimination or reduction of competition	Manufacturing	15	1.56	1.05	–0.93
	Service	14	1.79	0.97	
Factor 5: Acquiring strategic resources	Manufacturing		3.21	0.95	–0.36
	Service		3.29	0.92	
Acquire complementary resources	Manufacturing	7	2.97	1.34	–0.71
	Service	7=	3.21	1.29	
Gain strategic assets	Manufacturing	1	3.53	1.29	1.79
	Service	10	2.93	1.36	
Gain new capabilities	Manufacturing	5	3.14	1.31	–2.13***
	Service	2	3.76	1.02	
Factor 6: Product diversification	Manufacturing				
	Service				
Enable product diversification	Manufacturing	10	2.58	1.62	–1.75**
	Service	7=	3.21	1.23	

Notes: The mean for the factors is the mean of the factor scores; the mean for the individual motives is the average on a scale of 1 (no importance) to 5 (very important); * $p < 0.1$; ** $p < 0.05$; *** $p < 0.01$.

operate and compete effectively in the foreign manufacturing sector. Thus, acquisition allows UK firms to obtain necessary and/or new technological resources and other strategic assets in order to seize opportunities in foreign markets (Caves, 1990).

The highest-ranked motive in the service sector is to enable faster entry into the market, while this motive is ranked only fourth in the manufacturing sector. It appears that it is more of a priority for UK firms to enable faster entry into the service sector than in the manufacturing sector. The importance of faster entry into the service sector supports Kang and Johansson's (2000) study, where the growth of cross-border M&As in the service sector – that is, telecommunications, media and financial services – was seen in terms of the efforts of firms to capture new markets quickly and to offer more integrated global service.

The increase market power motive is ranked third for acquisitions in the service sector, whereas it is ranked ninth in the manufacturing sector. It appears that it is relatively more important for UK firms to increase market power in the service sector than in the manufacturing sector. If industry competition is higher in the service sector than in the manufacturing sector, a UK firm may choose to acquire an existing company in the service sector in order to increase industry concentration.

There is moderate support for Hypothesis 2, in that two of the six factors have mean scores that are significantly different – market power ($p < 0.01$) and product diversification ($p < .05$) – with both mean higher in the service sector. Two of the three individual motives constituting the market power factor – increase market power ($p < 0.01$) and increase market share ($p < 0.01$) – show means that are significantly higher for international acquisition in the service sector compared to those in the manufacturing sector. The market power factor and the individual motives to increase market power, to increase market share and to eliminate or reduce competition may be viewed as a set of largely defensive motives designed to consolidate and protect the UK firms' positions in foreign markets. Given that this set of motives is relatively more important for international acquisitions in the service sector than it is for motives in the manufacturing sector, it may be argued that international acquisitions in the service sector are more of a pro-reactive response to competitive pressure than is the case for international acquisitions in the manufacturing sector.

The finding that market power as a strategic motive is relatively more important for international acquisitions in the service sector than those in the manufacturing sector is consistent with McCann (1996) and Kreitl and Oberndorfer (2004). McCann found that the M&A motive of increasing the firm's market share is very highly ranked in service sectors such as transportation and travel, financial services, professional service sectors and so on. Kreitl and Oberndorfer found market share was the third-highest-ranked motive in the consulting service sector. They argued that market share provides a consulting firm with name recognition and reputation for its expertise, a factor which reduces cost in marketing and sales.

The individual motive constituting the product diversification factor – enable product diversification ($p < 0.05$) – shows a mean significantly higher for international acquisition in the service sector compared to that in manufacturing sector.

It appears that it is more of a priority for UK firms to enable product diversification in the service sector than in the manufacturing sector.

On the whole, there is moderate support for Hypothesis 2, indicating that motives for international acquisitions do vary according to the sector of acquisition, at least to some extent.

Strategic motives and pre-acquisition performance of foreign firms

The rank order of strategic motivation according to the pre-acquisition performance of target firms is shown in Table 3.5. Some of the motives have similar ranks between profitable target firm and not-profitable firm, although there are some differences in rank order according to the pre-acquisition performance of the target firm. The highest-ranked motive when acquiring a profitable firm is to facilitate international expansion, whereas this motive is ranked fourth in the case of an unprofitable firm. It appears that it is more of a priority for UK firms to acquire a profitable firm than to acquire an unprofitable firm for facilitating international expansion. This is not surprising, as acquiring a profitable firm can facilitate international expansion more easily than acquiring an unprofitable firm.

Similar variation exists in the rank order of other motives. The motive to increase market share is ranked sixth for acquiring a profitable firm. The same motive is ranked tenth for acquiring an unprofitable firm. It appears that it is relatively more important for UK firms to acquire a profitable firm than to acquire an unprofitable firm in order to increase market share. The market share of a profitable firm is expected to be higher than that of an unprofitable firm. Thus, acquiring a profitable firm can result in a relatively higher market share for the acquiring firm.

Despite some variation in ranking, Table 3.5 indicates weak support for Hypothesis 3, in that only one of the six factors – target improvement ($p < 0.1$) – has mean scores that are significantly different, with the mean unsurprisingly higher for acquisition of unprofitable firms. One of the three individual motives constituting the target improvement factor – turn around failing acquired firm ($p < 0.01$) – shows a mean significantly higher for international acquisitions of unprofitable firms compared with those of profitable firms. This is to be expected as an acquirer may be motivated to acquire a poorly performing foreign firm with a view to turning it around, for example by replacing inefficient management. This result is consistent with the improved management hypothesis, which holds that poorly managed firms have a greater likelihood of becoming takeover targets (Manne, 1965). Gaughan (1991) argues that some takeovers are motivated by a belief that the acquiring firm's management can better manage the target's resources. Thus, a UK acquirer may feel that its management skills are such that the value of the target will rise under its control.

Brealey and Myers (2003) suggest that cash is not the only asset that can be wasted by poor management. Firms with unexploited opportunities to cut costs and increase sales and earnings are natural candidates for acquisition by other firms with better managements. The authors also suggest that sometimes an acquisition is the

TABLE 3.5 Strategic motives for international acquisitions: performance of target firms

Factors	*Group*	*Rank*	*Mean*	*SD*	*T-value*
Factor 1: Synergies	Profitable		2.43	1.00	0.92
	Unprofitable		2.16	0.90	
Obtain economies of large-scale production	Profitable	12	2.24	1.27	0.81
	Unprofitable	13	1.93	1.28	
Obtain non-manufacturing scale economies	Profitable	11	2.38	1.17	0.88
	Unprofitable	12	2.07	1.28	
Gain efficiency through synergies	Profitable	8	3.14	1.38	0.49
	Unprofitable	8	2.93	1.48	
Cost reduction	Profitable	13	1.98	1.16	.73
	Unprofitable	15=	1.73	1.03	
Factor 2: Market development	Profitable		3.54	1.27	0.11
	Unprofitable		3.51	0.94	
To facilitate international expansion	Profitable	1	3.60	1.55	0.74
	Unprofitable	4=	3.27	1.38	
To enable presence in new markets	Profitable	2=	3.52	1.46	–.40
	Unprofitable	1	3.67	1.17	
To enable faster entry to market	Profitable	2=	3.52	1.63	–.16
	Unprofitable	2	3.60	1.84	
Factor 3: Target improvement	Profitable		1.46	0.53	–1.73*
	Unprofitable		1.91	0.96	
Turn around failing acquired firm	Profitable	17	1.38	.667	–2.41***
	Unprofitable	11	2.40	1.59	
Replace inefficient management of acquired firm	Profitable	16	1.48	0.86	–.99
	Unprofitable	15=	1.73	0.88	
Redeploy assets to the acquisition	Profitable	15	1.52	0.70	–.35
	Unprofitable	17	1.60	0.98	
Factor 4: Market power	Profitable		2.64	0.95	0.35
	Unprofitable		2.51	1.30	
Increase market power	Profitable	6=	3.16	1.46	0.68
	Unprofitable	9	2.87	1.40	
Increase market share	Profitable	6=	3.16	1.39	0.74
	Unprofitable	10	2.80	1.69	
Elimination or reduction of competition	Profitable	14	1.60	0.92	–0.88
	Unprofitable	14	1.87	1.30	
Factor 5: Acquiring strategic resources	Profitable		3.25	0.93	0.03
	Unprofitable		3.24	0.96	
Acquire complementary resources	Profitable	9	3.10	1.24	0.25
	Unprofitable	7	3.00	1.55	
Gain strategic assets	Profitable	5	3.26	1.36	–0.01
	Unprofitable	4=	3.27	1.33	
Gain new capabilities	Profitable	4	3.40	1.22	–0.18
	Unprofitable	3	3.47	1.24	
Factor 6: Product diversification	Profitable				
	Unprofitable				
Enable product diversification	Profitable	10	2.76	1.50	–1.00
	Unprofitable	6	3.20	1.42	

Notes: The mean for the factors is the mean of the factor scores; the mean for the individual motive is the average on a scale of 1 (no importance) to 5 (very important); * $p < 0.1$; ** $p < 0.05$; *** $p < 0.01$.

only simple and practical way to improve management, because the incumbent managers are naturally reluctant to fire or demote themselves, and stockholders of large public firms do not usually have much direct influence on how the firm is run or who runs it.

Overall, there is weak support for Hypothesis 3, suggesting that most of the motives for international acquisitions vary little according to pre-acquisition performance of the target firm. However, there are significant differences with respect to the motive of target improvement, as expected.

Summary and conclusions

This study identifies the main strategic motives driving CBM&As by UK firms. International acquisitions are seen primarily as a means to enable presence in new markets, to enable faster entry to market, to facilitate international expansion, to gain new capabilities, to gain strategic assets, to increase market power, to gain efficiency through synergies, to acquire complementary resources and to increase market share. In terms of underlying theoretical explanations, the main strategic motives are underpinned by the theories of strategic positioning and the resource-based view of the firm. The first three ranked motives are concerned with improving the firm's competitive position through the use of acquisition that may be characterised as most importantly allowing the UK firms to enter new foreign markets at speed and/or consolidating existing market positions. The leading set of motives also lends support to the RBV of acquisition, particularly when it is recognised that the acquisition takes place because the acquirer lacks the necessary capabilities or assets required to remain competitive in the foreign market. Where one firm wishes to acquire a capability that it does not have but is possessed by a target firm, the acquisition may facilitate obtaining these capabilities.

The study also finds that "enable overcoming of regulatory restrictions" and "tax reasons (savings)" appear to be relatively unimportant motives for international acquisitions by UK firms. This is not surprising as most of the regulatory restrictions were removed before 2000 (the acquisitions were completed in the 2000 to 2004 period). Regulatory reform and deregulation in the 1990s in industries such as telecommunications, electricity and finance played a significant role in the remarkable increases in M&As in both developed and developing countries (UNCTAD, 2000). Thus, the regulatory restrictions are now less important factors to be considered for making an acquisition overseas.

The study found little support for Hypothesis 1, indicating that the relative importance of the strategic motives does not vary significantly between the regional origin of the target firm. However, the rank order of the strategic motives suggests that there is some variation between the motives for acquisition in North America and Europe.

The findings indicate that the relative importance of the strategic motives varies to a moderate extent with the sector of acquisition activity, providing some support for Hypothesis 2. This is further supported in that there is some variation in ranking between the motives in the manufacturing sector and the motives in the service sector.

There is limited support for Hypothesis 3, in that there is little variance in the relative importance of the strategic motives with pre-acquisition performance of the target firm. However, in the key motive of target improvement there is a significant difference in means, with a significantly higher mean for acquisition of unprofitable firms. Also, the rank order of the strategic motives indicates that there are some variations in strategic motives between the acquisition of profitable firms and the acquisition of unprofitable firms.

In general, there is little variation in the relative importance of the motivating factors across the characteristics of the sample. Where there is variation, while this is sometimes readily explainable, it is not always obvious. Further investigation of the relative importance of the strategic motives between industries would help in providing a deeper understanding of the way in which strategic motives vary across these characteristics. Moreover, this study investigated the strategic motives for international acquisition by UK firms in the developed countries of North America and Europe. Future study could investigate the relative importance of the strategic motives in the context of developed and developing country acquisitions.

References

Almor, T., Tarba, S. Y. and Benjamini, H. 2009. Unmasking integration challenges: The case of Biogal's acquisition by Teva Pharmaceutical Industries. *International Studies of Management and Organization*, Vol. 39 (3): 33–53.

Almor, T., Tarba, S.Y. and Margalit, A. 2014. Maturing, technology-based, born global companies: Surviving through mergers and acquisitions. *Management International Review*, Vol. 54 (4): 421–444.

Anand, J., and Singh, H. 1997. Asset redeployment, acquisitions, and corporate strategy in declining industries. *Strategic Management Journal*, Vol. 18 (S1): 99–118.

Armitstead, L. 2006. British firms go on £62bn global spending spree. Business Section, *Sunday Times*, 1 January, p. 3.

Aw, M. and Chatterjee, R. 2004. The performance of UK firms acquiring large cross-border and domestic takeover targets. *Applied Financial Economics*, Vol. 14: 337–349.

Barkema, H. G. and Vermeulen, F. 1998. International expansion through start-up or acquisition: A learning perspective. *Academy of Management Journal*, Vol. 41 (1): 7–27.

Berkovitch, E., and Narayanan, M. P. 1993. Motives for takeovers: An empirical investigation. *Journal of Financial and Quantative Analysis*, Vol. 28 (3): 347–362.

Bradley, M., Desai, A. and Kim E. H. 1988. Synergistic gains from corporate acquisitions and their division between the stockholders of target and acquiring firms. *Journal of Financial Economics*, Vol. 21(1): 3–40.

Brealey, R. A. and Myers, S. C. 2003. *Principles of Corporate Finance.* 7th edition. New York: McGraw-Hill.

Bresman, H., Birkinshaw, J. and Nobel, R. 1999. Knowledge transfer in international acquisitions. *Journal of International Business Studies*, Vol. 3: 439–462.

Brouthers, K. D., van Hastenburg, P. and van den Ven, J. 1998. If most mergers fail why are they so popular? *Long Range Planning*, Vol. 31 (3): 347–353.

Buckley, P. J., Elia, S. and Kafouros, M. 2014. Acquisitions by emerging market multinationals: Implications for firm performance. *Journal of World Business*, Vol. 49: 611–632.

Calipha, R., Tarba, S. Y. and Brock, D. M. 2010. Mergers and acquisitions: A review of phases, motives, and success factors. *Advances in Mergers and Acquisitions*, Vol. 9: 1–24.

Caves, R. E. 1990. Corporate mergers in international economic integration. Working paper, Centre for Economic Policy Research, Harvard University.

Caves, R. E. 1996. *Multinational Enterprise and Economic Analysis*. 2nd edition. Cambridge: Cambridge University Press.

Cavusgil, T. S. and Zou, S. M. 1994. Marketing strategy–performance relationship: An investigation of the empirical link in export market ventures. *Journal of Marketing*, Vol. 58(1): 1–21.

Chen, C. and Findlay, C. 2003. A review of cross-border mergers and acquisitions in APEC. *Asian-Pacific Economic Literature*, Vol. 17 (2): 14–38.

Child, J., Falkner, D. and Pitkethly, R. 2001. *The Management of International Acquisitions*. Oxford: Oxford University Press.

Cycyota, C. S. and Harrison, D. A. 2002. Enhancing survey response rates at the executive level: Are employee- or consumer-level techniques effective? *Journal of Management*, Vol. 28 (2): 151–176.

Cui, L., Meyer, K. E. and Hu, H. W. 2014. What drives firms' intent to seek strategic assets by foreign direct investment? A study of emerging economy firms. *Journal of World Business*, Vol. 49: 488–501.

Danbolt, J. 2004. Target company cross-border effects in acquisitions into the UK. *European Financial Management*, Vol. 10 (1): 83–108.

Datta, D. and Puia, G. 1995. Cross-border acquisitions: An examination of the influence of relatedness and cultural fit on shareholder value creation in US acquiring firms. *Management International Review*, Vol. 35: 337–359.

Deng, P. 2009. Why do Chinese firms tend to acquire strategic assets in international expansion? *Journal of World Business*, Vol. 44: 74–84.

Deshpande, R. 1982. The organizational context of market research use. *Journal of Marketing*, Vol. 46 (3): 91–101.

Economist, The. 1999. Business: faites vos jeux. *The Economist*, 353 (8148): 63.

Eun, C. S., Kolodny, R. and Scheraga, C. 1996. Cross-border acquisitions and shareholder wealth: Tests of the synergy and internalization hypotheses. *Journal of Banking and Finance*, Vol. 20: 1559–1582.

Forbes (2015) Strong Q4 Activity Makes 2014 the Best Year for M&A since Downturn. Forbes Online. Accessed on 15 February 2015. Available at: http://www.forbes.com/sites/greatspeculations/2015/01/07/strong-q4-activity-makes-2014-the-best-year-for-ma-since-downturn/.

Gaughan, P. A. 1991. *Mergers and Acquisitions*. New York: John Wiley and Sons.

Gomes, E., Angwin, D., Weber, Y. and Tarba, S. Y. 2013. Critical success factors through the mergers and acquisitions process: Revealing pre- and post-M&A connections for improved performance. *Thunderbird International Business Review*, Vol. 55: 13–36.

Gomes, E., Weber, Y., Brown, C., and Tarba, S.Y. (2011). *Mergers, Acquisitions and Strategic Alliances: Understanding the Process*. London and New York: Palgrave Macmillan.

Graham, J. R. and Harvey, C. R. 2001. The theory and practice of corporate finance: Evidence from the field. *Journal of Financial Economics*, Vol. 60 (2): 187–243.

Granstrand, O. and Sjolander, S. E. 1990. Managing innovation in multi-technology corporations. *Research Policy*, Vol. 19: 35–60.

Haleblian, J., Devers, C. E., McNamara, G., Carpenter, M. E. and Davison, R. B. 2009. Taking stock of what we know about mergers and acquisitions: A review and research agenda. *Journal of Management*, Vol. 35: 469–502.

Harzing, A. 1997. Response rates in international mail surveys: Results of a 22 country study. *International Business Review*, Vol. 6 (6): 641–665.

Hennart, J. F. and Park, Y. R. 1993. Greenfield versus acquisition: The strategy of Japanese investors in the United States. *Management Science*, Vol. 39: 1054–1070.

Hill, C. W. L., Hwang, P. and Kim, W. C. 1990. An eclectic theory of the choice of international entry mode. *Strategic Management Journal*, Vol. 11: 117–128.

Hitt, M. A., Harrison, J. S. and Ireland, R. D. 2001. *Mergers and Acquisitions: A Guide to Creating Value for Stakeholders*. New York: Oxford University Press.

Hopkins, H. D. 1999. Cross-border mergers and acquisitions: Global and regional perspectives. *Journal of International Management*, Vol. 5: 207–239.

Ingham, H., Kran, I. and Lovestam, A. 1992. Mergers and profitability: A managerial success story? *Journal of Management Studies*, Vol. 29 (2): 195–208.

Jansson, K., Kirk-Smith, M. and Wightman, S. 1994. The impact of the single European market on cross-border mergers in the UK manufacturing industry. *European Business Review*, Vol. 94 (2): 8–13.

Kang, N. and Johansson, S. 2000. Cross-border mergers and acquisitions: Their role in industrial globalisation. Working paper, Directorate for Science, Technology and Industry, OECD.

Kesner, I. F., Shapiro, D. L. and Sharma, A. 1994. Brokering mergers: An agency theory perspective on the role of representatives. *Academy of Management Journal*, Vol. 37 (3): 703–721.

Kohli, R. and Mann, B. J. S. 2012. Analyzing determinants of value creation in domestic and cross-border acquisitions in India. *International Business Review*, Vol. 21: 998–1016.

KPMG Management Consulting 1998. *Mergers and Acquisitions in Europe*. Research report.

Kreitl, G. and Oberndorfer, W. 2004. Motives for acquisitions among engineering consulting firms. *Construction Management and Economics*, Vol. 22: 691–700.

Levy, H. and Sarnat, M. 1970. Diversification, portfolio analysis and the uneasy case for conglomerate merger. *Journal of Finance*, Vol. 25: 795–802.

Madhok, A. 1997. Cost, value and foreign market entry: The transaction and the firm. *Strategic Management Journal*, Vol. 18 (1): 39–63.

Manne, H. 1965. Mergers and the market for corporate control. *Journal of Political Economy*, Vol. 73 (2): 110–120.

Martin, X., Swaminathan, A. and Mitchell, W. 1998. Organizational evolution in the interorganizational environment: Incentives and constraints on international expansion strategy. *Administrative Science Quarterly*, Vol. 43: 566–601.

McCann, J. E. 1996. The growth of acquisitions in services. *Long Range Planning*, Vol. 29 (6): 835–841.

Moeller, S. B. and Schlingemann, F. P. 2005. Global diversification and bidder gains: A comparison between cross-border and domestic acquisitions. *Journal of Banking and Finance*, Vol. 29 (3): 533–564.

Mueller, D. C. 1969. A theory of conglomerate mergers. *Quarterly Journal of Economics*, Vol. 83: 643–659.

Mukherjee, T. K., Kiymaz, H. and Baker, H. K. 2004. Merger motives and target valuation: A survey of evidence from CFOs. *Journal of Applied Finance*, Fall/Winter: 7–24.

Nicholson, R. R. and Salaber, J. 2013. The motives and performance of cross-border acquirers from emerging economies: Comparison between Chinese and Indian firms. *International Business Review*, Vol. 22: 963–980.

Ohmae, K. 1989. The global logic of strategic alliances. *Harvard Business Review*, March–April: 143–154.

ONS. 2014. Mergers and acquisitions involving UK companies, Q4 2013. Office for National Statistics UK. Accessed on 15 February 2015. Available at: http://www.ons.gov.

uk/ons/rel/international-transactions/mergers-and-acquisitions-involving-uk-companies/q4-2013/stb-m-a-q4-2013. html#tab-Transactions-Abroad-by-UK-Companies.

Papadakis, V. M. and Thanos, I. C. 2010. Measuring the performance of acquisitions: An empirical investigation using multiple criteria. *British Journal of Management*, Vol. 21: 859–873.

Park, B. and Ghauri, P. N. 2011. Key factors affecting acquisition of technological capabilities from foreign acquiring firms by small and medium sized local firms. *Journal of World Business*, Vol. 46: 116–125.

Pfeffer, J. and Salancik, G. R. 1978. *The External Controls Of Organizations: A Resource Dependence Perspective*. New York: Harper and Row.

Porter, M. E. 1987. From competitive advantage to corporate strategy. *Harvard Business Review*, Vol. 65 (3): 43–59.

Ravenscraft, D. J. and Scherer, F. M. 1987. *Mergers, Sell-offs, and Economic Efficiency*. Washington, DC: The Brookings Institution.

Roll, R. 1986. The hubris hypothesis of corporate takeovers. *Journal of Business*, Vol. 59 (2): 197–216.

Rostand, A. 1994. Optimizing managerial decisions during the acquisition integration process. Paper presented at the 14th Annual Strategic Management Society International Conference, Paris.

Rugman, A. M. 1982. *New Theories of multinational Enterprise*. New York: St. Martin's Press.

Rui, H. and Yip, G. S. 2008. Foreign acquisitions by Chinese firms: A strategic intent perspective. *Journal of World Business*, Vol. 43: 213–226.

Schmitz, P. W. and Sliwka, D. 2001. On synergies and vertical integration. *International Journal of Industrial Organization*, Vol 19: 1281–1295.

Schoenberg, R. and Seow, L. M. 2005. Cross-border acquisitions: A comparative analysis. Paper presented at the 47th Annual Conference of the Academy of International Business, Quebec.

Servaes, H. 1991. Tobin's Q and the gains from takeovers. *Journal of Finance*, Vol. 46: 409–419.

Seth, A. 1990. Value creation in acquisition: A re-examination of performance issues. *Strategic Management Journal*, Vol. 11: 99–111.

Seth, A., Song, K. P. and Pettit, R. 2000. Synergy, managerialism or hubris? An empirical examination of motives for foreign acquisitions of US firms. *Journal of International Business Studies*, Vol. 31 (3): 387–405.

Shimizu, K., Hitt, M., Vaidyanath, D. and Pisano, V. 2004. Theoretical foundations of cross-border mergers and acquisitions: A review of current research and recommendations for the future. *Journal of International Management*, Vol. 10: 307–353.

Sirower, M. 1997. *The Synergy Trap*. New York: The Free Press.

Sudarsanam, P. S. 1995. *The Essence of Mergers and Acquisitions*. New Jersey: Prentice-Hall.

Trautwein, F. 1990. Merger motives and merger prescriptions. *Strategic Management Journal*, Vol. 11 (4): 283–295.

Uddin, M. and Boateng, A. 2011. Explaining the trends in the UK cross-border mergers and acquisitions: An analysis of macro-economic factors. *International Business Review*, Vol. 20: 547–556.

UNCTAD. 2000. *World Investment Report 2000: Cross-border Mergers and Acquisitions and Development*. New York and Geneva: United Nations.

Vasconcellos, G. M. and Kish, R. J. 1998. Cross-border mergers and acquisitions: The European–US experience. *Journal of Multinational Financial Management*, Vol. 8: 431–450.

Vermeulen, F., and Barkema, H. 2001. Learning through acquisitions. *Academy of Management Journal*, Vol. 44 (3): 457–476.

Walter, G. A. and Barney, J. B. 1990. Research notes and communications: Management objectives in mergers and acquisitions. *Strategic Management Journal*, Vol. 11 (1): 79–86.

Weber, Y. and Tarba, S. Y. 2011. Exploring culture clash in related mergers: Post-merger integration in the high-tech industry. *International Journal of Organizational Analysis*, Vol. 19 (3): 202–221.

Weber, Y., Tarba, S. Y. and Öberg, C. 2014. *A Comprehensive Guide to Mergers and Acquisitions: Managing the Critical Success Factors across Every Stage of the M&A Process*. New York and London: Pearson and Financial Times Press.

Weber, Y., Tarba, S. Y. and Reichel, A. 2009. International mergers and acquisitions performance revisited: The role of cultural distance and post-acquisition integration approach implementation. *Advances in Mergers and Acquisitions*, Vol. 8: 1–18.

Weber, Y., Tarba, S. Y. and Reichel, A. 2011. International mergers and acquisitions performance: Acquirer nationality and integration approaches. *International Studies of Management and Organization*, Vol. 41 (3): 9–24.

Weber, Y., Tarba, S. Y. and Rozen-Bachar, Z. 2011. Mergers and acquisitions performance paradox: The mediating role of integration approach. *European Journal of International Management*, Vol. 5 (4): 373–393.

Weber, Y., Tarba, S. Y. and Rozen-Bachar, Z. 2012. The effects of culture clash on international mergers in the high-tech industry. *World Review of Entrepreneurship, Management and Sustainable Development*, Vol. 8 (1): 103–118.

Weston, J. and Weaver, S. 2001. *Mergers and Acquisitions*. New York: McGraw-Hill.

Weston, J., Siu, J. A. and Johnson, B. 2001. *Takeovers, Restructuring and Corporate Governance*. New York: Prentice-Hall.

Williamson, O. E. 1975. *Market and Hierarchies: Analysis and Antitrust Implications*. New York: The Free Press.

Zheng, N., Wei, Y., Zhang, Y. and Yang, J. 2016. In search of strategic assets through cross-border merger and acquisitions: Evidence from Chinese multinational enterprises in developed economies. *International Business Review*, Vol. 25 (1): 177–186.

4

STRATEGIC MERGERS IN THE PUBLIC SECTOR

Comparing universities and hospitals

Rómulo Pinheiro, Timo Aarrevaara, Laila Nordstrand Berg, Lars Geschwind, and Dag Olaf Torjesen

Introduction

This chapter addresses the following research question: what can be learnt from public sector mergers that could assist in the planning and execution of successful strategic mergers more broadly? In so doing, we have undertaken a comprehensive literature review across two sectors of the economy – health and higher education – by investigating merger dynamics involving public hospitals and universities. Earlier reviews of mergers and acquisitions in different sectors have identified several gaps of knowledge. A meta-analysis of post-acquisition performance does not provide any evidence that acquisitions have a significant effect on financial performance or guarantee long-term financial gain (King *et al.* 2004), and there is a need for a better understanding of the conditions or variables related to acquisitions that will influence performance. Sarala *et al.* (2016) point out that sociocultural factors are determinants of outcomes, but there is an incomplete understanding of the role of such factors in mergers and acquisitions. Gaps revealed through their review include the need for a theoretically grounded examination of the role of sociocultural inter-firm linkages (complementary employee skills, trust, collective teaching and cultural integration), flexibility in human resources (employee skills, behaviour and practices) and different organizational cultural differences. By addressing these gaps, Sarala *et al.* (2016) developed a model which could be tested empirically. There is also a need to evaluate critical success factors at different phases in the merger process (Gomes *et al.* 2013; Haleblian *et al.* 2009). Another gap in the literature relates to interdisciplinary reviews (Gomes *et al.* 2013); in particular, management studies could benefit by synthesizing contributions from different fields and methodologies (Haleblian *et al.* 2009). There is little knowledge of the antecedents of acquisitions as an example, whether the motive is profit or managerial self-interest. Haleblian *et al.* (2009) also encourage exploring processes which foster effective integration, and the dynamics between the involved management teams. The gaps we address in this chapter are: (a) the rationale for merging; (b) the merger process; and (c) the tangible effects.

The rationale for comparing universities and hospitals is fourfold: first, they represent significant parts of the domestic GDP in many countries; second, both sectors are thought to be critical actors in the context of an ageing, knowledge-based economy underpinned by the global competition for talent, skills and novel ideas (innovation); third, both sectors have been at the forefront of policy agendas with the strategic aim of modernizing providers' internal structures, missions, functions and institutional profiles; and, fourth, both are professional bureaucracies characterized by increasingly hybrid forms of organizing and strong (legitimatized) professional groups – doctors, nurses, academics and so on.

As a phenomenon, mergers can be traced back to the US's manufacturing industry during the period 1895–1904, when the consolidation of an estimated 1,800 firms occurred (Choi 2011; Lamoreaux 1985). Globally, waves of mergers have occurred in different industries and across countries and world regions throughout the twentieth century (Amin 2011). In recent years, mergers have returned to the forefront of policy and strategic agendas. Although mergers involving public sector organizations can be traced back to the 1950s (Pinheiro *et al.* 2013; 2016a), we are particularly interested in investigating such strategic processes that have occurred in the last two decades or so, partly as a result of government-led efforts towards modernizing the public sector more broadly (Christensen and Lægreid 2011). Before doing so, a few important caveats about studying public sector mergers are necessary.

First, the determination of price and the economic benefits of mergers involving public organizations is a problematic undertaking. Such figures may be associated with the promise of benefits that never come to pass. The *rules* that might be appropriate for one sector (e.g. healthcare) might not necessarily apply in merger situations involving institutions belonging to other sectors, like higher education (see Pinheiro *et al.* 2016b). Similarly, differences within sectors are relevant, too. For example, why should the same merger rules work in small and large specialized multi-faculty universities? From a structural point of view, the idea is that an administrative federalism model will strengthen the capacity of the local public sector to take responsibility for the provision of welfare services (Christensen *et al.* 2007). For example, in the division of work between hospitals and local government, it is still unclear how the local public sector fits as regards the responsibility for the provision of healthcare services (Moisio 2012).

Second, instead of the classic arguments based on resources (constraints and assets) and competitive advantages (Barney 1991), it is reasonable to focus on the social benefits of performance instead. Determining what benefits will ensue from a new mode of operation across the public sector is, nonetheless, an ambiguous undertaking, not to mention the tensions associated with abolishing (de-institutionalization) the practices emanating from the previous organization (Oliver 1992). For example, within universities, new regulatory and strategic frameworks can make a broader scope of services more complex and ambiguous than was the case in the past (Enders and Boer 2009).

Third, whilst understanding change dynamics across the public sector, attention should be paid to the motives of the key actors involved, and their respective roles – direct and indirect – in processes of change or lack thereof. In the public sector it is typical for the managers responsible for everyday management also to be in charge of change management more broadly (Meek *et al.* 2010). That said, as many such managers do not belong to the traditional professional groups (doctors, nurses, academics, etc.) working at universities and hospitals, their authority and legitimacy are often challenged and scrutinized to an extent that is not the case in the private sector.

The chapter is organized as follows. In the next section we sketch out the literature pertaining to public sector mergers with a focus on the two aforementioned sectors. We then discuss the key findings across the sectors, and conclude by suggesting avenues for future research.

Public sector mergers

The literature on public sector mergers reveals significant variations across disciplines and schools of thought. Economic theorists examine mergers from the economies of scale point of view, and find utility in the efficiency and dynamics of work. In contrast, the organization theory school is critical of this approach, and emphasizes that transaction costs are higher when units (size) are enlarged. As public activity is controlled by means of regulation, mergers have complex consequences for public organizations. A change of unit size does not necessarily affect an organization's income and expenditure, thus the notion of an optimally sized unit does not necessarily make sense within the context of public sector mergers.

In the public sector, mergers can be pursued for reasons other than calculations-based optimizations, such as stronger management structures and more flexible pools of resources (Harman 2000). Financial resources as such are not necessarily an obstacle once it has been decided that there should be a merger. In contrast to the private sector, the price-setting objective is not the key issue facing two or more public organizations that wish to merge. The main actors involved can demonstrate their approaches without clear policy guidance to provide structure, thus creating inconsistent development plans and opportunities (Goddard and Palmer 2010). Yet, as is the case in the private sector, cost savings are often the main rationale behind public sector mergers. What is more, mergers are an important strategic avenue for developing public services in realms such as education, healthcare, local government and social work (Moisio 2012; OECD 2010).

The problems faced by public organizations in merger processes have been sketched in the literature. For example, the merger (2005–2006) between the employment and national insurance services has led to the creation of the Norwegian labour and welfare administration (NAV). This is by far the largest of the central government's reorganizations in the last decade. The evaluative literature on NAV reports that the greatest risks surrounding the merger process were threefold, pertaining to: the choice of reference organizations; overlapping stages; and the appointment of management (Askim *et al.* 2008, 2011). Various studies report a strong confidence in the central government's ability to implement wider reform programmes for public administration (Pollitt and Bouckaert 2011), with a rather optimistic view as regards the timetable for public sector mergers. It is clear, however, that building a "whole-of-government system" across organizational boundaries takes time, and that major reforms are far from being neutral administrative techniques (Christensen *et al.* 2009).

Mergers involving higher education institutions

Merger rationales and drivers

There are a variety of reasons or rationales for mergers among higher education institutions. At the level of the *superstructure* (Clark 1983) or central government, and as a policy instrument mergers are expected to: enhance system integration (rationalization); improve the quality of teaching and research; address equity considerations (e.g. enrolment contraction) as well as improve the (cost-)efficiency of domestic higher education systems (Harman 1986; Kyvik 2002).

A recent review of the literature, covering the period from the 1970s to the 1990s, identified the most important reasons for merging as relating to the need to:

- boost efficiency and effectiveness;
- deal with organizational fragmentation;
- broaden student access and implement equity strategies;
- increase government control over higher education systems;
- enhance decentralization (autonomy); and
- establish larger organizations (Ahmadvand *et al.* 2012).

All in all, mergers are thought to have the potential to produce substantial long-term benefits for individual providers and the system as whole. These include, but are not limited to: (a) the establishment of larger and more comprehensive institutions; (b) stronger academic programmes; (c) improved student services; (d) enhanced student choice; (e) greater institutional flexibility; and (f), under certain conditions, increased efficiencies and cost savings (Harman and Harman 2003; Harman and Meek 2002). A common rationale for resorting to mergers of academic institutions is based on the establishment of larger units, in the form of academic and administrative *economies of scale* (Norgard and Skodvin 2002; Pinheiro 2012).[1]

At the level of the individual higher education institution, the rationale and motivation for embracing mergers as a strategic management/planning mechanism (Toma 2010) pertains to the urge to address financial problems and emerging external threats, such as falling student demand and fiercer competition

(Goedegebuure and Meek 1994; Harman and Harman 2003; Pinheiro and Stensaker 2014), in addition to the changing needs and demands of key external stakeholder groups (Pinheiro 2012; Pinheiro *et al.* 2012b). In comparison, studies from the private higher education sector (period 1960–1994 and employing statistical regression analysis) reveal that mergers are more likely to occur amidst rises in faculty salaries and the decline in tuition rates (Bates and Santerre 2000).

Mergers can be broadly categorized as either *voluntary* (institutionally driven) or *forced* (mandated) by government (Harman and Harman 2003). Qualitative studies from Australia in the 1980s suggest that voluntary amalgamations tend to take place when institutions fear governments will mandate restructuring (Curri 2002). More recently, and in a number of countries, there has been a shift from mergers initiated from the "top down" by government as a means of dealing with so-called "problem cases" towards institution-initiated amalgamation processes involving "strong" institutions with clear strategic objectives (Harman and Harman 2008).

Goedegebuure and Meek (1994: 128) define a merger involving higher education institutions as pertaining to

> the combination of two or more separate institutions into a single new organizational entity, in which control rests with a single governing body and a single chief executive body, and whereby all assets, liabilities, and responsibilities of the former institutions are transferred to the single new organization.

These authors also make a distinction between mergers and takeovers or acquisition. The former is considered to be a takeover only if one of the organizations involved retains its original form and thereafter does not alter the legal base of its charter.

There have been several attempts to make typologies of higher education mergers, based on the institutional profiles and missions of the organizations involved. Goedegebuure and Meek (1994: 129; see also Cai *et al.* 2016) have proposed the following typology:

- Horizontal – similar academic fields, similar type of product;[2]
- Vertical – similar academic fields, different type of product;
- Diversification – different academic fields, similar type of product; and
- Conglomerate – different academic fields, different kind of product.

The process

Similar to what is the case in the private sector, merger processes involving higher education institutions are something of a "black box" – that is under-researched phenomena. That said, it is generally recognized in the literature that mergers are a complex and painstaking activity for institutions and staff alike (Bresler 2007; Cartwright *et al.* 2007; Wan 2008). A number of key challenges come to the fore as far as merger processes are concerned. Not only do mergers bring profound leadership/managerial- related challenges (Goedegebuure 2011b), but coherent, cohesive and sustainable integration efforts tend to take a long time to materialize, usually about a decade (Mao *et al.* 2009).

Studies from South Africa on staff perceptions of mergers indicate that staff are not necessarily opposed to the process, but that careful consideration needs to be given to certain personal factors (e.g. staff fears and anxieties) in order to ensure an effective merger (Hay and Fourie 2002). More recent studies (from South Africa and the UK) highlight the stressful potential of the pre-merger period on the staff involved, as well as the positive role of consultation and involvement during the merger process, from design and implementation to evaluation (Becker *et al.* 2004; Cartwright *et al.* 2007).

Another crucial issue relates to the spatial aspects of mergers. Research in Australia indicates that integrated merged campuses provide more scope for tighter cultural integration (around the notion of "integrated communities") when compared with federal structures, and that expert leadership is a key condition for minimizing cultural conflict and the development of new loyalties around a shared sense of community (Harman 2002; for similars accounts from South Africa, see Kamsteeg 2011 and Bresler 2007). "A particular cultural challenge for higher education leaders is to manage the merging of divergent campus cultures into coherent educational communities that display high levels of cultural integration and loyalty to the new institution" (Harman and Harman 2003: 38; see also Pinheiro and Berg 2016).

Various studies from South Africa have provided statistical evidence of the effect of a drastic life-changing event like mergers in the actualization of academics' intellectual potential and emotional skills, thus accentuating the importance of timely and continued assessment of the ongoing functioning and well-being of academics involved in mergers (Maree and Eiselen 2004; see also Theron and Dodd 2011). In other contexts, there is evidence of the critical role played by certain agents during the design and implementation phases. For example, a merger leading to the establishment of the third largest public higher education institution in the state of Ohio, USA, points to "the efforts of a number of [key] individuals who recognized the potential advantages of a merger and worked quickly through challenges by early engagement of stakeholders [including local politicians] in the merger process" (McGinnis *et al.* 2007: 1187).

A UK-based study covering a total of thirty mergers instigated between the late 1980s and the mid-1990s found that in two out of three cases, the final formal decision to merge was preceded by a period of inter-institutional collaboration, yet the latter factor was not found to be critical for success per se (Rowley 1997; see also Kyvik and Stensaker 2013). Evidence from Australia suggests that, in order to achieve organizational change resulting from a merger, the congruence between a set of key factors is critical to achieve desired outcomes, with the data pointing to the relationship between dimensions such as leadership, restructuring, the management of staff relations, organizational development, external pressure for change and organizational change (Curri 2002). Similarly, in China, Cai (2007) has demonstrated how academic staff integration resulting from a merger between three separate institutions was aided by factors such as cultural compatibility amongst the pre-merger institutions and managerial transparency. In Australia, Gamage (1992: 89) cites the critical factors that aided the successful merger between two institutions in the mid-1980s as: the voluntary nature of the merger; the lengthy, deliberative and consultative period taken to finalize the agreement; and the pace at which this was executed.

A study adopting a social identity approach – suggesting that pre-merger group membership, socio-structural characteristics and underlying motivational processes affect people's responses to mergers – provides empirical evidence for the fact that discrepancies between what merger partners *want* and what they *get* out of the merger affects outcomes that are essential to merger success (Gleibs *et al.* 2013). On the basis of a government-mandated merger between two UK-based institutions, the authors were able to predict and demonstrate empirically that members of the university and polytechnic groups involved in the process desired merger patterns that would optimize their status in the newly merged organization (Gleibs *et al.* 2013). Whereas members of the "low-status" group (polytechnic) preferred a merger pattern where both groups were equally represented, members of the "high-status" group were keen on integration proportionality and assimilation. More specifically, it indicates that a negative outcome (loss of status) for the pre-merger group leads to decreased support for the merger. In contrast, misfit that indicates a positive outcome (gain in status) for the in-group was not found to have a negative effect on merger support. According to Cai (2006: 223):

> In a post-merger process, if the staff members feel that their organization has been transformed into one with higher prestige, the new identity will accordingly change their ways of thinking and their behaviour patterns . . . because pursuing higher academic status is a common value and behaviour tendency among academic staff.

A comprehensive review of the literature by Harman and Harman (2003) revealed the following:

- Voluntary mergers are easier to organize and tend to be more successful than forced ones, "largely because it is possible to achieve a substantial degree of staff involvement in negotiations and implementation, leading usually to a strong sense of ownership" (Harman and Harman 2003: 31–32).
- Consolidations (i.e. mergers involving similar institutions) are, generally speaking, more demanding and involve difficult trade-offs, such as choice of the new academic structure, the portfolio of courses to be offered and so on.
- Cross-sectoral mergers pose special dilemmas since institutions from different sectors often have distinct missions, roles and cultures, in addition to distinct funding bases.
- Finally, mergers of institutions possessing the same or a similar range of disciplinary fields often mean greater commonality in academic cultures, thus easing

cultural integration, yet they also tend to require considerable rationalization of course offerings in order to realize cost savings.

In short, some evidence points to the complexity of the process surrounding mergers, either voluntary or forced, and to the criticality of key variables in predicting successful outcomes. Nonetheless, scholars are careful not to draw bold conclusions from specific case situations and highlight the criticality of the contextual circumstances surrounding mergers; ranging from changes in national regulations, demographic trends and migration patterns, regional and national competition, institutional histories, resource dependencies, leadership structures, academic aspirations, timing, the role of external actors, and so on. (Cai 2007; Goedegebuure 2011a; Goedegebuure and Meek 1994; Kyvik 2002; Locke 2007; Pinheiro and Stensaker 2014; Pinheiro *et al.* 2016a; Stensaker *et al.* 2016).

Effects

What do we know when it comes to the mid- and long-term effects or outcomes of mergers involving higher education institutions? From a comparative standpoint, it is interesting to discuss what kinds of indicators and aspects are used in the assessment of mergers. Whether a specific merger has been "successful" is contingent on the criteria used.

Skodvin (1999) proposes the following three dimensions or levels of analysis: governance, management and administration; economics; and academic activities. Based on a comprehensive review of the literature (in the late 1990s), Skodvin indicates that many merged institutions result in a more professional and efficient *administration*. That said, it was also revealed that economies of scale are less common, due to both the legal framework (unions) and human resources (HR) policies. Furthermore, growth in organizational size was found to be positively correlated with increasing internal complexity. In the realm of *economics*, Skodvin concludes that, in the short run, mergers are rather costly, but also that there are economies of scale over the long term. On this point, the data suggest considerable differences between network organizations spread across different locations and those located within a specific geographic area, with much higher transaction costs in the former. Finally, regarding *academic activities*, the status and prestige of the departments/fields involved were found to be obstacles in some circumstances, but, on the whole, mergers were thought to result into broader and more multidisciplinary programmatic offerings. More specifically, as regards research activities, results were found to be uncertain yet mergers seem to trigger positive developmental activities. Overall, Skodvin concludes that the greater the differences in terms of size and scope, the higher the probability that mergers will be successful.

Whilst investigating the short-term effects (after three years) of the merger between two Australian institutions in the mid-1980s, Gamage (1992) found realizable synergies and shortcomings. On the positive front, significant progress had been made with respect to the upgrading of existing and the development of new academic programmes, as well as an enhanced institutional profile and market recognition (e.g. by becoming the sixth-largest university in the country) – reflected in increased student demand and membership of the prestigious domestic "League of Big Universities." Yet, despite this, academic integration in the realm of teaching (staff synergies) was found to be far from optimal; and, more importantly, economies of scale (financial efficacy) had not been realized (see also Aagaard *et al.* 2016).

In their review of the existing international literature, Harman and Harman (2003: 42) conclude the following with respect to the outcomes generated by mergers involving higher education institutions:

> Overall, well-planned and sensible merger efforts appear to have been largely successful, even if the merger proposals were strongly contested at the time. In many cases, mergers have resulted in larger and more comprehensive institutions, with stronger academic programmes and support service, more choice for students and increased capacity for organisational flexibility. While mergers generally involve additional expenditure rather than cost savings in the short term, often there have been substantial longer-term gains, although care needs to be taken with many of the claims made about potential economies of scale.[3]

In his study of merger processes (1987–1994) involving UK-based higher education institutions (thirty cases), Rowley (1997: 12) concludes that 90 per cent of the mergers can be considered rather successful. In retrospect, the author stresses that, "while most HE [higher education] mergers are the outcome of a rational planning process, like corporate mergers they include many unanticipated consequences, some of which are strategically significant."

In China, Wan and Peterson (2007) found that the most significant benefit of a merger dating back to 1994 was an enhanced *academic portfolio*, with limited gains when it came to administrative effectiveness. According to these authors:

> the integration of academic structure is now accomplished to a large extent, although not without tensions and conflicts in the process. The new institution now gives more breadth and choice to their students. There are clear indications that the merger has improved the academic position of the new institution, especially in regard to the breadth of different education.
>
> *(Wan and Peterson 2007: 695)*

Recent studies from South Africa (Eastern Cape Province) tentatively suggest that the synergic effects, both administrative and academic, emanating from mergers have the potential for a stronger degree of *academic engagement* with regional actors at a variety of levels, thus augmenting the potential benefits of the presence of a university (i.e. its various educational sites or multiple campuses) across a given geography (Pinheiro 2010, 2012; see also Pinheiro *et al.* 2012a). Other recent studies from Scandinavia illustrate how a perceived "new" university has the potential to attract significantly more students than the earlier HEIs (Geschwind *et al.* 2016). This effect appears immediately after the completed merger, preceding the foreseen quality boost as an outcome of the process.

Yet another way to discuss post-merger effects is based on the attitudes of staff. In a study of the long-term effects of a forced merger – the creation of the University of Ulster in 1984, described as "a shotgun marriage" – Pritchard and Williamson (2008) found that twenty years after the merger almost two-thirds of survey respondents thought the former organization was "a happier place." However, the general picture that mergers are always stressful for the people involved has been questioned by some scholars. In a study of two UK universities, Cartwright *et al.* (2007) found that employees were relatively healthy in terms of stress.

Mergers involving hospitals

Rationale

In the 1980s, the merger trend reached the healthcare sector, starting in the US (Choi 2011). To justify the mergers, financial and operational improvements were promised. That said, as is often the case, scholars disagree on the rationale for merging hospitals, with some arguing that they will improve efficiency, lower costs and enhance health outcomes, while others contend that there is little evidence to support this view (Cuellar and Gertler 2003).

In the Nordic countries, most of the healthcare is publicly owned and managed (Häkkinen and Jonsson 2009). Since the 1990s the sector has been characterized by new public management reforms, and the main drivers behind the reforms have been attempts to improve economy, efficiency and equity – that is, improve regional variations in quality and accessibility. There have been concerns regarding low productivity and increasing costs. The costs are financed through a publicly governed tax system (Magnussen *et al.* 2009; Rehnberg *et al.* 2009) and all citizens are offered "universal coverage," which does not specify the types of services included. Two major trends have occurred in the Nordic countries in recent years. Reforms with effects on the production side have been implemented in Norway and Denmark. Sweden has prepared a reform, and Finland has taken a decision on such a reform (Häkkinen and Jonsson 2009). The long tradition of decentralizing responsibility for healthcare to local government (Rehnberg *et al.* 2009) has been challenged through reforms focusing on the production side (Häkkinen and Jonsson 2009). Mergers and the centralization of decision-making authority have been the primary means to enhance productivity and control rising costs.

In Sweden major restructuring of the healthcare sector during the 1980s paved the way for mergers (Choi 2011), which became a common strategy in the mid-1990s (Häkkinen and Jonsson 2009). In the late 1990s a merger resulted in the establishment of Sahlgrenska University Hospital in the western part of the country;

in 2004, Karolinska University Hospital merged with Huddinge University Hospital; and in 2010 Skåne University Hospital was formed out of the amalgamation between two other university hospitals (Choi 2011). Healthcare legislation has not been substantially changed in Sweden, but there have been attempts to merge regional authorities which have responsibility for healthcare. In 2007 a proposal to reduce the number of authorities from eighteen counties and two regions to six–nine regional authorities by 2015 was introduced.

Similar debates, supported by the Ministry of Health, took place in Finland, but no changes in legislation have been introduced so far. Since the 1990s, there have been reforms aimed at merging health centres and regional hospitals with the purpose of enhancing cooperation between primary and secondary healthcare and social welfare services. A few voluntary mergers have occurred, including the merger of three hospitals in the Helsinki area in 2007. During the 1990s, the central government made several recommendations regarding the internal organization of health units (Häkkinen and Jonsson 2009), but the municipalities did not cooperate. This resulted in a reform project which ended with the enactment of a new law in 2007, under the terms of which municipalities that decide to merger voluntarily receive financial support. As a result, in 2009 the number of municipalities was reduced from 415 to 348. This has had an impact on primary healthcare, but hospital care is still organized under federations of municipalities.

In Norway the number of hospitals fell from eighty before the reform in 2002 (HD 2001) to twenty in 2012 (Kjekshus and Bernstrøm 2010, 2013). This was achieved partly by merging existing hospitals and partly by closures. The country is divided into four health regions, organized as health enterprises. The strategic aim behind the merger processes was to enhance performance, quality, efficiency, and equity. Stronger central government control and responsibility were the main tools, together with clearer defined responsibilities for the enterprises, and increased operational flexibility (Lægreid *et al.* 2005).

Finally, in Denmark no major reforms affecting the number of public hospitals have been undertaken (Häkkinen and Jonsson 2009). That said, in tandem with the structural reform in 2007 – which led to the reduction of regional authorities from fourteen counties to four regions, and 275 municipalities to 98 (Häkkinen and Jonsson 2009) – there is also a political desire to concentrate hospital activities in larger entities (Kristensen *et al.* 2010). The regions have responsibility for hospitals, but the 2007 reform transferred responsibility for rehabilitation and health prevention to the municipalities.

Moving beyond the Nordic region, in the UK the focus of hospital politics changed after the Labour Party came to power in 1997 (Gaynor *et al.* 2012). The Conservative governments from 1979 to 1997, including those under Margaret Thatcher, emphasized *competition*, whereas Labour (1997–2010) put a premium on *cooperation*. The latter party sought to deal with the problems in the sector by merging hospitals that had failed to reach financial or qualitative goals, as defined by waiting times (Gaynor *et al.* 2012). Between 1997 and 2006, a total of 112 public hospitals were forced to merge.

On the other side of the Atlantic, in the USA, more than 900 hospital mergers and acquisitions occurred throughout the 1990s (Capps *et al.* 2002). One purpose for merging was to eliminate duplicated services and capacity, a strategic response to the increasing shift from *in-patient* care to *out-patient* care from the 1980s onwards. A second motive, which was barely mentioned, was to enhance market power or choice.

The process

Few studies have been concerned with process- and implementation-related issues surrounding mergers involving public hospitals. That said, we were able to identify a handful of studies, from the Nordic and English contexts, that were concerned with such matters.

A major bottleneck or barrier for the implementation of mergers involving Norwegian hospitals pertains to the lack of autonomy among the CEOs in terms of decision-making and strategy (Hippe and Trygstad 2012). There is a culture of consultative decisions in the hospital sector, with the central actors being local politicians, employee representatives, professionals and users. Although this is considered to be a barrier for implementation, it also works as a quality assurance mechanism for the decisions that are taken, in addition to increasing legitimacy and facilitating the implementation of the decisions. One of the main organizational solutions in the wake of the Norwegian health enterprise reform is the *multidivisional* form and enterprise, with its alleged advantages (Kjekshus and Bernstrøm 2013). Most hospitals in Norway have adapted to the divisionalized structure. The latter has paved the way for a significant amount of centralization, structural rationalization and functional specialization in the forms of: (a) formal mergers between hospitals; (b) a significant reduction of activities; and (c) closing down local hospitals (Bykjeflot and Neby 2008; Kvåle and Torjesen 2014). Such measures have been met with much antagonism by civic society, local politicians and grassroots movements. This kind of resistance can be identified as grassroots resistance and organized civic resistance against strategic measures from the top down (Spicer and Böhm 2007). This movement has especially been triggered by health enterprises' decisions or proposals to close or reduce the scale of emergency treatment units and obstetrics and maternity wards in local hospitals. This, in turn, resulted in local torchlight processions all over the country and even a national protest march in Oslo on December 7, 2010.

In contrast to Denmark and Sweden, the actions and rhetoric of the local hospital movement in Norway clearly show that health and the distribution of care and treatment are important political issues and a manifestation of local communities insisting on maintaining decentralization as a strong value and tradition in Norwegian local democracy (Baldersheim and Rose 2010). The irony is that the 2002 hospital reform, which was partially meant to depoliticize the sector at the local level by handing it to professional managers, seems to have created a situation that is more politically charged than was the case before (Kvåle and Torjesen 2011, 2014). In the wake of the health enterprise reform in 2002 extensive restructuring in the university hospital sector received considerable public attention. Three hospitals were merged into the "new" University Hospital of North Norway in 2006. In this case, national quality indicators showed unchanged or improved results after the merger process was finalized in 2011: waiting times for patients had increased, but so had productivity (measured in DRG points per employee-month); financial outcome had improved by 12 per cent; and most of the employees were satisfied with their jobs after the merger (Ingebrigtsen *et al.* 2012). Similarly, Kronborg and Tangen (2014) found that the 2002 mergers did not have any significant effect on either volume or quality of care.

The merger of the university hospitals in Oslo from 2009 has created far more turbulence and conflict. The Office of the Auditor General of Norway concluded in a report in 2011 that Norwegian health authorities were unaware of the challenges a merger of three university hospitals in the Oslo region may generate, especially as the consequences for patients were not sufficiently examined and clarified beforehand. Later, the merger of Oslo's university hospitals became a scandal that ended in a public hearing in parliament. The CEO of the regional health enterprise was held accountable and had to leave her position (Riksrevisjonen 2012).

In Sweden a study of mergers involving the Karolinska University Hospital pointed out that management at all levels played an important role in both the development and the outcome of the merger process (Choi 2011). Moreover, although the process was planned as a top-down exercise – from hospital level to clinical level – it contributed to unintended or unexpected results, which has led researchers to describe it as a non-linear, uncontrolled and unpredictable process. Choi (2011) suggests a bottom-up approach with incremental and emergent steps as a post-merger strategy. This process works better for a professional organization (like a hospital) due to the lack of knowledge of the professional activities among management. The professionals are viewed as autonomous experts, and there is a risk that they will leave the organization following top-down implementation. Internal changes therefore depend on both the willingness and trustworthiness of these autonomous experts (Choi 2011; Montgomery 2001), and findings from the above study reveal that health professionals do take part in the early stages of mergers. "Horizontal" cultural differences between merged organizations is expected to be the main challenge in mergers, but this study shows that the main conflict lines occurred in the vertical hierarchy (Choi 2011). The main barriers detected were the competing *institutional logics* (Thornton and Ocasio 2008) between managerialism and professionalism. It is challenging to build trust among physicians as the key profession among health professionals, and the above study claims that this is a primary explanatory factor for the success of mergers (Choi 2011).

Similarly, studies of mergers involving hospitals in the UK have shed light on the criticality of management, and specifically the management of human resources (Shield *et al.* 2002). The conclusions from this study indicate that the lack of proper human resource policies and strategies results in problems surrounding the evaluation of the merger process as such. Management was found to be an important element not only when it came to achieving successful merger outcomes, but also with respect employees' overall job satisfaction.

Effects

The bulk of the literature on hospital mergers focuses on the accrued effects as well as the possible explanations for the observed (positive, neutral or negative) effects.

A study comparing merger effects in the Nordic countries has revealed that the Finnish hospitals appear to be more efficient than the others – 10 per cent more efficient than those in Denmark and Norway, and 25 per cent more efficient than Swedish hospitals. One explanation for this is the Finnish system of cost control exercised via the municipalities, which are the main funders of public hospitals via taxation. According to the authors, the former is more efficient than either governmental or regional control (Häkkinen and Jonsson 2009). That said, it must be stated that the authors do not compare quality outcomes.

In the period 1992–2000, seventeen Norwegian hospitals merged into seven hospitals. Studies of the effects of these mergers show a significant negative effect on cost efficiency of about 2.5 per cent. In general, there was also no effect on technical efficiency (Kjekshus and Hagen 2003, 2007). Others enquiries shed light on the short-term effects of health reforms in Norway, which include: increased productivity; shorter waiting lists and better accessibility; a decline on the performance variations between hospitals, yet ongoing regional variations (Häkkinen and Jonsson 2009). A more recent study comparing cost efficiency between Norwegian hospitals that have merged with that of non-merged hospitals shows that mergers do not necessarily have a positive effect on economics of scale (Brakestad and Sjåstad 2013). The same study, which was carried out between 2002 and 2011, reveals that some hospitals experienced a positive effect after merger whereas others suffered a negative effect.

The 1996 merger between Sweden's Karlskrona County Hospital and Karlshamn General Hospital, which led to the establishment of Blekinge Hospital, was driven by the conviction that larger hospitals lead to improved clinical quality and lower average costs (Ahgren 2008). However, this case study revealed that the interviewed staff did not believe that costs were reduced after the merger. The quality of care has, on the other hand, increased slightly, but the health professionals involved believed that evidence-based medicine and care had a greater impact on quality when compared to the increased volume of patients.

In Denmark the government is investing more than €5.3 billion in hospitals this decade alone. The hospital sector is expected to undergo a major restructuring culminating with the closure of larger hospitals. A study calculating the potential gains from the mergers predicts significant cost reductions and technical efficiency due to better practice and the exploitation of economies of scale, but, at the same time, points to the risk that some hospitals might become too large (complex) and, as a result, will experience diseconomies of scale (Kristensen *et al.* 2010).

A Norwegian review of the merger literature, including cases from the USA, the UK and Norway, concludes that, all things being equal, hospital mergers can result in a 10 per cent cost reduction (Ingebrigtsen 2010). However, it is pointed out that this reduction comes as a direct result of reduced rises in costs, rather than reductions in per unit costs per se. The growth in costs can be effected by avoiding duplication of services and aided by the development of a shared organization culture.

A study of British hospitals that merged between 1997 and 2006 shows that in the long run their overall financial situation worsened (Gaynor *et al.* 2012). There were no reductions in numbers of administrative staff, and no significant productivity increases (e.g. as regards hospitalization rates). Waiting times increased slightly, as did the numbers of patients on the waiting lists. Lastly, there was no improvement in quality, measured by re-hospitalization and mortality rates among particular patient groups. A literature review by Posnett (1999; see also Posnett 2002) shows that there is no empirical support for the assumption that larger UK hospitals (run under the National Health Service) lead to benefits in the realms of economies of scale or improved patient outcomes. As far as economies of scale go, there is evidence to suggest that mergers of small hospitals (fewer than 200 beds) give the best results, and that hospitals with 200–400 beds are the most cost effective, while costs per treated patient tend to increase when the number of beds surpasses 600.

Notwithstanding the existing evidence, it is worth outlining that there are several biases surrounding studies of mergers in the public hospital sector (Dafny 2009). Dafny (2006) contends that one way of overcoming this is to include in the study sample the merged hospitals as well as the hospitals with which the merged institutions were competing in a certain geographically area. By comparing data from the period 1989–1996, it was revealed that prices increased by 40 per cent following the mergers of rival hospitals near by. Finally, the author points out that there have been only a few studies concerning quality outcomes from mergers.

A case study from North Carolina, USA, focusing on in-patient claims to four care insurers to calculate the effects of mergers on in-patient prices shows mixed results (Thompson 2011). For two of the insurers, the prices increased substantially; there was no particular effect on the third insurer; while the fourth insurance company had a significant price reduction. The differences in results between the insurers can be explained by different opportunities to bargain, the different types of plan offered, and the kind of service provided. The merged hospitals had less competition from other hospitals, due to the relative distance to the next hospital (twenty miles), and this factor alone, the author argues, might have contributed to a rise in average prices. Thompson (2011) also questions whether the hospitals' "non-profit" status might have contributed to the lack of exercised market power. Finally, a decrease in costs might be explained by the consolidation of medical specialties, which also improves quality of care.

Similarly, other findings support the claim that mergers often lead to increased costs. The merger of the non-profit Sutter and Summit hospitals in Oakland, California, in 1999 turned out to be anti-competitive (Tenn 2011). The question being investigated relates to geographic distances and, more specifically, whether travel costs to nearby hospitals limit competitive pricing. The data show that the merger led to increased prices due to the fact that the larger (merged) hospital improved its bargaining power to negotiate with health insurers. These findings are corroborated by other enquiries, for example into the merger between a non-profit hospital and a for-profit hospital in Santa Cruz, California in 1990, which also resulted in increased costs and a market power that led to price–cost mark-ups (Vita and Sacher 2001).

Finally, a review of sixty hospital mergers in the USA surveyed in 1991 focuses on mergers as an expeditious possibility to change hospitals' internal organizational structures (Bogue *et al.* 1995). In this scenario, the mergers served as strategic mechanisms to transform acute in-patient functions into other types of treatment. This was done by merging direct competitors located in the same geographic areas. Another strategy was to expand networks of acute care. This was preferred in larger geographically areas and became a major factor in managed healthcare contracting.

Discussion: lessons learned across public sector mergers

The evidence provided above suggests that mergers involving public sector organizations, such as universities and hospitals, occur in waves or phases. In the Nordic countries, the recent wave of public sector mergers was driven both by macro-economic considerations (economic recession) as well as governmental policies – inspired by NPM ideologies – favouring larger units and large-scale municipal federations, as a means of enhancing efficiency through economies of scale, in addition to fostering excellence, quality and responsiveness.

In the Nordic countries the traditional local government structure is the basis for the production of services paid for by federations of municipalities and state-run enterprises or institutions. This development can be explained by notions emanating from *public choice theory* claiming that all public and private institutional arrangements and transactions can be mediated (Wilkins 2012). The key economic argument against Wilkins's hypothesis is that transaction cost explanations associated with increased size (larger units) always include methodological shortcomings. It is, however, important to underline that the above observations focus on the public sector, which, in principle, is funded by the taxpayer and presents a situation similar to a quasi-market (Teixeira *et al.* 2004). In the case of the private sector, the diversification and actions surrounding more "genuine markets" (open competition) tends to focus on merger models (e.g. acquisitions and hostile takeovers) that are less emphasized in the public sector.

The major tensions surrounding public sector mergers relate to the fact that they involve a wide array of stakeholder groups (Christensen *et al.* 2007) and must be seen as legitimate in the eyes of both internal and external constituencies (Drori and Honig 2013), and that their execution or implementation often take place at the same time as new organizational templates are being considered and tested (Pinheiro and Stensaker 2014). Notwithstanding this, the literature clearly shows that for both hospitals and higher education institutions, mergers represent unprecedented strategic opportunities to implement reforms under a situation of resistance by employees, stakeholders and so on (Ford and Ford 2009; Oliver 1991).

It is possible to make broader generalizations, as the mergers of hospitals and higher education institutions are perceived as tools or *instruments* (Maassen and Olsen 2007) for enacting change within the context of a broader modernization or reform agenda for the public sector (Christensen and Lægreid 2011; Christensen *et al.* 2007). Furthermore, it is feasible to draw some broader conclusions for each of the two public sectors described above when it comes to the three aspects investigated here: namely, *rationale*, *process* and the *effects* of mergers.

The *rationale* feature of the merger processes refers to how mergers are conceived by their architects – that is, the internal and external actors who drive change or reform processes. The Nordic countries provide compelling examples in this respect. In both Sweden and Denmark, mergers between public universities and between hospitals have been taking place since the 1980s as part of a much larger government-driven effort towards modernizing the provision of public services. For example, in Sweden, mergers across the health and higher education sectors have been supported by significant legislative reforms aimed at reducing the number of authorities responsible for operational issues across these sectors. Similar reforms to those that took place in Sweden over the last decade are currently taking place in the Finnish healthcare system, pointing to the importance of policy transfers and the 'travelling' of ideas from one context to another (Czarniawska-Joerges and Sevón 2005; Gornitzka and Maassen 2011).

An important aspect to note is the issue of *resource dependencies* or the degree of external control (Pfeffer and Salancik 2003). In contrast to the private sector, public sector organizations rely on the government for the bulk of their funding, so they must be accountable to the public (Stensaker and Harvey 2011). Another aspect is the fact that "top-down" mergers are not necessarily as successful in publicly funded organizations as they are in the private sector. Hospitals and higher education institutions are *hybrid organizations* (Pache and Santos 2013) that are composed of cadres of highly skilled professionals who enjoy a relatively high degree of decision-making autonomy. Thus, traditional top-down (centralized) management systems are not necessarily fit for purpose in the context of hybrid organizational cultures (Locke 2007; Mintzberg 2000) characterized by an amalgamation of different (often conflicting) *institutional logics* (Greenwood *et al.* 2010). What is more, evidence suggests that public sector mergers often give rise to local resistance, as illustrated by internal coalition building and social movements in the Nordic region against closing down local hospitals and regionally based higher education providers.

There are similarities across the two sectors as far as process-related issues are concerned: dynamics within both hospitals and universities are affected by *competitive logic*, illustrated by the managerialism–professionalism dilemma (Salminen 2003; Berg and Pinheiro 2016). In the case of hospitals, *physicians* are the key profession; in higher education institutions it is the members of the *academic profession*. Their engagement or buy-in is the key factor for merger success and the primary reason for post-merger integration failures.

The literature on mergers also reports typical post-merger integration failures, such as insufficient managerial attention (Melkonian *et al.* 2011). These post-merger management activities are visible in management functions such as superior routines, incentive mechanisms and management methods (Puranam and Srikanth 2007). One of the key characteristics here is the limited opportunity that managers have to implement reforms required by strategies. In hospitals, this is largely due to the lack of structural autonomy in decision-making and strategy. In higher education institutions it is due to bottom-heavy decision-making that limits the management's ability to implement merger strategies. From this perspective, the strongest resistance towards reform processes comes not from the employees but from senior management, which is simultaneously responsible for performance (accountability) during the merger process and directly accountable for the effects of the reforms. Therefore, external causes initiated in a top-down strategic merger will often change during the merger process, whereas bottom-up approaches towards mergers will tend to focus on the post-merger strategy.

Finally, when it comes to the *effects* of mergers across these two public sectors, much attention is paid to measuring economic efficiency – by policy-makers and institutional leaders alike – to the detriment of other qualitative aspects, such as quality, accountability, accessibility and so on. However, for both hospitals and higher education institutions there is no clear evidence of the positive efficiency effects of mergers in the form of economies of scale. When it comes to the outcomes of mergers, one of the weaknesses present in the existing literature on public sector mergers lies in the fact that most studies tend to access effects at a given point in time rather than approaching the issue in an evolutionary fashion (longitudinal design), which, obviously, requires gathering pertinent data at several points in time.

Conclusion

Mergers are important strategic instruments for change across the public sector. That said, the literature sheds light on the complexities associated with merger processes that involve hybrid, professional organizations, such hospitals and universities. Merger "fever" seems to be on the rise, suggesting that this is seen as a global recipe or blueprint for modernizing government and for enhancing the provision of public – welfare and educational – services more generally. Despite the traditional arguments for efficiency, the existing data on the effects of mergers are rather inconclusive, suggesting that context and the ways in which success is measured or accessed play important roles. As far as the merger process is concerned, there are significant gaps in the literature, yet the overriding impression is of a process that is laden with complexity and underpinned by a series of nested tensions and volitions (Pinheiro *et al.* 2014), not least when it comes to the need to balance conflicting institutional logics and the demands of various stakeholder groups.

Going forward, we propose three avenues for future research. First, comparative studies across countries and sectors are warranted to gain a more holistic understanding of dynamics and to control for the importance of context. Second, researchers need to investigate the "black box" of merger processes. Important aspects in this respect include, but are not limited to, the role of leaders (formal and informal), active (and passive) processes of resistance (e.g. coalition building, public protests and so on), communication – both internal and external – resource distribution and conflict resolution/compromise. Finally, we need more studies that shed light on the various aspects underpinning mergers across the public sector over periods of time (longitudinal perspectives) as well as mixed methodologies in order to understand the intricacies associated with merger processes and their short-, medium- and long-term effects at the micro (sub-units), meso (whole organization) and macro (sector and society) levels.

Notes

1 For a discussion on economies of scale (and scope) in higher education, consult Koshal and Koshal (1999).
2 By "product," the authors mean core academic activities, such as teaching and research.
3 In the UK, Rowley (1997) found that although a few case institutions saw the potential for rationalization and for achieving economies of scale, this was not the main driver behind the merger.

References

Aagaard, K., Hansen, H. F., and Rasmussen, J. G. (2016). "Different faces of Danish Higher Education mergers." In R. Pinheiro, L. Geschwind, and T. Aarevaara (eds.), *Mergers in Higher Education: The Experience from Northern Europe* (pp. 195–210). Dordrecht: Springer.

Ahgren, B. (2008). "Is it better to be big? The reconfiguration of 21st century hospitals: Responses to a hospital merger in Sweden." *Health Policy*, 87, 92–99.

Ahmadvand, A., Heidari, K., Hosseini, S. H., and Majdzadeh, R. (2012). "Challenges and success factors in university mergers and academic integrations." *Archives of Iranian Medicine*, 15(12), 736–740.

Amin, A. (2011). *Post-Fordism: A Reader.* Oxford: Blackwell.

Askim, J., Christensen, T., Fimreite, A. L., and Lægreid, P. (2008). "Implementation of merger: Lessons from the Norwegian welfare bureaucracy". Working Paper 11/2008. Bergen: Rokkansenteret.

Askim, J., Fimreite, A. L., Moseley, A., and Pedersen, L. H. (2011). "One stop shops for social welfare: The adaptation of an organizational form in three countries." *Public Administration*, 89(4), 1451–1468.

Baldersheim, H., and Rose, L. E. (2010). "The staying of power of the Norwegian periphery." In H. Baldersheim and L. E. Rose (eds.), *Territorial Choice: Politics of Boundaries and Borders.* New York: Macmillan.

Barney, J. (1991). "Firm resources and sustained competitive advantage." *Journal of Management*, 17(1), 99–120.

Bates, L. J., and Santerre, R. E. (2000). "A time series analysis of private college closures and mergers." *Review of Industrial Organization*, 17(3), 267–276.

Becker, L. R. *et al.* (2004). "The impact of university incorporation on college lecturers." *Higher Education*, 48(2), 153–172.

Berg, L., and Pinheiro, R. (2016). "Handling different institutional logics in the public sector: Comparing management in Norwegian universities and hospitals." In R. Pinheiro, F. Ramirez, K. Vrabæk, and L. Geschwind (eds.), *Towards a Comparative Institutionalism: Forms, Dynamics and Logics across Health Care and Higher Education Fields*. Bingley: Emerald

Bogue, R. J., Shortell, S. M., Sohn, M.-W., Manheim, L. M., Bazzoli, G., and Cheeling, C. (1995). "Hospital reorganization after merger." *Medical Care*, 33(7), 676–686.

Brakestad, A. S., and Sjåstad, M. R. (2013). *Fusjoner og kostnadseffektivitet i sykehussektoren*. Master's thesis, Norges Handelshøyskole, Bergen.

Bresler, N. (2007). "The challenge to reposition three divergent higher education institutions as a new comprehensive institution." *South African Journal of Economic and Management Sciences*, 10(2), 195–206.

Bykjeflot, H., and Neby, S. (2008). "The end of the decentralised model of healthcare governance? Comparing developments in the Scandinavian hospital sectors." *Journal of Health Organization and Management*, 22(4), 331–349.

Cai, Y. (2006). "A case study of academic staff integration in a post-merger Chinese university." *Tertiary Education and Management*, 12(3), 215–226.

Cai, Y. (2007). *Academic Staff Integration in Chinese Post-Merger Chinese Higher Education Institutions*. Tampere: University of Tampere.

Cai, Y., Pinheiro, R., Geschwind, L., and Aarrevaara, T. (2016). "Towards a novel conceptual framework for understanding mergers in higher education." *European Journal of Higher Education*, 6(1), 7–24. doi: 10.1080/21568235.2015.1099457

Capps, C. S., Dranove, D., Greenstein, S., and Satterthwaite, M. (2002). "Antritrust policy and hospital mergers: Recommendations for a new approach." *Antitrust Bulletin*, 47, 677.

Cartwright, S., Tytherleigh, M., and Robertson, S. (2007). "Are mergers always stressful? Some evidence from the higher education sector." *European Journal of Work and Organizational Psychology*, 16(4), 456–478.

Choi, S. (2011). *Competing Logics in Hospital Mergers: The Case of Karolinska University Hospital*. Ph.D. thesis, Karolinska Institutet, Stockholm.

Christensen, T., and Lægreid, P. (2011). *The Ashgate Research Companion to New Public Management*. Surrey: Ashgate.

Christensen, T., Knuth, M., Lægreid, P., and Wiggan, J. (2009). "Reforms of welfare administration and policy: A comparison of complexity and hybridization: An introduction." *International Journal of Public Administration*, 32(12), 1001–1005.

Christensen, T., Lægreid, P., Roness, P. G., and Røvik, K. A. (2007). *Organization Theory and the Public Sector: Instrument, Culture and Myth*. Abingdon: Taylor & Francis.

Clark, B. R. (1983). *The Higher Education System: Academic Organization in Cross-National Perspective*. Los Angeles: University of California Press.

Cuellar, A. E., and Gertler, P. (2003). "Trends in hospital consolidation: The formation of local systems." *Health Affairs*, 22(6), 77–87.

Curri, G. (2002). "Reality versus perception: Restructuring tertiary education and institutional organizational change – a case study." *Higher Education*, 44(1), 133–151.

Czarniawska-Joerges, B., and Sevón, G. (2005). *Global Ideas: How Ideas, Objects and Practices Travel in a Global Economy*. Copenhagen: Liber and Copenhagen Business School Press.

Dafny, L. (2006). "Estimation and identification of merger effects: An application to hospital mergers." National Bureau of Economic Research Working Paper No. 1167.

Dafny, L. (2009). "Estimation and identification of merger effects: An application to hospital mergers." *Journal of Law and Economics*, 52, 523–550.

Drori, I., and Honig, B. (2013). "A process model of internal and external legitimacy." *Organization Studies*, 34(3), 345–376.

Enders, J., and Boer, H. (2009). "The mission impossible of the European university: Institutional confusion and institutional diversity." In A. Amaral, G. Neave, C. Musselin, and P. Maassen (eds.), *European Integration and the Governance of Higher Education and Research*. Dordrecht: Springer.

Ford, J. D., and Ford, L. W. (2009). "Decoding resistance to change." *Harvard Business Review*, 87(4), 99–103.

Gamage, D. T. (1992). "Recent reforms in Australian higher education with particular reference to institutional amalgamations." *Higher Education*, 24(1), 77–91.

Gaynor, M., Laudichella, M., and Propper, C. (2012). "Can governments do it better? Merger mania and hospital outcomes in the English NHS." *Journal of Health Economics*, 31(3), 528–543.

Geschwind, L., Melin, G., and Wedlin, L. (2016). "Branding in practice: The making of the Linnaeus University." In R. Pinheiro, L. Geschwind, and T. Aarrevaara (eds.), *Mergers in Higher Education: The Experience from Northern Europe*. Cham/Heidelberg/New York/Dordrecht/London: Springer.

Gleibs, I. H., Tauber, S., Viki, G. T., and Giessner, S. R. (2013). "When what we get is not what we want: The role of implemented versus desired merger patterns in support for mergers." *Social Psychology*, 44(3), 177–190.

Goddard, S., and Palmer, A. (2010). "An evaluation of the effects of a National Health Service trust merger on the learning and development of staff." *Human Resource Development International*, 13(5), 557–573.

Goedegebuure, L. (2011a). "Mergers and more: The changing tertiary education architecture in the 21st century." HEIK Working Papers 1(1).

Goedegebuure, L. (2011b). "Mergers and more: The changing tertiary education architecture in the 21st century." Paper presented at 10th Anniversary Higher Education Development Association Conference, Oslo.

Goedegebuure, L., and Meek, L. (1994). "A resource dependence perspective on mergers: Comparing institutional amalgamations in Australia and the Netherlands." *Comparative Policy Atudies in Higher Education*, 19, 127–143.

Gomes, E., Angwin, D. N., Weber, Y., and Tarba, S. Y. (2013). "Critical success factors through the mergers and acquisitions process: Revealing pre- and post-M&A connections for improved performance." *Thunderbird International Business Review*, 55(1), 13–35.

Gornitzka, Å., and Maassen, P. (2011). "University governance reforms, global scripts and the 'Nordic Model': Accounting for policy change?" In J. Schmid, K. Amos, and A. T. J. Schrader (eds.), *Welten der Bildung? Vergleichende Analysen von Bildungspolitik und Bildungssystemen*. Baden-Baden: Nomos Verlagsgesellschaft.

Graebner, M.E., & Eisenhardt, K.M. (2004). "The seller's side of the story: Acquisition as courtship and governance as syndicate in entrepreneurial firms." *Administrative Science Quarterly*, 49, 366–403.

Greenwood, R., Díaz, A. M., Li, S. X., and Lorente, J. C. (2010). "The multiplicity of institutional logics and the heterogeneity of organizational responses." *Organization Science*, 21(2), 521–539.

Häkkinen, U., and Jonsson, P. (2009). "Harnessing diversity of provision." In J. Magnussen, K. Vrangbæk, and R. B. Saltman (eds.), *Nordic Health Care Systems: Recent Reforms and Current Policy Challenges*. Berkshire: Open Univeristy Press.

Haleblian, J., Devers, C. E., McNamara, G., Carpenter, M. A., and Davison, R. B. (2009). "Taking stock of what we know about mergers and acquisitions: A review and research agenda." *Journal of Management*, 35, 1–34.

Harman, G. (1986). "Restructuring higher-education systems through institutional mergers: Australian experience, 1981–1983." *Higher Education*, 15(6), 567–586.

Harman, G. (2000). "Institutional mergers in Australian higher education since 1960." *Higher Education Quarterly*, 54(4), 343–366.

Harman, G., and Harman, K. (2003). "Institutional mergers in higher education: Lessons from international experience." *Tertiary Education and Management*, 9(1), 29–44.

Harman, G., and Harman, K. (2008). "Strategic mergers of strong institutions to enhance competitive advantage." *Higher Education Policy*, 21(1), 99–121.

Harman, K. (2002). "Merging divergent campus cultures into coherent educational communities: Challenges for higher education leaders." *Higher Education*, 44(1), 91–114.

Harman, K., and Meek, V. L. (2002). "Introduction to special issue: 'Merger revisited: international perspectives on mergers in higher education.'" *Higher Education*, 44(1), 1–4.

Hay, D., and Fourie, M. (2002). "Preparing the way for mergers in South African higher and further education institutions: An investigation into staff perceptions." *Higher Education*, 44(1), 115–131.

HD (2001). "Sykehusreformen." Oslo: Norwegian Ministry of Healthcare. Online at: www.regjeringen.no/no/tema/helse-og-omsorg/sykehus/sykehusreformen-20012002/id226436/, accessed 30 August 2016.

Hippe, J. M., and Trygstad, S. C. (2012). *Ti år etter. Ledelse, ansvar og samarbeid i norske sykehus.* Oslo: Fafo.

Ingebrigtsen, T. (2010). "Helseøkonomiske effekter av sykehussammenslåinger." *Tidsskrift for Den norske legeforening*, 130, 940–942.

Ingebrigtsen, T., Lind, M., Krogh, T., Lægland, J., Andersen, H., and Nerskogen, E. (2012). "Sammenslåing av tre sykehus til ett universitetssykehus." *Tidsskrift for Den norske legeforening*, 132(7), 813–817.

Kamsteeg, F. H. (2011). "Transformation as social drama: Stories about merging at North West University, South Africa." *Anthropology Southern Africa*, 34(1–2), 51–61.

King, D. R., Dalton, D. R., Daily, C. M., and Covin, J. G. (2004). "Meta-analyses of post-acquisition performance: Indications of unidentitied moderators." *Strategic Management Journal*, 25, 187–200.

Kjekshus, L. E., and Bernstrøm, V. (2010). *Helseforetakenes interne organizering og ledelse.* Intorg 2009 report. Oslo: Universitetet i Oslo.

Kjekshus, L. E., and Bernstrøm, V. (2013). *Helseforetakenes interne organizering og ledelse.* Intorg 2012 report. Oslo: Universitetet i Oslo.

Kjekshus, L. E., and Hagen, T. (2003). "Ga sammenslåing av sykehus bedre effektivitet? Erfaringer fra Norge i 1990-årene." Health Organization Research Programme Norway. Oslo: Universitetet i Oslo.

Kjekshus, L. E., and Hagen, T. (2007). "Do hospital mergers increase hospital efficiency? Evidence from a National Health Service country." *Journal of Health Services and Policy*, 12(4), 230–235.

Koshal, R. K., and Koshal, M. (1999). "Economies of scale and scope in higher education: A case of comprehensive universities." *Economics of Education Review*, 18(2), 269–277.

Kristensen, T., Bogetoft, P., and Pedersen, K. M. (2010). "Potential gains from hospital mergers in Denmark." *Health Care Management Science*, 13, 334–345.

Kronborg, I. H., and Tangen, J. (2014). *Effekter av norske sykehusfusjoner Medfører sykehusfusjoner læringseffekter og høyere kvalitet?* Bergen: Norges Handelshøyskole.

Kvåle, G., and Torjesen, D. O. (2011). "Social movements and organizations: Managerialism, localism and the hospital movement." Paper presented at the 6th Organization Studies Summer Workshop, Abbaye de Vauz de Cernay, Paris.

Kvåle, G., and Torjesen, D. O. (2014). "Sjukehusrørsla – kampen om tryggleik til individer og stader." In O. Bukve and G. Kvåle (eds.), *Kvalitet og samhandling i helseorganizasjonar*. Oslo: Universitetsforlaget.

Kyvik, S. (2002). "The merger of non-university colleges in Norway." *Higher Education*, 44(1), 53–72.

Kyvik, S., and Stensaker, B. (2013). "Factors affecting the decision to merge: The case of strategic mergers in Norwegian higher education." *Tertiary Education and Management*, 19(4), 323–337. doi: 10.1080/13583883.2013.805424

Lægreid, P., Opedal, S., and Stigen, I. M. (2005). "The Norwegian hospital reform: Balancing political control and enterprise autonomy." *Journal of Health Politics, Policy and Law*, 30(6), 1035–1072.

Lamoreaux, N. R. (1985). *The Great Merger Movement in American Business, 1895–1904*. Cambridge: Cambridge University Press.

Locke, W. (2007). "Higher education mergers: Integrating organizational cultures and developing appropriate management styles." *Higher Education Quarterly*, 61(1), 83–102.

Maassen, P., and Olsen, J. P. (2007). *University Dynamics and European Integration*. Dordrecht: Springer.

Magnussen, J., Vrangbæk, K., and Saltman, R. B. (2009). *Nordic Health Care Systems: Recent Reforms and Current Policy Changes*. Buckinghamshire: Open University Press.

Mao, Y.-Q., Du, Y., and Liu, J.-J. (2009). "The effects of university mergers in China since 1990s: From the perspective of knowledge production." *International Journal of Educational Management*, 23(1), 19–33.

Maree, J. G., and Eiselen, R. J. (2004). "The emotional intelligence profile of academics in a merger setting." *Education and Urban Society*, 36(4), 482–504.

McGinnis, R. A., McMillen, W., and Gold, J. P. (2007). "Merging two universities: The Medical University of Ohio and the University of Toledo." *Academic Medicine*, 82(12), 1187–1195.

Meek, V. L., Goedegebuure, L., Santiago, R., and Carvalho, T. (2010). *The Changing Dynamics of Higher Education Middle Management*. Dordrecht: Springer.

Melkonian, T., Monin, P., and Noorderhaven, N. G. (2011). "Distributive justice, procedural justice, exemplarity, and employees' willingness to cooperate in M&A integration processes: An analysis of the Air France–KLM merger." *Human Resource Management*, 50(6), 809–837.

Mintzberg, H. (2000). "The professional bureaucracy." In I. Jenniskens (ed.), *Management and Decision-making in Higher Education Institutions*. New York: Lemma.

Moisio, A. (2012) "Municipal partnerships: The experience of the Nordic countries." In N. Bosch and A. Solé-Olle (eds.), *IEB Report on Fiscal Federalism 2011*. Barcelona: Center for Research in Economics.

Montgomery, K. (2001). "Physician executives: The evolution and impact of a hybrid profession." *Advances in Health Care Management*, 2, 215–241.

Norgard, J. D., and Skodvin, O. J. (2002). "The importance of geography and culture in mergers: A Norwegian institutional case study." *Higher Education*, 44(1), 73–90.

OECD (2010). *OECD Economic Surveys: Finland 2010*. Paris: Organization for Economic Development and Cooperation.

Oliver, C. (1991). "Strategic responses to institutional processes." *Academy of Management Review*, 16(1), 145–179.

Oliver, C. (1992). "The antecedents of deinstitutionalization." *Organization Studies*, 13(4), 563–588.

Pache, A.-C., and Santos, F. (2013). "Inside the hybrid organization: Selective coupling as a response to competing institutional logics." *Academy of Management Journal*, 56(4), 972–1001.

Pfeffer, J., and Salancik, G. R. (2003). *The External Control of Organizations: A Resource Dependence Perspective*. Stanford, CA: Stanford Business Books.

Pinheiro, R. (2010). *Nelson Mandela Metropolitan University: An Engine of Economic Growth for South Africa and the Eastern Cape Region?* Cape Town: CHET.

Pinheiro, R. (2012). *In the Region, for the Region? A Comparative Study of the Institutionalisation of the Regional Mission of Universities*. Oslo: University of Oslo.

Pinheiro, R., and Berg, L. (2016). "Categorizing and assessing multi-campus universities in contemporary higher education." *Tertiary Education and Management, Online first*. doi: 10.1080/13583883.2016.1205124

Pinheiro, R., Benneworth, P., and Jones, G. A. (2012a). *Universities and Regional Development: A Critical Assessment of Tensions and Contradictions*. Abingdon and New York: Routledge.

Pinheiro, R., Geschwind, L., and Aarevaara, T. (2013). "Mergers in higher education: What do we know and what are we lacking?" Paper presented to the EAIR Annual Conference, Rotterdam.

Pinheiro, R., Geschwind, L., and Aarrevaara, T. (2014). "Nested tensions and interwoven dilemmas in higher education: The view from the Nordic countries." *Cambridge Journal of Regions, Economy and Society*, 7(2), 233–250.

Pinheiro, R., Geschwind, L., and Aarrevaara, T. (eds.). (2016a). *Mergers in Higher Education: The experience from Northern Europe* (Vol. 46). Cham/Heidelberg/New York/Dordrecht/London: Springer.

Pinheiro, R., Geschwind, L., Ramirez, F., and Vrangbæk, K. (eds.) (2016b). *Towards a Comparative Institutionalism: Forms, Dynamics and Logics across the Organizational Fields of Health Care and Higher Education*. Bingley: Emerald.

Pinheiro, R., Ouma, G., and Pillay, P. (2012b). "The dynamics of university transformation: A case study in the Eastern Cape Province of South Africa." *Journal of Higher Education in Africa*, 10(1), 95–120.

Pinheiro, R., and Stensaker, B. (2014). "Designing the entrepreneurial university: The interpretation of a global idea." *Public Organization Review*, 14(4), 497–516.

Pollitt, C., and Bouckaert, G. (2011). *Public Management Reform: A Comparative Analysis – New Public Management, Governance, and the Neo-Weberian State*. Oxford and New York: Oxford University Press.

Posnett, J. (1999). "Is bigger better? Concentration in the provision of secondary care." *British Medical Journal*, 319(1063), 1.

Posnett, J. (2002). "Are bigger hospitals better?" In M. McKee and J. Healy (eds.), *Hospital in a Changing Europe*. Buckinghamshire and Philadelphia, PA: Open University Press.

Pritchard, R. M., and Williamson, A. P. (2008). "Long-term human outcomes of a 'shotgun' marriage in higher education: Anatomy of a merger, two decades later." *Higher Education Management and Policy*, 20(1), 47.

Puranam, P., and Srikanth, K. (2007). "What they know vs. what they do: How acquirers leverage technology acquisitions." *Strategic Management Journal*, 28(8), 805–825.

Rehnberg, C., Magnussen, J., and Luoma, K. (2009). "Maintaing fiscal sustainability in the Nordic countries." In J. Magnussen, K. Vrangbæk, and R. B. Saltman (eds.), *Nordic Health Care Systems: Recent Reforms and Current Policy Challenges*. Berkshire: Open University Press.

Riksrevisjonen (2012). "Riksrevisjonens kontroll med forvaltningen av statlige selskaper for 2011." Dokument 3:2 (2012–2013). Bergen: Fagbokforlaget AS.

Rowley, G. (1997). "Strategic alliances: United we stand: A strategic analysis of mergers in higher education." *Public Money and Management*, 17(4), 7–12.

Salminen, A. (2003). "New public management and Finnish public sector organizations: The case of universities." In A. Amaral, V. L. Meek, and I. M. Larsen (eds.), *The Higher Education Managerial Revolution?* Dordrecht: Springer.

Sarala, R. M., Junni, P., Cooper, C. L., and Tarba, S. Y. (2016). "A sociocultural perspective on knowledge transfer in mergers and acquisitions." *Journal of Management*, 42(5), 1230–1249.

Shield, R., Thorpe, R., and Nelson, A. (2002). "Hospital mergers and psycological contracts." *Strategic Change*, 11, 357–367.

Skodvin, O.-J. (1999). "Mergers in higher education: Success or failure?" *Tertiary Education and Management*, 5(1), 63–78.

Spicer, A., and Böhm, S. (2007). "Moving management: Theorizing struggles against the hegemony of management." *Organization Studies*, 28(11), 1667–1698.

Stensaker, B., and Harvey, L. (2011). *Accountability in Higher Education: Global Perspectives on Trust and Power.* New York: Taylor & Francis.

Stensaker, B., Persson, M., and Pinheiro, R. (2016). "When mergers fail: A case study on the critical role of external stakeholders in merger initiatives." *European Journal of Higher Education*, 16, 56–70.

Teixeira, P., Jongbloed, B., Dill, D., and Amaral, A. (2004). *Markets in Higher Education: Rhetoric or Reality?* Berlin: Kluwer Academic.

Tenn, S. (2011). "The price effects of hospital mergers: A case study of Sutter-Summit transaction." *International Journal of the Economics of Business*, 18(1), 65–82.

Theron, A. V., and Dodd, N. M. (2011). "Organizational commitment in a post-merger situation." *South African Journal of Economic and Management Sciences*, 14(3), 333–345.

Thompson, A. (2011). "The effect of hospital mergers on inpatient prices: A case study of the New Hanover–Cape Fear transaction." *International Journal of the Economics of Business*, 18(1), 91–101.

Thornton, P., and Ocasio, W. (2008). "Institutional logics." In R. Greenwood, C. Oliver, S. K. Andersen, and R. Suddaby (eds.), *Handbook of Oranizational Institutionalizm.* Thousand Oaks, CA: Sage.

Toma, J. D. (2010). *Building Organizational Capacity: Strategic Management in Higher Education.* Baltimore, MD: Johns Hopkins University Press.

Vita, M. G., and Sacher, S. (2001). "The competitive effects of not-for-profit hospital mergers: A case study." *Journal of Industrial Economics*, 49(1), 63–84.

Wan, Y. (2008). *Managing Post-merger Integration: A Case Study of a Merger in Chinese Higher Education.* Ann Arbor: University of Michigan Press.

Wan, Y., and Peterson, M. W. (2007). "A case study of a merger in Chinese higher education: The motives, processes, and outcomes." *International Journal of Educational Development*, 27(6), 683–696.

Wilkins, A. (2012). "School choice and the commodification of education: A visual approach to school brochures and websites." *Critical Social Policy*, 32(1), 69–86.

5

CHINESE CROSS-BORDER M&A INTO INDUSTRIALIZED COUNTRIES

The case of Chinese acquisitions in Germany

Marina Schmitz, Fabian Jintae Froese, and Winno V. Wangenheim

Introduction

Chinese enterprises had established more than 25,400 entities in 184 foreign countries by the end of 2013 (Ministry of Commerce, 2014). In terms of outward foreign direct investment (OFDI), China ranks third worldwide, contributing a share of 8.6 per cent to worldwide OFDI, which highlights its growing importance as a foreign investor (UNCTAD, 2015). While the main target of Chinese OFDI is still South and East Asia (Ministry of Commerce, 2010; Morck *et al.*, 2008), OFDI into industrialized countries is rapidly increasing. Cross-border mergers and acquisitions (M&As) accounted for 63.9 per cent of the total Chinese OFDI in 2013 (Ministry of Commerce, 2014), and are the most common ways of Chinese OFDI entering industrialized countries. As Chinese OFDI is increasingly motivated by the

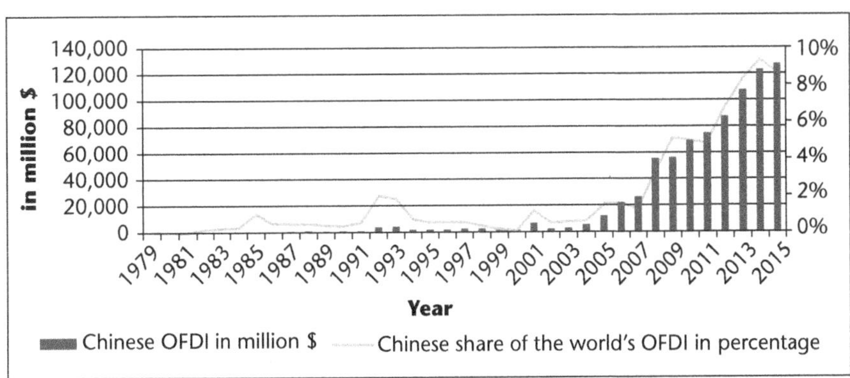

FIGURE 5.1 Chinese outward foreign direct investment (OFDI)

Source: UNCTAD (2016)

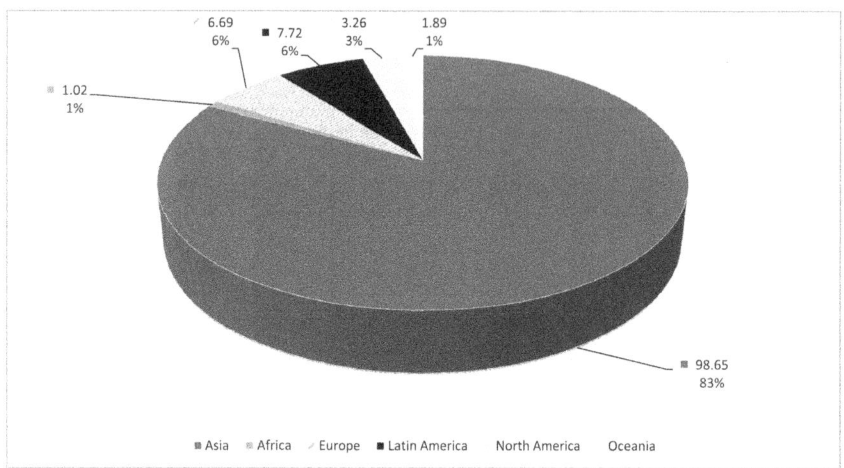

FIGURE 5.2 Destinations of Chinese OFDI in 2014 (in billion US$)

Source: 2015 China Statistical Yearbook

procurement of intangible assets, M&As are a rapid and highly efficient route to increase knowledge and technology and to gain reputation through the acquisition of well-reputed brands.

In the last decade, China's cross-border M&A transactions have mainly targeted Europe and North America due to its growing interest in strategic assets, including intangible assets, such as the acquisition of advanced technology in high-end manufacturing and brands, marketing, R&D knowledge, and advanced managerial strategies (e.g. Boateng *et al.*, 2008; Child and Rodrigues, 2005; Cui and Jiang, 2010; Luo and Tung, 2007; Luo *et al.*, 2010; Morck *et al.*, 2008). By addressing the shortage in the aforementioned areas, China is trying to overcome the problem of being an international latecomer (Boateng *et al.*, 2008; Child and Rodrigues, 2005). By increasing strategic assets through acquisition, China is now in a position to increase its international reputation and prestige (Deng, 2009), as well as firm-specific intangible assets, such as superior resources and skills that are not available at home (UNCTAD, 2006).

Although opportunities for China's internationalization have increased recently, partly due to the global financial crisis, challenges abroad raised by host country governments (e.g. CSR, transparency, environment protection) are mounting (Ministry of Commerce, 2013; Sauvant, 2013). These new challenges are in addition to existing challenges of liability of foreignness, cultural integration, acquisition of knowledge and integration to improve post-M&A innovative performance (Deng, 2009). Furthermore, China still suffers from a shortage of internationally experienced managers to run foreign companies. Time will tell whether the post-acquisition process, and the aforementioned challenges, can be handled successfully.

Despite the increasing importance of Chinese M&A (Cui and Jiang, 2010; Hong and Sun, 2006), little research exists on the outward M&A of Chinese and other emerging market multinational enterprises (EM MNEs). The small amount of research that exists has usually merely touched upon either some aspects of the pre-M&A phase or the post-M&A phase. This nascent body of research suggests that the M&A motivations and implementation of EM MNEs differ from that of MNEs from industrialized economies. Thus, more research is clearly needed. To fill this void, the purpose of this chapter is to increase our understanding of the cross-border M&As of Chinese MNEs into industrialized countries. Responding to the call for an understanding of the whole process of M&As (Gomes *et al.*, 2013) we investigate both the pre-M&A and post-M&A integration phases. We integrate M&A, FDI and China-specific literature to develop a conceptual model of Chinese outward M&As. In addition, we use the Sany-Putzmeister acquisition, one of the most well-known Chinese M&A acquisitions in Germany, as a case to illustrate our model. To gain further insight, we use the LexisNexis database for a press and media analysis. Altogether, we analysed forty-five articles that were published in 2012 and 2013 – up to two years after the acquisition was announced.

Our contributions are threefold. First, we build on and extend established M&A models (Birkinshaw *et al.*, 2000, Larsson and Finkelstein, 1999; Nahavandi and Malekzadeh, 1988) by integrating and linking them to crucial factors of the pre-M&A stage, as a holistic M&A process is a complex and understudied phenomenon (Gomes *et al.*, 2013). As for the pre-M&A stage, we focus on the motivations for internationalization, because motivations largely vary between EM MNEs and MNEs from industrialized countries and have a profound impact on the post-M&A integration phase. Second, we extend eclectic theory to the context of Chinese MNEs by adding context specific variables such as government influence and explore them in the context of EM MNEs' M&As targeting industrialized economies. Third, we develop our model by combining the strategic management and organizational behaviour streams of research in an M&A context with the existing FDI literature, with a focus on highlighting the success factors of Chinese cross-border M&As, deriving important practical and theoretical recommendations.

The remainder of this chapter is structured as follows. First, we provide an overview of the development of Chinese OFDI, M&As and the Putzmeister case, providing the grounding for our conceptual model. Second, we discuss patterns of the pre-merger decision and motivations by drawing on eclectic theory, and then the post-merger process by drawing on acculturation theory. Based on these theories and China-specific evidence, we develop a number of propositions. Finally, we conclude by discussing the findings and suggest implications for Chinese and other EM MNEs.

The development of Chinese outward foreign direct investment and M&As

OFDI is no longer a one-way street from industrialized to developing countries (Klossek *et al.*, 2012). Chinese OFDI started after the launch of the opening policy initiated by the Chinese government in 1978, a number of years before the well-known cases of Lenovo's acquisition of the IBM computer business and follow-up acquisitions by, for example, Haier, TCL and the China National Offshore Oil Corporation (CNOOC) (Morck *et al.*, 2008).

Chinese OFDI was reinvigorated in 1999 when the Chinese government initiated the going-out strategy as part of the 10th Five-Year Plan (2001–2005), which facilitated OFDI (Child and Rodrigues, 2005; Luo *et al.*, 2010). This strategy promoted the overseas investment of Chinese enterprises in those regions and industries that were classified as strategically important.

Although direct political guidance by the Chinese government plays a minor role in corporate investment decisions, the government does have a guiding influence and is responsible for the approval of internationalization decisions. It is currently trying to simplify the approval process for OFDI (Li, 2014), as well as incentivizing the internationalization and growth of promising – mostly state-owned – enterprises, for example by offering low-interest loans and tax deductions or even allocating banks to the respective companies (Buckley *et al.*, 2007; Luo *et al.*, 2010; Zhang and Daly, 2011). In 2003, privately owned enterprises, such as Lenovo, Huawei and Haier, were granted permission to apply for overseas investments (Buckley *et al.*, 2008), a privilege that was previously granted only to Chinese SOEs (Morck *et al.*, 2008). The current trend shows that mainly Chinese non-SOEs or enterprises with limited bureaucratic interference are those that are internationalizing (Child, 2011; Child and Rodrigues, 2005).

The going-out strategy is consistent with China's need to spend its foreign currency reserves, caused by a consistent trade surplus and a large savings–investment gap (Chen and Young, 2010; Hong and Sun, 2006). According to UNCTAD (2016), the annual investment flows from China have increased significantly since the launch of the strategy (also see Figure 5.1). The 12th Five-Year Plan (2011–2015) aimed to accelerate the going-out strategy, with plans to improve the legal environment, management learning and innovation in the M&A context. The further development of the OFDI curve and the associated political regulations which predominantly shaped it in the past are summarized in more detail in Buckley *et al.* (2007), Luo *et al.* (2010) and Zhang and Daly (2011). In more recent years, the financial crisis, by damaging the world's economies, has put less affected Chinese companies in a position to acquire ailing Western businesses (Chen and Young, 2010; Deng, 2009).

Chinese foreign acquisitions show several distinctive features: first, a tenfold increase in volume between 2005 and 2012 (UNCTAD, 2013); second, acquiring companies are mainly large Chinese enterprises with international experience; third, target firms are located mainly in industrialized countries and face strategic and/ or financial difficulties, and are generally concentrated in the 'seven strategic pillar' industries (resource, energy, telecommunications, electronics, machinery, home appliances and automobiles), as communicated in the Five-Year Plans (Rui and Yip, 2008). China's motivation for these acquisitions is its desire to address its competitive disadvantage and to 'catch up' with industrialized countries (Boateng *et al.*, 2008; Child and Rodrigues, 2005; Luo and Tung, 2007; Luo *et al.*, 2010; Rui and

Yip, 2008), and also to counter-attack the presence of large foreign MNEs in the Chinese market, bypass stringent trade barriers, alleviate domestic institutional constraints, secure preferential treatment offered by home governments, and exploit their advantage in other developing markets (Luo and Tung, 2007).

Chinese investments in Germany tripled between 2005 and 2010, offering a bright outlook for the next decade, rising from almost zero at the beginning of the 1990s and reaching a volume of US$1.43 billion by 2014 (OECD, 2014). Prime targets of Chinese M&A investment are German small and medium-sized enterprises (SMEs), because they possess the desired intangible skills and can be acquired easily due to the fact that 37 per cent of German family-owned SMEs face serious problems in appointing successors (DIHK, 2011). One major case that possesses such characteristics is that of Putzmeister. Facing financial difficulties and failing to identify a successor, Putzmeister's owner and founder Karl Schlecht announced in January 2012 that he had decided to sell the company to the Sany Heavy Industry Group, a Chinese competitor (see Table 5.1). This transaction caused a sensation in the German media, as it was the first time a German global market leader had been acquired by a Chinese company. Some of the public outcry following the announcement of the deal was characterized by prejudice; other criticisms focused on the potential collapse of 'Germany's economic backbone', the German 'Mittelstand' (SMEs).

Without first informing employees, who heard the news from the media, Schlecht sold his company to its largest Chinese rival. This surprising announcement triggered a wave of uncertainty and anxiety, fuelled partly by prejudice, leading to demonstrations encouraged by the works council. Hence, the preconditions for the integration of Putzmeister into the Sany Heavy Industry Group were rather poor. One factor that made the transaction necessary was the fact that the German firm's sales had decreased by 63 per cent during the global economic crisis. As Putzmeister's CFO stated, the firm now needed a 'strategic partner', especially as a large portion of worldwide growth in the construction industry was generated within China, and Putzmeister had an inadequate presence there. In an interview, Schlecht explained

TABLE 5.1 Comparison of the Sany Heavy Industry Group and Putzmeister in 2011

	Sany Heavy Industry Co., Ltd.	*Putzmeister GmbH*
Founded	1989	1958
Products	Heavy machinery (e.g. excavators, cranes) for construction industry	Concrete pumps and related modules
Origin	Changsha, Hunan Province	Aichtal, Baden-Württemberg County
Ownership	Privately owned (LIANG Wengen)	Family owned (Karl Schlecht)
Employees	Approx. 50,000	Approx. 3,000
Sales	€9.5 billion	€0.6 billion
Vision	'Quality changes the world'	'Be happy while serving, improving and creating values'

Source: Homepage of Putzmeister GmbH and Sany Heavy Industry Co., Ltd.

the strategic necessity of his sale of Putzmeister. He claimed that the firm was not sufficiently diverse to compete over the long term and asserted that the main reason for this was its business model's sensitivity to the overall economic performance of the cyclical industry in which it competed.

Theory and proposition development

The purpose of this chapter is to develop a model for the whole process of M&A for the case of Chinese M&As in industrialized countries (see Figure 5.3). To do so, we combine relevant theories from the pre- and post-merger phases. We explain the underlying theories, constructs and relationships in more detail in the following subsections.

Pre- and post-M&A based on eclectic and acculturation theories

The eclectic theory of direct investment provides a comprehensive theoretical explanation and framework of why firms engage in OFDI, including cross-border M&A (Dunning, 1977). According to the logic of the framework, firms go abroad if they meet three conditions. First, they need to have an ownership advantage – that is, tangible or intangible assets (e.g. advanced technology, exclusive access to inputs or a high capacity for innovation) that provide them with advantages over firms in a foreign market. Second, when exploiting ownership advantages, this must involve less transaction costs in order to internalize this advantage within the organization, rather than selling the ownership advantage to other firms. Third, decision-makers need to ask themselves whether their firm can exploit certain locational advantages in the respective host country, such as network linkages (Chen and Chen, 1998, 2004; Child and Rodrigues, 2005), favourable legislation, low input prices or an efficient infrastructure.

However, the eclectic theory, by providing an economic rather than a political or social view of the internationalization process (Child and Rodrigues, 2005), cannot fully explain the Chinese OFDI paradigm as it overlooks the role of government, which is a dominant actor in the M&A process of EM MNEs, as well as the motivations regarding internationalization decisions, which are different from what we know of the Western context. Therefore, researchers have already pointed out the need for an extended framework of internationalization theories, regarding internationalization solely as the logical consequence of a competitive advantage over firms in another market, to meet the distinctive features of developing country multinationals (Athreye and Kapur, 2009; Child and Rodrigues, 2005; Fortanier and Tulder, 2009; Kumar, 2009; Narula, 2012; Zhang and Daly, 2011). Government influence or entrepreneurial choice of internationalization or a co-evolution of the two, which would foster exchange and development of the usual path dependency (Rodrigues and Child, 2003) proposed in the eclectic theory, are regarded as distinctive features. EM MNEs can be especially motivated to use international expansion as a springboard to tackle ownership disadvantage. This view is consistent

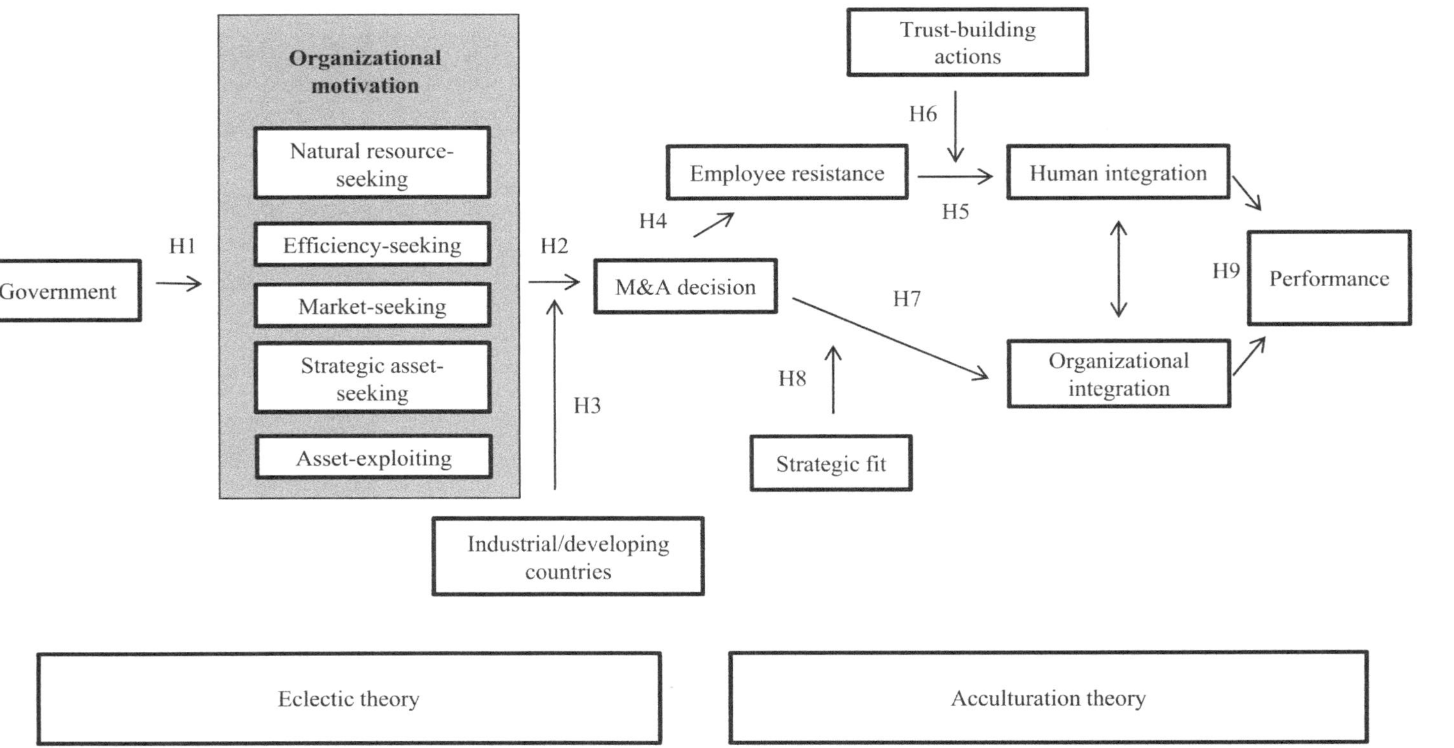

FIGURE 5.3 Model

with the existing literature, distinguishing between an asset-seeking and an asset-exploiting perspective of internationalization (Makino *et al.*, 2002). Regarding the Chinese context, OFDI, mostly in the form of M&A, is both asset-exploiting *and* augmenting (Chen and Young, 2010; Cui and Jiang, 2010; Dunning, 2006; Luo and Tung, 2007; Yiu *et al.*, 2007) – for example, Lenovo's acquisition of IBM – providing a platform for market entrance as well as the acquisition of technological knowledge. Dunning himself acknowledged this weakness, stating that there are 'two groups of reasons why any firm would engage in OFDI: the first is to exploit existing assets or competitive capabilities, and the second is to augment them' (Dunning and Lundan, 2008: 187).

A major challenge for cross-border M&A is the potential clash of cultures (e.g. Brannen and Peterson, 2009; Froese *et al.*, 2008) during the post-acquisition phase. Although diverse terminology exists for the various acculturation phases (e.g. Haspeslagh and Jemison, 1991), we follow Berry (1980) and Nahavandi and Malekzadeh (1988), who categorize the cultural change process following M&A into four different types: integration; assimilation; separation; and deculturation. Integration refers to a process whereby the acquiring company intends to maintain some of the characteristics of the target company, while implementing some of its own elements. Assimilation refers to a process where the acquiring firm imposes all or most of its practices on the target firm. Separation implies that the target company remains almost untouched. In deculturation, a completely new culture, different from those of the acquiring and target companies, is created. Chinese MNEs in industrialized countries tend to follow the separation and integration approaches. Acquired companies, such as Putzmeister, remain almost unchanged, and are therefore characterized by a 'light-touch integration' (Liu and Woywode, 2013). This integration form resembles a combination of the separation and integration approaches.

Pre-merger phase

According to Gomes *et al.* (2013), the main success factors in the pre-merger stage are: choice and evaluation of the strategic partner, pay the right price, size mismatches and organization, overall strategy and accumulated experience on M&A, courtship, communication before the merger, and future compensation policy. However, prior research draws on M&As from industrialized countries in the Western Hemisphere. Therefore, we intend to highlight success factors of pre- and post-M&A stages of EM MNEs in the following paragraphs.

Government and OFDI

In China, investments abroad, including cross-border M&As, are still heavily sponsored, supported and controlled by governmental institutions (Wang *et al.*, 2012a, 2012b; Zhang *et al.*, 2011), the most influential of which are the State Council, Ministry of Commerce (MOC), People's Bank of China, State Administration of Foreign Exchange (SAFE), State-owned Assets Supervision and

Administration Commission (SASAC), and State Development and Reform Commission (Luo *et al.*, 2010). However, the influence of government involvement is largely dependent on the level of government affiliation and the degree of state ownership (Wang *et al.*, 2012b). The high involvement of governmental institutions sometimes makes it necessary to align the OFDI strategy with the strategy of the respective company. However, this alignment is impeding entrepreneurial innovation, development and freedom (Child and Rodrigues, 2005; Cui and Jiang, 2010; Deng, 2009). Due to the sometimes differing political motivations behind internationalization (Chen and Young, 2010; Luo and Tung, 2007), principal–principal governance conflicts can arise between the major shareholders, mostly consisting of Chinese governmental institutions (Morck *et al.*, 2008), and other (non-governmental) minor shareholders. Given this backdrop, one of the emerging questions is whether the motivation behind internationalization is institutionally embedded or independently (entrepreneurially) driven (Child and Rodrigues, 2005; Rui and Yip, 2008).

In the case of Chinese cross-border M&As, all the internationalization drivers present in the organization are strongly influenced by the government. Among the Chinese companies benefiting from governmental support, there are several firms that are now able to compete internationally (Deng, 2009), as indicated by the number of Chinese companies that were present in the *Fortune* Global 500 list in 2013 (*CNN Money*, 2013). Chinese companies which are successful in the domestic market are increasingly willing to establish themselves as global players, venturing abroad mostly through the means of cross-border M&A (Deng, 2009; Luo and Tung, 2007).

The original OLI framework does not account for government influence, which is a crucial factor, especially for EM MNEs (Child and Rodrigues, 2005; Dunning and Narula, 1996) that are highly dependent on support from the government to account for lacking competitiveness. Even in the case of the *privately* owned Sany Heavy Industry Group, bonds and close contacts with the Communist Party are favourable and contribute positively to the corporate strategy (CNN, 2011). Additionally, mechanical engineering is one of the encouraged sectors, enjoying 'preferential policy and government support associated with funding, tax collection, foreign exchange, customs, streamlined approval process and others' (Wang *et al.*, 2012a: 431), thereby creating synergy effects between government policy and firm strategy. As the impact of government affiliation is indirect through networks, even private firms' decisions to internationalize might be driven, at least to some degree, by the government (Wang *et al.*, 2012b), which can have an influence on location, type and level of OFDI. As the government is able to influence the ability and willingness of EM MNEs to internationalize, its field of influence concerns, for example, strategic objectives and decisions, availability and costs of various resources, usage of these resources, capabilities, provision of valuable knowledge, information and intermediary services, as well as transaction costs associated with the cross- border expansion of the firm (Wang *et al.*, 2012b). In addition to the degree of involvement, motivations to support the institutionalization of specific firms can vary in terms of government level (e.g. state or provincial level versus city or county level) (Wang *et al.*, 2012b).

> *Proposition 1: Chinese government institutions/policies influence the motivations of Chinese cross-border M&As.*

The motivations for cross-border M&As

The eclectic theory literature suggests four possible motivations for OFDI (Dunning, 1977, 1993). First, OFDI can be driven by natural resource-seeking motivations. For example, such motivations can be observed in the various cases of Chinese firms in African countries (Dupasquier and Osakwe, 2006). Second, efficiency-seeking motivations are related to a firm's search for competitiveness. Efficiency can be enhanced by exploiting country-specific advantages, such as low labour costs, which is a less relevant factor for Asian companies moving to industrialized countries (Child and Rodrigues, 2005; Zhang, 2003). Third, a firm's internationalization can be driven by market-seeking motivations. Certain markets might be attractive because of their size, growth, per capita income or certain aspects of consumer behaviour. Sometimes there is also an interplay of home country market imperfections, institutional constraints (Child and Rodrigues, 2005; Deng, 2009; Zhang and Daly, 2011), domestic market competition (Chen and Young, 2010) and host country market advantages. Finally, a driver for OFDI can be the search for strategic assets. These can be assets that empower a company's strategy and provide advantages in the long term, and are acquired to enhance the firm's portfolio and ease the imbalance caused, for example, by superior technology available in firms in industrialized markets. In sum, as Wang *et al.* (2012b) argue, government involvement influences the level of overseas investment, its location (industrialized or developing countries) and its form (various asset-seeking or -exploiting motivations).

In the case of the Sany Heavy Industry Group's acquisition of Putzmeister, the most prevalent motivation was strategic asset-seeking – the pursuit of Putzmeister's concrete pump technology (a technology against which Sany had tried – and failed – to compete for almost twenty years). Furthermore, market-seeking motivations played a role because Putzmeister's brand name facilitated access to other relevant markets, providing further evidence for the theoretical reasoning by Makino *et al.* (2002) and Yiu *et al.* (2007) that strategic asset-seeking and market-seeking motivations play significant roles in investments in industrialized countries. Additionally, most companies from developing countries have no experience in operations in the international business context. Therefore, they rely heavily on the comparably highly skilled staff of the potential target firm.

For a correct understanding of the model, it should be added that OFDI is driven in practice by a number of these factors, not by a single one. The four motivations mentioned by Dunning (1993) include only situations in which a firm seeks certain assets in a foreign market. However, as conventional international business theory suggests, there are also situations in which a firm already has an advantage and internationalizes its activities in order to exploit these firm-specific ownership advantages in new settings (Child and Rodrigues, 2005; Guillén and García-Canal, 2009; Yiu *et al.*, 2007). Asset-exploiting motivations mainly play a role when internationalizing into developing countries, although some EM MNEs have succeeded in exploiting their assets in industrialized countries (Luo and Tung, 2007).

> *Proposition 2: Chinese cross-border M&As have asset-seeking organizational motivations (natural resource, efficiency, market and strategic asset-seeking) as well as asset-exploiting motivations.*

Country context

The strategic motivations explained above vary depending on the economic development level of the target countries. Asset-exploiting motivations are drivers of internationalization decisions in other developing countries, located for instance in Southeast Asia or Africa, particularly those that are less developed than China and have lower labour costs, which have become comparably higher in China. In regards to asset-seeking motivations, industrialized countries offer more opportunities to increase their assets, not only in regard to natural resources or market access, but nowadays more in the context of strategic assets, such as brand reputation, higher management skills and innovative and high-quality technologies. Chinese and other EM MNEs are still lacking these assets and need to absorb them in order to become global players. Therefore, the motivations differ depending on the target country.

The Sany Heavy Industry Group was already well established in the domestic market; however, it was eager to develop its competitive advantage in order to do business abroad. Therefore, Sany aimed to invest in industrialized countries, such as Germany, that were able to offer it the vital strategic assets (e.g. superior technology and brand reputation) it needed. Thus, Sany acquired Putzmeister.

Privately owned EM MNEs tend to invest into industrialized countries, and are often driven by their own limited legitimacy (e.g. lack of relationships to government officials) and their experience of discriminatory policies in their domestic market (Wang *et al.*, 2012b). Enhancing competitiveness and capabilities in industrialized markets is a common driver of companies affiliated with high levels of government that are eager to generate innovativeness and address competitive disadvantages, for example through the acquisition of foreign technology (Cui and Jiang, 2012; Wang *et al.*, 2012b).

> *Proposition 3: The economic level of the target country moderates the motivations of Chinese cross-border M&As, insofar as asset-exploiting motivations lead to investment in developing countries, whereas asset-seeking motivations lead to investment in industrialized countries.*

Post-merger phase

The post-merger integration phase is essential for the success of an M&A. However, the post-merger integration is challenging due to cultural and institutional differences and the resistance of various stakeholders, for example government institutions and employees in the target country (Björkman *et al.*, 2007; Datta, 1991; Froese *et al.*, 2008; Stahl and Voigt, 2008). Substantial research has examined the antecedents and mechanisms of M&A success (e.g. Almor *et al.*, 2009; Dauber, 2012; Weber and Tarba, 2011; Weber *et al.*, 2009, 2011). However, little research has investigated the post-merger phase of acquiring Chinese and EM MNEs, not to mention the link between pre-M&A motivations and post-outcomes. In the following subsections, we develop several propositions concerning the underlying mechanisms and moderating factors leading to successful organizational and human integration and, ultimately, M&A success.

Cross-border M&A and employee resistance

Organizational change typically follows M&A deals which can have negative consequences for the employees of the acquired firm (e.g. layoffs, relocation, career disruption) and cause negative reactions among this cohort, such as uncertainty, anxiety, distrust, tension and even hostility (Larsson and Finkelstein, 1999). Hence, when uncertainty about the individual employee's future (e.g. rumours about layoffs) is paired with prejudiced-induced uncertainty about the nature and characteristics of the acquiring firm, employee resistance is likely to be high (Morck *et al.*, 2008).

Further, when the two cultures collide, negative behavioural patterns influencing firm performance, such as lower productivity, absenteeism, lower job satisfaction and commitment, may arise (Froese and Goeritz, 2007; Jöns *et al.*, 2007). In the case of Sany and Putzmeister, these psychological and behavioural patterns, known as 'merger syndrome', occurred immediately after the announcement of the acquisition. Sometimes individual articles can display both negative and positive attitudes to foreign acquisition. For instance, a piece in the German newspaper *TAZ* had the rather pejorative headline 'When communists go shopping' but then went on to say: 'We prefer the Chinese because they have a long-term strategy, whereas Anglo-Saxon private equity firms are all about a quick turnaround' (Von Leesen, 2012). Political manoeuvring or demonstrations, as in the Putzmeister case, can exacerbate negative feelings, such as hostility, towards the acquiring firm (Seo and Hill, 2005) and also harm production because of employees' absence from work. Although Sany faced some trouble during the initiation phase, researchers have observed that, in general, acquisitions by privately owned firms are less troublesome than those by SOEs, which often invest in utilities and infrastructure industries (Zhang *et al.*, 2011).

Prejudice towards acquiring companies, based on a lack of knowledge about foreign cultures, can increase the level of anxiety, potentially endangering the acquisition of the desired assets (Child and Rodrigues, 2005). The psychic distance between the Chinese company and the German context further increases the liability of foreignness and results in a strategic disadvantage for MNCs operating abroad (Child *et al.*, 2002; Child and Rodrigues, 2005; Zaheer, 1995). Sarala (2010) showed that cultural differences increase post-acquisition conflict, whereas partner attractiveness reduces post-acquisition conflict. According to acculturation theory, this psychological acculturation phenomenon leads to a shift in the behaviour of the individual after undergoing the processes of culture shedding, culture learning and culture conflict (Berry, 1997). The first two stages imply a degree of 'unlearning' of one's own cultural aspects, and simultaneous 'replacement by behaviours that allow the individual a better *fit* with the society of settlement' (Berry, 1997: 18). In our case, the employees needed to adjust to the new environment of the M&A, which would likely result in initial employee resistance.

> *Proposition 4: Employee resistance is a major challenge for Chinese outward M&A decisions.*

Employee resistance and human integration

Human integration, a crucial part of the integration process, is defined as 'the creation of positive attitudes towards the integration among employees on both sides' (Birkinshaw *et al.*, 2000: 400). Employee resistance, often caused by cultural differences between the two companies involved, is an influential factor that is especially important in the M&A context, which challenges human resource management during the integration phase of the merger. Drawing on evidence from research on foreign subsidiaries, localization is beneficial for organizational commitment among host country nationals (Hitotsuyanagi-Hansel *et al.*, 2016), which further suggests that consideration of the host country employees is vital. These findings can also be transferred and applied to the M&A context, with its diverse cultures. However, research has also shown that national cultural differences are not as problematic as is often assumed, and, in addition to organizational differences, may even be positively associated with knowledge transfer (Vaara *et al.*, 2012). Additionally, the limited operational integration of Putzmeister might have helped to reduce the likelihood of post-acquisition cultural problems. As Shenkar (2001: 527–528) mentioned: 'how different one culture is from another has little meaning until those cultures are brought into contact with one another'.

According to acculturation theory, human integration can be accomplished only if the groups involved are free to choose whether to adopt the integration mode. However, in our M&A context, employee resistance impedes mutual accommodation and acceptance by both groups (Berry, 1997). As the management is a crucial player with respect to employees' reactions towards the M&A (Hildisch *et al.*, 2015), it has the potential to foster positive adaptation to the new cultural context between the employees (Berry, 1997). The 'light-touch integration' approach of the Chinese acquirer was meant to overcome the pre-merger conflicts and acculturative stress by keeping the operations of the two companies separate.

Proposition 5: Employee resistance hinders Chinese post-M&A human integration.

Trust-building actions

By 'trust-building actions', we mean actions undertaken by both sides, including trust and respectful communication, involvement in the organizational structure, as well as measures to reduce cultural distance, which will be explained in more detail below.

In addition to the findings of the Putzmeister case, prior studies found that trust-building actions can be a success factor for the integration of an acquired firm (Björkman *et al.*, 2007). Communication is a crucial factor to develop trust among employees during the integration (DiFonzo and Bordia, 1998), which subsequently avoids negative outcomes for the organization (Bordia *et al.*, 2004). Stress and resistance can be reduced through culturally active communication, participation and commitment (Froese and Goeritz, 2007). All of these efforts help to build trust among the employees of target companies.

Therefore, after the rough start and soon after the protests, the Sany Heavy Industry Group launched a number of trust-building actions. It communicated that no one would be laid off. Moreover, Wengen Liang, the founder and chairman of the Sany Heavy Industry Group, expressed his admiration and respect for the entrepreneurial achievements of Putzmeister whenever the opportunity arose. For example, when he met Schlecht for the first time, Liang said: 'You are my teacher' (Fischer, 2012; Klawitter and Wagner, 2012). Further signs of mutual trust can be found on both sides. For instance, Liang declined to conduct a due-diligence audit, which is usually a prerequisite in an acquisition of this size. This decision strongly impressed Putzmeister's top management and employees. Furthermore, Schlecht was invited to become a 'superior consultant' for the Sany Heavy Industry Group. (He accepted the offer but refused to be paid.) Additionally, Schlecht publicly highlighted his respect for the Chinese and for Sany's corporate culture. He emphasized the congruence between the values of his firm and the values that Sany defined in its corporate statements. Additionally, he praised China's Confucian heritage, which he said was apparent in the natural and courteous way in which Sany wanted to learn from Putzmeister. Even on lower hierarchical levels, the relationship between the two firms was respectful and trustful. Another sign of trust was the appointment of Putzmeister's CEO to Sany's board, which made him the only German on a Chinese board of directors at that time (Hirn, 2013).

Due to employee resistance, the willingness to adopt the acquirer's culture and practices was low, whereas the will to preserve one's own culture was high, leading to the separation mode of acculturation. However, changes in the acculturation mode constitute the dynamic nature of the M&A integration process, and make a continuous adjustment important (Nahavandi and Malekzadeh, 1988). Notably, intercultural training and Chinese language courses were immediately offered to the employees in order to decrease the perceived cultural distance to the unknown Chinese company.

> *Proposition 6: Trust-building actions moderate the relationship between employee resistance and human integration in that increased trust-building actions reduce the negative effect of employee resistance.*

M&A decision and organizational integration

Acquiring companies can pursue different levels of integration, usually simplified as a high versus low level of integration (Haspeslagh and Jemison, 1991). The organizational integration adopted by the Chinese MNEs is mostly characterized by a 'light-touch integration' (Liu and Woywode, 2013), which does not involve too many changes and comprises a loose integration, giving Putzmeister greater autonomy. This autonomy is reflected by the physical absence of Sany Heavy Industry Group managers at Putzmeister's headquarters (Hirn, 2013), as well as an absence of intercompany exchange among production workers or mid-level management. In daily business, the changes for Putzmeister's employees were marginal. However, Putzmeister recruits German engineers for Sany. Also, Sany sends delegations to Germany on a regular basis and tries to learn from Putzmeister. Many of the German manufacturer's processes have been adopted in China (Klooß, 2013). Consequently, the Chinese CEO made the following statement: 'It feels like they bought us and not the other way around' (Simon, 2012). Additionally, the two organizations agreed on a separation of markets: while the Sany Heavy Industry Group concentrates on the Chinese market, Putzmeister covers the rest of the world. Thus, there is less potential for conflict, and competences and areas of activity are clear. The businesses are kept autonomous and independent, and little cultural or behavioural assimilation takes place.

According to acculturation theory, a fit between culture and strategy is of the utmost importance in order to achieve organizational effectiveness. Furthermore, factors determining the course of acculturation are the choice of degree of relatedness (diversification strategy) and perception of the attractiveness of the acquirer (Appelbaum *et al.*, 2000; Nahavandi and Malekzadeh, 1988). In the case of Putzmeister, the two companies involved are related in their business. However, against the usual assumption of acculturation theory regarding the relatedness of business, there has been no desire to intervene in daily business operations, and the acquirer has not imposed its culture on the acquired company (Nahavandi and Malekzadeh, 1988), as already discussed in the previous proposition.

Due to the initial protests and prejudices against Sany, which were shared by most of the employees of the acquired firm, the perceived attractiveness of Sany, the acquirer, was low, whereas the wish of employees to preserve their own (German) culture was high, suggesting a separation of businesses. We assume that the strategic fit in this case is limited to financial issues on the side of Putzmeister and to technological and symbolic images on the side of Sany. To accomplish these benefits, only limited organizational change is needed.

> *Proposition 7: Chinese outward M&A decisions pursue a low organizational integration approach.*

Strategic fit

According to Schlecht's analysis, the alternative to the corporate sale would have been bankruptcy. Thus, the strategic fit from Putzmeister's perspective applies not only to its employees, who, in the long-term perspective, gained job security, but also to the owner, who reached his personal altruistic goals. Putzmeister retained its financial strength after undergoing a restructuring process following the economic and financial crisis. The Sany Heavy Industry Group not only covered all existing debts immediately, but also gave Putzmeister funds for further acquisitions and thereby fostered investment and growth. As a strategy expert stated in the press, 'the two companies are a good match, and if the managers can get along we could see the first Chinese–German success story' (Simon, 2012).

For the Sany Heavy Industry Group, an important benefit of the acquisition was the access to Putzmeister's technology, in particular the construction plans of the concrete pumps, which provided it with a competitive advantage. Additionally, the central location in Germany and the possibility to use Putzmeister's sales and service infrastructure facilitated access to the entire European market for Sany. In turn, Sany now sells Putzmeister's concrete pumps in China as a 'premium product'. Furthermore, the Chinese firm was able to gain a lot of public attention, which led to greater prominence and a higher reputation in Europe.

Moreover, synergies were expected, and joint research and development activities were planned. According to Putzmeister's CEO, product quality between China and Germany would have to be adjusted to accomplish equal standards. The Sany Heavy Industry Group is now considering to serve as a component supplier (e.g. hydraulic cylinders) for Putzmeister's concrete pumps (Klooß, 2013), which fosters a vertical integration of its supply chain and might generate cost advantages. Taken together, a strategic fit on both sides is crucial for the success of M&As.

> *Proposition 8: Strategic fit between the acquiring and the acquired company moderates the relationship between the M&A decision and organizational integration insofar as higher strategic fit leads to greater organizational integration.*

Human and organizational integration and performance

To achieve a successful acquisition, organizational and human integration should both be of a high level. The future success of the Putzmeister acquisition is a matter of mutual development of both human and organizational integration. However, as the integration strategy is an ongoing process, this phase may last up to seven years (Birkinshaw *et al.*, 2000). In general, human integration has been proven to be a favourable basis on which to establish organizational integration (Froese and Goeritz, 2007). This is especially important in the context of an Asian acquirer that is culturally influenced by Confucian values, seeing the human being as the basis of organizational integration (high-context culture). In line with prior research (e.g. Birkinshaw *et al.*, 2000; Froese and Goeritz, 2007), we propose that both human and organizational integration are important for M&A success.

Proposition 9: Human and organizational integration positively affect performance.

Discussion

Based on a comprehensive literature review and illustrated by drawing on the Putzmeister–Sany case, we developed a conceptual model of how motivations behind M&A decisions and the post-integration approach influence M&A success. Compared to MNEs from industrialized Western countries, Chinese MNEs face a very different institutional environment in their home country (Meyer *et al.*, 2009; Peng *et al.*, 2008; Yang *et al.*, 2009), have different motivations (Child and Rodrigues, 2005; Deng, 2004, 2007; Rui and Yip, 2008) and firm competitive advantages (Buckley *et al.*, 2007; Morck *et al.*, 2008), eventually leading to different post-M&A integration challenges and approaches. Our study suggests that government has a strong influence on Chinese MNEs' cross-border decisions, not only on state-owned enterprises but also on privately owned firms, depending on their government affiliation level (e.g. Child and Rodrigues, 2005; Lu *et al.*, 2011; Wang *et al.*, 2012a, 2012b).

In addition, we identified several key factors that are crucial for a successful post-M&A integration process, such as trust-building actions and strategic fit to facilitate the human as well as organizational integration. If strategic and organizational fit factors are considered before the M&A deal and integration decision, M&A performance can be increased (Gomes *et al.*, 2013).

Theoretical implications

Despite the long history of M&A research (Cartwright and Schoenberg, 2006) there have been few attempts to provide a holistic picture of a pre- and post-M&A process. We extended the models of post-merger integration processes by also integrating and linking them to crucial internationalization drivers and motivation. Combining the M&A and FDI literature sheds a different light on prior research. Our integrative, conceptual model can increase sensitivity to possible pitfalls and give guidance concerning areas of importance while planning an acquisition. Additionally, adding internationalization drivers, motivation and agents (e.g. government) as an antecedent to the conventional pre- and post-M&A stages (Gomes *et al.*, 2013) is particularly important in the context of outward cross-border M&As of EM MNEs.

Nahavandi and Malekzadeh (1988) applied acculturation theory to the M&A context. However, regarding the case of Putzmeister, we would add further specifications and extensions, such as the 'light-touch integration', typical of EM MNEs, constituting an interactive outcome of absorptive capacity and cultural influences (Liu and Woywode, 2013). This approach seems to find recent empirical support, as the need for integration decreases when the target country is more industrialized, as in our case (Bauer and Matzler, 2014). The same applies with respect to eclectic theory, where we added the government as a driving force regarding the internationalization decisions of EM MNEs. Government is one of the agents that is pulling the strings and is therefore able to leave an unnoticed footprint on the whole integration phase. Therefore, we call for a more detailed observation of government in the whole process of the internationalization of companies, differing by ownership (Wang *et al.*, 2012b). We feel that this theoretical extension is also relevant for other developing countries, where governments play a vital role in guiding economic development.

We combined knowledge of the strategic management and organizational behaviour streams of research in the M&A context and introduced the FDI literature to gain a new understanding of the agents, processes and decisions involved. Our research shows that post-M&A integration is strongly based on pre-M&A internationalization motivations. Additionally, we explored various factors accounting for the success or failure of cross-border M&As that were in our context, trust-building actions, as well as the strategic fit of the two merging companies. Additionally, the mutual understanding of the two company leaders contributed a great deal to the successful outcome. This leads to the observation that although the cultural distance between China and Germany is high, the common ground between the leaders contributed to a lower demand for structural integration (Bauer and Matzler, 2014; Puranam *et al.*, 2009), offering 'acquirers an alternate path to achieving coordination that may be less disruptive than structural integration' (Puranam *et al.*, 2009: 326). In summary, more than one single factor is responsible for successful M&A, so further investigation of its interdependencies is required (Bauer and Matzler, 2014).

Practical implications

We can provide several practical implications for the various stakeholders (policy-makers, managers and employees) involved in Chinese cross-border M&As in industrialized countries.

As for policy implications, the size and frequency of mostly horizontal acquisitions are both increasing. Policy-makers should be prepared for an increase of investment in high-technology-intensive industries rather than the traditional manufacturing sector (Chen and Young, 2010). Additionally, the target industries for investment show a slight shift towards technology, real estate and food after investing almost solely in natural resources in the past (CCTV, 2013). Future M&A deals will involve a higher percentage of private enterprises, which are increasingly encouraged and financially supported by the government, pointing to a 'golden era' for their investment abroad (Li, 2013). Chinese private companies have a less complex organizational structure than SOEs, provide more transparency, and have faster decision-making processes and stronger willingness to learn, making them much easier to work with (Liu and Woywode, 2013). However, target firms and countries need to be aware that government affiliation level and motivations behind the investment are not always visible at first glance. Therefore, due to strong government influence in internationalization decisions, we would advise policy-makers to pay increased attention to announcements related to guidelines, such as the going-out strategy or the Five-Year Plan, to deduce possible future development and react more promptly towards these changes. As costs in China continue to rise, global industrial production will be moved to cheaper countries. To counter this threat, the Chinese government's goals are to move up the value chain through internationalization and create more sustainable competitive advantages by accessing already industrialized markets, technology and brands, as well as enlarging their networks (Buckley *et al.*, 2007). Therefore, in the future, we will see an increase in Chinese cross-border M&A deals targeting companies from industrialized countries. Additionally, future acquisition intentions from private Chinese companies should be less subject to suspicion, because the Chinese government will often not be the majority owner of the firm.

As for managerial implications, the intelligent signalling and cultural intelligence of the Chinese and German sides led to a relatively harmonious integration process without any known major conflicts, contributing to a reduction of employee resistance, which led to better post-acquisition firm performance. Therefore, the dedication and effort of top managers, supervisors and executives contribute significantly to a successful M&A process (Appelbaum *et al.*, 2000), especially if employees perceive support from this cohort (Hildisch *et al.*, 2015). The light-touch integration approach is also greatly beneficial for Western firms insofar as high autonomy is preserved and strategic resources are leveraged (Liu and Woywode, 2013). Additionally, employee expectations are crucial to the success of M&As. Therefore, managers should enquire about these expectations by using specific tools, such as joint activities or employee surveys (Froese *et al.*, 2008). To reduce the likelihood of strikes and demonstrations further, practitioners will have to maintain strong links to unions in order to avoid potential impacts on the firm's performance. Above all, the timing of communication is essential as any delays in communication foster hostile feelings of employees towards M&As, hampering future communication and integration (Appelbaum *et al.*, 2000).

As for implications for foreign (e.g. German) employees in industrialized countries, the latter should not be too worried about layoffs as Chinese companies prefer light-touch integration, and do not tend to initiate significant changes following a merger. Less organizational integration leads to reduced employee resistance. However, if employee resistance does develop, trust-building actions could reduce it.

As for Chinese policy implications, the growing scepticism towards Chinese M&A deals makes it necessary to restructure the going-out policy and requires paying considerably more attention to the promotion of sustainable OFDI, meaning OFDI that contributes as much as possible to the economic, social and environmental development of host countries and takes place in the context of fair governance, including contracts in natural resources (Sauvant, 2013).

Regarding the practical implications for Chinese companies, we would suggest acquiring firms extending their evaluation criteria for potential target firms by 'mutual strategic fit', meaning that the two merging companies should complement each other in terms of industrial sector or strategic goals behind the M&A decision – a less obvious success factor of cross-border M&As. Additionally, it was shown that not only strategic and organizational integration aspects are crucial for the outcome, but also the human side of the merger. Managers should also consider the identified success factor of trust-building actions – measures that have to be planned carefully in advance and must be tailored to the target firm's organizational and national culture. It was shown how prejudices can multiply anxiety among employees. Positive experiences with Chinese cross-border M&As can improve the image of Chinese companies abroad and mitigate prejudices against Chinese firms and provide opportunities for future M&A decisions in industrialized countries. Findings and recommendations include transparent management communication and participation in decision-making (Bordia *et al.*, 2004; Napier, 1989), stress management training (Matteson and Ivancevich, 1990), and employee assistance programmes ('town meetings') before, during and after an acquisition (Fugate *et al.*, 2002).

Limitations and avenues for future research

As our conceptual model mainly draws evidence from one single case in the Chinese–German context, the applicability and generalizability to other country and industry contexts need to be further investigated and empirically supported. However, we suggest that our framework is relevant and can be applied to other emerging economies with strong governmental control and thus higher involvement in internationalization strategies and decisions. Additionally, as our case is based on a privately owned Chinese company, conclusions about other diverse ownership types of companies are difficult to draw. However, as our argument is mainly based on government affiliation level, the de facto ownership type is of minor concern. Still, future research needs to investigate differences and similarities more closely, as Li *et al.* (2014) have already observed differences between central and local SOEs and OFDI strategies.

Possible avenues for future research are the elaboration and further investigation of a holistic M&A process, as the pre-M&A decision and its antecedents have an influence on various factors during post-merger stages. Developing a generalizable framework that is applicable to other forms of OFDI and other cultural settings could be a valuable area of investigation. Additionally, future research should try to embrace and incorporate further research streams that are relevant to the topic, such as financial economics or the process perspective of the post-merger.

Due to the scarcity of research on a holistic M&A process in general and regarding the context of EM MNEs specifically, we suggest further theoretical investigation and encourage researchers in the field to conduct a large-scale study, providing quantitative support based on our theoretical arguments and case study observations. Furthermore, additional studies have to investigate the double-faced nature of EM MNEs, as parallels between their own driving forces and resources to internationalize and institutional motivations lead to exploitation of these complementarities (Wang *et al.*, 2012b). To provide evidence for the generalizability of our framework, other economies showing a hybrid industrial structure of traditional central planning system and market economy regarding the degree of market imperfection, structural uncertainty and government interference (Wang *et al.*, 2012a) need to be further investigated. In the course of economic development, the question remains whether the role of government institutions remains stable over time or whether entrepreneurship will increase in power in the future (Lu *et al.*, 2011; Yiu *et al.*, 2007).

References

Almor, T., S. Y. Tarba and H. Benjamini, 'Unmasking integration challenges: The case of Biogal's acquisition by Teva Pharmaceutical Industries', *International Studies of Management and Organization*, Vol. 39, No. 3, 2009, pp. 32–52.

Appelbaum, S. H., J. Gandell, H. Yortis, S. Proper and F. Jobin, 'Anatomy of a merger: Behavior of organizational factors and processes throughout the pre–during–post-stages (part 1)', *Management Decision*, Vol. 38, No. 9, 2000, pp. 649–662.

Athreye, S. and S. Kapur, 'Introduction: The internationalization of Chinese and Indian firms – trends, motivations and strategy', *Industrial and Corporate Change*, Vol. 18, No. 2, 2009, pp. 209–221.

Bauer, F. and K. Matzler, 'Antecedents of M&A success: The role of strategic complementarity, cultural fit, and degree and speed of integration', *Strategic Management Journal*, Vol. 35, No. 2, 2014, pp. 269–291.

Berry, J. W., 'Acculturation as varieties of adaptation', in: A. M. Padilla (ed.), *Acculturation: Theory, models, and some new findings*, Boulder, CO: Westview Press, 1980, pp. 9–26.

Berry, J. W., 'Immigration, acculturation, and adaptation', *Applied Psychology*, Vol. 46, No. 1, 1997, pp. 5–34.

Birkinshaw, J., H. Bresman and L. Håkanson, 'Managing the post-acquisition integration process: How the human integration and task integration processes interact to foster value creation', *Journal of Management Studies*, Vol. 37, No. 3, 2000, pp. 395–425.

Björkman, I., G. K. Stahl and E. Vaara, 'Cultural differences and capability transfer in cross-border acquisitions: The mediating roles of capability complementarity, absorptive capacity, and social integration', *Journal of International Business Studies*, Vol. 38, No. 4, 2007, pp. 658–672.

Boateng, A., W. Qian and Y. Tianle, 'Cross-border M&As by Chinese firms: An analysis of strategic motives and performance', *Thunderbird International Business Review*, Vol. 50, No. 4, 2008, pp. 259–270.

Bordia, P., E. Hunt, N. Paulsen, D. Tourish and N. DiFonzo, 'Uncertainty during organizational change: Is it all about control?', *European Journal of Work and Organizational Psychology*, Vol. 13, No. 3, 2004, pp. 345–365.

Brannen, M. Y. and M. F. Peterson, 'Merging without alienating: Interventions promoting cross-cultural organizational integration and their limitations', *Journal of International Business Studies*, Vol. 40, No. 3, 2009, pp. 468–489.

Buckley, P. J, L. J. Clegg, A. R. Cross, X. Liu, H. Voss and P. Zheng, 'The determinants of Chinese outward foreign direct investment', *Journal of International Business Studies*, Vol. 38, No. 4, 2007, pp. 499–518.

Buckley, P. J., A. R. Cross, H. Tan, L. Xin and H. Voss, 'Historic and emergent trends in Chinese outward direct investment', *Management International Review*, Vol. 48, No. 6, 2008, pp. 715–748.

Cartwright, S. and R. Schoenberg, 'Thirty years of mergers and acquisitions research: Recent advances and future opportunities', *British Journal of Management*, Vol. 17, No. S1, 2006, pp. S1–S5.

CCTV, 'Chinese overseas acquisitions', 2013. Available at http://usa.chinadaily.com.cn/business/2013-10/28/content_17063425.htm (accessed 2 May 2014).

Chen, H. and T.-J. Chen, 'Network linkages and location choice in foreign direct investment', *Journal of International Business Studies*, Vol. 29, No. 3, 1998, pp. 445–467.

Chen, X.-P. and C. C. Chen, 'On the intricacies of the Chinese guanxi: A process model of guanxi development', *Asia Pacific Journal of Management*, Vol. 21, No. 3, 2004, pp. 305–324.

Chen, Y. Y. and M. N. Young, 'Cross-border mergers and acquisitions by Chinese listed companies: A principal–principal perspective', *Asia Pacific Journal of Management*, Vol. 27, No. 3, 2010, pp. 523–539.

Child, J., 'China and international business', in: A. M. Rugman and T. L. Brewer (eds), *Oxford Handbook of International Business*, New York: Oxford University Press, 2011, pp. 648–686.

Child, J., S. H. Ng and C. Wong, 'Psychic distance and internationalization: Evidence from Hong Kong firms', *International Studies of Management and Organization*, Vol. 32, No. 1, 2002, pp. 36–56.

Child, J. and S. B. Rodrigues, 'The Internationalization of Chinese firms: A case for theoretical extension?', *Management and Organization Review*, Vol. 1, No. 3, 2005, pp. 381–410.

CNN, 'China's richest man hopes to join the political elite', 29 September 2011. Available at http://edition.cnn.com/2011/09/29/business/china-liang-wengen-communist-party/ (accessed 25 April 2014).

CNN Money, '*Fortune* Global 500 2013', 2013. Available at http://money.cnn.com/magazines/fortune/global500/2013/full_list/ (accessed 2 April 2014).

Cui, L. and F. Jiang, 'Behind ownership decision of Chinese outward FDI: Resources and institutions', *Asia Pacific Journal of Management*, Vol. 27, No. 4, 2010, pp. 751–774.

Cui, L. and F. Jiang, 'State ownership effect on firms' FDI ownership decisions under institutional pressure: A study of Chinese outward-investing firms', *Journal of International Business Studies*, Vol. 43, No. 3, 2012, pp. 264–284.

Datta, D. K., 'Organizational fit and acquisition performance: Effects of post-acquisition integration', *Strategic Management Journal*, Vol. 12, No. 4, 1991, pp. 281–297.

Dauber, D., 'Opposing positions in M&A research: Culture, integration and performance', *Cross-Cultural Management: An International Journal*, Vol. 19, No. 3, 2012, pp. 375–398.

Deng, P., 'Outward investment by Chinese MNCs: Motivations and implications', *Business Horizons*, Vol. 47, No. 3, 2004, pp. 8–16.

Deng, P., 'Investing for strategic resources and its rationale: The case of outward FDI from Chinese companies', *Business Horizons*, Vol. 50, No. 1, 2007, pp. 71–81.

Deng, P., 'Why do Chinese firms tend to acquire strategic assets in international expansion?', *Journal of World Business*, Vol. 44, No. 1, 2009, pp. 74–84.

DiFonzo, N. and P. Bordia, 'A tale of two corporations: Managing uncertainty during organizational change', *Human Resource Management*, Vol. 37, Nos. 3–4, 1998, pp. 295–303.

DIHK, *'Fachkraft Chef' gesucht!, DIHK-Report zur Unternehmensnachfolge 2011*, 2011. Available at www.leipzig.ihk.de/fileadmin/user_upload/Dokumente/EuU/DIHK-Nachfolgereport_2011.pdf (accessed 17 March 2014).

Dunning, J. H., 'Trade, location of economic activity and the MNE: A search for an eclectic approach', in: B. Ohlin, P.-O. Hesselborn and P. M. Wijkman (eds), *The International Allocation of Economic Activity: Proceedings of a Nobel Symposium Held at Stockholm*, London: Macmillan, 1977, pp. 395–418.

Dunning, J. H., *Multinational Enterprises and the Global Economy*, Reading, MA, and Menlo Park, CA: Addison Wesley, 1993.

Dunning, J., 'Comment on Dragon multinationals: New players in 21st century globalization', *Asia Pacific Journal of Management*, Vol. 23, No. 2, 2006, pp. 139–141.

Dunning, J. H. and S. M. Lundan, *Multinational Enterprises and the Global Economy*, Cheltenham: Edward Elgar, 2008.

Dunning, J. and R. Narula (eds), *Foreign Direct Investment and Governments: Catalysts for Economic Restructuring* London: Routledge, 1996.

Dupasquier, C. and P. N. Osakwe, 'Foreign direct investment in Africa: Performance, challenges, and responsibilities', *Journal of Asian Economics*, Vol. 17, No. 2, 2006, pp. 241–260.

Fischer, H., 'Die Betonmischer: Die Kräfteverhältnisse zwischen West und Ost verschieben sich: Warum der chinesische Konzern Sany den deutschen Betonpumpenbauer Putzmeister übernommen hat', *Impulse*, No. 3, 2012, pp. 40–47.

Fortanier, F. and R. v. Tulder, 'Internationalization trajectories – a cross-country comparison: Are large Chinese and Indian companies different?', *Industrial and Corporate Change*, Vol. 18, No. 2, 2009, pp. 223–247.

Froese, F. J. and L. E. Goeritz, 'Integration management of Western acquisitions in Japan', *Asian Business and Management*, Vol. 6, No. 1, 2007, pp. 95–114.

Froese, F. J., Y. S. Pak and L. C. Chong, 'Managing the human side of cross-border acquisitions in South Korea", *Korean Issue*, Vol. 43, No. 1, 2008, pp. 97–108.

Fugate, M., A. J. Kinicki and C. L. Scheck, 'Coping with an organizational merger over four stages', *Personnel Psychology*, Vol. 55, No. 4, 2002, pp. 905–928.

Gomes, E., D. N. Angwin, Y. Weber and S. Y. Tarba, 'Critical success factors through the mergers and acquisitions process: Revealing pre- and post-M&A connections for improved performance', *Thunderbird International Business Review*, Vol. 55, No. 1, 2013, pp. 13–35.

Guillén, M. F. and E. García-Canal, 'The American model of the multinational firm and the new multinationals from emerging economies', *Academy of Management Perspectives*, Vol. 23, No. 2, 2009, pp. 23–35.

Haspeslagh, P. C. and D. B. Jemison, *Managing Acquisitions: Creating Value through Corporate Renewal*, New York: Free Press, 1991.

Hildisch, A. K., F. J. Froese and Y. S. Pak, 'Employee responses to a cross-border acquisition in South Korea: The role of social support from different hierarchical levels', *Asian Business and Management*, Vol. 14, No. 4, 2015, pp. 327–347.

Hirn, W., 'Neue Herren aus China: Wie sich Putzmeister und Sany die Welt aufteilen', 2013. Available at www.manager-magazin.de/unternehmen/artikel/a-900147.html (accessed 20 January 2015).

Hitotsuyanagi-Hansel, A., F. J. Froese and Y. S. Pak, 'Lessening the divide in foreign subsidiaries: The influence of localization on the organizational commitment and turnover intention of host country nationals', *International Business Review*, No. 25, 2016, pp. 569–578.

Hong, E. and L. Sun, 'Dynamics of internationalization and outward investment: Chinese corporations' strategies', *China Quarterly*, No. 187, 2006, pp. 610–634.

Jöns, I., F. J. Froese and Y. S. Pak, 'Cultural changes during the integration process of acquisitions: A comparative study between German and German–Korean acquisitions', *International Journal of Intercultural Relations*, Vol. 31, No. 5, 2007, pp. 591–604.

Klawitter, N. and W. Wagner, 'Götterdämmerung: Die Chinesen übernehmen den Betonpumpenhersteller Putzmeister und damit erstmals ein deutsches Unternehmen von Weltgeltung. Es dürfte nicht das letzte gewesen sein.', *Der Spiegel*, No. 6, 2012, pp. 68–69.

Klooß, K., 'Putzmeister-Chef Norbert Scheuch: Die Globalisierung trägt uns weg von Deutschland', 2013. Available at www.manager-magazin.de/unternehmen/industrie/a-889073-2.html (accessed 18 August 2014).

Klossek, A., B. M. Linke and M. Nippa, 'Chinese enterprises in Germany: Establishment modes and strategies to mitigate the liability of foreignness', *Focus on China Special Section*, Vol. 47, No. 1, 2012, pp. 35–44.

Kumar, N., 'How emerging giants are rewriting the rules of M&A', *Harvard Business Review*, Vol. 87, No. 5, 2009, pp. 115–121.

Larsson, R. and S. Finkelstein, 'Integrating strategic, organizational, and human resource perspectives on mergers and acquisitions: A case survey of synergy realization', *Organization Science*, Vol. 10, No. 1, 1999, pp. 1–26.

Li, J., 'Overseas investment set for "golden era"', 2013. Available at http://usa.chinadaily.com.cn/business/2013-12/12/content_17170070.htm (accessed 2 May 2014).

Li, J., 'State planners relax outward investment regulations', 2014. Available at http://usa.chinadaily.com.cn/epaper/2014-01/09/content_17226582.htm (accessed 2 May 2014).

Li, M. H., L. Cui and J. Lu, 'Varieties in state capitalism: Outward FDI strategies of central and local state-owned enterprises from emerging economy countries', *Journal of International Business Studies*, Vol. 45, No. 8, 2014, pp. 980–1004.

Liu, Y. and M. Woywode, 'Light-touch integration of Chinese cross-border M&A: The influences of culture and absorptive capacity', *Thunderbird International Business Review*, Vol. 55, No. 4, 2013, pp. 469–483.

Lu, J., X. Liu and H. Wang, 'Motives for outward FDI of Chinese private firms: Firm resources, industry dynamics, and government policies', *Management and Organization Review*, Vol. 7, No. 2, 2011, pp. 223–248.

Luo, Y. and R. L. Tung, 'International expansion of emerging market enterprises: A springboard perspective', *Journal of International Business Studies*, Vol. 38, No. 4, 2007, pp. 481–498.

Luo, Y., Q. Xue and B. Han, 'How emerging market governments promote outward FDI: Experience from China', *Journal of World Business*, Vol. 45, No. 1, 2010, pp. 68–79.

Makino, S., C.-M. Lau and R.-S. Yeh, 'Asset-exploitation versus asset-seeking: Implications for location choice of foreign direct investment from newly industrialized economies', *Journal of International Business Studies*, Vol. 33, No. 3, 2002, pp. 403–421.

Matteson, M. T. and J. M. Ivancevich, 'Merger and acquisition stress: Fear and uncertainty at mid-career', *Prevention in Human Services*, Vol. 8, No. 1, 1990, pp. 139–158.

Meyer, K. E., S. Estrin, S. K. Bhaumik and M. W. Peng, 'Institutions, resources, and entry strategies in emerging economies', *Strategic Management Journal*, Vol. 30, No. 1, 2009, pp. 61–80.

Ministry of Commerce, *Statistical Bulletin of China's Outward Foreign Direct Investment*, Beijing: Ministry of Commerce, 2010.

Ministry of Commerce, 'MOFCOM holds press conference on CSR of Chinese companies operating abroad', 2013. Available at http://english.mofcom.gov.cn/article/zt_review2013/column3/201401/20140100455061.shtml (accessed 2 May 2014).

Ministry of Commerce, *Joint Report on Statistics of China's Outbound FDI 2013*, 2014. Available at http://english.mofcom.gov.cn/article/newsrelease/significantnews/201409/20140900727958.shtml (accessed 16 June 2016).

Morck, R., B. Yeung and M. Zhao, 'Perspectives on China's outward foreign direct investment', *Journal of International Business Studies*, Vol. 39, No. 3, 2008, pp. 337–350.

Nahavandi, A. and A. R. Malekzadeh, 'Acculturation in mergers and acquisitions', *Academy of Management Review*, Vol. 13, No. 1, 1988, pp. 79–90.

Napier, N. K., 'Mergers and acquisitions, human resource issues and outcomes: A review and suggested typology', *Journal of Management Studies*, Vol. 26, No. 3, 1989, pp. 271–290.

Narula, R., 'Do we need different frameworks to explain infant MNEs from developing countries?', *Global Strategy Journal*, Vol. 2, No. 3, 2012, pp. 188–204.

OECD, 'FDI financial flows by partner country BMD4', 2014. Available at www.oecd.org/corporate/mne/statistics.htm (accessed 16 June 2016).

Peng, M. W., D. Y. L. Wang and Y. Jiang, 'An institution-based view of international business strategy: A focus on emerging economies', *Journal of International Business Studies*, Vol. 39, No. 5, 2008, pp. 920–936.

Puranam, P., H. Singh and S. Chaudhuri, 'Integrating acquired capabilities: When structural integration is (un)necessary', *Organization Science*, Vol. 20, No. 2, 2009, pp. 313–328.

Rodrigues, S. and J. Child, 'Co-evolution in an institutionalized environment', *Journal of Management Studies*, Vol. 40, No. 8, 2003, pp. 2137–2162.

Rui, H. and G. S. Yip, 'Foreign acquisitions by Chinese firms: A strategic intent perspective', *Journal of World Business*, Vol. 43, No. 2, 2008, pp. 213–226.

Sarala, R. M., 'The impact of cultural differences and acculturation factors on post-acquisition conflict', *Scandinavian Journal of Management*, Vol. 26, No. 1, 2010, pp. 38–56.

Sauvant, K. P., *Challenges for China's outward FDI*, 2013. Available at http://usa.chinadaily.com.cn/opinion/2013-10/31/content_17070440.htm (accessed 30 April 2014).

Seo, M.-G. and N. S. Hill, 'Understanding the human side of merger and acquisition: An integrative framework', *Journal of Applied Behavioral Science*, Vol. 41, No. 4, 2005, pp. 422–443.

Shenkar, O., 'Cultural distance revisited: Towards a more rigorous conceptualization and measurement of cultural differences', *Journal of International Business Studies*, Vol. 32, No. 3, 2001, pp. 519–535.

Simon, H., 'Sany-Putzmeister takeover – a sign of Mittelstand deals to come', 2012. Available at http://blogs.ft.com/beyond-brics/2012/02/02/sany-putzmeister-a-sign-of-mittelstand-deals-to-come/?Authorised=false (accessed 18 August 2014).

Stahl, G. K. and A. Voigt, 'Do cultural differences matter in mergers and acquisitions? A tentative model and examination', *Organization Science*, Vol. 19, No. 1, 2008, pp. 160–176.

UNCTAD, *World Investment Report 2006: FDI from Developing and Transition Economies: Implications for Development*, New York: United Nations, 2006.

UNCTAD, *World Investment Report 2013: Global Value Chains: Investment and Trade for Development*, New York: United Nations, 2013.

UNCTAD, *World Investment Report 2015: Reforming International Investment Governance*, New York: United Nations, 2015.

UNCTAD, *World Investment Report 2016: Investor Nationality: Policy Challenges*, New York: United Nations, 2016.

Vaara, E., R. M. Sarala, G. K. Stahl and I. Björkman, 'The impact of organizational and national cultural differences on social conflict and knowledge transfer in international acquisitions', *Journal of Management Studies*, Vol. 49, No. 1, 2012, pp. 1–27.

Von Leesen, G., 'Putzmeister in Kommunistenhand', 2012. Available at www.kontextwochenzeitung.de/wirtschaft/45/putzmeister-in-kommunistenhand-1192.html (accessed 18 August 2014).

Wang, C., J. Hong, M. Kafouros and A. Boateng, 'What drives outward FDI of Chinese firms? Testing the explanatory power of three theoretical frameworks', *International Business Review*, Vol. 21, No. 3, 2012a, pp. 425–438.

Wang, C., J. Hong, M. Kafouros and M. Wright, 'Exploring the role of government involvement in outward FDI from emerging economies', *Journal of International Business Studies*, Vol. 43, No. 7, 2012b, pp. 655–676.

Weber, Y. and S. Y. Tarba, 'Exploring integration approach in related mergers: Post-merger integration in the high-tech industry', *International Journal of Organizational Analysis*, Vol. 19, No. 3, 2011, pp. 202–221.

Weber, Y., S. Y. Tarba and A. Reichel, 'International mergers and acquisitions performance revisited: The role of cultural distance and post', *Advances in Mergers and Acquisitions*, Vol. 8, 2009, pp. 1–17.

Weber, Y., S. Y. Tarba and A. Reichel, 'A model of the influence of culture on integration approaches and international mergers and acquisitions performance', *International Studies of Management and Organization*, Vol. 41, No. 3, 2011, pp. 9–24.

Yang, X., Y. Jiang, R. Kang and Y. Ke, 'A comparative analysis of the internationalization of Chinese and Japanese firms', *Asia Pacific Journal of Management*, Vol. 26, No. 1, 2009, pp. 141–162.

Yiu, D. W., C. Lau and G. D. Bruton, 'International venturing by emerging economy firms: The effects of firm capabilities, home country networks, and corporate entrepreneurship', *Journal of International Business Studies*, Vol. 38, No. 4, 2007, pp. 519–540.

Zaheer, S., 'Overcoming the liability of foreignness', *Academy of Management Journal*, Vol. 38, No. 2, 1995, pp. 341–363.

Zhang, J., C. Zhou and H. Ebbers, 'Completion of Chinese overseas acquisitions: Institutional perspectives and evidence', *International Business Review*, Vol. 20, No. 2, 2011, pp. 226–238.

Zhang, X. and K. Daly, 'The determinants of China's outward foreign direct investment', *Emerging Markets Review*, Vol. 12, No. 4, 2011, pp. 389–398.

Zhang, Y., *China's Emerging Global Businesses: Political Economy and Institutional Investigations*, Basingstoke: Palgrave Macmillan, 2003.

6

POST-MERGER INTEGRATION IN THE PHARMACEUTICAL AND BIOTECHNOLOGY INDUSTRIES

A practical approach

Lars Schweizer

Introduction

Mergers and acquisitions (M&As) have been a popular strategy for firms during the last few decades. On the one hand, they offer various advantages such as direct access to technologies, products, distribution channels, and market positions. On the other hand, M&As can provide access to knowledge and bring into a company capabilities that are hard to develop (Schweizer 2005). Still, many M&As have not been successful and have failed to achieve their objectives, particularly due to difficulties in the post-acquisition integration process (Agrawal and Jaffe 2000; Aktas *et al.* 2009, 2011; Haleblian *et al.* 2009; King *et al.* 2004; Sirower 1997). Moreover, Gomes *et al.* (2013) argue that, despite a lot of M&A research in different disciplines, the M&A research field suffers from a lack of connectedness between these different research streams.

The desire to obtain valuable resources, including know-how, technologies, and capabilities possessed by target firms has always been a driver of M&A activities (Chaudhuri and Tabrizi 1999). Especially in industries characterized by rapid innovation, technological complexity, and highly specialized skills and know-how, firms may not be able to develop all the necessary technologies and capabilities internally in order to maintain their competitive position (Schweizer 2005, 2012). As a result, the number of M&As during the 1990s and 2000s rose dramatically in high-technology sectors such as biotechnology (BioCentury 2007; Schweizer 2012).

Schweizer (2012) has analyzed the development of the biotechnology industry and has come to the conclusion that there will be increased M&A activities due to several reasons. First, the technological frontier of biotechnology is advancing with a knowledge, skill, and competence base that is fundamentally different from prior know-how (Patzelt and Brenner 2008; Powell 1996), so biotechnology and pharmaceutical firms face the need to search constantly for new knowledge and technologies. Second, the pattern of inter-firm collaboration in biotechnology is more extensive than in any other industry, and M&A deals are one important strategy in that context (Patzelt *et al.* 2012), subsequently forcing biotechnology firms to deal with the command and control structure of big pharmaceutical companies (Schweizer 2005, 2012). Third, startup firms in this research-intensive, high-technology industry require not only substantial financial resources, but also competencies in different scientific and technological fields (Jones *et al.* 2001), while at the same time having a high risk of failure during the first few years of their existence.

This problematic issue is also reflected in the following two practitioner statements, which were made to the author during personal conversations. On the one hand, a managing director of a big pharmaceutical company said: "If a biotechnology company has a promising technology or product, big pharma simply will buy it." On the other hand, a CEO and founder of a young German biotechnology company stated: "We do not want to be taken over, we prefer to remain independent, because this company is our life's work." Given these obviously controversial perspectives, the high failure rate of M&A activities (Haleblian *et al.* 2009; King *et al.* 2004, 2008), as well as the need for further research on post-acquisition integration in the pharmaceutical and biotechnology industries (Patzelt *et al.*, 2012; Schweizer 2012), the following theoretical and at the same time very practical research question can be formulated:

> *How can the post-acquisition integration of acquired biotechnology companies into the structure of big pharmaceutical companies be successfully realized without endangering their innovative competencies and flexibility?*

This chapter is exploratory in nature and tries to provide a (practical) answer to that question by presenting and discussing the post-acquisition integration case of Boston-based Lexigen Pharmaceuticals Corp., which was acquired by the German pharmaceutical company Merck (not to be mistaken for the U.S.-based Merck and Co.).

Review of existing post-merger integration literature

The complexity of the post-merger integration phase led to the development of many contingency frameworks or typologies (e.g., Angwin 2012; Haspeslagh and Jemison 1991; Schweiger *et al.* 1993; Schweiger and Weber 1989). The best-known post-acquisition integration framework has been developed by Haspeslagh and Jemison (1991). In their book, they propose four integration styles (symbiotic, preservation, absorption, holding) each comprising different levels of intended synergy and, thus, human integration (Birkinshaw *et al.* 2000). Building on that, Almor *et al.* (2009) suggest that an adopted post-acquisition integration approach depends on the cultural differences between combining entities and the (expected) synergy potentials of the deal. For example, Weber and Tarba (2011) present the post-acquisition integration problems that arise from a cultural clash between two merging entities in a high-tech industry. In a further step, Schweizer (2005) argues that in order for synergies to be realized, it may be necessary to transfer tacit knowledge and capabilities requiring a high degree of post-acquisition integration. However, this high level of post-acquisition integration may lead to the loss of the autonomy of the acquired unit, so that the desired capabilities could be destroyed (Puranam *et al.* 2006). This not only highlights a key problem for the successful realization of a post-acquisition integration strategy, but requires the detailed analysis of the context in which the intended transaction is supposed to take place.

This argumentation of Schweizer (2005) is in line with other studies which come to the conclusion that the extent of post-acquisition integration needed to achieve synergy realization may ultimately lead to the destruction of the acquired firm's knowledge, resource, and capability base through employee turnover, disruption of organizational routines, and dissolution of embedded ties in the acquired firm (Puranam *et al.* 2006, 2009; Puranam and Srikanth 2007; Ranft 2006; Spedale *et al.* 2007). In a recent study, Sarala *et al.* (2014) analyze the sociocultural factors that determine M&A outcomes. The authors argue that sociocultural interfirm linkages (like, e.g., complementary employee skills, trust, collective teaching, as well as cultural integration) between the merging firms have a significant impact on the level of knowledge transfer in M&As. In a previous study, Weber and Tarba (2010), building on a knowledge-based view of acquisitions, suggest that an acquiring firm should make use of its HR practices (like training and communication) in order to develop post-merger integration capabilities. In another study, Weber *et al.* (2009) analyze the effect of cultural distance on different post-acquisition integration approaches and propose a framework of how to deal with this challenge. In a follow-up study (Weber *et al.* 2011), the same authors develop a theoretical model that simultaneously deals with the effects of corporate culture, national culture, and synergy potential on various integration approaches, as well as their influence on M&A performance.

Besides the above-mentioned articles, other studies have discussed key success factors and challenges for successful post-acquisition integration, including speed (Haspeslagh and Jemison 1991; Kitching 1967; Schweizer and Patzelt 2012), organizational and cultural fit (Datta 1991; Nahavandi and Malekzadeh 1988), human resources retention, and management integration (Hambrick and Canella 1993; Walsh 1988). Despite the popularity and frequent coverage of M&A, studies of the post-acquisition integration process are rather fragmented and lack sufficient rigorous empirical research (Inkpen *et al.* 2000). In particular, researchers have considered several isolated aspects and typologies but have failed to address the complexities and multidimensional facets of integration (Bower 2001; Haspeslagh and Jemison 1991; Schweizer 2005). Moreover, researchers have insufficiently linked integration problems to the types of organizational resources and capabilities acquired (Haspeslagh and Jemison 1991), so that there is a need to look beyond single integration approaches (Puranam *et al.* 2006; Schweizer 2005).

Looking at the specific pharmaceutical and biotechnology context, it is important to consider the observation of Bower (2001: 99–100), who pointed out that "many of the pharmaceuticals' R&D acquisitions have yet to pay off' because biotech products and technologies are organic and far more difficult to integrate than computer or chip components (Schweizer 2005). It is quite obvious that intangible assets like know-how and intellectual property do not passively translate into tangible revenue. Following that, Bradfield and El-Sayed (2009) emphasize that M&As of competing pharmaceutical and biotechnology firms, rather than resolving the problems of the acquiring firms, create new ones. Similarly, Danzon *et al.* (2007) conclude that mergers may be a response to trouble for firms operating in the biotechnology and pharmaceutical industries, but they are not a solution. Following this, Graebner *et al.* (2010) come to the conclusion that there are a number of challenges to a successful post-acquisition integration of biotechnology M&A activities. This latter point provided the motivation for the present study.

Research design, case presentation and analysis

Research design

Following the argumentation of the previous section, specific post-acquisition integration activities – especially in the pharmaceutical and biotechnology industries – are still under-researched (Patzelt *et al.* 2012; Schweizer 2012). Miles and Huberman (1994) suggest that researchers should use a qualitative research design when there is a clear need for an in-depth understanding, for local contextualization, and for the points of view of the people under study. Thus, the present study is based on a detailed analysis of a single, exploratory case study. This is in line with Yin (1994), who states that case studies can be used for exploratory, descriptive, or explanatory purposes. This is also supported by the argumentation of Eisenhardt (1989, 1991).

In the context of M&A, Larsson (1990) argued that case studies are particularly appropriate for the study of M&A integration processes, given the need for detailed, contextual descriptions of very sensitive data. Moreover, the use of case studies in the context of M&As is in line with Bower's (2001, 2004) recommendations as well as those of Hunt (1990), Javidan *et al.* (2004), and Napier (1989). During the last decade, using a qualitative approach in M&A research has become increasingly popular. Graebner (2004, 2009) and Graebner and Eisenhardt (2004) have used a qualitative approach for their analysis of M&A in the entrepreneurial high-technology sector. Melkonian *et al.* (2011) and Monin *et al.* (2013) have used a qualitative case-study in their analysis of the post-merger integration process between Air France and KLM. Riad and Vaara (2011), Vaara and Tienari (2011), and Riad *et al.* (2012) have also employed a qualitative approach in the context of international M&A activities.

We conducted preliminary unstructured interviews with industry experts to obtain an appropriate degree of relevance and structure. We applied semi-structured interviews to gain comparative qualitative data for the present case study. In addition to that, we analyzed archival documents and detailed write-ups, all included in a case-study database, and collected additional documents, such as annual reports, press releases, internal memos, procedures, and documents. To insure internal validity, we used multiple iterations and follow-ups during the analysis. Looking at multiple companies and analyzing comparative findings established external validity.

As noted before, our principal research question is: how do pharmaceutical firms successfully integrate acquired biotechnology firms during the post-acquisition process? The framework selected for the within-case analysis is based on the semi-structured questionnaire used for the interviews. The within-case analysis utilized a matrix technique for comparative analysis across interviews within one case (Miles and Huberman 1994). The resulting matrices allow visual identification of patterns in the post-acquisition integration process. The topics chosen for the questionnaire have been developed by making a first review of the post-merger/post-acquisition and M&A literature and studies as well as preliminary discussions with industry experts and has also been continuously updated based on useful remarks which came up during the different interviews.

All interviews were fully taped and transcribed into a protocol. Each interview was then structured and coded to facilitate within-case analysis. Based on the within-case analysis – using the above-mentioned matrix technique (Miles and Huberman 1994) – we developed a comprehensive case description based on identified patterns and summarized our findings in a practical post-acquisition integration framework.

Corporate profiles

The roots of Merck KGaA reach back into the seventeenth century, when, in 1668, Friedrich Jacob Merck purchased the Engel-Apotheke in Darmstadt. In 1827, Heinrich Emanuel Merck began the large-scale production of alkaloids, followed by plant extracts and many other chemicals. By the end of the nineteenth century, Merck offered about 10,000 products, which were exported to many countries, and had founded subsidiaries throughout the world. In 1889, Georg Merck took over the office in New York and established Merck and Co., which started the local production of chemicals in the U.S. ten years later. After World War I, Merck lost many of its foreign affiliates, among them its U.S. affiliate Merck and Co., which became an independent American company. Since then, the latter has become one of the largest pharmaceutical companies in the world. Both companies agreed that the name "Merck" is exclusively used in the U.S. and Canada by Merck and Co. and in Europe and the rest of the world by Merck KGaA. In 1999, EMD Pharmaceuticals Inc. was founded by Merck KGaA in order to manage the North American pharmaceutical operations. In 1995, the legal form of Merck – until then managed as an OHG (open partnership) – was transformed into a KGaA (partnership limited by shares). The Merck Group's operating activities are grouped under Merck KGaA, in which E. Merck, holding the Merck family's equity interest, is a general partner with a 74 percent stake, while the shareholders have a 26 percent stake.

At the time of the acquisition, the Merck Group, still headquartered in Darmstadt, conducted its international business in four business sectors – pharmaceuticals, laboratory products, laboratory distribution, and specialty chemicals – with sales of €6.7 billion in 2000. Merck is represented by 209 operating activities in 52 countries and employs 33,000 people worldwide. Fifty-two percent of its employees work in Europe, 30 percent in North and Latin America, and 18 percent in Asia, Australia, and Africa. In fiscal 2000, Merck reported an operating profit of €0.7 billion on sales of €6.7 billion. Europe accounted for 38 percent of sales, North and Latin America 45 percent, and Asia, Australia, and Africa the remaining 17 percent. Figure 6.1 provides a simplified overview of Merck's organizational structure.

Merck's pharmaceutical sector consists of three main business segments: ethicals, generics, and consumer healthcare. In the ethicals segment the different therapeutic areas are: cardiovascular, metabolism/diabetes, women's health, central nervous system, and (notably) cancer/oncology. Following a strategic review of its pipeline, the group's strategic focus in the pharmaceuticals business sector lays in cardiovascular diseases and metabolism/diabetes. Moreover, Merck aims to gain a leadership position in the field of oncology and strengthen its position in the growth market of women's health. The pharmaceuticals business sector invested €453 million in the research and development of new drugs in 2000, which represents 16 percent of the total sales in this segment, and around 83 percent of the total R&D expenditure of the Merck Group. Sales in the pharmaceuticals business sector rose by 2 percent in 2000 to €2.914 million (previous year: €2.8 billion), representing 43 percent of the Merck Group's total sales.

Lexigen Pharmaceuticals Corp. (formerly Fuji Immuno Pharmaceuticals Corp.) was founded in 1992 by Professor Susumu Tonegawa, winner of the 1987 Nobel Prize for Medicine, and Harvard Professor Lan Bo Chen. The company is engaged in the development of drugs and genetically engineered products to treat cancer, immune system disorders, and other diseases. Apart from that, Lexigen has developed a broad technology platform with the aim of generating new therapies. The company develops certain immunocytokines as cancer treatments, and simultaneously works on the immunocytokine concept as a broad, proprietary technology base. Lexigen is developing two particular immunocytokines for the treatment of cancer, both of which are in clinical trials. One is for the treatment of gastrointestinal, pancreatic, and prostate cancers, and a second is for the treatment of small lung cancers and melanoma. Lexigen has also developed an active substance, FP-21399, for use in the treatment of AIDS. This anti-AIDS compound inhibits fusion of the virus with its target cell. Moreover, Lexigen is developing a new diagnostic procedure that is capable of identifying cancer cells in the bloodstream with the help of computer-analysis methods. Besides some academic relationships with universities in the Boston area, Lexigen had no industrial collaborations prior to the takeover. Figure 6.2 summarizes the most important phases of Lexigen's history.

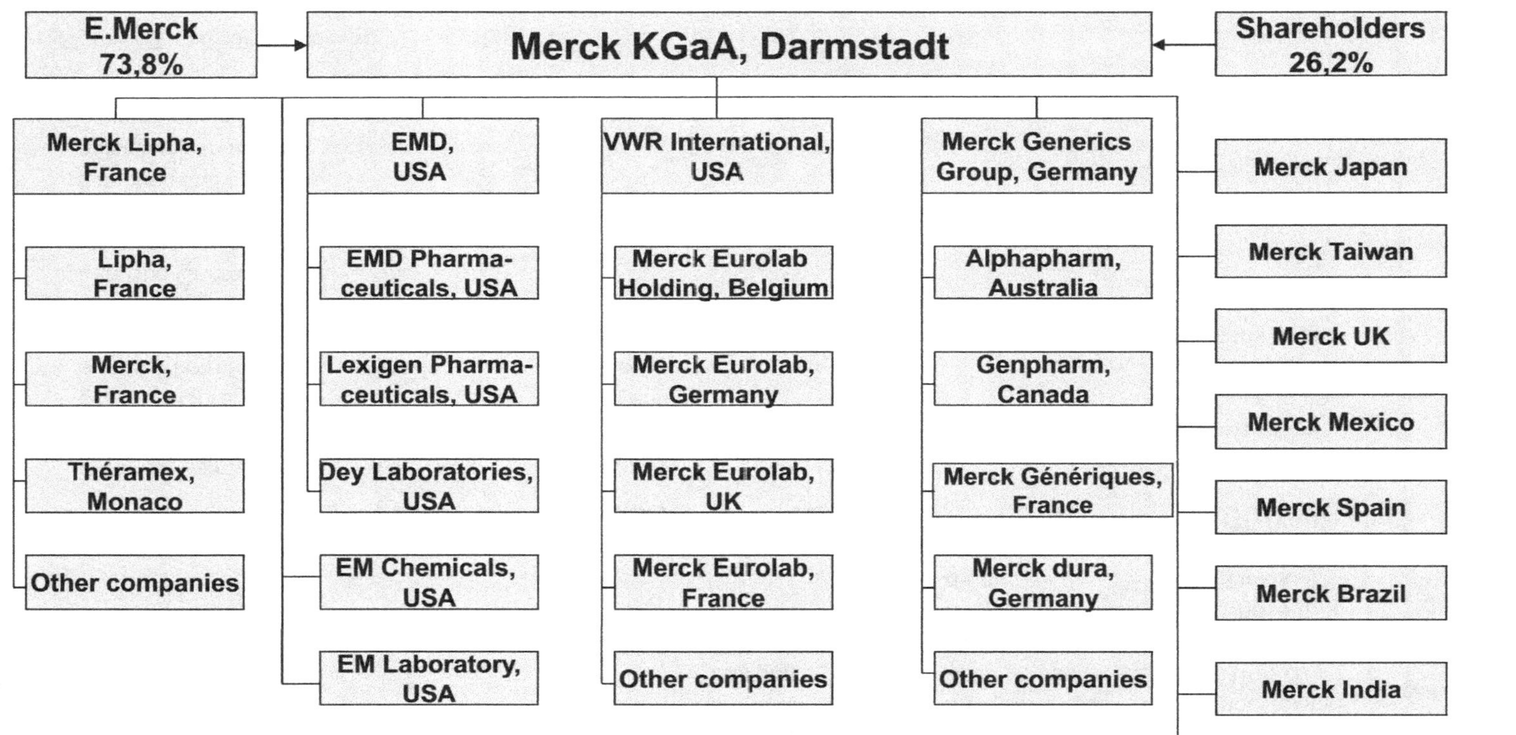

FIGURE 6.1 Merck's organizational structure

Source: Merck KGaA (2001), p. 59

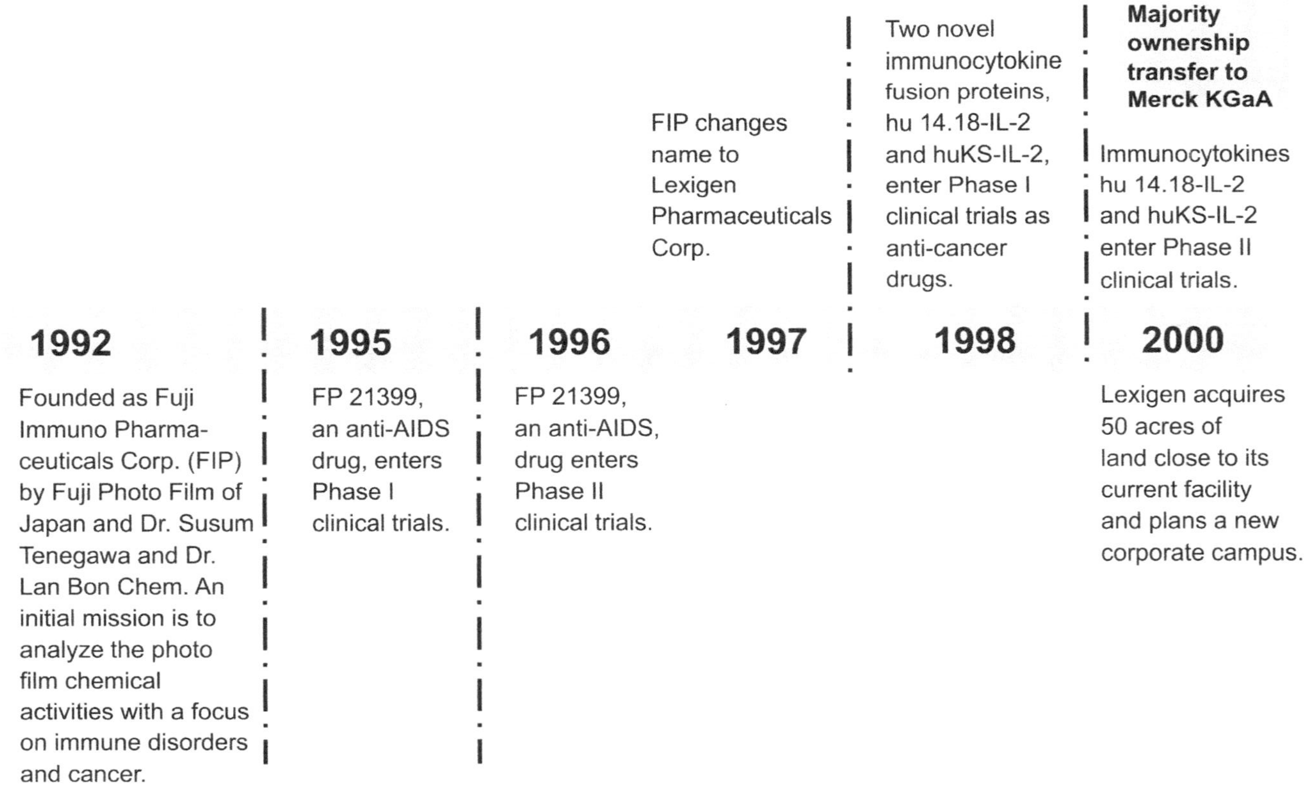

1992

Founded as Fuji Immuno Pharmaceuticals Corp. (FIP) by Fuji Photo Film of Japan and Dr. Susum Tenegawa and Dr. Lan Bon Chem. An initial mission is to analyze the photo film chemical activities with a focus on immune disorders and cancer.

1995

FP 21399, an anti-AIDS drug, enters Phase I clinical trials.

1996

FP 21399, an anti-AIDS, drug enters Phase II clinical trials.

1997

FIP changes name to Lexigen Pharmaceuticals Corp.

1998

Two novel immunocytokine fusion proteins, hu 14.18-IL-2 and huKS-IL-2, enter Phase I clinical trials as anti-cancer drugs.

2000

Majority ownership transfer to Merck KGaA

Immunocytokines hu 14.18-IL-2 and huKS-IL-2 enter Phase II clinical trials.

Lexigen acquires 50 acres of land close to its current facility and plans a new corporate campus.

FIGURE 6.2 History of Lexigen

Source: www.lexigenpharm.com

Description of the M&A and integration process

Acquisition process and motives

On 16 December 1998, Merck announced that it had acquired 57 percent of Lexigen Pharmaceuticals Corp., located in Lexington, MA. The purchase comprised the exclusive rights to new technologies and important fundamental patents for pharmaceutical research, including a new diagnostic process to identify cancer cells in the blood with the help of computer analysis. At that moment, Lexigen had a total of twenty-seven employees on its payroll. Merck did not disclose the purchase price for the shareholding.

The acquisition of Lexigen was carried out for several reasons. In a first step, this acquisition must be regarded from a broader strategic perspective, which can best be expressed in the words of Hans Joachim Langmann, a member of Merck's executive board (Merck KGaA 2000: 4):

> The 23% increase in our research expenditure . . . was used to boost the development of new drugs for treating cancer in particular. The same strategy was also behind the acquisition of the U.S. research company Lexigen and the conclusion of key license agreements. We aim to become one of the leading companies in the oncology sector.

Thus, Merck is striving to become a leader in the area of cancer research in the future. It attacks cancer with four diverse therapeutic approaches: angiogenesis inhibitors; monoclonal antibodies; immunotherapeutics; and immunocytokines.

Besides this general motive, the second major motive behind the acquisition was that Lexigen had an interesting technology platform in the field of immunocytokines, to which Merck wanted to gain access. At that point in time, Lexigen had two oncology products undergoing Phase I clinical trials, and Merck hoped to launch them by 2005 as potential blockbusters. One of the products is designed for the treatment of gastrointestinal, pancreatic, and prostate cancer, and the other is for the treatment of small cell lung cancer and melanoma. Apart from that, Lexigen has developed a new diagnostic procedure that is able to identify cancer cells in the bloodstream with the help of computer-analysis methods.

The third major reason was that Merck wanted to strengthen its pharmaceutical position in the U.S., which it considered one of the most important markets. It was expected that Lexigen's presence in the Boston research community and its links to renowned research centers would lead to an increase in creativity and innovative capacity.

> Lexigen had a patent issued on a certain technology, the technology of immunocytokines. This was a technology Merck wanted to get a license for, because Merck needed it for its own oncology research. Then it turned out that Lexigen itself had some financial problems and was up

> for sale. At Merck, it was decided to acquire the company with the aim of establishing a pharmaceutical pillar in the U.S.; more precisely, in the Boston area.
>
> *(Integration manager)*

For Lexigen, this acquisition provided access to the vast resources that can be provided only by a large pharmaceutical company. Lexigen needed these resources due to the fact that it was in the middle of clinical Phases I/II, which required a lot of money that Lexigen did not have. Therefore, the company was searching for a potential buyer or investor. Helped by the fact that there had already been some preliminary negotiations between Merck and Lexigen concerning a specific patent in the field of immunocytokines, Merck finally acquired Lexigen.

Organizational integration

As far as the organizational integration is concerned, a distinction between the original intended plan and the final structure must be made, as the structure of Merck's pharmaceutical business itself changed only a few months after the acquisition. Thus, the description of the organizational integration and the different organizational elements mainly focuses on the structure that was finally established, rather than the original integration plans, which were never implemented. A Lexigen executive described this rather troublesome process as follows:

> In reality, there is not a very good definition of what the responsibilities and structure are, or how the interaction should be. It is about two years since the acquisition of Lexigen by Merck and more than one and a half since the creation of EMD. And yet, there is still a lot of time and effort being spent on defining what the roles are, and what the responsibilities will be.
>
> *(Anonymous interviewee)*

According to the original plan, Lexigen was to cover nearly the whole pharmaceutical value chain, including basic R&D as well as clinical development and marketing. In addition, the company was meant to retain a lot of autonomy, as the following quotation indicates:

> When the small company was first acquired there was a very clear statement from the CEO of Merck that the small company should retain some of the attributes that make it small, dynamic and very fast; that these, by themselves, are assets to Merck and that they should not become the same operating procedures as Merck. The same day that this comment was made, we began to receive instructions from other divisions within Merck about how we should operate to be like Merck . . . So, there continues to be an expectation within Merck that we will do things in conformity, as they are done in

> Merck, but also an expectation that we should operate with a high level of independence and some level of separateness.
>
> *(Anonymous interviewee)*

This original plan was short lived. In fact, it was never really implemented, because half a year later Merck announced a substantial reorganization of its pharmaceutical business, with a special focus on its presence in the U.S. Thus, this reorganization must be kept in mind when discussing the further organizational integration. This reorganization changed the role that was to be attributed to Lexigen in a fundamental way. Merck had set up a separate company to focus on growth in its pharmaceutical business in the U.S.: EMD Pharmaceuticals, Inc., located in Durham, N.C., now serves as the North American headquarters for the Merck Pharma Division. On 1 June 1999, Matthew Emmens was named president and CEO of the newly created company. The new headquarters, located near Research Triangle Park, has the task of creating relationships with researchers at important research centers and of coordinating Merck's North American drug development, marketing, and sales activities, including those of Lexigen. To enhance the organizational effectiveness, the management structure of the Pharma Division was streamlined and the number of board members was reduced. An integration manager commented on this reorganization:

> It was decided that most of the biologic research is to be with Lexigen. Their main responsibility lies in biological research, especially everything that has to do with proteins. It can be seen as a center of excellence. From that point of view it was not a bad decision to separate research from clinical development. I don't know if a local separation was really necessary. However, the separation and to say that Lexigen should do this, what it does best, was an appropriate decision. But it wasn't the original intention at the beginning. And this reorganization caused quite a stir.

Thus, at this specific moment – with the creation of EMD as the new North American headquarters for the Merck Pharma Division – the role of Lexigen was redefined. Ever since, Lexigen has been considered one of Merck's key research facilities as well as an entry point into the U.S. pharmaceutical market and the Boston scientific community. Henceforth, Lexigen is considered Merck's worldwide center of excellence for biological entities. It is to generate drug candidates through its research, while EMD is providing the development and commercialization expertise and Merck supplies its global presence and management capabilities. Lexigen's role centers on basic research and on acting as a "kind of supplier":

> At the beginning, everything was supposed to be in the hands of Lexigen, including clinical development. Now, one can rather call it a "disintegration." Lexigen is an important research facility for Merck, one of the most important suppliers for the biotech platforms. The research unit Lexigen

> will play only a supportive role for the clinical development of the projects, which will be done at Durham.
>
> *(Integration manager)*

From a strategic point of view, only the president of Lexigen, Stephen Gillies, is involved in the process of clinical development, because he is at the same time vice-president for research at EMD, and therefore participates in the respective strategy meetings. Lexigen itself is "only" a research unit and, thus, not really involved in overall strategy-making. However, as far as its research activities are concerned, Lexigen has a high degree of autonomy and its own research budget. The company has to undergo a general review process and has to fulfill certain objectives, but it carries out its research completely on its own.

> People at Lexigen are part of the worldwide research team at Merck. Lexigen itself – besides Stephen Gillies – is not part of the strategy-making process. A decision has been made that EMD will take over that part and coordinate the further development.
>
> *(Integration manager)*

In terms of reporting and controlling systems, Lexigen has no responsibility at all, because everything is centrally managed by EMD. Lexigen only controls the research budget, which is granted by EMD.

> As far as reporting and controlling is concerned, everything is managed by EMD. Lexigen receives its money from EMD via a specific allocation mechanism. Lexigen is now part of EMD and doesn't belong directly to Merck any more. At Lexigen, there are no controlling or reporting structures in place. A company like Lexigen which started with fifteen people does not have the necessary departments to handle eighty people. Lexigen has its own research budget and its own president, and that's it.
>
> *(Integration manager)*

As far as the general collaboration between Lexigen and Merck is concerned, there is a wide gap between the two sides' expectations. Lexigen wants to continue to work efficiently, as it has done in the past. This means very little expenditure but high risk. In contrast, Merck wants to make everything as secure as possible, which has led to some delays in terms of decision-making. Although Merck provides the necessary know-how and resources for the next steps of the development process, this obvious contradiction has created some problems from the point of view of Lexigen, as the following quotation reveals:

> Biotech does not operate by being conservative. Biotech operates by taking risks, by being dynamic, by moving very quickly, by trying different ideas on a trial basis. If it works, you continue. If it doesn't work, you try something else. It moves very, very quickly. The expectations for the development of ideas and the development of products both go faster than

> the operational tempo of a large corporation or the operational tempo of a large conservative corporation.
>
> *(Anonymous interviewee)*

This quotation shows that the day-to-day business of the biotech company changed completely. On the one hand, this has one important advantage because the company has more resources than before. On the other hand, however, there is a severe drawback for the future management of such a company because there is a clear change in the way of doing business:

> If a small biotech company fails to achieve a goal for two years, that means the death of the company. In the structure of a big company, that is not true. It is acceptable to continue to fail to meet a goal, because it is not just a small biotech company any more; it is also part of a large corporation. There is money to support it. So, having the structure behind it allows failure happen that could not take place if we were on our own . . . This is good and bad. On the one hand, it allows time, which is necessary to develop ideas; on the other hand, it allows us to adopt a slower operational tempo and not accomplish goals that we would have achieved otherwise. That is not necessarily a benefit.
>
> *(Anonymous interviewee)*

At first, responsibility for Lexigen came under the auspices of the oncology business team at Merck's headquarters in Darmstadt, especially its head Klaus Hoenneknoewel. In addition, the decision to acquire Lexigen was advocated by this team. The reorganization of the Phama Division had been decided at the top of the company and not by the oncology team. Aside from that, this reorganization resulted in a change of responsibility for Lexigen, because the company was put under the auspices of EMD in Durham, N.C. Hence, the president of Lexigen, Stephen Gillies, reports directly to the president and CEO of EMD, Matthew Emmens, who in turn reports directly to the chairman of Merck's Executive Board in Darmstadt, Bernhard Scheuble. This reporting structure provoked some discontent at Lexigen, because "you have three different visions of how one area – the oncology area – should work and within the space of one and a half years there are three different major structural changes" (anonymous interviewee).

With regard to a possible transfer of knowledge or a specific technology from Lexigen to Merck, it can be said that there was no real transfer, because the biotech expertise is within Lexigen. Instead, some of the projects in the field of biologics at Merck were stopped and transferred to Lexigen.

From a cultural point of view, different levels must be distinguished. In a first step, there is a difference in terms of country culture between the U.S. and Germany which is reflected in different ways of working:

> In the U.S. – irrespective of the industry – you think much more in a matrix structure and work together as a team . . . more than you do in

> Germany. In Germany, the matrix structure is well known, but it is the line function which gives the directives and defines roles and responsibilities . . . Interactive communication and collaboration as a team are very difficult in a context where the line function is dominant. It took me a lot of time and effort to get the team members – who were really top people in their respective fields – to work effectively together. But in the end, it worked out quite well.
>
> *(Integration manager)*

Apart from this general difference, people expected problems resulting from the fact that big pharma needs to collaborate with "small biotech." This is reflected in various employees' statements, such as "Now we have to cope with the Germans and big pharma" (from a Lexigen employee) and "Those people at Lexigen have no clue about what it really means to develop a drug" (from a Merck employee). Obviously, the two sides had different opinions on how to do business. If Lexigen had remained independent, it would have continued to pursue the strategy of developing a medicine and then building up the corresponding organization. In contrast to this traditional biotech strategy, Merck takes a big pharma approach, which consists of building the structure and organization first and then developing the product. In consequence, one of the executives at Lexigen concluded that "because of the corporate structure and culture within Merck, there is an inability to make decisions" (anonymous interviewee).

At the moment of the acquisition, Lexigen had twenty-seven employees, none of whom left after the deal was done. There were several reasons for this. Lexigen itself was mainly dominated by one person, its president and owner of all its major patents, Stephen Gillies. The whole organization was more or less tailor-made for him and he had everything under his control. Nothing really changed too much after the acquisition for Lexigen's employees, because the company was granted autonomy in the field of research, with Gillies remaining in charge of everything. So he remained the employees' boss and only contact. Apart from the fact that a few other important employees were contractually bound, the overall situation for the company improved as they now had access to resources they had never enjoyed before. Thus, they continued to do what they had always done – research.

> Stephen Gillies continued to be their boss. They did not care about the integration, because they were not affected. Only those involved in the development project, about four or five people, were affected. But they were bound by contract.
>
> *(Integration manager)*

Organization of the integration process

The organization of the integration process was not as easy and straightforward as expected. There was some kind of integration process immediately after the acquisition. However, because of the reorganization decision of Merck's Pharma Division, this integration never became effective. Thus, the following description tries to combine both approaches by comparing some of the immediate actions with later decisions.

The original integration was a relatively short process because only twenty-seven people at Lexigen were involved. A merger team was created under the direction of Klaus Hoenneknoewel, head of the oncology business team in Darmstadt, consisting of four people from his team and four from Lexigen. This merger team carried out the integration by bringing together people from the different groups and preparing the collaboration. Most of the integration was to be done on a day-to-day working relationship. In this context, one integration manager took a leading role and served as an interface manager between Lexigen and Merck, and then between Lexigen and EMD. This integration manager was a German scientist who had worked in the U.S. and he was employed by Lexigen on the recommendation of Merck's headquarters in Darmstadt. His main task was to get people to work together in teams and ensure the exchange of relevant skills and knowledge.

Apart from that, there was no real transfer of employees to or from either side during the integration process. For instance, no executive from Darmstadt was sent to Lexigen in order to make them familiar with the company's systems and structure, because a new structure was created through the formation of EMD, changing roles and expectations with regard to Lexigen. This decision was not made (and not really supported) by the oncology business team; rather, it was made by Merck's Executive Board. An executive at Lexigen described the situation as follows:

> I do know that there has been a series of indecisive events . . . [and] some decisions that were made were short-lived. So, a particular vision is defined, discussed. The vision is made, we pursue that vision, and then a few months later it changes. And a few months after that it changes again. And a few months later it changes again, which of course prevents effective integration . . . I think that within the different companies people are finding it difficult, because they don't know what their sphere of operations is and how it is related to the others. So, at the individual level, at the group level within the company here, within the company EMD, the goals for those personnel may change all of a sudden.
>
> *(Anonymous interviewee)*

This reveals that people at Lexigen were not content with the decisions that were being made at the top of the group. Moreover, it highlights one of the major lessons Merck learned concerning the acquisition and especially the subsequent integration process: decisions must be made as quickly and as clearly as possible in order to prevent insecurity at the individual level. Furthermore, there was no clear communication about these issues, which exacerbated the sense of insecurity. Another problem was the difference in opinion over how to run the business. While big pharmaceutical companies prefer to establish the necessary organization first and then develop the product, small biotech companies tend to do the opposite. Hence, it is necessary to ensure a smooth transition from the early phases of the development process, which had already been carried out at Lexigen, to the later ones, which were subsequently under the control of Merck.

> The first integration process was carried out quickly . . . OK, a few experts were missing – [they] were at neither Merck nor Lexigen and the responsibility for them was also not well defined. That was a mistake, but the integration process itself was initiated as quickly as possible and could also have been run that way, if there had not been the creation of EMD. But that is another story, which of course clearly affects the integration of Lexigen and needs to be taken into account. Hence, it is difficult to say whether the original plan would have been successful or not.
>
> *(Integration manager)*

Analysis of the M&A and integration process

This section analyzes the M&A deal between Merck and Lexigen. It should be remembered that the original integration plans were never really implemented (which happens quite often in M&As), but rather were replaced by a major reorganization within Merck a few months after the acquisition.

First, the motives for the M&A transaction will be analyzed. As we saw above, Merck wanted to cement its position in the oncology sector and strengthen its presence in the U.S. pharmaceutical market by gaining access to the Boston research community. From this, the first major motive can be derived by concluding that the acquisition of Lexigen contributed to the long-run strategic objectives of Merck. In addition, Lexigen had a very interesting technology platform and two oncology products undergoing clinical trials with very promising sales potential (perhaps even the chance of becoming blockbusters) and therefore a substantial positive impact on operational results. Furthermore, Merck needed the immunocytokines patent in order to continue with its own research. Thus, the second major motive was more short term. Lexigen accepted the takeover offer because it needed money in order to proceed with its clinical trials. In addition, it gained access to a large pharmaceutical company's resources.

While analyzing the organizational integration and the different elements of organizational/structural integration, knowledge/competence integration and transfer as well as cultural and personnel integration, it is necessary to keep in mind the two identified major motives because they explain an important aspect of the integration and the subsequent reorganization. It is very difficult to determine whether there were two basic organizational integration strategies or whether there was one organizational integration strategy at two different levels. In the oncology business team's original plan, the intention was that Lexigen should retain a high degree of autonomy in nearly every stage of the pharmaceutical value chain.

This meant that Lexigen was to assume responsibility for R&D, clinical development, and sales and marketing in the U.S.

In this context, two points should be noted: Lexigen's focus was solely on oncology; and Lexigen was a small biotechnology company with only twenty-seven employees at the time of the takeover, and it had no experience in clinical development or in running a larger pharmaceutical business. Therefore, it is quite easy to understand the rationale for the reorganization decision. The crucial question for Merck's Executive Board was whether Lexigen – given its specific situation – would be able to ensure the long-run objective of strengthening Merck's position in the whole U.S. pharmaceutical business sector, not merely oncology. The Executive Board decided that it would not, so they set up a separate company, EMD Pharmaceuticals. After that decision was made, Lexigen was free to play the role of a center of excellence for biological entities with the aim of conducting basic research and generating promising new drugs. These drugs would then be developed and commercialized by EMD in the U.S., with Merck supplying a global presence, management capabilities, and support. By establishing this structure, the Executive Board at Darmstadt hoped to meet the long-term objective of increasing Merck's presence in the U.S.

What did this mean for the overall organizational integration strategy? The organizational integration strategy needs to be considered in close connection with the degree of autonomy that was granted. Research was clearly separated from development and commercialization. As far as basic research and the generation of new drugs were concerned, Lexigen was granted maximum autonomy and remained in full control of those aspects of the business. This was reflected in the fact that the president of Lexigen was also made vice-president of EMD, with responsibility for U.S.-wide research. Once Lexigen has identified a promising new drug, EMD takes over and assumes full responsibility for the further development and commercialization of the product; Lexigen has no role to play in this. Therefore, it is possible to draw the conclusion that the level of responsibility varies due to position along the pharmaceutical value chain. During the early stages of research, Lexigen has overall responsibility as well as a high degree of autonomy. Thus, it can be considered a "strategic leader" in that context (Bartlett and Ghoshal 1989). However, as soon as a promising drug has been identified – which represents a degree of progression along the pharmaceutical value chain – EMD assumes full responsibility for the product's further development. Lexigen merely offers some support, if requested and needed. From this, it follows that the current clinical trials are managed by EMD at Durham, N.C., so the second major motive of the acquisition has been realized in accordance with the overall strategic direction.

In terms of strategy-making as well as reporting and budgeting, the decisions are made at EMD after consultation with Merck. Lexigen does not even have designated departments to perform these functions. It is involved only to the extent that Stephen Gillies is vice-president for research at EMD, in addition to being president of Lexigen. Furthermore, everything relating to reporting, controlling and human resources is managed by EMD on Lexigen's behalf.

With regard to a possible knowledge transfer, it must be stressed that there was no transfer of knowledge from Lexigen to Merck. Instead, projects at Merck with a clear link to biologics and proteins were wound down and transferred to Lexigen because the latter is now the center of excellence within Merck for everything that has to do with biologics. "They [Lexigen] had people who had much more experience and knowledge in the field of proteins than the people at Merck" (integration manager). Thus, when asking who was the best in this field and who had the necessary knowledge, know-how and competence within the company, the clear answer was "Lexigen." This made perfect sense, because it reflected one of the principal motives for the acquisition – the know-how and technology that Lexigen had at its disposal. Figure 6.3 summarizes Lexigen's new role and how it developed.

Another question is how the clinical development of promising drugs will be carried out in the future. The answer to that question relates to the reorganization process and has nothing to do with the original integration plans. It is now the task of the dedicated "interface manager," whose role has changed over time. At first he was more of an integration manager, whereas after the reorganization he became an interface manager, as he was responsible for the transfer of knowledge needed at Durham. In addition, Stephen Gillies, the holder of Lexigen's major patents, will support future development activities at EMD. Moreover, so-called "translation research teams" will be introduced in order to support development activities at Durham. This new relationship is presented from a value chain perspective in Figure 6.4.

The cultural analysis can be subdivided into two different dimensions. First, there is the obvious cultural gap on a country level between U.S.-based Lexigen and the German company Merck. In this context, some problems arose due to different thinking with respect to command and control structures. In the U.S., the matrix

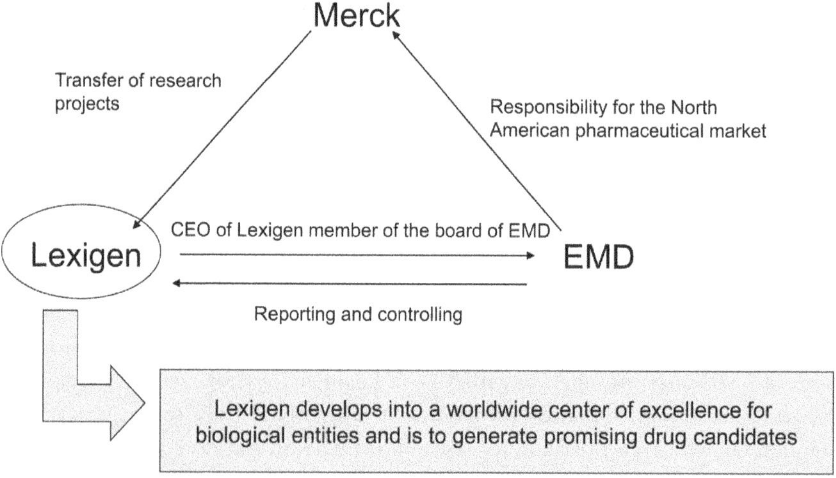

FIGURE 6.3 Relationship between Lexigen, Merck, and EMD

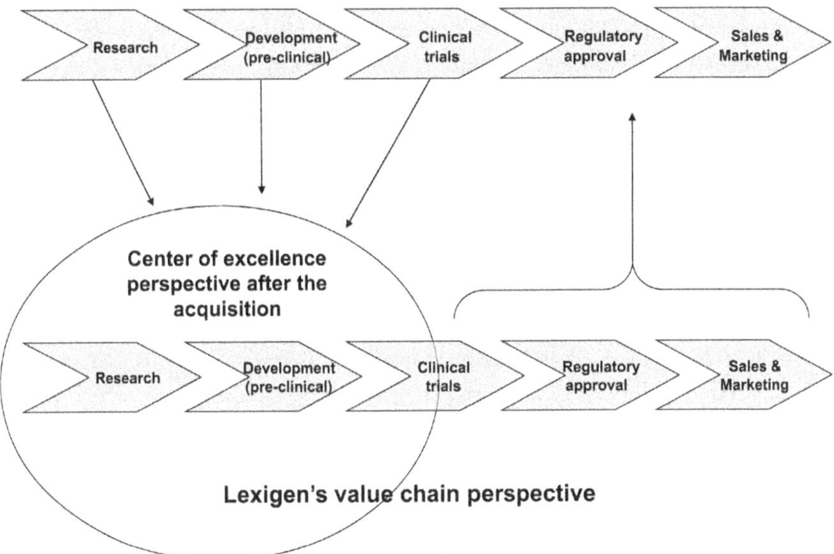

FIGURE 6.4 Value chain and center of excellence perspective

Source: Based on Schweizer (2005)

structure and teamwork across different line functions is the dominant system. By contrast, in Germany, although the matrix structure exists, the line function is preeminent. This resulted in a few coordination and communication problems, but these were quickly resolved by the integration team.

Second, there is a very wide gap between the structure and thinking of big pharma – like Merck – and the way business is conducted at a small biotechnology company, such as Lexigen. Big pharmaceutical companies try to avoid risk, or at least reduce it as far as possible. This thinking underpins Merck's approach to tackling a project or developing a drug: it first builds up the necessary structure and organization for the whole value chain and only then focuses on the development of the product. By contrast, small biotech companies, in this case Lexigen, develop the product first and then establish the necessary organization. One of the important reasons why they adopt this approach is that they do not have the necessary resources to build up elaborate structures before identifying a potential revenue generator. Now that Lexigen is part of Merck it is no longer the fast-acting, highly dynamic and high-risk-taking small biotechnology company it once was. It has become part of a much larger entity that acts according to different rules. Bearing this in mind, Lexigen employees' complaints that "it is the expectation of a large corporation that the small company operates like them" (anonymous interviewee) are understandable because their company is no longer a small, independent firm. Its role within Merck therefore needs to be newly defined, and it takes more time to reach decisions than it did when Lexigen was an independent, small biotechnology company.

Notwithstanding these problems that were due to the cultural gap, both sides also gained from their liaison. On the one hand, Lexigen now has access to the money it needs to continue its research and push its products through clinical trials. This is done with the help of Merck, as Lexigen itself never went through the process of gaining regulatory approval when it was an independent company. On the other hand, Merck now has access to new technologies and some promising new drugs. The question is how the two organizations get along with each other in order to get the best out of the deal. All of the decisions relating to the realization of these advantages are made at Merck, not at Lexigen. The reorganization of Merck's pharma business segment resulted in the definition of Lexigen's role as a center of excellence for research within Merck (see Figure 6.4). Thus, Lexigen was tasked with undertaking basic research and generating promising drugs which would then be developed by EMD.

This reorganization has had an impact on the way Lexigen sees itself, although it always takes some time before such a change is fully accepted. One can draw the conclusion that Lexigen is no longer supposed to act in the same entrepreneurial way as it did before its acquisition. If Merck had not acquired Lexigen, the latter would have had to develop a product, push it through clinical trials, bring it to the market, and generate revenue from it. Since the acquisition, Lexigen can focus exclusively on undertaking basic research and generating promising new drugs. Therefore, its employees need to cultivate a spirit of discovery rather than a spirit of entrepreneurialism. Accepting this argumentation and the likelihood that the cultural gap between Merck and Lexigen will diminish, it is possible to go one step further and conclude that Lexigen – because its activities are now confined to the research field and it no longer has any role to play in the rest of the pharmaceutical value chain – has lost some of its former identity. This brings it closer to Merck, and, in turn, brings Merck closer to the fulfillment of the goals it had in mind when deciding to acquire Lexigen and subsequently reorganize its pharma business segment.

Given that Lexigen had only twenty-seven employees at the time of the deal and that it was not listed on any stock exchange (implying that stock option programs did not exist), any analysis of personnel integration issues is sure to be relatively short and straightforward. As mentioned earlier, no Lexigen employees left the company after the acquisition, probably because nothing changed for them. They kept their boss, Stephen Gillies, and they were assured that they could continue to undertake their research. Moreover, they had access to unprecedented resources, provided by Merck; and the top four or five Lexigen scientists were bound by specific contracts.

At this point, analysis of the organization of the integration process needs to be taken into account. It is again necessary to point out that the integration process cannot be separated from the subsequent reorganization process. Thus, both dimensions are covered in this analysis. The case description reveals one major problem in terms of responsibility. The acquisition and the early integration efforts were initiated and carried out by Merck's oncology business team. At first, this team was put in charge of Lexigen. However, the subsequent reorganization decision of the Pharma Division was made at the very top of the company, not at the level of the oncology business team. As a result of this reorganization, responsibility for Lexigen was transferred from the oncology business team to EMD. This reveals that the original integration plans of the oncology business team did not enjoy the full support of Merck's Executive Board.

The change in responsibility was one of the major reasons why the final integration of Lexigen following the reorganization decision took so long to complete and generated such uncertainty among Lexigen's employees. This uncertainty is reflected in the following statement: "The problem can only be solved if someone is willing to realize a vision with the support of top management within Merck, and is willing to implement decisions and the vision from the top down" (anonymous interviewee). This comment not only reveals Lexigen employees' frustration over the sluggishness of decision-making after the acquisition, but indicates that they held top management responsible for the problem. For example, the original integration efforts of the first merger team under the direction of Klaus Hoenneknoewel, head of the oncology business team, were never really effective. The first integration process itself was carried out quite quickly, but the subsequent reorganization – which implied some kind of "reintegration" – took much longer and was not communicated clearly to the employees.

Conclusion and practical post-acquisition integration framework

The biotechnology industry has witnessed a continuous increase in M&A activity over the last few decades (BioCentury 2007; Schweizer 2012). In an industry where developing a successful product is no guarantee that it will ever happen again (Urbig *et al.* 2013), firms frequently have to look outside for new products in order to fill their pipelines (Schweizer 2014). Returning to the statement of the managing director from a large pharmaceutical company in the introductory section of this chapter, it is often cheaper and more effective to buy these missing parts than to build them internally. Still, pharmaceutical firms and their managers face some key obstacles to the successful realization of a post-acquisition integration strategy (Almor *et al.* 2009; Graebner *et al.* 2010). Because of that, a detailed analysis of the context in which the intended transaction is supposed to take place and the pursued motives needs to be undertaken (Larsson 1990). Thus, the study at hand provides managers of pharmaceutical firms with detailed steps and concepts relating to how to conduct the acquisition of a biotechnology company. Therefore, this study can be considered a response to calls for more research on how to integrate an acquired biotechnology firm from a practical point of view (Bradfield and El-Sayed 2009; Danzon and Epstein 2007; Graebner *et al.* 2010). From a theoretical perspective, this study extends the existing knowledge base in M&A integration by developing a detailed theoretical – and practical – post-acquisition integration approach. Thus, it can also be considered a response to calls in the literature for more research on post-acquisition integration activities (Bower 2001; Patzelt *et al.* 2012; Schweizer 2005, 2012).

The acquiring pharmaceutical company needs to make sure that the employees of the biotechnology firm who stay within the company, remain committed (Schweizer and Patzelt 2012) and do not leave (Ranft and Lord 2000, 2002). This indicates the importance of human integration (Birkinshaw *et al.* 2000; Weber and Tarba, 2010). As was shown in the discussed M&A case, it is necessary to maintain a balance between granting the acquired biotechnology firm the necessary autonomy in relation to all R&D activities (Schweizer 2005) while at the same time supporting it during all of the other important steps in the pharmaceutical value chain, as the R&D activities need to be nurtured throughout the post-acquisition integration process (Larsson and Finkelstein 1999). Even if a deal seems to put the merged entity on a new growth curve, it will take a long time to realize the intended synergies because the development cycles in biotech companies are very long (Urbig *et al.* 2013).

Based on the case analysis, Figure 6.5 suggests how to go forward as a pharmaceutical company when integrating an acquired biotechnology firm.

At this point in the analysis, it becomes obvious that we need to combine and integrate the new role of Lexigen (see Figure 6.3) and the value chain and center of excellence perspective (Figure 6.4) with the different M&A typologies (e.g., Haspeslagh and Jemison 1991), as discussed in the literature review section earlier. This combination leads to the development and justification of the proposed practical integration framework in Figure 6.5. The case analysis reveals that the application of a single post-acquisition integration approach is insufficient. Rather, there is a clear need to go beyond single integration approaches (Puranam *et al.* 2006; Schweizer 2005). In order to overcome the challenges of the post-acquisition integration process, as detailed by Graebner *et al.* (2010), our analysis shows that the integration of an acquired biotechnology firm requires the simultaneous application of two distinct integration approaches concerning R&D and non-R&D-related portions (Puranam *et al.* 2006).

In order to integrate an acquired biotechnology company and, at the same time, preserve its autonomy so as not to endanger its capabilities, pharmaceutical companies need to apply a hybrid integration approach with segmentation across different functions and value chain steps (Puranam *et al.* 2006, 2009; Schweizer 2005). There is a clear need for cooperation between the biotech and pharmaceutical companies after the acquisition in order to create value (Haspeslagh and Jemison 1991; Sirower 1997). This raises the problems of how to coordinate and combine the two organizations (Birkinshaw *et al.* 2000) and how to allocate control among the firms after the acquisition (Borys and Jemison 1989).

Responding to the need to go beyond single integration approaches (Puranam *et al.* 2006; Schweizer 2005), a slow preservation strategy granting the acquired biotech company a high degree of autonomy is applied in all R&D-related areas.

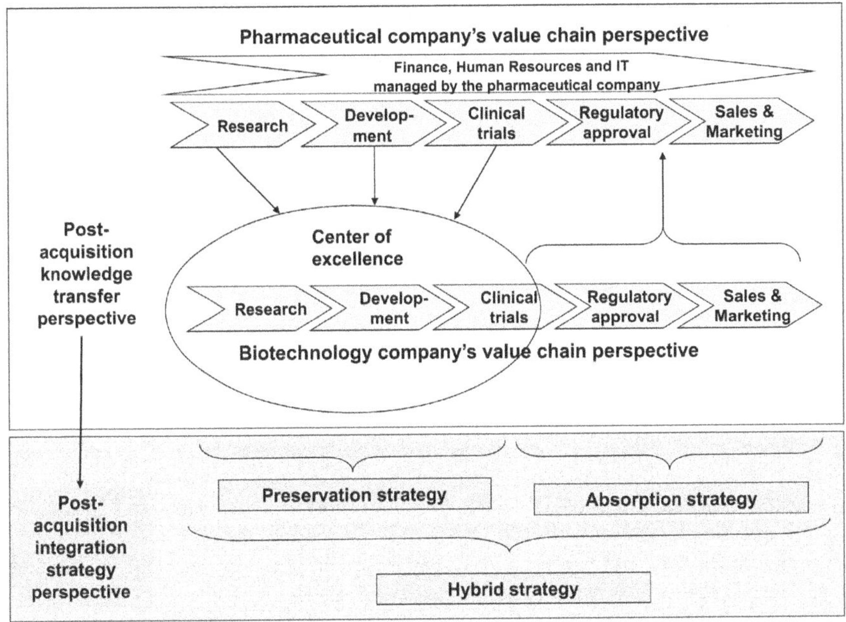

FIGURE 6.5 Practical integration framework

Source: Based on Schweizer (2005)

This is also done in order to realize the long-term strategy of supporting overall growth strategies by accessing biotechnology know-how and technologies (Ranft 2006) and/or enter a specific market. However, a rapid absorption strategy is applied in the contexts of clinical trials, regulatory affairs, and sales and marketing. This reflects the realization of the short-term strategy of improving the acquiring pharmaceutical company's market position by filling its R&D pipelines and gaining potential blockbusters (Puranam *et al.* 2009). In addition, supporting functions (such as finance, HR and IT) are carried out by the pharmaceutical company, because it usually has more sophisticated systems. Thus, it is obvious that the speed of integration is an important element that needs to be considered in more detail (Homburg and Bucerius 2005, 2006; Kitching 1967; Schweizer and Patzelt 2012).

Of course, there are some limits to the generalizability of our findings, and these should be addressed in future research. Because of the relatively small size and scope of the sample (it is a single case study), we recommend additional empirical efforts to validate our findings statistically with quantitative data. Moreover, industries with different attributes and characteristics might show different results, mechanisms, or attributes that need to be considered. Further research could also consider the acquisition performance and financial success of M&A within the context of cross-border M&As or examine how companies deal with the complexities of cross-border M&As and overcome cultural differences.

In sum, we have attempted to contribute to the literature on M&A and provide best-practice examples for practitioners by addressing the call for research into post-acquisition integration and the implications for managing foreign-acquired resources and capabilities (Haspeslagh and Jemison 1991; Schweizer 2005). Our work links acquisition motives, appropriate post-acquisition strategies, and specific integration approaches based on the types of acquired resources and capabilities (Ranft 2006; Puranam and Srikanth 2007). We hope this study provides perspectives for fruitful future research that will contribute to a more widespread understanding of the dynamics of cross-border M&As.

References

Agrawal, A. and Jaffe, J. F. (2000). The post-merger performance puzzle. In C. Cooper and A. Gregory (Eds.), *Advances in mergers and acquisitions*. New York: Elsevier Science, pp. 7–42.

Aktas, N., de Bodt, E., and Roll, R. (2009). Learning, hubris and corporate serial acquisitions. *Journal of Corporate Finance*, 15, 543–561.

Aktas, N., de Bodt, E., and Roll, R. (2011). Serial acquirer building: an empirical test of the learning hypothesis. *Journal of Corporate Finance*, 17, 18–32.

Almor, T., Tarba, S. Y., and Benjamini, H. (2009). Unmasking integration challenges: the case of Biogal's acquisition by Teva Pharmaceutical Industries. *International Studies of Management and Organization*, 39(3), 33–53.

Angwin, D. N. (2012). Typologies in M&A research. In D. Faulkner, S. Teerikangas, and R. Joseph (Eds.), *Oxford handbook of mergers and acquisitions*. Oxford, England: Oxford University Press, pp. 40–70.

Bartlett, C. A. and Ghoshal, S. (1989). *Managing across borders: the transnational solution*. Boston, MA: Harvard Business School Press.

BioCentury (2007). M&A upside. *BioCentury*, 15, pp. A1–A7.

Birkinshaw, J., Bresman, H., and Hakanson, L. (2000). Managing the post-acquisition integration process: how the human integration and task integration processes interact to foster value creation. *Journal of Management Studies*, 37, 395–425.

Borys, B. and Jemison, D. B. (1989). Hybrid arrangements as strategic alliances: theoretical issues in organizational combinations. *Academy of Management Review*, 14, 234–249.

Bower J. L. (2001). Not all M&As are alike – and that matters. *Harvard Business Review*, 79, 93–101.

Bower, J. L. (2004). When we study M&A, what are we learning? In A. Pablo and M. Javidan (Eds.), *Mergers and acquisitions: creating integrative knowledge*. Oxford: Blackwell Publishing, pp. 235–244.

Bradfield, R. and El-Sayed, H. (2009). Four scenarios for the future of the pharmaceutical industry. *Technology Analysis and Strategic Management*, 21, 195–212.

Chaudhuri, S. and Tabrizi, B. (1999). Capturing the real value in high-tech acquisitions. *Harvard Business Review*, 77, 123–130.

Danzon, P. M., Epstein, A., and Nicholson, S. (2007). Mergers and acquisitions in the pharmaceutical and biotech industries. *Managerial and Decision Economics*, 28, 307–328.

Datta, D. K. (1991). Organizational fit and acquisition performance: effects of post-acquisition integration. *Strategic Management Journal*, 12, 281–297.

Eisenhardt, K. M. (1989). Building theory from case study research. *Acadamy of Management Review*, 14, 488–511.

Eisenhardt, K. (1991). Better stories and better constructs: the case for rigor and comparative logic. *Academy of Management Review*, 16(3), 620–627.

Gomes, E., Angwin, D., Weber, Y., and Tarba, S. Y. (2013). Critical success factors through the mergers and acquisitions process: revealing pre- and post-M&A connections for improved performance. *Thunderbird International Business Review*, 55, 13–36.

Graebner, M. E. (2004). Momentum and serendipidity: how acquired firm leaders create value in the integration of technology firms. *Strategic Management Journal*, 25(8–9), 751–777.

Graebner, M. (2009). Caveat venditor: trust asymmetries in acquisitions of entrepreneurial firms. *Academy of Management Journal*, 52(3), 435–472.

Graebner, M. E. and Eisenhardt, K. M. (2004). The other side of the story: acquisition as courtship and governance as syndicate in entrepreneurial firms. *Administrative Science Quarterly*, 49, 366–403.

Graebner, M. E., Eisenhardt, K. M., and Roundy P. T. (2010). Success and failure in technology acquisitions: lessons for buyers and sellers. *Academy of Management Perspectives*, 24, 73–92.

Haleblian, J., Devers, C. A., McNamara, G., Carpenter, M. A., and Davison, R. B. (2009). Taking stock of what we know about mergers and acquisitions: a review and research agenda. *Journal of Management*, 35, 469–502.

Hambrick, D. C. and Canella, A. A. (1993). Relative standing: a framework for understanding departures of acquired executives. *Academy of Management Journal*, 36, 733–762.

Haspeslagh, P. C. and Jemison, D. B. (1991). *Managing acquisitions: creating value through corporate renewal*. New York: Free Press.

Homburg, C. and Bucerius, M. (2005). A marketing perspective on mergers and acquisitions: how marketing integration affects postmerger performance. *Journal of Marketing Research*, 69, 95–113.

Homburg, C. and Bucerius, M. (2006). Is speed of integration really a success factor of mergers and acquisitions? An analysis of the role of internal and external relatedness. *Strategic Management Journal*, 27, 347–367.

Hunt, J. W. (1990). Changing pattern of acquisition behaviour in takeovers and the consequences for acquisition processes. *Strategic Management Journal*, 11, 69–77.

Inkpen, A. C., Sundaram, A. K., and Rockwood, K. (2000). Cross-border acquisitions of U.S. technology assets. *California Management Review*, 42, 50–71.

Javidan, M., Pablo, A., Singh, H., Hitt, M., and Jemison, D. (2004). Where we've been and where we're going. In A. Pablo and M. Javidan (Eds.), *Mergers and acquisitions: creating integrative knowledge*. Oxford: Blackwell Publishing, pp. 245–261.

Jones, G. K., Lanctot, A., and Teegen, H. J. (2001). Determinants and performance of external technology acquisition. *Journal of Business Venturing*, 16, 255–283.

King, D. R., Dalton, D. R., Daily, C. M., and Covin, J. G. (2004). Meta-analysis of post-acquisition performance: indications of unidentified moderators. *Strategic Management Journal*, 25, 187–200.

King, D. R., Slotegraaf, R. J., and Kesner I. (2008). Performance implications of firm resource interactions in the acquisition of R&D-intensive firms. *Organization Science*, 19, 327–340.

Kitching, J. (1967). Why do mergers miscarry? *Harvard Business Review*, 45(6), 84–101.

Larsson, R. (1990). Coordination of action in mergers and acquisitions: interpretive and systems approaches towards synergy. Doctoral dissertation, University of Lund, Sweden.

Larsson, R. and Finkelstein, S. (1999). Integrating strategic, organizational, and human resource perspectives on mergers and acquisitions: a case survey of synergy realization. *Organization Science*, 10, 1–26.

Melkonian, T., Monin, P., and Noorderhaven, N. G. (2011). Distributive justice, procedural justice, exemplarity, and employees' willingness to cooperate in M&A integration processes: an analysis of the Air France–KLM merger. *Human Resource Management*, 50(6), 809–837.

Merck KGaA (2000). *Annual report 1999*. Darmstadt: Merck KGaA.

Merck KGaA (2001). *Annual report 2000*. Darmstadt: Merck KGaA.

Miles, M. B. and Huberman, A. M. (1994). *Qualitative data analysis: an expanded sourcebook* (2nd edn.). Beverly Hills, CA: Sage.

Monin, P., Noorderhaven, N., Vaara, E., and Kroon, D. (2013). Giving sense to and making sense of justice in postmerger integration. *Academy of Management Journal*, 56(1), 256–284.

Nahavandi, A. and Malekzadeh, A. R. (1988). Acculturation in mergers and acquisition. *Academy of Management Review*, 13, 79–90.

Napier, N. K. (1989). Mergers and acquisitions: human resource issues and outcomes: a review and suggested typology. *Journal of Management Studies*, 26, 271–289.

Patzelt, H. and Brenner, T. (2008). Introduction. In H. Patzelt and T. Brenner (Eds.), *Handbook of bioentrepreneurship*. New York: Springer, pp. 1–6.

Patzelt, H., Schweizer, L., and Behrens, J. (2012). Biotechnology entrepreneurship. *Foundations and Trends in Entrepreneurship*, 8, 63–140.

Powell, W. (1996). Inter-organizational collaboration in the biotechnology industry. *Journal of Institutional and Theoretical Economics*, 152, 197–215.

Puranam, P., Singh, H., and Chaudhuri, S. (2009). Integrating acquired capabilities: when structural integration is (un)necessary. *Organization Science*, 20(2), 313–328.

Puranam, P., Singh, H., and Zollo, M. (2006). Organizing for innovation: managing the coordination–autonomy dilemma in technology acquisitions. *Academy of Management Journal*, 49(2), 263–280.

Puranam, P. and Srikanth, K. (2007). What they know vs. what they do: how acquirers leverage technology acquisitions. *Strategic Management Journal*, 28(8), 805–825.

Ranft, A. L. (2006). Knowledge preservation and transfer during post-acquisition integration. *Advances in Mergers and Acquisitions*, 5, 51–67.

Ranft, A. L. and Lord, M. D. (2000). Acquiring new knowledge: the role of retaining human capital in acquisition of high-tech firms. *Journal of High Technology Management Research*, 11, 295–319.

Ranft, A .L. and Lord, M. D. (2002). Acquiring new technologies and capabilities: a grounded model of acquisition implementation. *Organization Science*, 13, 420–441.

Riad, S. and Vaara, E. (2011). Varieties of national metonymy in media accounts of international mergers and acquisitions. *Journal of Management Studies*, 48(4), 737–771.

Riad, S., Vaara, E., and Zhang, N. (2012). The intertextual production of international relations in mergers and acquisitions. *Organization Studies*, 33(1), 121–148.

Sarala, R.M., Junni, P., Cooper, C. L., and Tarba, S. Y. (2014). A socio-cultural perspective on knowledge transfer in mergers and acquisitions. *Journal of Management*, 16 April. Available at http://jom.sagepub.com/content/early/2014/04/16/0149206314530167.full.pdf+html (accessed 11 August 2016).

Schweiger, D. M., Csiszar, E., and Napier, N. K. (1993). Implementing international mergers and acquisitions. *Human Resource Planning*, 16, 53–70.

Schweiger, D. M. and Weber, Y. (1989). Strategies for managing human resources during mergers and acquisitions: an empirical investigation. *Human Resource Planning*, 12, 69–86.

Schweizer, L. (2005). Organizational integration of acquired biotechnology companies into pharmaceutical companies: the need for a hybrid approach. *Academy of Management Journal*, 48, 1051–1074.

Schweizer, L. (2012). Characteristics of biotechnology mergers and acquisitions. In D. Faulkner, S. Teerikangas, and R. J. Joseph (Eds.), *The handbook of mergers and acquisitions*. Oxford: Oxford University Press, pp. 638–658.

Schweizer, L. (2014). Strategic alliances or M&A as the road to innovation for pharmaceutical companies. *Journal of Entrepreneurship and Organization Management*, 3(2), 116–117.

Schweizer, L. and Patzelt, H. (2012). Employee commitment in the post-acquisition integration process: the effect of leadership style and integration speed. *Scandinavian Journal of Management*, 28, 298–310.

Sirower, M. L. (1997). *The synergy trap: how companies lose the acquisition game*. New York: Free Press.

Spedale, S., van Den Bosch, F. A. J., and Volberda, H. W. (2007). Preservation and dissolution of the target firm's embedded ties in acquisitions. *Organization Studies*, 28(8), 1169–1196.

Urbig, D., Bürger, R., Patzelt, H., and Schweizer, L. (2013). Investor reactions to new product development failures: the moderating role of product development stage. *Journal of Management*, 39(4), 985–1015.

Vaara, E. and Tienari, J. (2011). On the narrative construction of multinational corporations: an antenarrative analysis of legitimation and resistance in a cross-border merger. *Organization Science*, 22(2), 370–390.

Walsh, J. P. (1988). Top management turnover following mergers and acquisitions. *Strategic Management Journal*, 9, 173–183.

Weber, Y. and Tarba, S. Y. (2010). Human resource practices and performance of mergers and acquisitions in Israel. *Human Resource Management Review*, 20, 203–211.

Weber, Y. and Tarba, S. Y. (2011). Exploring integration approach in related mergers. *International Journal of Organizational Analysis*, 19(3), 202–221.

Weber, Y., Tarba, S. Y., and Reichel, A. (2009). International mergers and acquisitions performance revisited: the role of cultural distance and post-acquisition integration approach implementation. *Advances in Mergers and Acquisitions*, 8, 1–18.

Weber, Y., Tarba, S. Y., and Reichel, A. (2011). A model of the influence of culture on integration approaches and international mergers and acquisitions performance. *International Studies of Management and Organization*, 41(3), 9–24.

Yin, R. K. (1994). *Case study research, design and methods* (2nd edn.). Thousand Oaks, CA: Sage.

7

HUMAN RESOURCE MANAGEMENT IN THE CONTEXT OF MERGERS AND ACQUISITIONS

Fang Lee Cooke

Introduction

Since the mid-1980s, mergers and acquisitions (M&As) have been a popular strategy for organizations to survive, expand and gain competitive advantage in an increasingly complex business environment. However, M&As often fail to achieve the anticipated organizational outcome, not because of financial or strategic reasons but because of the poor management of people-related issues (e.g. Schuler and Jackson 2001; Waring 2005; Stahl *et al.* 2013). This chapter examines a number of specific human resource management (HRM) problems and challenges encountered in domestic and cross-border M&As. It draws on empirical examples of extant studies on M&As in different organizational, industrial, national and international contexts to illustrate the complexity and difficulties M&A partners may experience. It also outlines some of the key HR activities throughout the M&A process. In doing so, the chapter reveals the dynamics of political, institutional, cultural and psychological factors at play in post-M&A integration.

The terms 'mergers' and 'acquisitions' are often used interchangeably in the literature. However, in this chapter, a 'merger' is used for the combination of two entities into a new organization, whereas an 'acquisition' is 'the takeover of a target organization by a lead entity' (Marks and Mirvis 2011: 874–875). We use the term 'merger' or 'acquisition' when discussing specific cases, and the term 'M&A' for more general discussion. A merger has been likened to an entity that consists of two animals, whereas an acquisition may take place in either a friendly or a hostile manner. This indicates the daunting task of post-M&A integration. Cross-border acquisition is a popular form of foreign direct investment (United Nations Conference on Trade and Development 2013). This enables the acquiring firm to access various resources and fulfil its strategic goals in the host country (e.g. Lin *et al.* 2009). However, cross-border acquisitions tend to be politically sensitive, particularly when they involve key industries with natural resources and national security implications, as was demonstrated in several failed attempts by Chinese firms to acquire business stakes in various parts of the world (e.g. White 2005; Garnaut 2009). Even when acquisition deals have gone through, post-acquisition integration may present insurmountable challenges, as discussed below.

This chapter consists of three main sections. The first identifies the political and socio-psychological dimensions of M&As and how organizational and national traditions may be affected following an M&A. The second section highlights a number of M&A-related challenges to HRM which may have a knock-on effect on post-M&A integration and organizational performance. In particular, we focus on organizational identity and employee commitment, and the integration of organizational culture and cross-cultural management issues. In the third section, we provide insights into the strategic and operational role of the HR function, what factors may impact on its role, as well as some of the HR activities in M&As.

The political and socio-psychological dimensions of M&As

While M&As often take place for business reasons to enhance shareholders' value, such as creating or strengthening corporate competitive advantage through the acquisition/synergy of resources, accessing new markets and/or products, lowering cost and so forth, M&As 'are inevitably also a political process' (Olcott 2008: 1570) that is 'best understood as a manifestation of the struggle for corporate control rather than merely the search for immediate profits' (Walter 1985: 302). Very few M&As are conducted on an equal footing in reality. And staff within the 'weaker' partner, especially the acquired business, are often expected to adopt the procedures and practices of the dominant entity in the new set-up. Even when new rules are developed in the new set-up, the acquired staff may feel that their voices are less heard. Such a perceived power imbalance not only affects the socio-psychological wellbeing of the staff, but also influences their workplace behaviour in the post-M&A integration. As Olcott (2008: 1570) argued, 'political arrangements play an important part in explaining the organizational outcome' of M&As.

For example, Marmenout's (2011: 803) experimental study of collective rumination, 'defined as repetitively and passively discussing organizational problems and their negative consequences with a group of peers', found that such workplace behaviour could lead to employees' dysfunctional reactions to mergers. Such reactions often derive from employees' experience of fear of uncertainty, perception of lack of control, and anxiety of job losses or deterioration of employment terms and conditions. These feelings are common in major organizational changes, particularly when information that is relevant to the affected employees is limited and perceived to be untrustworthy.

By contrast, Melkonian *et al.*'s (2011: 830) study of the Air France–KLM merger found that perceived distributive justice 'has had a significant and lasting influence on Air France–KLM employees' willingness to cooperate', although it was more than a year before 'perceived procedural justice progressively emerged as another powerful predictor of employees' willingness to cooperate'. The same study revealed that commitment from the top management (CEOs) to open communication and positive management behaviour are instrumental in shaping employees' willingness to 'cooperate with each other in a respectful, fair, and trustful manner' (Melkonian *et al.* 2011: 830). Melkonian *et al.*'s (2011) findings underline the importance of managing employees' distributive justice perceptions through the adequate distribution of justice-relevant information related to M&As and management behaviour, especially during the early stages of an M&A.

In an international acquisition context, post-acquisition changes may weaken the institutionalized national employment system embedded in the acquired firms. For example, Olcott's (2008) case study of Japanese firms that have been taken over by Western firms found that the new management did not favour two distinct Japanese corporate norms: commitment to lifelong employment and seniority-based rewards. While the new management did not openly challenge the traditional system, their attitude 'led to a general erosion of the legitimacy of institutionalized practices' (Olcott 2008: 1582).

M&As and key challenges to HRM

While M&As continue to be an important corporate activity in the twenty-first century, the ability to create and harvest value from them is largely contingent upon the ability to retain and mobilize the human resources of the entities involved (Kiessling *et al.* 2012). M&As are major organizational changes, and, as such, inevitably present HRM challenges. In this section, we will discuss a number of key HR issues, drawing on empirical studies from various national and industrial contexts. We focus on issues related to organizational identity and employee commitment. We also highlight problems that stem from cultural differences. For clarity, some of the challenges to HR practices will be discussed in the next section, which covers HR activities.

Organizational identity and employee commitment

Existing research evidence suggests that employees' reactions to M&As tend to vary, underpinned, amongst other things, by the employees' perceptions of the extent to which their pre-M&A organizational identity has been eroded (van Dick *et al.* 2006). Employees may find themselves confronted by the question 'Who are we?', particularly when two rival organizations with very different histories, cultures and practices merge (Clark *et al.* 2010). 'Identity ambiguity' may trigger a cognitive process amongst employees in an attempt to change identity; it may also give rise to counterproductive socio-political forces in the organization (Clark *et al.* 2010). Equally, frustrated organizational identification and poor adjustment to the new identity may lead to distorted workplace behaviour and work attitude, particularly amongst lower-level employees in the acquired or the weaker merger organization (Makri 2012).

For example, Maguire and Phillips' (2008) study of two large insurance companies in Citigroup revealed that the ambiguity of the new organization's identity undermined institutional trust. Meanwhile, Wickramasinghe and Karunaratne's (2009: 708) study of bank mergers in Sri Lanka found that, although employees did not feel 'as if they had been given false promises, the merger encouraged them to look for employment opportunities elsewhere' in part because of a loss of organizational identity. Cho *et al.*'s (2014) study of 222 employees in a merged Korean company also showed that employees who feel disadvantaged in organizational resource allocation (e.g. pay, promotion and job transfer) as a result of post-M&A integration may exhibit dysfunctional behaviour, such as withdrawing job effort and expressing an intention to quit. By contrast, van Dick *et al.*'s (2006: 77) study of the merger of two hospitals in Germany suggests that post-merger identification is positively related to employee attitudes and behaviour in that employees who have a strong identification with the new entity 'are more satisfied, less likely to withdraw and more willing to put in extra effort'. The authors conclude that ensuring a sense of belonging among the workforce and providing a positive basis for employees' social identity are key to the success of a merger (van Dick *et al.* 2006: 77).

Integration of organizational culture and cross-cultural management

Integration is a key aspect of post-M&A activities that may have a profound impact on individuals' lives and organizational performance. Pucik *et al.* (2015: 257) pointed out that 'the concept of "integration" has different meanings depending on the strategic logic' that underpins the M&A. For example, they differentiate acquisitions into five categories: preservation acquisitions; absorption acquisitions; reverse mergers; best of both; and transformation. According to Pucik *et al.* (2015: 257), while true integration involves the capture of 'hidden synergies by sharing and leveraging capabilities', many post-M&A integration processes are in fact 'assimilations'.

In recent years, research into the success and failure of M&As has moved from the traditional focus on financial and strategic factors to the role of socio-cultural and HR issues in the post-M&A integration (Björkman and Lu 2001; Cartwright and Price 2003; Marks and Mirvis 2011; Stahl *et al.* 2013). Cultural clashes and a failure to create a new corporate culture following the M&A have often been cited as the main reasons for the failure of domestic and international M&A deals (e.g. Teerikangas and Véry 2006; Weber and Tarba 2012; Stahl *et al.* 2013). This is because cultural mismatch undermines the development of trust and commitment, the alignment of strategic goals, and knowledge sharing/transfer (e.g. Drori *et al.* 2011). In unequal mergers and acquisitions, 'the dominant culture may be perceived as threatening and thus be rejected by the less dominant culture' (Drori *et al.* 2011: 628).

In domestic M&As, studies have largely focused on the (in)compatibility of organizational culture – for example, norms and values shared within the organizations engaging in the M&As (Stahl *et al.* 2013). Cultural differences between

M&A partners have been found to result in reduced top management commitment and cooperation (Weber *et al.* 1996). It should be noted that not all domestic M&As are initiated by corporate leaders. In the 1990s and 2000s, many governments (at both national and local levels) have taken the initiative to merge public sector organizations, such as schools, universities and hospitals, in a bid to improve efficiency, accountability and service provision. In such mergers, organizational leaders often have very little influence over the process of merger and post-merger integration. As Kavanagh and Ashkanasy's (2006: S81) study of the mergers between three large multi-site public sector organizations in Australia revealed, 'in many cases the change that occurs as a result of a merger is imposed on the leaders themselves, and it is often the pace of change that inhibits the successful re-engineering of the culture'.

In cross-border M&As, studies of cultural difference tend to focus on the national level, highlighting cultural distance and incompatibility as key factors for post-M&A integration difficulties or M&A failure (e.g. Cartwright and Cooper 1993; Björkman *et al.* 2007; Drori *et al.* 2011; Stahl *et al.* 2013). For example, Dameron and Joffre's (2007: 2053) study of the integration team that was created to manage the post-merger integration of France Telecom Mobile and Orange UK found that the coexistence of the French and English cultures was 'never seen as an opportunity, a differentiation and a source of creativity'. Rather, 'cultural diversity was always experienced by the members of the integration team as a difficulty to overcome'.

In reality, cultural mismatch in international M&As is compounded by organizational as well as national cultures, even for ostensible mergers of equals. The Daimler–Chrysler merger is an often-cited example that illustrates how the operational and managerial differences between the German and the American companies led to the dominance of the German approach, which consequently led to Chrysler employees' disillusionment and undermined 'employees' shared understanding of every aspect of the organization, from strategy to employment practices' (Drori *et al.* 2011: 626).

Difficulties created by socio-cultural differences may be exacerbated by language barriers. As Teerikangas and Irrmann (2013) observed, the absence of a shared native language slows down cooperation, causes misunderstandings, and inhibits the development of a trust relationship. Here, the language barrier is not just linguistic but also cognitive and socio-cultural. This is particularly the case when a large number of expatriates from headquarters are sent to work in the acquired business units overseas. For instance, a Japanese energy (gas and oil) corporation acquired (part of) an Australian firm (an A$40 billion project). The new business unit consists of nearly 100 Japanese expatriates (all male), 500 (mostly Australians) employees and another 600 contingency workers. Japan is a relatively homogeneous nation, whereas Australia, being an immigrant country, is a multicultural society. It was reported that the Japanese managers lacked cultural sensitivity when dealing with the multicultural workforce. Other reported cultural differences included: the Japanese consensus approach versus the Australians' direct approach; and the Japanese slow meeting style versus the Australian quick and direct style. The Japanese expatriates tended to be deficient in English and received little prior training to prepare them for the Australian corporate world. Similarly, the Australian managers and key professional staff did not receive cross-cultural training after the acquisition to enable them to work effectively with their expatriate colleagues (author's interview with Australian HR manager 2014).

Nevertheless, not all cultural differences are detrimental to M&A successes. Cultural differences, rather than similarities, may form the basis for M&A partners to learn from each other to create synergy, expand the corporate knowledge base, and complement each other. In their study of corporate capability transfer, Björkman *et al.* (2007) found that a moderate level of cultural distance may create space for mutual learning and synergy realization, as long as the cognitive and normative gaps between the partners are bridgeable. It is also important to note that in post-M&A integration, cultural distance may evolve over time, although 'the measures of cultural change require development', as Stahl *et al.* (2013: 337) observed.

Given the significant role of culture in underpinning the success or otherwise of M&As – often measured by the post-M&A performance of the new entity – researchers of M&As have proposed a number of (new) research angles to pursue. For example, Teerikangas and Véry (2006: 2053) propose, 'instead of studying the simple performance impact of cultural differences in M&A', we should consider 'how cultural differences impact on the M&A process and its outcome'. They further argue that it is important to examine, from different intellectual perspectives, the coexistence and dynamics of sub-cultures at various levels as well as the interconnections and interactions between levels of cultures in order to develop a more nuanced understanding of the organizational culture reality in the M&A context.

Similarly, Drori *et al.* (2011: 629) suggest that the notions of cultural pluralism and cultural ambiguity may be seen as 'the hallmark of cultures' in the post-M&A integration context when the new cultures constructed by the M&As are contested, negotiated, and made sense of in 'an unsettled organizational period'. On a more optimistic note, based on their study of a merger of equals in the high-tech sector, Drori *et al.* (2011: 625) argue that social actors entering the merger may 'enact a culture of equality' by developing 'new aspirations and patterns of appreciation' and initiating 'practices and strategies that construct equality as an integral part of the merger'. This action 'transforms the meaning of "a merger of equals" to a more practical, pragmatic, and integrative equality, which takes into account the interests and the needs of the merged firm'.

Role of the HR function and HR activities in M&As

Given the centrality of HR issues in the success or otherwise of post-M&A integration, the role of HR is both strategically and operationally critical (e.g. Faulkner *et al.* 2002; Schroeder 2012). However, existing research has highlighted the fact that the HR department is often not (or at least insufficiently) involved in the strategic planning of the M&A, and the HR professionals often lack competence in handling HR issues related to the M&A (e.g. Jeris *et al.* 2002;

Björkman and Søderberg 2003; Antila and Kakkonen 2008; Wickramasinghe and Karunaratne 2009; Barratt-Pugh *et al.* 2013).[1] A number of authors have proposed HR frameworks and guidelines that cover different stages throughout the M&A process (e.g. Schuler and Jackson 2001; Marks and Vansteenkiste 2008; Schroeder 2012; Teerikangas *et al.* 2015). For example, Teerikangas *et al.* (2015) divide the HR function into two categories: strategic and transactional. For the strategic role, the HR function needs to participate from the outset in 'strategic decision making and transformational leadership' (Teerikangas *et al.* 2015: 446). For the transactional role, the HR function involves facilitating the post-M&A integration of HR policies and practices, such as payroll, benefits, rewards and pensions (Teerikangas *et al.* 2015). In this section, we discuss the strategic and operational role of the HR function as well as some of the HR activities that the in-house HR team may carry out as part of the post-M&A transition and integration.

Factors influencing the role of the HR function

Extant research has revealed several elements that have constrained the role of the HR function in the M&A process. First is top management's lack of awareness of the strategic importance of HR involvement, and therefore their low expectations of the strategic contribution of the HR function (e.g. Teerikangas *et al.* 2015). Instead, the HR function is expected to deal with specific HR matters arising from the M&A (e.g. Björkman and Søderberg 2003). For example, Tanure and Gonzalez-Duarte's (2007: 381) case study of bank acquisitions in the Brizilian context showed that:

> the top management, in particular its CEO, played a critical role in guaranteeing a consistency between discourse and practice concerning the relevance of people in both deals and, in consequence, opening the possibility for HR managers to play a more strategic role.

Second, the role of the HR function and specific HR issues are contingent upon the strategic intent of the M&A (e.g. Aguilera and Dencker 2004; Gomes *et al.* 2012). Third, the expectations of the role of the HR function amongst other members of the organization and how these expectations are met may affect the role of the HR team (e.g. Aguilera and Dencker 2004). Fourth, the strategic role of the in-house HR team may be hampered by the deployment of external business/HR consultants to facilitate the M&A management for various reasons (e.g. Antila and Kakkonen 2008). Fifth, if the M&A is small in scale and affects few people, or if the two entities remain separate both geographically and in their business orientations, with limited interactions between the two partners, then the HR function in the M&A may be limited (Antila and Kakkonen 2008). Finally, the speed of the M&A may affect the role of the HR function, as well as that of other functional teams, in the pre-M&A analysis (Antila and Kakkonen 2008).

Nevertheless, Antila and Kakkonen's (2008: 293) case study of the international M&A of three Finnish companies found that, while 'top management support has an impact on the role of HR managers in an organisation it does not determine the role of HR managers in the IM&A process'. Instead, the 'most important factor affecting the roles of HR managers was the ability of HR managers to show the importance of HR-related issues in the IM&A process'. This capability, as the authors observed, needs to be demonstrated in the HR team's competence in their day-to-day work and in their ability to provide HR guidelines and frameworks in the M&A situation and communicate these throughout the organization. Similarly, Barratt-Pugh *et al.*'s (2013: 761) study of the merger of two Australian state departments with very different cultures concluded that the HR department should 'focus on a strategic approach and not use all resources and energy on selection, grievance and out-placement activity. The emphasis should be on visibly leading the change, not on mopping up the casualties.' More broadly, Correia *et al.*'s (2013: 330) study, which draws on the 2005 Cranet survey containing data on HR policies and practices in private and public sector organizations in thirty-two (mainly European) countries, shows that in the case of bidder acquisitions, 'HRM strategic involvement and a shift of responsibility from line managers to HRM managers boost organizational performance'.

Gomes *et al.*'s (2012) study of nineteen merged banks in Nigeria at the peak of banking sector mergers in the country in the mid-2000s echoes some of the above findings, as they found that 'HRM issues are important during both pre- and post-merger phases'. According to these authors, while post-merger 'integration approaches appear to vary significantly between merging banks', for mergers involving fewer banks that succeeded (many more complex and larger mergers failed), 'certain HRM themes emerge as being of particular importance to overall outcome'. These included: '(1) the quality of HRM due diligence, (2) the existence and handling of regional cultural differences, (3) the extent and quality of communications, and (4) the use of integration advisors to facilitate the process' (Gomes *et al.* 2012: 2891).

HR activities

Strategic alignment

Of all the HR activities related to M&As, strategic alignment of the HR strategy with the business strategy is perhaps the most important to enhance the likelihood of M&A success (Aguilera and Dencker 2004). This includes the analysis of what types and level of human resources are needed, where they can be sourced, how their performance is evaluated and rewarded, what attitudes are required from the management and workforce, what type of organizational culture is to be promoted, and so forth. In the international M&A context, strategic HR alignment also includes whether, and if so how, the corporate HR strategy may be rolled out to – or adapted by – the overseas subsidiaries. In addition, given the cultural differences between the M&A partners and national settings, as discussed earlier, the alignment of the HR strategy and business strategy and the promotion of the corporate HR strategy in subsidiaries need to take into account the institutional, cultural and structural fit between the business units/partners.

Leadership/management development

Good leadership at all levels is crucial to successful post-M&A integration. For instance, Marmenout (2011) argues that while managers cannot prevent employees from discussing what may happen regarding the M&A amongst themselves (i.e. collective rumination), the managers can influence the way in which they discuss it through active involvement, distraction and positive leadership and therefore potentially reduce the collective rumination. For instance, they can encourage employees to 'engage in problem solving by working on a suitable solution for a particular integration issue'; distract employees' attention with pleasant or neutral activities; and provide positive leadership by creating an optimistic climate and developing trust relationships through open communication and timely diffusion of information (Marmenout 2011: 803). Similarly, Barratt-Pugh *et al.*'s (2013: 761) study of the Australian state department merger revealed the need for the HR department 'to focus resources on how managers operationalised the project, by orchestrating supportive development activity that builds leadership capability. Such actions generated change agency that made the change happen.' Schroeder (2012) also highlights the role of leadership training so that organizational leaders become champions of cultural change in post-M&A integration. Therefore, a key HR activity in M&A is to facilitate leadership development. In addition, international M&A as a form of expansion may trigger the need for a large group of expatriate senior managers and technical personnel with managerial responsibilities, as was the case in the Japanese–Australian energy case discussed earlier. This staffing arrangement creates training needs both ways: cross-cultural awareness and management for local staff and expatriate managers.

Communication

Open, timely and genuine communication is considered a must in change management to reduce uncertainty, mitigate negative attitudes amongst employees, develop shared understanding, perceived fairness and trust, and bridge cultural differences (e.g. van Dick *et al.* 2006). As Gomes *et al.* (2012: 2894) found, communication has helped develop inter-organizational linkages and mitigate the potential disruption of regional cultural differences in the Nigerian bank mergers in the process of enculturation – 'the creation and maintenance of organizational cultures and the assimilation of members into the organization'.

Managing cultural change

The importance of managing culture in the post-M&A integration phase was highlighted earlier. As Marks and Mirvis (2011: 863) pointed out, the 'message to

HR professionals is to be proactive in putting culture on the agenda', though their ability to do so is contingent upon the way the HR function is deployed in the M&A situation.[2] According to Weber and Tarba (2012: 300), corporate culture analysis is 'an important and influential milestone in the international business environment exploration'. In the cross-border M&A context, this involves 'cultural difference assessment during all stages of the M&A, including screening, planning and negotiation and enhanc[ing] the effectiveness of interventions carried out during post-merger integration process' (Weber and Tarba 2012: 300). Sarala *et al.* (2014) further argued that socio-cultural inter-firm linkages (e.g. complementary employee skills, trust, collective teaching, and cultural integration) between the merging firms influence the level of knowledge transfer in M&As, and that HR flexibility (e.g. flexibility in employee skills, flexibility in employee behaviour, and flexibility in HR practices) is vital for the development of socio-cultural inter-firm linkages in M&As. These views are echoed by Teerikangas *et al.* (2015: 442), who believe that the effectiveness of post-M&A integration in the cross-border context depends upon 'the extent to which differences in institutions, national cultures and language are recognized'. And recognizing and accommodating these differences requires relevant HR interventions.

Training and counselling

M&A as a major organizational change may trigger a high degree of anxiety amongst the workforce due to the turbulence and uncertainty the event is likely to cause, as discussed earlier. Motivation, commitment and organizational identification amongst the employees may be negatively affected. This requires a range of HR interventions, including training and counselling, to help individuals overcome these feelings and adapt to the change. Such training and counselling need to be tailored to the specific needs of the employees and may be provided by external professionals who are specialized in dealing with post-M&A integration (see, e.g., Schroeder 2012).

Staffing issues

Labour turnover, both involuntary and voluntary, is a common HR outcome following a merger or acquisition. Creating synergy and reducing cost are often strategic goals of M&As. Downsizing is inevitable. Existing research has found that over-downsizing may lead to the loss of organizational competence and create skill shortages in the workforce, as was found in a study of M&As in the Australian coal-mining industry (Waring 2005). HR due diligence is needed to identify what skills and competences are required for the business and to determine how downsizing should be managed, as the latter tends to cause workplace stress, lower morale and voluntary turnover due to employees' sense of violation of psychological contract (e.g. Hubbard and Purcell 2001; Waring 2005; Schroeder 2012).

Harmonization and transfer of HR practices

M&As may trigger the need for greater consistency of HR practices within the organization, such as pay and grading systems, pension and other welfare schemes, working time arrangements, leave entitlements, performance management systems, and so forth (e.g. Schroeder 2012). While harmonization of terms and conditions may be necessary in domestic M&As, transfer of HR practices may be attempted in international M&As for various reasons, such as dissemination of perceived good HR practice and standardization of corporate HRM for greater consistency and control. Existing studies of the transfer of HR practices have highlighted immense challenges to the transfer of HR practices from the headquarters to subsidiaries or across subsidiaries for political, institutional, cultural and/or organizational reasons (e.g. Rubery and Grimshaw 2003; Ferner *et al.* 2012). These challenges may be heightened in a cross-border M&A context. As such, total transfer may prove difficult to achieve; instead, partial transfer or adaptation may be more likely. For instance, Cooke and Huang's (2011) study of changes and continuity in the performance appraisal and reward systems of four Chinese IT firms after they were acquired by US-owned multinational corporations revealed that while the performance management and reward policies of the acquired firms have experienced changes, the structure of compensation remains largely unchanged. There was a high degree of resistance amongst the Chinese managers to the adoption of more sophisticated performance appraisal techniques and to widening the wage band to differentiate employees' performance. As a result, the post-acquisition strategic alignment of HR practices between the corporate and the Chinese subsidiaries was not achieved (Cooke and Huang 2011). Therefore, when transferring HR practices across national boundaries, a cautious and pragmatic approach may be necessary as full transfer may be unrealistic.

Employment relations and trade union negotiation

Where firms are unionized, consultation and negotiation with the union on a range of employment relations/HR issues, especially changes to employment terms and conditions, is another top priority for the HR function. While some organizations have a separate industrial/employment relations department to handle employment relations matters, this function may be assumed by the HR department in other organizations. In acquisition cases, the acquiring firm may not have experience in dealing with unions. This will increase the HR challenges in the post-acquisition integration. In a worst-case scenario, it may lead to serious damage to the business and the corporate reputation. The Shanghai Automotive Industry Corporation's (SAIC) acquisition of the South Korean Ssangyong Motor Company is a case in point. Fuelled by the ambition to become one of the top six global automotive firms by 2010, SAIC acquired a 51 per cent stake in Ssangyong in late 2004. In January 2009, after a record loss of over US$75.42 million, the company was placed into receivership and acquired by the Indian Mahindra and Mahindra Limited in August 2010. Disruptions in production due to a series of strikes amongst the Korean workers, organized by a union leader with over twenty years of organizing experience, was a main reason for the SAIC–Ssangyong failure. The SAIC management had no experience of dealing with trade unions or industrial relations issues and therefore had difficulty in handling the Korean union and the workers' militancy. Amongst other issues, the Korean workers' resentment of and resistance towards SAIC were fanned by post-acquisition redundancies, work reorganization, SAIC's alleged failure to provide promised investment and, later, its transfer of Ssangyong's technology to SAIC researchers (Chen 2009).

Interim HR practices

During the M&A integration, organizations may undergo a major period of uncertainty while stock-taking and attempting to create synergies. Uncertainty undermines morale and organizational commitment and increases staff turnover (intent). In order to retain and engage key employees, interim HR practices may be introduced to help the organization negotiate this period. For example, Clark *et al.*'s (2010) study found that creating a transitional organizational identity helps employees cope with the initial stages of the merger process and facilitates the creation of a new shared identity. According to Schroeder (2012), a bonus programme may be introduced to encourage the retention of key staff with skills and experience that are valuable to the organization. In addition, intrinsic methods, such as involvement in the development of integration plans, may be introduced. Finally, integration-related performance measures may be included in the performance management system so that individuals have a vested interest in achieving integration goals.

Conclusions

Mergers and acquisitions have been examined from a range of perspectives, including views from, for example, sociology, organizational behaviour, cross-cultural analysis, human resource management, and strategic management. Research studies of M&As have pointed to similar conclusions: that post-M&A integration tends to present enormous challenges to organizations and that HR issues are often obstacles to achieving M&A goals. In particular, the loss of organizational identity and cultural differences are two major challenges, especially for unequal M&A partners and cross-border M&As. M&A as a major organizational change may trigger multiple facets of emotional feelings amongst those who may be affected and result in poor individual and organizational performance. Establishing a 'mutual understanding on the roles and responsibilities', especially during unexpected organizational events, may help to develop psychological contracts and retain employees after the M&A (Kiessling *et al.* 2012: 88).

The role of the HR function in strategic planning, developing appropriate HR interventions and supporting line management is an important means to mitigate employees' perceived organizational injustice in the M&A process, enhance their wellbeing, and secure their commitment and engagement. As such, the HR team needs to play a strategic, administrative, advisory and facilitating role throughout the various stages of the M&A. This requires the team to develop the capability to convince the top management of its strategic role and the capacity to secure organizational resources and support for the HR professionals to perform their multiple roles. However, existing research has pointed to a similar conclusion: that the in-house HR team needs to be more proactive and innovative in order to play a more strategic role and add value to the M&A. In addition, in the cross-border M&A context, developing an understanding of the institutional and cultural contexts of the M&A partners will help reduce the risk of post-M&A integration failure (Stahl *et al.* 2013). This is where the HR function can add value to the M&A process through due diligence.

Successful management of HR and cultural issues have profound implications not only for M&A organizations but also for research and conceptualization of the M&A process (Clark *et al.* 2010; Stahl *et al.* 2013). M&A scholars have identified a number of avenues for future research. For example, Stahl *et al.* (2013) suggest the following four main unresolved issues in M&A research:

- the whole process of pre- and post-merger;
- the role of cultural differences in the socio-cultural dynamics of M&As;
- the role of prior M&A experience as organizational learning in current M&As; and
- how to assess performance in financial, economic, strategic, executive and regulatory terms.

Clark *et al.* (2010) call for more insights into the cognitive dynamics of organizational identity in an M&A process to understand the complexity of organizational identity change during post-M&A integration. An important research question posed by Clark *et al.* (2010: 429) is: 'under what conditions is organizational identity change facilitated by the emergence of a transitional identity?' In a similar vein, Cho *et al.* (2014: 423) point out that more attention should be paid to examining 'how turnover intention is formed in M&As with a more process-oriented framework that is applicable to employees of all ranks'.

Weber and Tarba (2012: 300) suggest that, instead of focusing only on post-M&A cultural integration, 'consideration of cultural differences is also essential in making the choice of the right partner for M&A and should be assessed and measured during pre-merger planning and negotiation stages'. Teerikangas and Véry (2006: S35) also argue that research into cultural differences should take into account cultures that manifest at all levels and their dynamic interactions in order to understand how 'diverse sources of complexity' underpin 'the relationship between culture and M&A performance'. They further call for research into the role of the integration strategy and the role of managerial efforts in mediating the culture–performance relationship. The knowledge of these issues is likely to be beneficial not only to the research community but also to organizations in their M&A activities.

Notes

1 See Teerikangas *et al.* (2015) for a more detailed discussion of the four scenarios of HR's involvement in M&As.
2 See Marks and Mirvis (2011) for a detailed framework on how the HR function can work with business partners in managing acculturation in M&As to achieve the 'cultural endstate' by applying the change management model.

References

Aguilera, R.V. and Dencker, J.C. (2004) 'The role of human resource management in cross-border mergers and acquisitions', *International Journal of Human Resource Management*, 5, 8, 1355–1370.

Antila, E.M. and Kakkonen, A. (2008) 'Factors affecting the role of HR managers in international mergers and acquisitions: a multiple case study', *Personnel Review*, 37, 3, 280–299.

Barratt-Pugh, L., Bahn, S. and Gakere, E. (2013) 'Managers as change agents: implications for human resource managers engaging with culture change', *Journal of Organizational Change Management*, 26, 4, 748–764.

Bartlett, C. and Ghoshal, S. (2000) *Managing across Borders: The Transnational Solution*, Boston, MA: Harvard Business School Press.

Björkman, I. and Lu, Y. (2001) 'Institutionalization and bargaining power explanations of human resource management in international joint ventures: the case of Chinese–Western joint ventures', *Organization Studies*, 22, 491–512.

Björkman, I. and Søderberg, A.-M. (2003) 'Quo vadis, HR? An analysis of the roles played by the HR function during the post merger process', in Søderberg, A.-M. and Vaara, E. (eds), *Merging across Borders: People, Cultures and Politics*, Copenhagen: Copenhagen Business School Press, pp. 177–202.

Björkman, I., Stahl, G.K. and Vaara, E. (2007) 'Cultural differences and capability transfer in cross-border acquisitions: the mediating roles of capability complementarity, absorptive capacity, and social integration', *Journal of International Business Studies*, 38, 658–672.

Cartwright, S. and Cooper, C. (1993) 'The role of culture compatibility in successful organizational marriage', *Academy of Management Executive*, 2, 57–69.

Cartwright, S. and Price, F. (2003) 'Managerial preferences in international mergers and acquisitions: an international comparison', *Advances in Mergers and Acquisitions*, 2, 81–95.

Chen, X. (2009) 'SAIC–Ssangyong: lose–lose ending'. Available at: http://news.sina.com.cn/c/sd/2009-08-20/144018476402.shtml, accessed 28 December 2014.

Cho, B., Lee, D. and Kim, K. (2014) 'How does relative deprivation influence employee intention to leave a merged company? The role of organizational identification', *Human Resource Management*, 53, 3, 421–443.

Clark, S.M., Gioia, D.A., Ketchen, D.J. Jr. and Thomas, J.B. (2010) 'Transitional identity as a facilitator of organizational identity change during a merger', *Administrative Science Quarterly*, 55, 397–438.

Collings, D., Wood, G. and Caligiuri, P. (eds) (2015) *The Routledge Companion to International Human Resource Management*, Abingdon: Routledge.

Cooke, F.L. and Huang, K. (2011) 'Post-acquisition evolution of the appraisal and reward systems: a study of Chinese IT firms acquired by US firms', *Human Resource Management*, 50, 6, 839–858.

Correia, M.F., Campos e Cunha, R. and Scholten, M. (2013) 'Impact of M&As on organizational performance: the moderating role of HRM centrality', *European Management Journal*, 31, 323–332.

Dameron, S. and Joffre, O. (2007) 'The good and the bad: the impact of diversity management on co-operative relationships', *International Journal of Human Resource Management*, 18, 11, 2037–2056.

Drori, I., Wrzesniewski, A. and Ellis, S. (2011) 'Cultural clashes in a "merger or equals": the case of high-tech start-ups', *Human Resource Management*, 50, 5, 625–649.

Faulkner, D., Pitkethly, R. and Child, J. (2002) 'International mergers and acquisitions in the UK 1985–94: a comparison of national HRM practices', *International Journal of Human Resource Management*, 13, 1, 106–122.

Ferner, A, Edwards, T. and Tempel, A. (2012) 'Power, institutions and the cross-national transfer of employment practices in multinationals', *Human Relations*, 65, 2, 163–187.

Garnaut, J. (2009) 'Chinalco, Rio deal collapses'. Available at: www.smh.com.au/business/chinalco-rio-deal-collapses-20090605-bxdc.html, accessed 20 December 2014.

Gomes, E., Angwin, D., Peter, E. and Mellahi, K. (2012) 'HRM issues and outcomes in African mergers and acquisitions: a study of the Nigerian banking sector', *International Journal of Human Resource Management*, 23, 14, 2874–2900.

Hubbard, N. and Purcell, J. (2001) 'Managing employee expectations during acquisitions', *Human Resource Management Journal*, 2, 1, 17–33.

Jeris, L.S., Johnson, J.R. and Anthony, C.C. (2002) 'HRD involvement in merger and acquisition decisions and strategy development: four organizational portraits', *International Journal of Training and Development*, 6, 1, 2–10.

Kavanagh, M.H. and Ashkanasy, N.M. (2006) 'The impact of leadership and change management strategy on organizational culture and individual acceptance of change during a merger', *British Journal of Management*, 17, 1, S81–S103.

Kiessling, T., Harvey, M. and Moeller, M. (2012) 'Supply-chain corporate venturing through acquisition: key management team retention', *Journal of World Business*, 47, 1, 81–92.

Lin, Z., Peng, M., Yang, H. and Sun, S. (2009) 'How do networks and learning drive M&As? An institutional comparison between China and the United States', *Strategic Management Journal*, 30, 10, 1113–1132.

Maguire, S. and Phillips, N. (2008) '"Citibankers" at Citigroup: a study of the loss of institutional trust after a merger', *Journal of Management Studies*, 45, 372–401.

Makri, E. (2012) 'Merger integration patterns, status of pre-merger organizations, stress, and employee health post-combination', *Journal of Business Studies Quarterly*, 4, 2, 113–127.

Marks, M.L. and Mirvis, P.H. (2011) 'A framework for the human resources role in managing culture in mergers and acquisitions', *Human Resource Management*, 50, 6, 859–877.

Marks, M.L. and Vansteenkiste, R. (2008) 'Preparing for organizational death: proactive HR engagement in an organizational transition', *Human Resources Management*, 47, 809–827.

Marmenout, K. (2011) 'Peer interaction in mergers: evidence of collective rumination', *Human Resource Management*, 50, 6, 783–808.

Melkonian, T., Monin, P. and Noorderhaven, N.G. (2011) 'Distributive justice, procedural justice, exemplarity, and employees' willingness to cooperate in M&A integration processes: an analysis of the Air France–KLM merger', *Human Resource Management*, 50, 6, 809–837.

Olcott, G. (2008) 'The politics of institutionalization: the impact of foreign ownership and control on Japanese organizations', *International Journal of Human Resource Management*, 19, 9, 1569–1587.

Pucik, V., Björkman, I., Evans, P. and Stahl, G.K. (2015) 'Human resource management in cross-border mergers and acquisitions', in Harzing, A. and Pinnington, A. (eds), *International Human Resource Management*, 4th edition, London: Sage, pp. 252–287.

Rubery, J. and Grimshaw, D. (2003) *The Organisation of Employment: An International Perspective*, London: Palgrave.

Sarala, R., Junni, P., Cooper, C.L. and Tarba, S. (2014) 'A socio-cultural perspective on knowledge transfer in mergers and acquisitions,' *Journal of Management*, 16 April. Available at: http://jom.sagepub.com/content/early/2014/04/16/0149206314530167.full.pdf+html, accessed 16 August 2016.

Schroeder, H. (2012) 'Post-merger integration the art and science way', *Strategic HR Review*, 11, 5, 272–277.

Schuler, R. and Jackson, S. (2001), 'HR issues and activities in mergers and acquisitions', *European Management Journal*, 3, 239–253.

Stahl, G.K., Angwin, D.N., Véry, P., Gomes, E., Weber, Y., Tarba, S.Y., Noorderhaven, N., Benyamini, H., Bouckenooghe, D., Chreim, S., Durand, M., Hassett, M.E., Kokk, G., Mendenhall, M.E., Mirc, N., Miska, C., Park, K.M., Reynolds, N., Rouzies, A., Sarala, R.M., Seloti, S.L. Jr., Søndergaard, M. and Yildiz, H.E. (2013) 'Sociocultural integration in mergers and acquisitions: unresolved paradoxes and directions for future research', *Thunderbird International Business Review*, 55, 4, 333–356.

Tanure, B. and Gonzalez-Duarte, R. (2007) 'Managing people in radical changes (M&As): the adoption of intrinsically consistent HRM strategies in Brazilian companies', *International Journal of Manpower*, 28, 5, 369–383.

Teerikangas, S. and Irrmann, O. (2013) 'Unbundling the linguistic dynamics in cross-border acquisitions', paper presented at the Annual Meeting of the Academy of Management, Orlando, FL, August.

Teerikangas, S., Stahl, G.K., Björkman, I. and Mendenhall, M.E. (2015) 'IHRM issues in mergers and acquisitions', in Collings, D., Wood, G. and Caligiuri, P. (eds), *The Routledge Companion to International Human Resource Management*, Abingdon: Routledge, pp. 423–456.

Teerikangas, S. and Véry, P. (2006) 'The culture–performance relationship in M&A: from yes/no to how', *British Journal of Management*, 17, 1, S31–S48.

United Nations Conference on Trade and Development (2013) *World Investment Report*, Geneva: United Nations.

van Dick, R., Ullrich, J. and Tissington, P.A. (2006) 'Working under a black cloud: how to sustain organizational identification after a merger', *British Journal of Management*, 17, 1, S69–S79.

Walter, G.A. (1985) 'Culture collisions in mergers and acquisitions', in Frost, J.P., Moore, L.F., Louis, M.R., Lunberg, C.C. and Martin, J. (eds), *Organizational Culture*, Beverly Hills, CA: Sage, pp. 301–314.

Waring, P. (2005) 'Some employment relations consequences of the merger and acquisition movement in the Australian black coal mining industry 1997–2003', *Australian Bulletin of Labour*, 31, 1, 72–89.

Weber, Y., Shenkar, O. and Raveh, A. (1996) 'National and corporate cultural fit in mergers and acquisitions: an exploratory study', *Management Science*, 42, 8, 1215–1227.

Weber, Y. and Tarba, S.Y. (2012) 'Mergers and acquisitions process: the use of corporate culture analysis', *Cross Cultural Management*, 19, 3, 288–303.

White, B. (2005) 'Chinese drop bid to buy US oil firm', *Washington Post*, 3 August. Available at: www.washingtonpost.com/wp-dyn/content/article/2005/08/02/AR2005080200404.html, accessed 20 December 2014.

Wickramasinghe, V. and Karunaratne, C. (2009) 'People management in mergers and acquisitions in Sri Lanka: employee perceptions', *International Journal of Human Resource Management*, 20, 3, 694–715.

8

THE ROLE OF HUMAN RESOURCE MANAGEMENT PRACTICES IN MERGERS AND ACQUISITIONS

Sut I Wong, Elizabeth Solberg, Paulina Junni, and Steffen Robert Giessner

Introduction

Mergers and acquisitions (M&As) have been increasingly used in the past decade as a strategic means for companies to gain competitive advantages (Lakshman 2011), such as knowledge capital management and international market penetration. Economic synergies obtained through domestic or international M&As are considered particularly important in the current global business environment (Lupina-Wegener 2013; Weber and Fried 2011). Notwithstanding this, M&As also come with challenges. It is well recognized that M&As are one of the most extreme forms of organizational change (Hogan and Overmyer-Day 1994). Research shows that approximately half of all M&As fail to achieve their anticipated outcomes and that the consequences of M&A failure are detrimental (Cartwright and Schoenberg 2006; Rees and Edwards 2009; Thanos and Papadakis 2012). The dysfunctional impact of M&A failure is not only evident in organizational outcomes, such as reduced productivity and market reputation (Paruchuri *et al.* 2006), but also in the reduced well-being of organizational members, as reflected in increased job insecurity and stress (Schweiger and Denisi 1991; Terry *et al.*1996).

For decades, scholars and practitioners have been investigating the factors that contribute to the success of M&As (e.g., King *et al.* 2004; Lupina-Wegener 2013; Faulkner *et al.* 2012; Gomes *et al.* 2013; Haleblian *et al.* 2009). It has long been recognized that the success or failure of M&As depends crucially on the post-acquisition integration process (Weber and Tarba 2010, 2011), for which human resource management (HRM) practices are considered an important means to manage the human side of integration (Bramson 2000). In fact, there is evidence of a direct correlation between HR involvement and M&A success (Lin *et al.* 2006). In particular, the role of HRM in maintaining workforce stability (Bryson 2003) and reducing employee distress (Marks and Mirvis 2001) during post-acquisition integration are identified as key contributors to M&A effectiveness (Bryson 2003). Yet the role of HRM has been largely neglected in the M&A integration literature, and only recently has its importance received increasing attention (Marks and Mirvis 2011; Nikandrou and Papalexandris 2007; Sarala *et al.* Forthcoming; Weber and Fried 2011; Weber and Tarba 2010). While recent studies have highlighted the importance of HRM in acquisitions (e.g., the *Human Resource Management* journal dedicated two special issues to this topic in 2011), there has been no systematic review to synthesize the existing studies on the role of HRM in M&A. Therefore, a more comprehensive picture of the role that HRM plays in M&A integration is needed to help future research in this area. Accordingly, in this chapter we review studies in four theoretical streams (resource-based view; social identity view; cultural view; and organizational sensemaking view) that have received much attention in the M&A integration literature, but have never been systematically linked to the role of HRM in M&A. By doing so, we aim to contribute to the field by providing an overview of the multifaceted role of HRM in M&A integration, and to identify important areas for future research.

The chapter is organized as follows. First, we review the literature of post-acquisition integration. After this, we discuss four relevant theoretical landscapes from which M&As are typically assessed—including the resource-based view, social identity theory, acculturation theory, and organizational sensemaking theory—to identify various ways in which HRM may help the M&A process and contribute to M&A success. Finally, we discuss three important HRM contingencies factors (HRM centrality, HRM power, and HRM ambiguity) that impact the effectiveness of HRM practices in facilitating the M&A integration process. We conclude by providing theoretical and practical implications for how HRM may be implemented in M&As and suggest areas for future research.

Post-acquisition integration

Post-acquisition integration refers to changes that are made to the merging firms' structures, practices, systems, and cultures in order to create acquisition synergies (Pablo 1994). Previous research has tended to view changes relating to firm structures, practices, and systems as broadly relating to operational or 'task' integration, whereas socio-cultural or 'human' integration concerns changes in the cultures and identities of the merging firms (e.g., Birkinshaw *et al.* 2000). Both task and human integration aim to create value post-acquisition. However, task integration is more formal and concerns strategic choices related to the extent and speed of integration between the merging firms (Haspeslagh and Jemison 1991), whereas human integration is considered the softer side of M&A integration, as it generally relates to managing employee experiences and attitudes toward the M&A.

Studies focusing on the task-related side of M&A integration have tended to draw on the resource-based view, arguing that the combination of the merging firms' resources post-acquisition is critical for value creation. The underlying assumption is that there is a 'strategic fit' between the acquiring and acquired firm, which allows them to create synergies from combining similar or complementary resources (e.g., Almor *et al.* 2009). The prevailing theme in these studies has related to the amount of integration versus autonomy needed in order to create synergies, and studies have shown that there is a trade-off between the two. While integration facilitates the transfer of knowledge and resources between the firms, the removal of autonomy accompanied by integration can disrupt the acquired firm, for example through higher employee turnover, which reduces the value of the expected synergies (Haspeslagh and Jemison 1991). For instance, autonomy removal can reduce the acquired firm's innovative capabilities (Puranam *et al.* 2006; Puranam and Srikanth 2007), impede the transfer of tacit knowledge from the acquired firm to the parent firm (Ranft 2006), and weaken the acquired firms' external ties (Spedale *et al.* 2007). Recent studies have shown that the degree of autonomy granted to the acquired firm can change over the course of integration. For instance, Almor *et al.* (2009) and Schweizer (2005) show that acquirers of biotech companies tend to grant more autonomy to the acquired firms at first, but then increase the degree of integration in selected areas as they get to know the acquired firm's operations. Furthermore, researchers have begun to explore the role of the acquired firm in M&A value creation (e.g., Graebner 2004; Graebner and Eisenhardt 2004). Graebner (2004) shows that the effect of autonomy on acquisition success depends on the acquired firm's management: autonomy enhances acquisition success when the acquired firm's managers take an active role during the integration process, whereas it impedes value creation if managers remain passive. While previous studies have mentioned the importance of considering HRM aspects in M&A task integration—such as staffing needs and turnover concerns (Chaudhuri and Tabrizi 1999), learning efforts needed to create synergies from knowledge transfer (Chaudhuri 2005; Ranft and Lord 2002), and target firm involvement (e.g., Graebner 2004)—we lack a systematic understanding of the strategic role that HRM plays in this aspect of M&A integration.

In contrast to task integration, socio-cultural or human aspects are more difficult to manage, as these relate to employee experiences and attitudes (e.g., Marks and Mirvis 2011). Studies on M&A's socio-cultural integration have tended to focus on how social identity (e.g., Colman and Lunnan 2011; Hogg and Terry 2000; Giessner *et al.* Forthcoming), culture (e.g., Stahl and Voigt 2008; Weber *et al.* 2009, 2011), and organizational sensemaking (e.g., Vaara 2002; Riad and Vaara 2011; Riad *et al.* 2012) impact employee experiences and reactions during M&A integration.

Studies focusing on social identity issues in M&A integration build on the notion that employees are more positively inclined to their own social group or 'in-group', while the acquisition partner is seen as a less attractive 'out-group' (e.g., Hogg and Terry 2000). This can lead to 'us versus them' thinking, which can impede M&A integration by causing resistance to collaboration and antipathy towards the members of the partner firm, particularly when organizational members perceive that their current identity is threatened (e.g., Giessner *et al.* Forthcoming; Ulrich *et al.* 2005; Van Knippenberg *et al.* 2002). However, recent studies have shown that identity threats can also lead to unexpected value creation by pushing acquired firm members to contribute their knowledge and skills to the acquiring firm in order to preserve and legitimize the acquired firm's existing identity (Colman and Lunnan 2011). While studies taking a social identity perspective have highlighted important employee reactions caused by identity changes, the M&A literature lacks studies that discuss how these employee reactions can be managed using concrete HRM practices.

Concerning cultural issues, several studies indicate that cultural differences can impede M&A integration effectiveness by causing social conflict (e.g., Stahl and Voigt 2008) and cultural clashes (Weber and Tarba 2011). Furthermore, Weber *et al.* (2009, 2011) develop propositions about how the acquiring firm's national culture impacts the appropriateness of task integration approaches described by Haspeslagh and Jemison (1991). They argue that acquiring firms need to modify the 'ideal' strategic integration approach to suit their own cultural style in order to bring about successful integration. While these propositions remain untested, a number of empirical studies show that the acquiring firm's integration approaches do indeed vary based on the acquiring firm's nationality (e.g., Calori *et al.* 1994; Child *et al.* 2000; Lubatkin *et al.* 1998). While a few studies have discussed the HRM practices that can mitigate problems caused by cultural differences—such as cultural due diligence (Harding and Rouse 2007) and deep-level cultural integration (Schweiger and Goulet 2005)—we lack a systematic understanding of the role of HRM in managing cultural issues.

The organizational sensemaking stream represents the most recent perspective on human integration. It represents a more critical perspective that is concerned with how individuals make sense of M&As. Many researchers have used discourse analysis in order to understand how individuals make sense of acquisition events (e.g., Riad 2005; Vaara 2002). This stream of research has aimed to provide a richer picture of the M&A integration process by showing how individuals socially construct meanings about M&A events. For instance, Riad (2007) examined how individuals constructed notions of 'organizational culture' to make sense of a merger and to provide (de)legitimacy for different integration issues. However, while the studies in this stream help us understand how individuals make sense of M&A processes, we lack studies that analyze how HRM practices can influence employee sensemaking.

Taken together, individual studies in each of the research streams discussed above (resource-based view; social identity view; cultural view; and organizational sensemaking view) have touched upon the topic of HRM. However, as a whole, these studies have tended to be fragmented, focusing either on the more strategic task side of M&A integration or on softer human aspects related to culture, social identity, or sensemaking. In order to provide a systematic and comprehensive view of the role HRM plays in M&A integration, we proceed to review HRM-related studies in each of these four research streams.

The roles of HRM in M&As

In this section, we review research that explains the role HRM practices can and do play in M&A integration processes, based on the four major theoretical frameworks outlined above. These theoretical frameworks are directed to distinct mechanisms in which HRM may be used as a strategic means to manage M&A integration. By looking at different theoretical frameworks, we encourage a pluralistic view on the function of HRM in M&As.

Resource-based view—enabling human capital to contribute to M&A success

The resource-based view (RBV) asserts that an organization's competitive advantage lies within the valuable, rare, inimitable and non-substitutable resources at its disposal (Barney 1991). These resources can reside in 'physical capital', such as technology and locations, or 'organizational capital', including internal structures, processes, and procedures. The organization's most precious resource, however, is arguably its ability to acquire and apply knowledge in order to get the best out of its physical and organizational capital, a capability that is inherent to the organization's 'human capital', or the knowledge, skills, and abilities possessed by its employees (Nordhaug and Gronhaug 1994; Penrose 1959; Prahalad and Hamel 1990).

The use of M&As to gain a competitive advantage through organizational resources appears in the earliest conceptions of the RBV (see Wernerfelt 1984). In line with this perspective, M&As are now widely viewed as a way for organizations to gain new markets, master new technologies, and gain operational efficiencies, both within and across borders. M&A is also increasingly used as a means to enhance the organization's human resource capabilities, particularly in knowledge-based organizations (Lin *et al.* 2006). Achieving a competitive advantage though M&As is a challenge, however, as many M&A initiatives fail to produce the intended results (Cartwright and Schoenberg 2006; Rees and Edwards 2009). On the other hand, empirical research indicates that combined organizations with high levels of human capital perform better than other merged organizations, which is likely due to their superior capability for inter-organizational learning and knowledge integration (Lin *et al.* 2006). Research also indicates that M&As are most successful when human capital issues resulting from the merger activity are managed effectively (Nikandrou and Papalexandris 2007; Schuler and Jackson 2001). As such, the role of HRM in facilitating M&A success by enabling human capital advantage is a topic about which there has been considerable discourse.

According to strategic HRM scholars, the primary role of HRM is to 'deliver "added-value" through the strategic development of the organization's rare, inimitable, and non-substitutable internal resources embodied—literally—in its staff' (Boselie *et al.* 2005: 71). Thus, building the organization's human capital and influencing the kind of employee behavior that constitutes a competitive advantage is a primary goal of HRM (Boxall and Steeneveld, 1999: 445). In M&As, in particular, HRM is shown to play a critical role in developing human capital and motivating the employee behaviors that are needed for M&A success. For example, training and development practices that prepare employees to respond effectively to job and technology changes imposed by M&A activity are indicated to differentiate top-performing merged organizations from their less effective counterparts (Nikandrou and Papalexandris 2007). Training can also be used to foster the self-awareness and cultural sensitivity that are necessary for successful integration of cross-national M&As (Harper and Cormeraie 1995).

HRM practices that are used to acquire and retain human capital resources, especially those 'exceptional human talent[s], latent with productive possibilities' (Boxall 1996: 81), are also necessary in M&As. High turnover rates plague many M&As, requiring sufficient selection procedures to be in place to fill important gaps (Nikandrou and Papalexandris 2007). Financial incentives and other transactional benefits could also be necessary to retain key employees, especially in the acquired organization (Schuler and Jackson 2001), although empirical findings of a positive relationship between the use of financial incentives and M&A success are inconsistent (see Nikandrou and Papalexandris 2007). Further, how selection and retention incentives are used will differ depending on the M&A strategy (Aguilera and Dencker 2004). While some M&As seek to create human capital synergies, others are aimed at reducing human capital overcapacity. In overcapacity M&As, HRM initiatives such as outplacement programs become more critical (Aguilera and Dencker 2004). In particular, programs that help individuals become more employable in the external job market could enable voluntary resignations and reduce negative feelings toward organizational change and dismissal (Baruch 2001; De Cuyper *et al.* 2008). However, even when human capital reduction is not the primary M&A strategy, layoffs in M&As are common, and the threat of redundancy and job insecurity can be very disruptive if these career concerns are not adequately addressed (Lupina-Wegener 2013; Nikandrou and Papalexandris 2007). Thus, the existence of career opportunities in the internal labor market and career management initiatives are necessary to improve employees' support for M&A initiatives as well as their retention (Appelbaum *et al.* 2002; Bourantas and Nikandrou 1998). Indeed, research indicates that providing internal career opportunities is a mark of top-performing M&As (Nikandrou and Papalexandris 2007).

Finally, HRM processes that facilitate knowledge sharing and transfer are necessary in order to realize the synergies sought in merging human capital (Aguilera and Dencker 2004; Ranft 2006; Schuler and Jackson 2001) while minimizing conflict between the combining groups (Weber and Fried 2011). Designing integration work around teams can encourage knowledge sharing by giving employees from each of the combining organizations the opportunity to work together (Cabrera and Cabrera 2007). Empirical research supports the proposition that the creation of integration teams across key areas of business, and the selection of an integration manager to oversee this activity, is often found in organizations that enjoy M&A success (Schuler and Jackson 2001). Formalized socialization programs also provide fora in which knowledge can be shared, while also facilitating the creation of shared norms that are important for successful M&A integration (Aguilera *et al.* 2006; Cabrera and Cabrera 2007). On the other hand, HRM practices aimed at appraising and rewarding knowledge sharing, while often found in successful mergers (Schuler and Jackson 2001), should be used with caution. Financial rewards in particular could be perceived as controlling, decreasing employees' intrinsic motivation for engaging in knowledge-sharing behavior (Gagné and Deci 2005). Offering rewards that are low in salience could signal to employees that knowledge sharing is valued, without appearing to be controlling (Cabrera and Cabrera 2007). Still, research extending beyond the M&A domain indicates that incentives that are provided based on group or organizational results, when coupled with internal labor markets, team building, and developmental performance appraisals (i.e., 'commitment-based HRM practices'), are better suited to facilitate knowledge exchange and application, as they create a social climate that emphasizes trust and cooperation (Collins and Smith 2006).

To summarize, the RBV provides a strategic perspective in explaining why organizations engage in M&A activity and utilize HRM practices to enable M&A success. However, while the above discussion indicates that there are some universal 'best practices' that can be applied to manage M&A integration effectively, the relationships between these practices and M&A success are not always consistent. Much of the extant research investigating the link between human capital-enhancing HRM practices and M&A success has been conducted in a single country or has made certain assumptions about the merger strategy. Research suggests, however, that both merger strategy and national culture could impact the effectiveness of certain HRM practices in generating human capital synergies and M&A performance (Aguilera and Dencker 2004; Weber and Fried 2011; Weber and Tarba 2010). Future empirical research that accounts for the interactions between HRM initiatives, M&A strategy, and national culture is therefore needed to improve our understanding of these contingencies.

Social identity theory—facilitating post-acquisition identification

M&As viewed through the lens of social identity theory draw attention to the fact that M&A success requires employees to accept a new 'post-acquisition identity' and that certain features of social context facilitate the internalization of the newly combined organization's values and goals into employees' self-concept. Social identity theory describes individuals as social beings whose self-concepts are influenced by the social groups to which they belong (Tajfel and Turner 1986), such as a work organization (Ashforth and Mael 1989; Hogg and Terry 2000). Identification with a favorable group can enhance an individual's sense of self-worth (Brown 2000). When a threat to a group's social identity is perceived, however, individuals are likely to try to protect their group identity in order to maintain their positive self-concept (Tajfel *et al.* 1971).

Perceived changes in organizational identity due to a merger (i.e., a low sense of continuity; see Rousseau 1989) are known to elicit feelings of a threatened social identity among employees (Bartels *et al.* 2006; Giessner 2011; Ullrich *et al.* 2005). This threat has been shown to trigger anxiety and stress in individuals (Buono and Bowditch 1989; Cartwright and Cooper 1993), change resistance (Jemison and Sitkin 1986), and generate organizational conflict (Marks and Mirvis 1985;

Olie 2005), all of which can negatively impact post-acquisition identification. Given that the two combining entities are usually unequal in terms of their status, it is often the case that the employees from at least one merger partner experience a discontinuity of their identity (Giessner *et al.* 2006). It is recognized that employees from organizations with higher statuses are prone to adopt an attitude of superiority and treat employees from the lower-status organization as inferior (see Hambrick and Cannella 1993; Jemison and Sitkin 1986), because they might feel threatened that the low-status organization's reputation will drag down their status (Hornsey *et al.* 2003). In contrast, employees of the low-status organization are most often dominated and feel that their position within the organization is less legitimate (Giessner *et al.* 2012). Feelings of social identity threat and distrust may be amplified by national cultural stereotyping and xenophobia in international M&As (Krug and Nigh 2001; van Knippenberg *et al.* 2002).

However, organizations that manage to have employees with stronger post-acquisition identification have been shown to increase job satisfaction (Terry *et al.* 2001; Van Dick *et al.* 2004), organizational citizenship behavior (Lipponen *et al.* 2004; Van Dick *et al.* 2004), and organizational commitment (Terry *et al.* 2001), as well as reduce turnover intentions (Van Dick *et al.* 2004). Pre-acquisition identification (Bartels *et al.* 2006; van Knippenberg *et al.* 2002), high group status, and inter-group permeability (Terry *et al.* 2001) have been shown to impact post-acquisition identification positively. As mentioned above, a sense of continuity can increase post-acquisition identification. However, as some employees are likely to experience a discontinuity of their identity (Giessner *et al.* 2006), researchers have also focused on further antecedents. A qualitative study by Ullrich *et al.* (2005) on mid-level managers during a large industrial merger found that some of the managers seemed to identify with the merged organization even when they perceived an observable change in social identity. What motivated them was a clear direction for the future and an outline of how to get there. Ullrich *et al.* termed this 'projected continuity'. Further research seemed to confirm this by showing that perceived utility or necessity of the merger can increase post-acquisition identification (Bartels *et al.* 2006; Lupina-Wegener *et al.* 2014). This provides a potential way for HRM communication efforts to increase post-acquisition identification for those employees experiencing a discontinuity of their observable identity (Giessner 2011). Thus, these findings indicate that communication efforts aimed at influencing employees' perceptions of the continuity of their identity, and the necessity and utility of the merger for the future of the organization, are important for eliciting post-acquisition identification.

In addition, perceptions that the distribution of resources and outcomes during the M&A process (i.e., distributive justice) are fair, as well as the practices used to facilitate the integration (i.e., procedural justice), represent central HRM efforts that are needed to increase and maintain post-acquisition identification during the M&A integration process (Lipponen *et al.*, 2004; Monin *et al.* 2013; see Giessner *et al.* Forthcoming for a review). Such indications resonate with the research of Bowen and Ostroff (2004), who argue that the perceived relevance and fairness of HRM initiatives are critical for creating a work climate that influences desired employee attitudes and behavior. Bowen and Ostroff's assertion builds on the assumption that perceived relevance promotes the internalization of externally sanctioned behavior into one's self-concept. Perceived relevance is said to be fostered by the prestige and ability of an influencing agent (e.g., the M&A integration manager) to provide expert knowledge, allocate resources, or apply sanctions (Bowen and Ostroff 2004). The fairness element of Bowen and Ostroff's model builds on the principles of organizational justice and research that links various justice perceptions to positive employee outcomes (see Colquitt *et al.* 2001 for a meta-analytic review of various justice perceptions and their correlates). This research generally indicates that being transparent about the rules of reward distributions and involving employees in decision-making processes can foster fairness perceptions (see also Citera and Rentsch 1993). A recent meta-analysis indicates that justice perceptions induce positive employee outcomes by fostering affective organizational commitment and other characteristic features of trust-based social exchange relationships (Colquitt *et al.* 2013). Organizational commitment is strongly related to the construct of organizational identification (Riketta 2005). Thus, there is considerable support for the suggestion that fairness perceptions could relate directly to identification with the merged organization and, in turn, provide positive post-acquisition outcomes (Lipponen *et al.* 2004; Edwards and Edwards 2012).

Acculturation—managing post-acquisition organizational culture

Organizational culture refers to a symbolic set of values, beliefs, and assumptions that are held by organizational members and guide the way in which they, and in aggregate the organization, operates (Denison 1996). While efforts to manage the organizational culture during the M&A process may concern the softer, human side of M&A integration, organizational culture can also be a strategic resource for deriving value and competitive advantage from the post-acquisition organization (Barney 1986). Indeed, research indicates that efforts that are aimed at managing post-acquisition organizational culture are critical to achieving desired M&A outcomes (Schweiger and Goulet 2005; Nahavandi and Malekzadeh 1988). Efforts aimed at hindering culture clashes between the combining entities are particularly important, as clashes are shown to negatively impact the realization of strategic M&A objectives (Cartwright and Price 2003; Very *et al.* 1996), effectiveness of system integration (Weber and Pliskin 1996), and post-acquisition stock price performance (Chatterjee *et al.* 1992). Despite its importance, however, companies do not often set a high priority on post-acquisition organizational culture management (Marks and Mirvis 2011).

Managing a post-acquisition organizational culture is not necessarily about creating a new, cohesive organizational culture (Seo and Hill 2005). In fact, four approaches to acculturation, referring to the cultural changes induced by one group or both, resulting in interactions between the two combining organizational cultures, have been identified (Marks and Mirvis 2011). 'Cultural transformation' involves the abandonment of previously held cultures and the adoption of new values and norms (Marks and Mirvis 2011). On the other hand, 'cultural pluralism' is concerned with the coexistence of cultures in the combining organizations and requires no or minimal culture changes (Marks and Mirvis 2011), 'cultural integration' involves blending together the current organizational cultures (Berry 1983), and 'cultural assimilation' refers to a unilateral process by which one culture absorbs the other (Nahavandi and Malekzadeh 1988).

There are two perspectives in the current literature concerning M&A culture management. On the one hand, scholars who value cultural differences believe that a variety of people and practices may facilitate innovative idea generation and implementation in organizations (Cox 1993). Further, the unique capabilities embedded in different organizational cultures create the positive conflicts needed for synergies and learning (Vermeulen and Barkema 2001), which, in turn, break down rigidities in the combining entities to enrich market and management knowledge (Schreyögg 2005; Olie and Verwaal 2004). Indeed, evidence from M&A research indicates that differences in style and practices can be positively related to post-M&A performance (Vermeulen 2005), sales growth (Morosini *et al.* 1998), reduced employee resistance (Larsson and Finkelstein 1999), creative problem solving, innovation (Mirvis and Marks 2003), and increased synergies (Weber *et al.* 1996). Another line of M&A research, however, looks at the 'dark side' of organizational culture differences. Scholars in this area suggest that the differences between two combining entities can lead to ethnocentrism, stereotyping, and domination of the higher-status group over the lower-status group (Sales and Mirvis 1984).

It is recognized that HRM has a role in facilitating the different approaches towards M&A acculturation (Lakshman 2011). The HR function can, for instance, help to map out potential cultural gaps between the two combining organizations (Marks and Mirvis 2011), design activities for social integration (Ranft and Lord 2002), manage the expectations of the two combining organizations to reduce acculturative stress (Marks 2003), create a safe environment for venting stress (Marks 2003), and coach leaders to align their model behaviors with the desired culture (Chatman and Cha 2003). The involvement of HRM in regards to culture management is vital to M&A success, not only in the implementation stage but also in the planning stage, when integration strategies are to be decided (Marks and Mirvis 2011).

Organization sensemaking—setting expectations via communication

Organizational sensemaking refers to a process of social construction in which organizational members interpret and explain what occurs in the environment in and through discursive interactions with others (Maitlis 2005). Sensemaking is a critical organizational activity (Weick 2005), particularly in ambiguous work contexts where people are thrust into unfamiliar roles and task settings (Weick 1993). Thus, it is understandable that sensemaking is an important activity to foster in the context of M&A integration.

The process of comparing M&A integration practices versus expectations could trigger sensemaking processes. Expectations are believed to be a directive element for sensemaking (Weick 2005). Employees constantly scan their environment, seeking information to help them form comparative judgments (Vidyarthi *et al.* 2010). The subsequent process of confirming one's expectations, which are grounded in one's own beliefs, versus what is interpreted from cues in the environment, is considered to be important for driving individual judgments of the situation and, in turn, behavior with regards to dealing with these situations (Weick 2005). Thus, the perception of M&A integration practices should elicit a comparison of perceived M&A experiences versus expectations (Oliver *et al.* 1994). The extent to which these expectations are met determines the perceived disconfirmation experience (Oliver 1977) in that a gap arises when the expectations are 'better than' or 'worse than' perceived experiences. Experiences that fall short of expectation (negative disconfirmation) foster disappointment and reduce satisfaction (Irving and Montes 2009).

Based on the above theory, setting expectations should be a crucial element in influencing employees' positive judgments of M&A integration. To this end, communication efforts aimed at conveying the strategic direction of the M&A to employees, and correcting any misconceptions, are particularly valuable. It is well recognized that effective internal organizational communication is important to achieve M&A success (Ager 2011; Armenakis and Bedeian 1999; Schweiger and Denisi 1991). Communication regarding the evolving stages and changes associated with M&As not only helps employees to form expectations of the M&A process (Hubbard and Purcell 2001), but also provides them with assurance and the ability to make informed choices on how to deal with this challenging situation (Schweiger and Denisi 1991; Seo and Hill 2005)

The involvement of the HR function in disseminating relevant communication regarding the M&A is vital not only in the implementation stage, but throughout the M&A process. Prior to the M&A, HR could inform employees about the practical plan of the M&A, future direction, and potential cultural changes associated with the new combined entity (Schweiger and Denisi 1991). Post-acquisition, HR can inform employees about the integration status and strategic direction (Jimmieson and White 2011). Various communication media can be used to share up-to-date information about what is happening with the M&A, including face-to-face communication, company newsletters, and video displays. A study by Schweiger and Denisi (1991) demonstrates that firms that provide a realistic M&A review program, in which employees are informed using different means of communication, enjoy greater employee job satisfaction and organizational commitment and reduced job uncertainty. Other evidence shows that using communication mechanisms enables employees to raise their concerns and leads to successful post-acquisition integration (Nikandrou and Papalexandris 2007; Papadakis 2005). In addition, employees are more likely to perceive a positive atmosphere about the handling of differences in organizational culture (Appelbaum *et al.* 2002) and the successful management of the integration process (Hubbard 2001).

Critical contingency factors in M&A HRM implementation

In the previous section, we reviewed how different HRM practices may facilitate integration processes in M&As using four major theoretical frameworks. Clearly, HRM plays an important role in managing M&A integration, yet the relationship between HRM and M&A performance is not straightforward (Lin *et al.* 2006). It is thus important to look at the conditions under which HRM practices are likely to be more or less helpful. In this section, therefore, we review studies that have investigated the conditions under which the use of HRM in M&As has yielded more or less successful results.

HR centrality

The extent to which the HR function is involved in M&A strategy formation, referred to as HR centrality, is considered to be a primary condition that is necessary for HR to act as an intrinsic part of the integration team (Bramson 2000). There are two dimensions that define HR centrality: the degree of involvement in the firm's strategy; and the existence of an HR strategy (Becker and Gerhart 1996). HR centrality is high when HR managers take part in the firm's strategy formulation as members of top management teams (Nikandrou and Papalexandris 2007). This enables HR managers to have the most up-to-date information about the firm's business situation and to evaluate whether and how the firm's current human capital may serve strategic goals (Bramson 2000), both of which are necessary for HR strategy formation.

HR centrality is particularly important in M&As as HR managers can serve as strategic partners in the search for and evaluation of potential M&A partners (Galpin and Herndon 2000; Schuler and Jackson 2001). In this strategic role, HR managers also help the organization to align their human resource capabilities with business needs and trends (Brooks and Dawes 1999). Later in the M&A process, HR managers can help firms to evaluate the compatibility of corporate cultures and, more importantly, to analyze alternative integration options (Bramson 2000).

HR power

Previous studies have demonstrated that HR strategy formulization is positively related to firm (Tregaskis 1997) and individual performance (Weber and Drori 2011; Marmenout 2011). Nevertheless, its effectiveness is contingent. A study by Lupina-Wegner (2013) revealed that the strength of HR power, which refers to the quality of HR strategy development and its execution effectiveness, may moderate the way in which employees of the combining organizations respond to M&A integration. HR power tends to be lower in international M&As, when there is a less clear understanding of the local context. Detrimental consequences of HR integration, such as perceived uncertainty and reduced autonomy, may emerge where there is low HR power. Supporting this, Smith *et al.* (2013) argue that the intended objective of an HR integration strategy of bringing people together may not necessarily lead to positive employee responses from the two combining firms when they see themselves as different from each other.

Ambiguity

In addition, HR initiatives set by management during M&As might not be evaluated as intended by employees (Khilji and Wang 2006; Risberg 1997). Previous studies provide evidence of discrepancies between the HR practices perceived by managers versus employees (Edgar and Geare 2005; Khilji and Wang 2006). Communication is considered an important means to spell out the meaning of HR practices and minimize potential misconceptions (Den Hartog *et al.* 2013). For instance, if organizations can get employees to see how the intended HR practices address their concerns, it is more likely that they may respond positively to M&A activity (Lupina-Wegener 2013; Giessner 2011; Ullrich *et al.* 2005).

Further, giving employees a meaningful rationale and acknowledging conflicting feelings regarding the M&A could foster employee acceptance of organizational change (Gagné *et al.* 2000). Self-determination theory and research support the proposal that the internalization of externally sanctioned activities, such as those required by M&As, occurs when individuals are placed in an 'autonomy-supportive' social context where they are provided with a meaningful rationale for engaging in the activity, they perceive that their feelings concerning the activity are acknowledged, and they have discretion with regards to when or how to carry it out (Deci *et al.* 1994).

Conclusions

While previous studies have touched upon HRM in M&As, research on this topic has been scarce, and we have lacked a systematic overview of what role HRM plays in M&A integration. We have reviewed four theoretical streams (resource-based view; social identity view; cultural view; organizational sensemaking view) in order to provide a more comprehensive overview of the role of HRM practices in M&A integration. We have also identified important contingency factors that are likely to impact the success of HRM practices in M&As. Overall, previous research provides clear evidence that the involvement of HRM in M&As at both the operational and strategic levels helps organizations to integrate and allocate resources to achieve better organizational and employee outcomes. Furthermore, our review shows that HRM plays a multifaceted role in facilitating M&A integration, and that the centrality and power of HR managers and the ambiguity of intended HRM efforts constitute critical contingencies that impact the extent to which HRM practices are likely to contribute to successful M&A integration. Based on the review, we outline

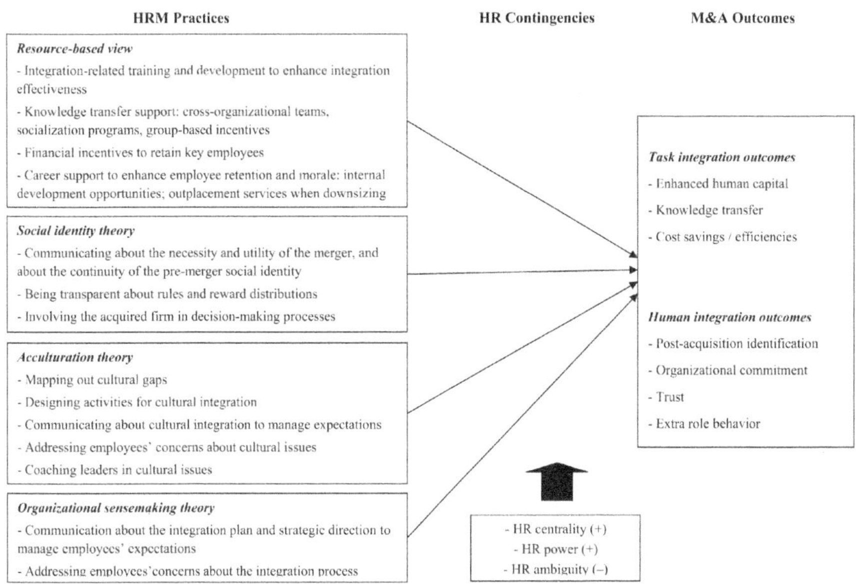

FIGURE 8.1 The role of HRM practices in M&A integration

managerial recommendations concerning the role of HRM in M&As. These recommendations, as well as the conceptual model, are depicted in Figure 8.1.

Strategic human capital management is increasingly important to gain competitive advantage in today's knowledge-based economy. A growing number of companies are using M&A as a strategic means to acquire unique human capital (e.g., Lin *et al.* 2006). Thus, organizations are advised to involve HR during both strategic M&A planning and implementation. In practice, HR managers should consider providing integration-related training and development (Nikandrou and Papalexandris 2007) to enhance integration effectiveness and make the most of the acquired human capital. Furthermore, cross-organizational teams (Cabrera and Cabrera 2007), socialization (e.g., Aguilera *et al.* 2006), and group-based knowledge transfer incentives (Collins and Smith 2006) can be effective means for enhancing knowledge transfer between the combined firms. HR managers can also address staffing needs and retention issues by providing compelling incentives to key employees. While findings on the impact of financial incentives have been mixed, our review suggests that enhancing employees' perceived career opportunities may also be effective for motivating them to stay with the merged firm (e.g., Nikandrou and Papalexandris 2007).

Organizations should also pay attention to softer, human-related factors that may influence the success of post-acquisition integration. Underestimating the potential effect of social identification may jeopardize the intended outcomes of the M&A. In the integration process, HR should function as the anchor that mitigates potential identity threats between the two combining organizations, and design action plans to tackle these threats to minimize potential negative impacts of 'us versus them' thinking. Communicating about the necessity and the benefits of the acquisition can increase the attractiveness of the merger and, hence, employee integration (Giessner 2011). Furthermore, communicating about plans to let the pre-acquisition firms' identities continue may dampen fears related to identity loss (e.g., Ullrich *et al.* 2005). Because distributive and procedural justice can influence employee identification and commitment (e.g., Lipponen *et al.* 2004), it is important that the acquiring firm is transparent concerning the distribution of key positions and rewards, and that the acquired firm is included in the decision-making process.

In addition, HR should provide strategic guidance to organizations and managers on how they can reach a desirable cultural end state. More specifically, HR managers should help to identify and map out cultural gaps (Marks and Mirvis 2011). Based on this, HR managers can design integration activities that facilitate cultural integration, such as seminars where the partner firms' cultures are discussed, including which parts of their cultures should be preserved and which should be changed (e.g., Marks and Mirvis 2011; Schweiger and Goulet 2005). Informal socialization events and opportunities to get together outside of the work environment can also help employees understand the partner firm's unwritten norms and beliefs (e.g., Schweiger and Goulet 2005). It is also important that HR managers communicate the meaning of the M&A and desired post-acquisition organizational culture to employees, in order to manage expectations and reduce anxiety related to cultural change (Marks 2003). Communication should run both ways, though, as employees' concerns need to be heeded and addressed (Marks 2003). The HR function can play an important role in facilitating both types of communication and in involving employees in the cultural change process. However, employees often turn to their direct supervisors for information and support. Therefore, it is critical that leaders receive training and coaching in how to deal with potential cross-cultural issues (Chatman and Cha 2003).

During integration, organizational members create their own meanings of the acquisition, its aims, and potential outcomes. It can be difficult to impact how employees make sense of the acquisition, as organizational sensemaking is influenced by personal political motives (Vaara 2002), and information presented by the merging firms' managers (Riad 2005, 2007; Vaara 2002), the media (Riad and Vaara 2011; Riad *et al.* 2012), and peers (Marmenout 2011). Nevertheless, the HR function can try to help employees make sense of the acquisition by engaging in frequent two-way communication concerning the acquisition goals, plans, and processes, as well as changes along the way (e.g., Hubbard and Purcell 2001).

HR has the potential to play an important and multifaceted role in M&A integration. However, in practice, this is easier said than done, as the implementation of HR practices in M&As is complex and contingent upon the overall role of HR in the merging firms. In order to add strategic value, it is crucial that the HR function occupies a central position in the acquiring firm prior to the acquisition (e.g., Bramson 2000). HR is likely to have a stronger impact on M&A outcomes when HR's power is high (Weber and Drori 2011)—that is, when HR practices and processes are well developed, formalized, and clearly communicated. In contrast, ambiguity and different interpretations (Risberg 1997) of HR practices can make their implementation harder and the outcomes less predictable. HR managers should therefore pay attention to communicating to employees about the intended HR strategy for integrating the merging firms.

In addition to the managerial recommendations discussed above, this study has important theoretical implications. Depending on the chosen theoretical perspective, it is possible to identify distinct, critical HRM practices that are likely to aid M&A integration. Taken together, the four theoretical perspectives applied in this review show that HRM plays a multifaceted role in M&As. The HR function plays an important role in achieving greater strategic task integration by optimizing the use of human capital. In addition, the HR function can act as a bridge between managers and employees and between the merging organizations, to help manage the softer human side of integration by providing information and support. This highlights the strategic and socio-cultural role of HRM, and points to the need for combining several theoretical perspectives in order to gain a comprehensive understanding of the phenomenon under study. In this review, we also identified critical contingencies that are likely to impact the role of HRM in M&As. How much value HRM can add to M&As is likely to depend on how central, powerful, and clear (or ambiguous) the HR function and its activities are from the outset. We therefore call for future research to examine the impact of these contingencies on the role of HRM in M&As.

While this study has provided a systematic and comprehensive review of the role of HRM in M&A integration based on four theoretical research streams, it has not elaborated on the inter-linkages between these streams. Such links should be explored in future research. For instance, social identities (Zaheer *et al.* 1998) and employee sensemaking (Riad 2005; Vaara 2002) are often influenced by national and organizational cultures. Therefore, cultural changes brought about by the acquisition are likely to trigger identity and sensemaking processes among organizational members. It would therefore be interesting to examine how and when HR managers should get involved in order to help organizational members navigate through these softer integration issues. In addition, there may be a balance between HR managers having a strategic task-oriented role in M&A integration versus accounting for more human aspects. In order to be seen as strategically relevant, HR managers must understand the needs of the business and the interests of top-level managers. However, this strategic focus may steer HR away from softer employee needs 'on the ground'. Future studies could examine whether such trade-offs exist, and how the degree of HR specialization (versus having a broader role) impacts M&A integration success in different types of acquisitions. Finally, many empirical studies reviewed in this chapter are based on qualitative case studies that have taken a specific and narrow focus on certain HR aspects. Future studies should draw on larger empirical samples in order to test the impact of the outlined HRM practices on M&A outcomes. It is also important to examine under which contingencies different HRM practices are likely to be more or less useful. Finally, while we have suggested three critical contingencies (HR centrality, HR power, HRM practice ambiguity), future studies could consider other moderators, such as acquisition characteristics (e.g., acquisition aims, acquisition experience, previous relationship between the merging firms) and industry characteristics (e.g., market turbulence).

To conclude, we set out to provide a systematic and comprehensive review of the role of HRM in M&A integration. We reviewed four theoretical research streams (resource-based view; social identity view; cultural view; organizational sensemaking view), and identified critical contingency factors that may impact the success of implementing HRM practices in M&As. We hope that this review has provided inspiration for future research that aims to uncover how HR can add value in M&As.

References

Ager, D., 'The emotional impact and behavioral consequences of post-M&A integration: an ethnographic case study in the software industry'. *Journal of Contemporary Ethnography* 40, 2011, 199–230.

Aguilera, R.V. and J.C. Dencker, 'The role of human resource management in cross-border mergers and acquisitions'. *International Journal of Human Resource Management* 15, 2004, 1355–1370.

Aguilera, R.V., J.C. Dencker and Z.Y. Yalabik, 'Institutions and organizational socialization: connectivity in the human side of post-merger and acquisition integration'. In A.Y. Lewin, S.T. Cavusgil, T.M. Holt and D.A. Griffith (Eds.), *Thought leadership in advancing international business research*, Basingstoke: Palgrave Macmillan, 2006, pp. 153–189.

Almor, T., S.Y. Tarba and H. Benjamini, 'Unmasking integration challenges: the case of Biogal's acquisition by Teva Pharmaceutical Industries'. *International Studies of Management and Organization* 39, 2009, 33–53.

Appelbaum, S.H., A. Heather and B.T. Sharipo, 'Career management in information technology: a case study'. *Career Development International* 7, 2002, 142–158.

Armenakis, A.A. and A.G. Bedeian, 'Organizational change: a review of theory and research in the 1990s'. *Journal of Management* 25, 1999, 293–315.

Ashforth, B.E. and F. Mael, 'Social identity theory and the organization'. *Academy of Management Review* 14, 1989, 20–39.

Barney, J.B., 'Organizational culture: can it be a source of competitive advantage?' *Academy of Management Review* 11, 1986, 656–665.

Barney, J.B., 'Firm resources and sustained competitive advantage'. *Journal of Management* 17, 1991, 99.

Bartels, J.D., R. Jong, M. Jong and A. Pruyn, 'Organizational identification during a merger: determinants of employees' expected identification with the new organization'. *British Journal of Management* 17, 2006, 49–67.

Baruch, Y., 'Employability: a substitute for loyalty'. *Human Resource Development International* 4, 2001, 543–566.

Becker, B. and B. Gerhart, 'The impact of human resource management on organizational performance: progress and prospects'. *Academy of Management Journal* 39, 1996, 779–801.

Berry, J.W., 'Acculturation: a comparative analysis of alternative forms'. *Perspectives in Immigrant and Minority Education* 5, 1983, 66–77.

Birkinshaw, J., H. Bresman and L. Håkanson, 'Managing the post-acquisition integration process: how the human integration and task integration processes interact to foster value creation'. *Journal of Management Studies* 37, 2000, 395–425.

Boselie, P., G. Dietz and C. Boon, 'Commonalities and contradictions in HRM and performance research'. *Human Resource Management Journal* 15, 2005, 67–94.

Bourantas, D. and I. Nikandrou, 'Modelling post-acquisition employee behavior: typology and determining factors'. *Employee Relations* 20, 1998, 73–91.

Bowen, D.E. and C. Ostroff, 'Understanding HRM–firm performance linkages: the role of the "strength" of the HRM system'. *Academy of Management Review* 29, 2004, 203–221.

Boxall, P., 'The strategic HRM Debate and the resource-based view of the firm'. *Human Resource Management Journal* 6, 1996, 59–75.

Boxall, P. and M. Steeneveld, 'Human resource strategy and competitive advantage: a longitudinal study of engineering consultancies'. *Journal of Management Studies* 36, 1999, 443–463.

Bramson, R.N., 'HR's role in mergers and acquisitions'. *Training and Development* 54, 2000, 59.

Brooks, I. and J. Dawes, 'Merger as a trigger for cultural change in the retail financial services sector'. *Services Industries Journal* 19, 1999, 194–206.

Brown, R., 'Social identity theory: past achievements, current problems and future challenges'. *European Journal of Social Psychology* 30, 2000, 745–778.

Bryson, J., 'Managing HRM risk in a merger'. *Employee Relations* 25, 2003, 14–30.

Buono, A.F., and J.L. Bowditch, *The human side of mergers and acquisitions*, San Francisco, CA: Jossey-Bass, 1989.

Cabrera, E.F. and A. Cabrera, ' Fostering knowledge sharing thorugh people management practices'. *International Journal of Human Resource Management* 16, 2007, 720–735.

Calori, R., M. Lubatkin and P. Very, 'Control mechanisms in cross-border acquisitions: an international comparison'. *Organization Studies* 15, 1994, 361–379.

Cartwright, S. and C.D. Cooper, 'The psychological impact of mergers and acquisitions on the individual: a study of building society managers'. *Human Relations* 46, 1993, 327–347.

Cartwright, S. and F. Price, 'Managerial preferences in international merger and acquisition partners revisited: how are they influenced?' *Advances in Mergers and Acquisitions* 2, 2003, 81–95.

Cartwright, S. and R. Schoenberg, 'Thirty years of mergers and acquisitions research: research advances and future opportunities'. *British Journal of Management* 17, 2006, 1–5.

Chatman, J. and S. Cha, 'Leading by leveraging culture'. *California Management Review* 45, 2003, 14.

Chatterjee, S., M. Lubatkin, H. Schweiger, M. David and Y.Weber, 'Cultural differences and shareholder value: explaining the variability in the performance of related mergers'. *Strategic Management Journal* 13, 1992, 319–334.

Chaudhuri, S., 'Managing human resources to capture capabilities: case studies in high-technology acquisitions'. In G.K. Stahl and M.E. Mendenhall (Eds.), *Mergers and acquisitions: managing culture and human resources*, Stanford, CA: Stanford University Press, 2005, pp. 277–301.

Chaudhuri, S. and B. Tabrizi, 'Capturing the real value in high-tech acquisitions'. *Harvard Business Review* 77, 1999, 123–130.

Child, J., D. Faulkner and R. Pitkethly, 'Foreign direct investment in the UK 1985–1994: the impact on domestic management practice'. *Journal of Management Studies* 37, 2000, 141–166.

Citera, M. and J.R. Rentsch, 'Is there justice in organizational acquisitions? The role of distributive and procedural fairness in corporate acquisitions'. In R. Cropanzano (Ed.), *Justice in the workplace: approaching fairness in human resource management*, Hillsdale, NJ: Lawrence Erlbaum, 1993, pp. 211–230.

Collins, C.J. and K.G. Smith, 'Knowledge exchange and combination: the role of human resource practices in the performance of high-technology firms'. *Academy of Management Journal* 49, 2006, 544–560.

Colman, H.L. and R. Lunnan, 'Organizational identification and serendipitous value creation in post-acquisition integration'. *Journal of Management* 37, 2011, 839–860.

Colquitt, J.A., D.E. Conlon, M.J. Wesson, C.O. Porter and K.Y. Ng, 'Justice at the millennium: a meta-analytic review of 25 years of organizational justice research'. *Journal of Applied Psychology* 86, 2001, 425–445.

Colquitt, J.A., B.A. Scott, J.B. Rodell, D.M. Long, C.P. Zapata, D.E. Conlon and M.J. Wesson, 'Justice at the millennium, a decade later: a meta-analytic test of social exchange and affect-based perspectives'. *Journal of Applied Psychology* 98, 2013, 199–236.

Cox, T., *Cultural diversity in organizations: theory, research and practice*, San Francisco, CA: Berrett-Koehler, 1993.

Deci, E.L., H. Eghrari, B.C. Patrick and D.R Leone, 'Facilitating internalization: the self-determination theory perspective'. *Journal of Personality* 62, 1994, 119–142.

Deci, E.L. and R.M. Ryan, 'The "what" and "why" of goal pursuits: human needs and the self-determination of behavior'. *Psychological Inquiry* 11, 2000, 227–268.

De Cuyper, N., C. Bernhard-Oettel, E. Berntson, H.D. Witte and B. Alarco, 'Employability and employees' well-being: mediation by job insecurity'. *Applied Psychology* 57, 2008, 488–509.

Den Hartog, D.N., C. Boon, R.M. Verburg and M.A. Croon, 'HRM, communication, satisfaction, and perceived performance: a cross-level test'. *Journal of Management* 39, 2013, 1637–1665.

Denison, D.R., 'What is the difference between organizational culture and organizational climate? A native's point of view on a decade of paradigm wars'. *Academy of Management Review* 21, 1996, 619–654.

Edgar, F. and A. Geare, 'HRM practice and employee attitudes: different measures – different results'. *Personnel Review* 34, 2005, 534–549.

Edwards, M.R. and T. Edwards, 'Procedural justice and identification with the acquirer: the moderating effects of job continuity, organisational identity strength and organisational similarity'. *Human Resource Management Journal* 22, 2012, 109–128.

Faulkner, D., S. Teerikangas and R.J. Joseph, *The handbook of mergers and acquisitions*, Oxford: Oxford University Press, 2012.

Gagné, M. and E.L. Deci, 'Self-determination theory and work motivation'. *Journal of Organizational Behavior* 26, 2005, 331–362.

Gagné, M., R. Koestner and M. Zuckerman 'Facilitating acceptance of organizational change: the importance of self-determination'. *Journal of Applied Social Psychology* 30, 2000, 1843–1852.

Galpin, T.J. and M. Herndon, *The complete guide to mergers and acquisitions: process tools to support M&A integration at every level*, San Francisco, CA: John Wiley & Sons, 2000.

Giessner, S.R., 'Is the merger necessary? The interactive effect of perceived necessity and sense of continuity on post-merger identification'. *Human Relations* 64, 2011, 1079–1098.

Giessner, S.R., K.E. Horton and S.I.W. Humborstad, 'Identity management during organizational mergers: empirical insights and practical advice'. *Social Issues and Policy Review* Forthcoming.

Giessner, S.R., T. Viki, S. Otten, D.J Terry and S. Tauber, 'The challenge of merging: merger patterns, premerger status, and merger support'. *Personality and Social Psychology Bulletin* 32, 2006, 339–352.

Giessner, S.R., J. Ullrich and R. Van Dick, *A social identity analysis of mergers and acquisitions*, Oxford: Oxford University Press, 2012.

Gomes, E., D. Angwin, Y. Weber and S.Y. Tarba, 'Critical success factors through the mergers and acquisitions process: revealing pre- and post-M&A connections for improved performance'. *Thunderbird International Business Review* 55, 2013, 13–36.

Graebner, M.E., 'Momentum and serendipidity: how acquired firm leaders create value in the integration of technology firms'. *Strategic Management Journal* 25, 2004, 751–777.

Graebner, M.E. and K.M. Eisenhardt, 'The other side of the story: acquisition as courtship and governance as syndicate in entrepreneurial firms'. *Administrative Science Quarterly* 49, 2004, 366–403.

Haleblian, J., C.E. Devers, G. McNamara, M.E. Carpenter and R.B. Davison, 'Taking stock of what we know about mergers and acquisitions: a review and research agenda'. *Journal of Management* 35, 2009, 469–502.

Hambrick, D.C. and A.A. Cannella, 'Relative standing: a framework for understanding departures of acquired executives'. *Academy of Management Journal* 36, 1993, 733–762.

Harding, D. and T. Rouse, 'Human due diligence'. *Harvard Business Review* 85, 2007, 124–131.

Harper, J. and S Cormeraie, 'Mergers, marriages and after: how can training help?' *Journal of European Industrial Training* 19, 1995, 24–29.

Haspeslagh, P. and D.B. Jemison, *Managing acquisitions: creating value through corporate renewal*, New York: The Free Press, 1991.

Hogan, E.A. and L. Overmyer-Day, 'The psychology of mergers and acquisitions'. *International Review of Industrial and Organizational Psychology* 9, 1994, 247–247.

Hogg, M.A. and D.I. Terry, 'Social identity and self-categorization processes in organizational contexts'. *Academy of Management Review* 25, 2000, 121–140.

Hornsey, M.J., E. van Leeuwen and W. Van Santen, 'Dragging down and dragging up: how relative group status affects responses to common fate'. *Group Dynamics: Theory, Research, and Practice* 7, 2003, 275.

Hubbard, N., *Acquisition strategy and implementation*, West Lafayette, IN: Purdue University Press, 2001.

Hubbard, N. and J. Purcell, J. 'Managing employee expectations during acquisitions'. *Human Resource Management Journal* 11, 2001, 17–33.

Irving, P.G. and S.D. Montes, 'Met expectations: the effects of expected and delivered inducements on employee satisfaction'. *Journal of Occupational and Organizational Psychology* 82, 2009, 431–451.

Jemison, D.B. and S.B. Sitkin, 'Corporate acquisitions: a process perspective'. *Academy of Management Review* 11, 1986, 145–163.

Jimmieson, N.L. and K.M White, 'Predicting employee intentions to support organizational change: an examination of identification processes during a re-brand'. *British Journal of Social Psychology* 50, 2011, 331–341.

Khilji, S.E. and X. Wang, '"Intended" and "implemented" HRM: the missing linchpin in strategic human resource management research'. *International Journal of Human Resource Management* 17, 2006, 1171–1189.

King, D.R., D.R. Dalton, C.M. Daily and J.G. Covin, 'Meta-analyses of post-acquisition performance: indications of unidentified moderators'. *Strategic Management Journal* 25, 2004, 187–200.

Krug, J.A. and D. Nigh, 'Executive perceptions in foreign and domestic acquisitions: an analysis of foreign ownership and its effect on executive fate'. *Journal of World Business* 36, 2001, 85–105.

Lakshman, C., 'Postacquisition cultural integration in mergers & acquisitions: a knowledge-based approach'. *Human Resource Management* 50, 2011, 605–623.

Larsson, R. and S. Finkelstein, 'Integrating strategic, organizational, and human resource perspectives on mergers and acquisitions: a case survey of synergy realization'. *Organization Science* 10, 1999, 1–26.

Lin, W., S.C. Hung and P.C. Li, 'Mergers and acquisitions as a human resource strategy – evidence from US banking firms'. *International Journal of Manpower* 27, 2006, 126–142.

Lipponen, J., M.E. Olkkonen and M. Moilanen, 'Perceived procedural justice and employee responses to an organizational merger'. *European Journal of Work and Organizational Psychology* 13, 2004, 391–413.

Lubatkin, M., R. Calori, P. Very and J.F. Veiga, 'Managing mergers across borders: a two-nation exploration of a nationally bound administrative heritage'. *Organization Science* 9, 1998, 670–684.

Lupina-Wegener, A.A., 'Human resource integration in subsidiary mergers and acquisitions: evidence from Poland'. *Journal of Organizational Change Management* 26, 2013, 286–304.

Lupina-Wegener, A., F. Drzensky, J. Ullrich and R. Van Dick, 'Focusing on the bright tomorrow? A longitudinal study of organizational identification and projected continuity in a corporate merger'. *British Journal of Social Psychology* 53, 2014, 752–772.

Maitlis, S., 'The social processes of organizational sensemaking'. *Academy of Management Journal* 48, 2005, 21–49.

Marks, M.L., *Charging back up the hill: workplace recovery after mergers, acquistions, and downsizing*. San Francisco, CA: Jossey-Bass, 2003.

Marks, M.L. and P. Mirvis, 'Merger syndrome: stress and uncertainty', *Mergers and Acquisitions*, 1985, 50–55.

Marks, M.L. and P.H. Mirvis, 'Making mergers and acquisitions work: strategic and psychological preparation'. *Academy of Management Executive* 15, 2001, 80–92.

Marks, M.L. and P. H. Mirvis, 'A framework for the human resources role in managing culture in mergers and acquistions'. *Human Resource Management* 50, 2011, 859–877.

Marmenout, K., 'Peer interaction in mergers: evidence of collective rumination'. *Human Resource Management* 50, 2011, 783–808.

Mirvis, P.H. and M.L. Marks, *Managing the merger: making it work*, Washington, DC: Beard Books, 2003.

Monin, P., N. Noorderhaven, E. Vaara and D. Kroon, 'Giving sense to and making sense of justice in postmerger integration'. *Academy of Management Journal* 56, 2013, 256–284.

Morosini, P., S. Shane and H. Singh, 'National cultural distance and cross-border acquisition performance'. *Journal of International Business Studies* 29, 1998, 137–158.

Nahavandi, A. and A.R. Malekzadeh, 'Acculturation in mergers and acquisitions'. *Academy of Management Review* 13, 1988, 79–90.

Nikandrou, I. and N. Papalexandris, 'The impact of M&A experience on strategic HRM practices and organisational effectiveness: evidence from Greek firms'. *Human Resource Management Journal* 17, 2007, 155–177.

Nordhaug, O. and K. Gronhaug, 'Competences as resources in firms'. *International Journal of Human Resource Management* 5, 1994, 89–106.

Olie, R., 'Integration processes in cross-border mergers: lessons learned from Dutch–German mergers'. *Mergers and Acquisitions: Managing Culture and Human Resources*, 2005, 323–350.

Olie, R. and E. Verwaal, 'The effects of cultural distance and host country experience on the performance of cross-border acquisitions'. Paper presented at Academy of Management Conference, New Orleans, LA, 2004.

Oliver, R.L., 'Effect of expectation and disconfirmation on postexposure product evaluations: an alternative interpretation'. *Journal of Applied Psychology* 62, 1977, 480.

Oliver, R.L., P.V. Balakrishnan and B. Barry. 'Outcome satisfaction in negotiation: a test of expectancy disconfirmation'. *Organizational Behavior and Human Decision Processes* 60, 1994, 252–275.

Pablo, A., 'Determinants of acquisition integration level: a decision-making perspective'. *Academy of Management Journal* 37, 1994, 803–836.

Papadakis, V.M., 'The role of broader context and the communication program in merger and acquisition implementation success'. *Management Decision* 43, 2005, 236–255.

Paruchuri, S., A. Nerkar and D.C. Hambrick, 'Acquisition integration and productivity losses in the technical core: disruption of inventors in acquired companies'. *Organization Science* 17, 2006, 545–562.

Penrose, E., *The theory of the growth of the firm*, Oxford: Oxford University Press, 1959.

Prahalad, C.K. and G. Hamel, 'The core competence of the corporation'. *Harvard Business Review* 68, 1990, 79–91.

Puranam, P., H. Singh and M. Zollo, 'Organizing for innovation: managing the coordination–autonomy dilemma in technology acquisitions'. *Academy of Management Journal* 49, 2006, 263–280.

Puranam, P. and K. Srikanth, 'What they know vs. what they do: how acquirers leverage technology acquisitions'. *Strategic Management Journal* 28, 2007, 805–825.

Ranft, A.L., 'Knowledge preservation and transfer during post-acquisition integration'. *Advances in Mergers and Acquisitions* 5, 2006, 51–67.

Ranft, A.L. and M.D. Lord, 'Acquiring new technologies and capabilities: a grounded model of acquisition implementation'. *Organization Science* 13, 2002, 420–441.

Rees, C. and T. Edwards, 'Management strategy and HR in international mergers: choice, constraint and pragmatism'. *Human Resource Management Journal* 19, 2009, 24–39.

Riad, S., 'The power of "organizational culture" as a discursive formation in merger integration'. *Organization Studies* 26, 2005, 1529–1554.

Riad, S., 'Of mergers and cultures: what happened to "shared values and joint assumptions"?' *Journal of Organizational Change Management* 20, 2007, 26–43.

Riad, S. and E. Vaara, 'Varieties of national metonymy in media accounts of international mergers and acquisitions'. *Journal of Management Studies* 48, 2011, 737–771.

Riad, S., E. Vaara and N. Zhang, 'The intertextual production of international relations in mergers and acquisitions'. *Organization Studies* 33, 2012, 121–148.

Riketta, M., 'Organizational identification: a meta-analysis'. *Journal of Vocational Behavior* 66, 2005, 358–384.

Risberg, A., 'Ambiguity and communication in cross-cultural acquisitions'. *Leadership and Organization Development Journal* 18, 1997, 257–266.

Rousseau, D.M., 'Psychological and implied contracts in organizations'. *Employee Responsibilities and Rights Journal* 2, 1989, 121–139.

Sales, A.L. and P.H. Mirvis, 'When cultures collide: issues in acquisition'. In J.R. Kimberly and R. Quinn (Eds.), *Managing Organizational Transitions*, Homewood, IL: Irwin, 1984, pp. 107–133.

Sarala, R.M., P. Junni, C.L. Cooper and S.Y. Tarba, 'A socio-cultural perspective on knowledge transfer in mergers and acquisitions'. *Journal of Management* Forthcoming.

Schreyögg, G., 'The role of corporate culture diversity in integrating mergers and acquisitions'. In G. Stahl and M.E. Mendenhall (Eds.), *Mergers and acquisitions: managing culture and human resources*. Stanford, CA: Stanford University Press, 2005, pp. 108–126.

Schuler, R.S. and S.E. Jackson, 'HR issues and activities in mergers and acquisitions'. *European Management Journal* 19, 2001, 239–253.

Schweiger, D.M. and A.S. Denisi, 'Communication with employees following a merger: a longitudinal field experiment'. *Academy of Management Journal* 34, 1991, 110–135.

Schweiger, D.M. and P.K. Goulet, 'Facilitating acquisition integration through deep-level cultural learning interventions: a longitudinal field experiment'. *Organization Studies* 26, 2005, 1477–1499.

Schweizer, L., 'Organizational integration of acquired biotech companies into pharmaceutical companies: the need for a hybrid approach'. *Academy of Management Journal* 48, 2005, 1051–1074.

Seo, M.G. and N.H. Hill, 'Understanding the human side of merger and acquisition: an integrative framework'. *Journal of Applied Behavioral Science* 41, 2005, 422–443.

Smith, P., J.V. Da Cunha, A. Giangreco, A. Vasilaki and A. Carugati, 'The threat of dis-identification for HR practices: an ethnographic study of a merger'. *European Management Journal* 31, 2013, 308–321.

Spedale, S., F.A.J. van den Bosch and H.W. Volberda, 'Preservation and dissolution of the target firm's embedded ties in acquisitions'. *Organization Studies* 28, 2007, 1169–1196.

Stahl, G.K. and A. Voigt, 'Do cultural differences matter in mergers and acquisitions? A tentative model for examination'. *Organization Science* 19, 2008, 160–176.

Tajfel, H., M.G. Billig, R.P. Bundy and C. Flament, 'Social categorization and intergroup behaviour'. *European Journal of Social Psychology* 1, 1971, 149–178.

Tajfel, H. and J.C. Turner, 'The social identity theory of intergroup behaviour'. In W. G. Austin and S. Worchel (Eds.), *Psychology of intergroup relations*, 2nd edn. Chicago: Nelson-Hall, 1986, pp. 7–24.

Terry, D.D.J., V.J. Callan and G. Sartori, 'Employee adjustment to an organizational merger: stress, coping and intergroup differences'. *Stress Medicine* 12, 1996, 105–122.

Terry, D.J., C.J. Carey and V.J. Callan, 'Employee adjustment to an organizational merger: an intergroup perspective'. *Personality and Social Psychological Bulletin* 27, 2001, 67–280.

Thanos, I. and V. Papadakis, *Unbundling acquisition performance: how do they perform and how can this be measured?*, Oxford : Oxford University Press, 2012.

Tregaskis, O., 'The role of national context and HR strategy in shaping training and development practice in French and UK organizations'. *Organization Studies* 18, 1997, 839–857.

Ullrich, J., J. Wieseke and R.V. Dick, 'Continuity and change in mergers and acquisitions: a social identity case study of a German industrial merger'. *Journal of Management Studies* 42, 2005, 1549–1569.

Vaara, E., 'On the discursive construction of success–failure in narratives of post-merger integration'. *Organization Studies* 23, 2002, 211–243.

Van Dick, R., O. Christ, J. Stellmacher *et al.*, 'Should I stay or should I go? Explaining turnover intentions with orgainzational identification and job satisfaction'. *British Journal of Management* 15, 2004, 351–360.

van Knippenberg, D., B. van Knippenberg, L. Monden and F. de Lima, 'Organizational identification after a merger: a social identity perspective'. *British Journal of Social Psychology* 41, 2002, 233–252.

Vermeulen, F., 'How acquisitions can revitalize companies'. *Sloan Management Review* 46, 2005, 44–51.

Vermeulen, F. and H. Barkema, 'Learning through acquisitions'. *Academy of Management Journal* 44, 2001, 457–476.

Very, P., M. Lubatkin and R. Calori, 'A cross-national assessment of acculturative stress in recent European mergers'. *International Studies of Management and Organization* 26, 1996, 59–86.

Vidyarthi, P.R., R.C. Liden, S. Anand, B. Erdogan and S. Ghosh, ' Where do I stand? Examining the effects of leader–member exchange social comparison on employee work behaviors'. *Journal of Applied Psychology* 95, 2010, 849.

Weber, Y. and I. Drori, 'Integrating organizational and human behavior perspectives on mergers and acquisitions'. *International Studies of Management and Organization* 41, 2011, 76–95.

Weber, Y. and Y. Fried, 'The role of HR practices in managing culture clash during the postmerger integration process'. *Human Resource Management* 50, 2011, 565–570.

Weber, Y. and N. Pliskin, 'The effects of information systems integration and organizational culture on a firm's effectiveness'. *Information and Management* 30, 1996, 81–90.

Weber, Y., O. Shenkar and A. Raveh, 'National and corporate cultural fit in mergers/acquisitions: an exploratory study'. *Management Science* 42, 1996, 1215–1227.

Weber, Y. and S.Y. Tarba, 'Human resource practices and performance of mergers and acquisitions in Israel'. *Human Resource Management Review* 20, 2010, 203–211.

Weber, Y. and S.Y. Tarba, 'Exploring integration approach in related mergers'. *International Journal of Organizational Analysis* 19, 2011, 202–221.

Weber, Y., S.Y. Tarba and A. Reichel, 'International mergers and acquisitions performance revisited: the role of cultural distance and post-acquisition integration approach implementation'. *Advances in Mergers and Acquisitions* 8, 2009, 1–18.

Weber, Y., S.Y. Tarba and A. Reichel, 'A model of the influence of culture on integration approaches and international mergers and acquisitions performance'. *International Studies of Management and Organization* 41, 2011, 9–24.

Weick, K.E., 'The collapse of sensemaking in organizations: the Mann Gulch disaster'. *Administrative Science Quarterly* 38, 1993, 628–652.

Weick, K.E., K.M. Sutcliffe and D. Obstfeld, 'Organizing and the process of sensemaking'. *Organization Science* 16, 2005, 409–421.

Wernerfelt, B., 'A resource-based view of the firm'. *Strategic Management Journal* 5, 1984, 171–180.

Zaheer, A., B. McEvily and V. Perrone, 'Does trust matter? Exploring the effects of interorganizational and interpersonal trust on performance'. *Organization Science* 9, 1998, 141–159.

9

HOW DO COMMUNICATION AND CULTURAL DIFFERENCES EXPLAIN POST-MERGER IDENTIFICATION?

Evidence from two merged dairy firms

David Kroon

Introduction

Organizations frequently use mergers and acquisitions (M&As) as a strategy to expand and improve their competitive advantage (Makri, Hitt and Lane, 2010). However, M&As often fail to meet their objectives (Dyer, Kale and Singh, 2004; Seo and Hill, 2005). Scholars increasingly attribute poor M&A performance to issues that arise during the integration phase (Cording, Christmann and King, 2008; Epstein, 2005). Birkinshaw (1999: 34; italics added), for example, concludes that 'human integration', concerned primarily with 'the process of generating satisfaction – and ultimately *a shared identity* – among the employees of the merged company', is an important determinant of overall M&A success.

The extent to which employees of the merged company identify with the newly merged organization (i.e. post-merger identification) influences employees' willingness to strive for organizational goals, to stay with the organization, to spread a positive image of the organization and to cooperate with other organizational members (Bartels, Douwes, De Jong and Pruyn, 2006). Especially in times of considerable organizational restructuring (such as during post-merger integration), these aspects are of crucial importance. In this study, we therefore aim to provide more insight into the factors that explain the level of post-merger identification.

Although research on post-merger identification has flourished (Van Dick, Ullrich and Tissington, 2006; Van Knippenberg, Van Knippenberg, Monden and De Lima, 2002; Zaheer, Schomaker and Genc, 2003), several questions remain unanswered. First, we know little about how different pre-merger organizational cultures affect post-merger identification. Both researchers and practitioners frequently refer to cultural differences as causes of disappointing outcomes in domestic and international cooperation (Larsson and Lubatkin, 2001). Previous research has already illustrated that organizational identification (Ullrich and

Van Dick, 2007) and organizational culture (Teerikangas, 2007) are related, and that both are of crucial importance in post-merger integration times (Kroon, Noorderhaven and Leufkens, 2009). However, until now cultural differences and post-merger identification have been mostly studied in isolation from each other, or, at the other extreme, the concepts have been used interchangeably (Kroon *et al.*, 2009: 22).

Second, we need to know more about the role of employee communication in explaining the relationship between cultural differences and post-merger identification. Prior studies have identified that intensive communication is the key to a successful integration of two clashing cultures (DiGeorgio, 2002). Furthermore, employee communication has been shown to influence (expected) post-merger identification (Bartels *et al.*, 2006). But although scholars agree on the crucial importance of proper communication in the post-merger integration process (Clampitt, DeKoch and Cashman, 2000; Epstein, 2004; Sonenshein, 2010), the literature on its specific influence has remained scarce (Allatta and Singh, 2011).

By conducting a large-scale study of two dairy firms in the Netherlands, we contribute to the literature on 'human factors' in post-merger integration in several ways. First, our empirical findings show that both the perceived quality of communicated information ('merger communication') and the general communication climate (Bartels *et al.*, 2006; Bartels, Pruyn, De Jong and Joustra, 2007) are important determinants of post-merger identification. Moreover, we find that the perceived communication climate mediates the relationship between merger communication and post-merger identification. Second, we observe that merger communication moderates the negative relation between perceived cultural differences and post-merger identification. Finally, our study provides managers and practitioners engaged in M&As with some specific knowledge on how communication may help to make M&As more successful.

The remainder of this paper is organized as follows. The section below develops a theoretical framework, introduces the key variables of the study, and advances testable hypotheses. The next section describes our research design and the operationalization of the constructs. We test our hypotheses using questionnaire data from a large-scale merger between two dairy firms in the Netherlands. The chapter concludes with a discussion of the study's main theoretical and managerial implications as well as suggestions for future research opportunities.

Theoretical background

Post-merger identification and cultural differences

Social identification reflects the extent to which the self is defined in collective terms (Tajfel and Turner, 1986). It implies a 'merging' of the self and the group in a psychological sense. However, not all social groups are emotionally significant all the time. Self-categorization theory, seen by Hogg and Terry (2000) as a development of social identity theory, articulates the principles according to which different social identities become salient in a given situation (Turner, Hogg, Oakes, Reicher and Wetherell, 1987). The core element of self-categorization theory, according to Van Dick *et al.* (2006), is that an individual's social identity is not uniformly predictive of his or her behaviour. In other words, which aspect of one's identity is influential in a given situation is dependent on the context (e.g. a merger or an acquisition) and the group's salience in that context.

Applying social identity theory to an M&A context, we can define post-merger identification as the perception of oneness with or belongingness to the newly merged organization, where the individual defines him- or herself in terms of this organization (Mael and Ashforth, 1992). According to social identity theory and self-categorization theory, M&As may be perceived as a threat to the stability and continuation of employees' pre-merger organizational identities (Bartels *et al.*, 2006). There are also practical examples of mergers that failed because of 'us versus them' dynamics that prevail if employees do not relinquish their 'old' identities (Hogg and Terry, 2000). Terry and Callan (1998) argue that, because of the rejection of a new post-merger identity, negative responses and feelings toward the employees of the other organization may jeopardize the success of the merger. On the other hand, when employees do identify with the newly merged organization this is found to have positive effects on merger integration processes and outcomes (Van Knippenberg *et al.*, 2002; Terry, Carey and Callan, 2001; Seo and Hill, 2005). When organization members have a sense of belonging to or feel connected with the post-merger organization this results in more support for and cooperation in the merger integration process.

Similar to the 'us versus them' dynamics regarding the pre-merger organizational identities, differences in pre-merger organizational cultures can be seen as the root cause of many problems in M&A integration (Zaheer *et al.*, 2003). However, culture and identity are rarely examined together (Kroon *et al.*, 2009) and most previous work has focused on the theoretical relations between both concepts (Hatch and Schultz, 1997, 2000, 2002). More recently, Ravasi and Schultz (2006) and Kroon *et al.* (2009) have conducted empirical studies on the relationship between culture and identity. Ravasi and Schultz (2006) found that, when confronted with change (such as a merger or an acquisition), organizational culture supplies employees with cues for reinterpreting the defining characteristics of their organization and for making sense of their new organization's identity. In line with this, Kroon *et al.* (2009) found that post-merger identification mediates the relationship between organizational cultural differences and employees' willingness to cooperate.

Employee communication

M&As are associated with many unknowns and ambiguities, which are generally perceived as uncomfortable by employees (Corley and Gioia, 2004). In an M&A context, several sources of employee uncertainty exist. First, uncertainty about the consequences of the M&A including possible layoffs and new future roles for employees causes stress among organizational members. Second, organizational members are often uncertain about the continuation of their pre-merger organization in the post-merger culture and identity (Van Knippenberg *et al.*, 2002) and feel anxiety about losing their identity and organizational culture. Finally, according to Schweiger and DeNisi (1991), not the change itself but the means of communicating about it may cause stress and uncertainty.

Proper communication helps organizational members to cope with the experienced uncertainty, and thus reduce the negative outcomes often associated with M&As (Schweiger and DeNisi, 1991). Prior literature has generally acknowledged the importance of accurate and relevant communication during M&A processes (Ager, 2011; Appelbaum, Gandell, Yortis, Proper and Jobin, 2000; Sonenshein, 2010). Epstein (2004), for example, points to overcommunication as a major driver of success in post-merger integration

According to Smidts, Pruyn and Van Riel (2001), employee communication can be divided into two components: 'merger communication' (i.e. the content and quality of the information that is communicated to employees) and 'communication climate' (i.e. the overall quality of communication in the organization as a whole). In their study, Smidts *et al.* (2001) distinguish between communication about relevant organizational issues and communication about an employee's personal role in the organization. In an M&A context, relevant organizational issues include goals, objectives and achievements of the merger (Smidts *et al.*, 2001) as well as possible layoffs and other important consequences of the M&A (Papadakis, 2005). The latter type of communication implies what is expected of organizational members in the future with respect to their work and their contribution to merger success.

Whereas most previous work has focused on management and top-down communication about the merger, and because few studies have addressed the specific role of communication during post-merger integration (Bartels *et al.*, 2006), we examine both merger communication and the perceived communication climate in relation to employees' post-merger identification. The essence of our theoretical background is captured in the following research question:

> *How do perceived cultural differences, communication climate and merger communication influence employees' post-merger identification?*

Hypotheses development

Cultural differences and post-merger identification

Although positive effects – such as the benefits of increased diversity within the organization (Vaara, 1999) – are also found, the negative effects of cultural differences on organizational identification, including inter-group bias, are more profound. Inter-group bias means that members have a preference for the in-group over the out-group, and social identity theory asserts that certain contexts in particular provide ground for comparison between these groups (Ashforth and Mael, 1989; DeNisi and Shin, 2005). M&As in which organizational cultural differences are perceived constitute such a context in which employees' own organization is compared with and favoured over the partner organization. This is expected to decrease the identification with the newly merged organization, as members identify less with the post-merger organization since this entity comprises both the members' own and the more negatively perceived partner organization. This is in line with the findings of Kroon *et al.* (2009), who concluded that perceived organizational cultural differences indirectly influence behavioural intentions, such as willingness to cooperate in the merger through the more explicit organizational identification process. Therefore, we propose that perceived cultural differences have a negative effect on post-merger identification.

> *Hypothesis 1: Perceived cultural differences are negatively related to post-merger identification.*

Employee communication and post-merger identification

In earlier research, employee communication has been found to be related to organizational identification (Scott, 1997; Smidts *et al.*, 2001). According to Smidts *et al.* (2001), the adequacy of information about both employees' personal roles and the organization as well as a positive communication climate strengthen employees' identification with the post-merger organization. Bartels *et al.* (2006, 2007) also found evidence for the existence of this relationship in an M&A context. Whereas these authors examined the *expected* identification with the post-merger organization, we also expect this to hold for employees' *actual* identification with the post-merger organization.

As stated before, the communication climate consists of employees' perceptions about the quality of information in the organization (Smidts *et al.*, 2001; Bartels *et al.*, 2006) and the relevant dimensions of communication climate in a merging organization are employees' feelings of supportiveness, openness in communication, and participation in decision-making (Bartels *et al.*, 2006). These aspects constitute some individual needs that employees would like to have fulfilled in their organization. Since the number of individual needs that are satisfied within the organization are positively associated with the level of organizational identification (March and Simon, 1958), we propose that as employees have a higher feeling of supportiveness, of having voice and of being taken seriously in the newly merged organization, the strength of their identification with the post-merger organization will increase. Thus, based on the findings of Smidts *et al.* (2001) and Bartels *et al.* (2006), we develop the following hypothesis:

> *Hypothesis 2: The more positive employees' perceptions of the communication climate, the more they will identify with the post-merger organization.*

In addition to the effect of the communication climate on post-merger identification, Smidts *et al.* (2001) found that employees' perception of the quality of information about their personal roles and about the organization is positively related to organizational identification. Bartels *et al.* (2006) examined the role of communication in a merger context and concluded that the more positive employees' perceptions of the communication about the merger, the more organizational members identify with the post-merger organization. Hence, we argue that a positive perception of the content and quality of communication about the merger has a positive effect on post-merger identification.

> *Hypothesis 3: The more positive employees' perceptions of merger communication, the more they will identify with the post-merger organization.*

According to Smidts *et al.* (2001), communication climate mediates the effect of the perceived quality of information about employees' personal roles and about the organization on organizational identification, since communicating higher-quality information to employees leads to more positive employee perception of the communication climate of their organization. We also expect this finding to hold in an M&A context. In other words, better content and quality of information about the merger improves the perceived communication climate of the merged organization. As a result, employees' post-merger identification will increase. Thus, we expect that a perceived communication climate mediates the relationship between merger communication and identification with the post-merger organization.

> *Hypothesis 4: The positive effect of employees' perceived merger communication on post-merger identification is mediated by the communication climate.*

Cultural differences, merger communication and post-merger identification

Because of the salience of the in-group and the out-group boundary in an M&A setting, employees tend to engage more in inter-group cognitions, such as in-group favouritism and stereotyping (DeNisi and Shin, 2005; Ashforth and Mael, 1989). When organizational cultural differences are perceived, the prevalence of inter-group cognitions and the level of in-group favouritism in comparison with the out-group, the merging partner, will be exacerbated (Cartwright and Cooper, 1993; Haunschild, Moreland and Murrell, 1994). These inter-group cognitions tend to cause negative outcomes, including out-group discrimination, distrust of the merging partner, tensions and in-group rumours. In addition, inter-group cognitions tend to motivate non-cooperative behaviour (DeNisi and Shin, 2005). However, employee communication can compensate for these negative attitudes and behaviours. Schweiger and DeNisi (1991) point out that it is not so much the organizational change that is stressful for organizational members but rather how (well) that change is communicated. Moreover, realistic communication can help employees cope with the uncertainty as a result of a merger or an acquisition. According to Jimmieson, Terry and Callan (2004), the information supply about (forthcoming) organizational changes may help to reduce employees' feelings of uncertainty and threats caused by these changes. In other words, the appropriate communication policy is vital to bridge the differences in culture (Appelbaum *et al.*, 2000; Papadakis, 2005). These issues mainly deal with the content and quality of communication about the merger (i.e. merger communication). Therefore, we argue that positive perceptions of merger communication weaken the negative effect of perceived cultural differences on post-merger identification.

> *Hypothesis 5: The negative effect of employees' perceived cultural differences on post-merger identification is attenuated by positive perceptions of merger communication.*

Methods

Below, we describe how we test the developed hypotheses using data from a large-scale study of two merged dairy firms in the Netherlands.

Research setting

We studied the merger of two Dutch dairy firms. One pre-merger company was mainly located in the north of the Netherlands, whereas the other company's plants and offices were located in the south and east. Mergers are quite common in the dairy industry. The merger we studied was initiated by the dairy farmers, and in December 2007 the managements of both dairy cooperatives announced their intentions to merge. The European Commission started reviewing the merger in the beginning of 2008, a process that continued until the end of the year, when the Commission approved the merger under the condition that the new cooperative would divest some of its fresh dairy activities in the Netherlands. The official merger took place on 30 December 2008, resulting in a multinational dairy cooperative. This company is now located in twenty-five countries and provides dairy-based products to more than one hundred countries around the world. In 2011, sales amounted to over €9 billion. The company employs around 19,000 people.

Sample and data collection procedure

We first conducted some exploratory interviews with the Director Corporate Strategy and the Director Human Resources to gain some knowledge about the merger context and the phases and key events of the merger integration process. Next, our primary data was collected using a self-administered questionnaire, three years and five months after the implementation of the merger. Existing scales from previous research were used to measure the core variables of our study. Our sample consists of management and employees of the division that is most strongly affected by the merger. This sample is further restricted to contain only those organization members who were present in one of the pre-merger companies. The stratified systematic sampling technique is used to ensure that employees from each of the hierarchical levels and pre-merger organizations are represented proportionally within the sample.

A total of 411 surveys were distributed, with 142 sent to employees working at headquarters and 269 sent to employees working at the selected plants. Employees working at headquarters received an online questionnaire, whereas employees working in the plants received a hard-copy version. We assured both groups of the confidentiality of the findings and the anonymity of the respondents. Company involvement and salience of the topic were highlighted by adding a personal note from the Director Human Resources of the division. Ultimately, 142 surveys were returned (a response rate of 35 per cent). This is sufficient to obtain reliable results from statistical analyses, based on Hinkin's (1998) norm of approximately 150 responses.

The final type of data collected in this study consists of secondary data. It includes documents of the merger, such as communication material that was sent out (e.g. presentations, emails and letters), the annual reports of the merged company, the results of the culture research done by McKinsey in the pre-merger phase, and a document about the presentation of the new logo and the development of a new strategy. Furthermore, access to personnel databases helped in selecting a sample for the survey. These secondary data sources were primarily used for triangulation, for understanding the merger context and key events during the post-merger integration process.

Variables

The questionnaire contained several variables that are not relevant for the present context. We will describe only those scales that match the present theoretical framework. The Appendix presents the multi-item survey constructs that were used in this study, together with their factor loadings and Cronbach's alpha for scale reliability.

Post-merger identification, our dependent variable, is measured by five items derived from Mael and Ashforth's (1992) identification scale. These items were rated on a five-point Likert-type scale (1 'completely disagree' to 5 'completely agree'). Cronbach's alpha for the post-merger identification scale equals 0.87, which indicates good scale reliability.

The extent to which employees perceive organizational *cultural differences* is measured by using a seven-item Likert-type scale based on Kroon *et al.* (2009). The organizational cultural differences are calculated by taking the sum of the absolute differences between employees' perceived culture of their own pre-merger organization and the perceived culture of the 'new' post-merger organization for all seven items included in the scale. The reliability of the measure can be considered satisfactory (Cronbach's $\alpha = 0.77$). However, we can also argue that this is a formative, rather than a reflective, scale, in which case Cronbach's alpha is not a relevant measure (Diamantopoulos and Siguaw, 2006).

To measure the *communication climate* at the merged company, a nine-item Likert-type scale developed by Bartels *et al.* (2006) is used. Respondents were asked to indicate the extent to which they agreed with such statements as 'Generally speaking, everyone is honest with one another' and 'Colleagues genuinely listen to me when I say something'. Seven items remain after a factor analysis. The scale is reliable, as Cronbach's alpha equals 0.85.

The initial scale for *merger communication* is an eighteen-item, five-point Likert-type scale (1 'strongly disagree' to 5 'strongly agree') that measures employees' perceptions of the communication about the merger. This measure is based on the scale of Bartels *et al.* (2006). After a factor analysis, four items were deleted and the scale demonstrates excellent scale reliability (Cronbach's $\alpha = 0.95$).

Finally, several control variables are included in this study. Gender is included as a dummy variable (0 'male' and 1 'female'), as well as employees' pre-merger organization. In addition, age and tenure are included, with both expressed in years. Furthermore, we asked whether the respondent had changed location due to the merger. In addition to this question, the variable *integration impact* is measured with five items based on Shrivastava (1986), to assess the extent to which employees have been impacted by the merger. The scale can be considered reliable (Cronbach's $\alpha = 0.81$).

Analysis

We first conducted a confirmatory factor analysis using AMOS 6.0 (Byrne, 2001) to check for convergent and discriminant validity. As the data are not normally distributed, principal axis factoring is preferred (Costello and Osborne, 2005). The rotation method used is oblique rotation, since this allows factors to correlate – it treats constructs as dependent on each other – and provides the most accurate solution in a factor analysis. Subsequently, we performed hierarchical multiple regression analysis to examine post-merger identification. Before calculating the interaction term used to test Hypothesis 5, we mean-centred the variables involved (Aiken and West, 1991).

Results

Reliability and validity

All multi-item constructs display satisfactory levels of reliability, as can be seen from the Cronbach's alphas in the Appendix, which range from 0.81 to 0.95. Convergent validity is examined by looking at the item factor loadings (see Appendix). All of the standardized item loadings (λ) for the multi-item constructs are above the cut-off value of 0.50 (Hildebrandt, 1987), supporting convergent validity.

To assess discriminant validity, we performed a series of chi-square difference tests on the factor correlations. It is particularly important that discriminant validity would be achieved between the employee communication constructs, since these constructs were rather highly correlated. Therefore, we constrained the correlation between these constructs to 1.0 and then performed a chi-square difference test on the values obtained for the unconstrained and the constrained model. The significant difference in chi-square ($\Delta \chi^2 = 240.80$, $\Delta\, df = 1$, $p < 0.01$) between the unconstrained model and the constrained model, where we constrained the correlation between communication climate and merger communication to 1.0, indicates that discriminant validity is achieved. Moreover, the differences in goodness-of-fit and comparative-fit indexes between the constrained and unconstrained models are moderately large (Δ GFI = 0.08, Δ CFI = 0.09), again providing evidence for sufficient discriminant validity.[1]

Descriptive statistics

The means, standard deviations and intercorrelations of the variables used in this study are presented in Table 9.1.

Means of the perceived quality and content of communication regarding the merger, the perceived communication climate and the level of identification with the post-merger organization are all above the midpoint of a five-point Likert-type scale (means are 3.60, 3.74 and 3.71, respectively). Of the survey respondents, 80 per cent are men, whereas 20 per cent are women. The mean age of these respondents is forty-six years and, on average, employees had worked for more than twenty years at one of the pre-merger organizations. Both pre-merger organizations are represented approximately equally and the percentage of respondents that changed location after the merger is 56 per cent. This high percentage might be due to the fact that all employees working at headquarters, 43 per cent of the respondents, changed location after the merger as both of the previous headquarters were closed and replaced by a new headquarters.

Testing the hypotheses

First, we examine the relationship between post-merger identification and the control variables. From the results in Table 9.2 (Model 1), we can conclude that employees who had to change location as a result of the merger identify less with the post-merger organization.

To examine the effect of organizational cultural differences on post-merger identification, we introduced this variable in Model 2. The additional variance accounted for by the cultural differences variable is significant ($\Delta R^2 = 0.04$, $p < 0.05$). The coefficient of the cultural differences variable in Model 2 is significant and negative ($b = -0.04$, $p < 0.05$), providing support for Hypothesis 1. This is consistent with the findings of Kroon *et al.* (2009), who illustrate that the extent to which organizational members perceive cultural differences between organizations is negatively related to post-merger identification. However, as we will illustrate below, this result does not hold across all specifications of the model.

In order to test Hypotheses 2 and 3, the variables communication climate and merger communication were added to Model 3. Since a positive and significant effect is found for communication climate ($b = 0.35$, $p < 0.01$) as well as for merger

TABLE 9.1 Descriptive statistics and correlations matrix

Variables	*Mean*	*s.d.*	*1*	*2*	*3*	*4*	*5*	*6*	*7*	*8*	*9*
1. Post-merger identification	3.71	0.73									
2. Age	46.40	9.74	–.06								
3. Gender	0.21	0.41	.01	–.23*							
4. Company	0.54	0.50	.04	.14	–.12						
5. Location	0.44	0.50	–.15	.14	–.09	.17					
6. Tenure	20.60	12.59	–.11	.82*	–.17	.24*	.24*				
7. Integration impact	3.56	0.76	.07	.00	–.07	–.09	–.37*	–.05			
8. Cultural differences	3.72	3.47	–.14	–.13	–.03	–.16	–.11	–.19	.36*		
9. Merger communication	3.60	0.62	–.38*	–.07	–.00	–.03	–.13	–.02	–.05	–.29*	
10. Communication climate	3.74	0.48	.36*	–.14	–.03	–.08	–.01	–.11	–.13	–.20	.39*

Notes: N = 142; * $p < 0.01$.

TABLE 9.2 Results of multiple regression analysis for post-merger identification

Variables	*Post-merger identification*	*Post-merger identification*	*Post-merger identification*	*Post-merger identification*
Intercept	4.10** (0.64)	3.82** (0.66)	1.91* (0.83)	2.23** (0.82)
Age	–0.00 (0.01)	0.00 (0.01)	0.01 (0.01)	0.00 (0.01)
Gender	–0.06 (0.15)	–0.05 (0.15)	–0.02 (0.14)	–0.05 (0.14)
Company	0.21† (0.12)	0.17 (0.12)	0.19 (0.12)	0.13 (0.12)
Location	–0.23† (0.13)	–0.22† (0.13)	–0.15 (0.13)	–0.12 (0.13)
Tenure	–0.00 (0.01)	–0.01 (0.01)	–0.01 (0.01)	–0.01 (0.01)
Integration impact	–0.03 (0.08)	0.05 (0.09)	0.09 (0.09)	0.12 (0.09)
Main effects				
Cultural differences		–0.04* (0.02)	–0.02 (0.02)	–0.01 (0.02)
Merger communication			0.25* (0.11)	0.21* (0.10)
Communication climate			0.35** (0.12)	0.29* (0.12)
Interaction effect				
Cultural differences × merger communication				0.06** (0.02)
R^2	0.05	0.09	0.24	0.28
ΔR^2		0.04	0.19	0.31
ΔF		4.31	10.27	6.83

Notes:
N = 142.
The changes in R^2 in Models 2, 3 and 4 are in comparison to the value in Model 1. The changes in F-statistic are in comparison to the value in the previous model. The coefficients reported are unstandardized estimates, with standard errors in parentheses.
† $p < 0.10$.
* $p < 0.05$.
** $p < 0.01$.

communication ($b = 0.25$, $p < 0.05$), it can be argued that employee communication is an important determinant in explaining post-merger identification. More specifically, a more positive communication climate at the post-merger organization as perceived by employees results in higher levels of post-merger identification. In other words, as employees have higher feelings of supportiveness, of having a voice and of being taken seriously in the newly merged organization, they will identify more strongly with the post-merger organization. This is in line with the studies of Smidts *et al.* (2001) and Bartels *et al.* (2006, 2007), who found – in both a non-merger and a merger context – that as employees perceive the communication climate of their organization as more positive, they identify more strongly with that organization.

Hypothesis 3 is also supported. This finding is in line with the study of Smidts *et al.* (2001), who found that employees' perception of the quality of information about their personal roles and about organizational issues is positively related to post-merger identification. Furthermore, it is consistent with the conclusion

TABLE 9.3 Results of regression analysis for testing Hypothesis 5

Variables	*Dependent variable = post-merger identification*	*Dependent variable = communication climate*	R^2
Step 1:			
Merger communication	0.32** (0.10)		0.17
Step 2:			
Merger communication		0.33** (0.07)	0.20
Steps 3 and 4:			
Merger communication	0.25* (0.11)		0.24
Communication climate	0.35** (0.12)		

Notes:
N = 142.
The coefficients reported are unstandardized estimates, with standard errors in parentheses.
* $p < 0.05$.
** $p < 0.01$.

of Bartels *et al.* (2006) that positive perceptions of the quality of communication about the merger have a positive effect on identification with the post-merger organization.

In order to analyse the mediating role of the communication climate (Hypothesis 4), the causal step approach of Baron and Kenny (1986) is followed. According to Baron and Kenny (1986), three conditions should be met to establish mediation – all are tested by means of regression analysis (see Table 9.3 for a summary of the results).

The first step is to assess the effect of merger communication on post-merger identification. A positive and significant effect for perceived quality and content of communication about the merger is observed ($b = 0.32$, $p < 0.01$). Then, the relation between the independent variable and the mediator is examined using regression analysis, with communication climate as the dependent variable. The same control variables as were used before are included in this analysis. We found that the perceived quality and content of communication about the merger is positively and significantly related to the perceived communication climate ($b = 0.33$, $p < 0.01$). The third and final step is to examine the effect of communication climate on post-merger identification, when the independent variable merger communication is controlled for. A positive and significant effect is found ($b = 0.35$, $p < 0.01$). Since all three steps are met and the effect of the independent variable on the dependent variable is less in the third ($b = 0.25$, $p = 0.05$) than in the first regression analysis, a partial mediation model can be established. Thus, it can be argued that the communication climate partly mediates the relationship between merger communication and employees' identification with the post-merger organization. Furthermore, in addition to the approach of Baron and Kenny (1986), the mediation model is tested using Sobel's test – a significance test for the indirect effect of the independent variable on the dependent variable via the

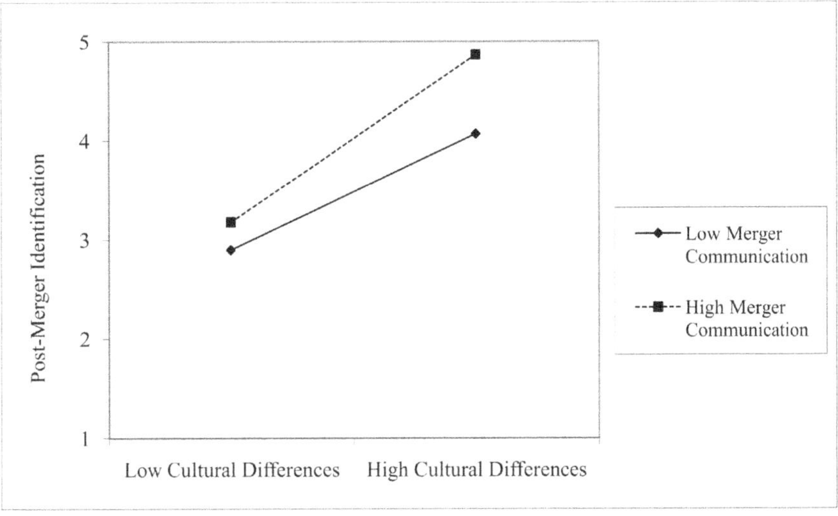

FIGURE 9.1 The relationship between cultural differences and post-merger identification moderated by merger communication

mediator (Baron and Kenny, 1986). Since Sobel's test statistic is significant (Sobel's test statistic = 2.48, $p < 0.05$), we can support Hypothesis 4.

To test whether the cultural differences variable is differentially related to post-merger identification across employees with varying perceptions of merger communication (Hypothesis 5), we regressed post-merger identification on *cultural differences*, *merger communication* and *cultural differences* × *merger communication*. As can be seen from Model 4 in Table 9.2, the coefficient of the interaction term *cultural differences* × *merger communication* is significantly positive ($b = 0.06$, $p < 0.01$), thereby supporting Hypothesis 5. To gain further insight into the differences between employees with varying perceptions of merger communication, we plotted the relationship between cultural differences and post-merger identification for employees with low (i.e. 'negative') and high (i.e. 'positive') perceptions of merger communication (see Figure 9.1).

The regression lines represent the post-merger identification values expected on the basis of unstandardized regression coefficients from the complete regression analysis in Table 9.2 (Model 4).

Discussion

Theoretical and managerial implications

The results of this study reveal that employee communication during a post-merger integration process is an important determinant of the extent to which employees identify with the newly merged organization. Both employees' positive perceptions of the content and quality of communication about the merger and the communication climate of the post-merger organization have positive effects on post-merger identification. Moreover, in our study a mediation effect is found of communication climate on the relationship between the perceived content and quality of communication about the merger and post-merger identification. Hence, better content and quality of communication about the merger improve the perceived communication climate in the post-merger organization and therefore the extent to which employees identify with the post-merger organization.

In the current study, the proposed relationship between perceived organizational cultural differences and post-merger identification is also found. This is consistent with the findings of Kroon *et al.* (2009), who concluded that perceived organizational cultural differences indirectly influence behavioural intentions, such as willingness to cooperate in the merger through the more explicit organizational identification process. Finally, we have observed an interesting interaction effect between merger communication and perceived cultural differences. That is, when organizational members feel that the content and quality of communication about the merger is correct and reliable, the relationship between cultural differences and post-merger identification is positively influenced.

Our study contributes to the literature on 'human factors' in post-merger integration. In previous literature it has been found that identification with the post-merger organization has a significant effect on post-merger integration outcomes, such as employee satisfaction, willingness to cooperate and turnover (intentions). In the current study, employee communication has a positive effect on post-merger identification, which implies that employee communication has an indirect effect on post-merger integration processes and M&A success.

Our study also contributes to social identity theory, which states that people derive part of their self-concept from the perceived membership in a relevant group or organization (Tajfel and Turner, 1986). The current study identifies additional antecedents of identification with the post-merger organization. Moreover, we clearly distinguish between identity and culture, two concepts which are often used interchangeably in the earlier literature. Finally, our findings illustrate how a mediation model and, in addition, a moderation model explain additional variance in our post-merger identification variable. These observations imply that multiple antecedents intricately interact to influence organizational identification in an M&A context. We therefore encourage further research to delve into the interactions of multiple determinants of organizational identification, including non-perceptual variables, such as changes in the leadership of the company.

Although communication problems are often seen as secondary concerns in post-M&A integration, they are apparent in most mergers and acquisitions (Vaara, 2003). Our study empirically shows how communication can influence employees' perceptions of the M&A integration process. We also acknowledge the multi-dimensional nature of employee communication and distinguish between merger communication and communication climate of the merged organization. These two foci significantly influence post-merger identification but they also influence each other. From a managerial point of view, our findings imply that managers should invest in open and honest communication about the M&A and provide information about the goals and objectives, the developments and the consequences of the merger to employees in a timely manner. Information that is perceived by employees as reliable and relevant can improve the extent to which employees identify with the newly merged organization, which in turn can influence important attitudinal (e.g. satisfaction) and behavioural (e.g. turnover) variables in a post-merger integration process. Previous research has already illustrated that the development of a communication strategy is important in addressing organizational uncertainty. In addition, a poor communication programme may create significant problems and could even lead to the failure of the M&A (Clampitt *et al.*, 2000; Papadakis, 2005).

Limitations and suggestions for future research

One important limitation of the current study is that the research was restricted to one particular post-M&A integration process. Single case studies place limitations on the generalizability of the results to other cases. Hence, there is no certainty that the findings are equally applicable to other research settings and contexts. However, we do feel that the findings can be used for 'naturalistic generalization', whereby one recognizes similarities between the findings of this research and those of other cases without making any statistical inference. We do encourage future research to examine other M&A settings and inter- and/or intra-organizational contexts in which radical organizational discontinuities occur.

A second limitation of our study is that we collected data at one point in time. Therefore, we have to be careful with a causal interpretation of the results. As previous studies have found support for the unstable and evolving nature of organizational identity, it would be interesting to examine changes in post-merger identification over time.

A final limitation concerns the nature of our data. We collected the independent and dependent variables using the same instrument. Hence, there is a risk of common method bias. However, Spector (2006) indicates that these method bias effects may be overstated. Moreover, support for Hypotheses 4 and 5 is unlikely to be an artefact of single respondent bias since it is implausible that respondents theorized such a mediated and moderated relationship when filling out the questionnaire. We also undertook procedural remedies against common method bias, such as protecting respondent anonymity and reducing item ambiguity.

In relation to our study's findings, previous research has found that organizational identification is a relatively explicit and conscious process, whereas organizational culture is more tacit and implicit (Cartwright and Cooper, 1993; Hatch and Schultz, 2000; Ravasi and Schultz, 2006). Therefore, employee communication, which is often of an explicit nature, might influence post-merger identification and perceived cultural differences differently. Merger communication might also play a different role for indirectly involved employees than for those directly involved in the merger or acquisition. These issues, amongst others, might be interesting to address and explore in future research.

Appendix

Multi-item survey constructs

Factor loadings (λ)	
Post-merger identification (Cronbach's α = 0.87)	
1. When someone criticizes (company A–B), it feels like a personal insult.	.71
2. I am very interested in what others think about (company A–B).	.70
3. When I talk about (company A–B), I usually say 'we' rather than 'they'.	.76
4. When someone praises (company A–B), it feels like a personal compliment.	.87
5. (Company A–B)'s successes are my successes.	.76
Merger communication (Cronbach's α = 0.95)	
1. I think the information I received about the merger was reliable.	.80
2. I think the information I received about the merger was true.	.80
3. Communication about the merger was open.	.81
4. I was sufficiently informed about the merger.	.77
5. I could easily get information about the merger.	.77
6. I received information about the merger on time.	.75
7. I think the information I received about the merger was useful.	.67
8. I am satisfied with the way I was informed about the latest developments of the merger.	.80
9. I am satisfied with the way I was informed about the objectives of the merger.	.72
10. I think the information I received about the merger was complete.	.76
11. I think the information I received about the merger was credible.	.73
12. Communication about the merger was honest.	.74
13. Openness and honesty about the merger were stimulated.	.65
14. I am satisfied with the communication about the merger at (company A–B).	.78
Communication climate (Cronbach's α = 0.85)	
1. Generally speaking, everyone at (company A–B) is honest with one another.	.81
2. I can discuss anything with colleagues at (company A–B).	.66
3. Generally speaking, everyone at (company A–B) is open to one another.	.74
4. If I talk with colleagues at (company A–B), I feel I am being taken seriously.	.62
5. Colleagues at (company A–B) are open to the opinions of others.	.56
6. Colleagues at (company A–B) genuinely listen to me when I say something.	.59
7. My suggestions are taken seriously by my colleagues at (company A–B).	.64
Integration impact (Cronbach's α = 0.81)	
1. My work has changed due to the merger.	.65
2. The structure has changed in the location I'm working at, due to the merger.	.77
3. Decision-making has changed in the location I'm working at, due to the merger.	.75
4. Systems and procedures have changed in the location I'm working at, due to the merger.	.70
5. Production technologies have changed in the location I'm working at, due to the merger.	.54

Note

1 Results for other construct combinations allow the same conclusion (i.e. discriminant validity is achieved).

References

Ager, D. L. (2011) 'The emotional impact and behavioral consequences of post-M&A integration: An ethnographic case study in the software industry', *Journal of Contemporary Ethnography*, 40: 199–230.

Aiken, L. S. and West, S. G. (1991) *Multiple regression: Testing and interpreting interactions*. Thousand Oakes, CA: Sage.

Allatta, J. T. and Singh, H. (2011) 'Evolving communication patterns in response to an acquisition event', *Strategic Management Journal*, 32: 1099–1118.

Appelbaum, S. H., Gandell, J., Yortis, H., Proper, S. and Jobin, F. (2000) 'Anatomy of a merger: Behavior of organizational factors and processes throughout the pre- during-post-stages (part 1)', *Management Decision*, 38: 649–661.

Ashforth, B. E. and Mael, F. A. (1989) 'Social identity and the organization', *Academy of Management Review*, 14: 20–39.

Baron, R. M. and Kenny, D. A. (1986) 'The moderator–mediator variable distinction in social psychological research: Conceptual, strategic and statistical considerations', *Journal of Personality and Social Psychology*, 51: 1173–1182.

Bartels, J., Douwes, R., De Jong, M. and Pruyn, A. (2006) 'Organizational identification during a merger: Determinants of employees' expected identification with the new organization', *British Journal of Management*, 17: S49–S67.

Bartels, J., Pruyn, A., De Jong, M. and Joustra, I. (2007) 'Multiple organizational identification levels and the impact of perceived external prestige and communication climate', *Journal of Organizational Behavior*, 28: 173–190.

Birkinshaw, J. M. (1999) 'Acquiring intellect: Managing the integration of knowledge-intensive acquisitions', *Business Horizons*, 42: 33–40.

Byrne, B. M. (2001) *Structural equation modeling with AMOS: Basic concepts, applications, and programming*. Mahwah, NJ: Lawrence Erlbaum.

Cartwright, S. and Cooper, C. L. (1993) 'The role of culture compatibility in successful organizational marriage', *Academy of Management Executive*, 7: 57–70.

Clampitt, P., DeKoch, R. and Cashman, T. (2000) 'A strategy for communicating about uncertainty', *Academy of Management Executive*, 14: 41–57.

Cording, M., Christmann, P. and King, D. R. (2008) 'Reducing causal ambiguity in acquisition integration: Intermediate goals as mediators of integration decisions and acquisition performance', *Academy of Management Journal*, 51: 744–767.

Corley, K. G. and Gioia, D. A. (2004) 'Identity ambiguity and change in the wake of a corporate spin-off', *Administrative Science Quarterly*, 49: 173–208.

Costello, A. B. and Osborne, J. (2005) 'Best practices in exploratory factor analysis: Four recommendations for getting the most from your analysis', *Practical Assessment Research and Evaluation*, 10: 1–9.

DeNisi, A. S. and Shin, S. J. (2005) 'Psychological communication interventions in mergers and acquisitions'. In G. K. Stahl and M. E. Mendenhall (eds), *Mergers and acquisitions: Managing culture and human resources* (pp. 228–236). Stanford, CA: Stanford University Press.

Diamantopoulos, A. and Siguaw, J. A. (2006) 'Formative versus reflective indicators in organizational measure development: A comparison and empirical illustration', *British Journal of Management*, 17: 263–282.

DiGeorgio, R. (2002) 'Making mergers and acquisitions work: What we know and don't know – Part I', *Journal of Change Management*, 3: 134–148.
Dyer, J. H., Kale, P. and Singh, H. (2004) 'When to ally and when to acquire', *Harvard Business Review*, 82: 108–115.
Epstein, M. J. (2004) 'The drivers of success in post-merger integration', *Organizational Dynamics*, 33: 174–189.
Epstein, M. J. (2005) 'The determinants and evaluation of merger success', *Business Horizons*, 48: 37–46.
Hatch, M. J. and Schultz, M. (1997) 'Relations between organizational culture, identity and image', *European Journal of Marketing*, 31: 356–365.
Hatch, M. J. and Schultz, M. (2000) 'Scaling the tower of Babel: Relational differences between identity, image, and culture in organizations'. In M. Schultz, M.J. Hatch and M.H. Larsen (eds), *The expressive organization* (pp. 11–35). Oxford: Oxford University Press.
Hatch, M. J. and Schultz, M. (2002) 'The dynamics of organizational identity', *Human Relations*, 55: 989–1018.
Haunschild, P. R., Moreland, R. L. and Murrell, A. J. (1994) 'Sources of resistance to mergers between groups', *Journal of Applied Social Psychology*, 24: 1150–1178.
Hildebrandt, L. (1987) 'Consumer retail satisfaction in rural areas: A reanalysis of survey data', *Journal of Economic Psychology*, 8: 19–42.
Hinkin, T. R. (1998) 'A brief tutorial on the development of measures for use in survey questionnaires', *Organizational Research Methods*, 1: 104–121.
Hogg, M. and Terry, D. J. (2000) 'Social identity and self-categorization processes in organizational contexts', *Academy of Management Review*, 25: 121–140.
Jimmieson, N. L., Terry, D. J. and Callan, V. J. (2004) 'A longitudinal study of employee adaptation to organizational change: The role of change-related information and change-related self-efficacy', *Journal of Occupational Health Psychology*, 9: 11–27.
Kroon, D. P., Noorderhaven, N. G. and Leufkens, A. S. (2009) 'Organizational identification and cultural differences: Explaining employee attitudes and behavioral intentions during postmerger integration'. In C. L. Cooper and S. Finkelstein (eds), *Advances in mergers and acquisitions* (pp. 19–42). Bingley: Emerald Group.
Larsson, R. and Lubatkin, M. (2001) 'Achieving acculturation in mergers and acquisitions: An international case survey', *Human Relations*, 54: 1573–1607.
Mael, F. A. and Ashforth, B. E. (1992) 'Alumni and their alma mater: A partial test of the reformulated model of organizational identification', *Journal of Organizational Behaviour*, 13: 103–123.
March, J. G. and Simon, H. A. (1958) *Organizations*. New York: Wiley.
Makri, M., Hitt, M. A. and Lane, P. J. (2010) 'Complementary technologies, knowledge relatedness, and invention outcomes in high technology mergers and acquisitions', *Strategic Management Journal*, 31: 602–628.
Papadakis, V. M. (2005) 'The role of broader context and the communication program in merger and acquisition implementation success', *Management Decision*, 43: 236–255.
Ravasi, D. and Schultz, M. (2006) 'Responding to organizational identity threats: Exploring the role of organizational culture', *Academy of Management Journal*, 49: 433–458.
Schweiger, D. M. and DeNisi, A. S. (1991) 'Communication with employees following a merger: A longitudinal field experiment', *Academy of Management Journal*, 34: 110–135.
Scott, C. R. (1997) 'Identification with multiple targets in a geographically dispersed organization', *Management Communication Quarterly*, 10: 491–522.
Seo, M. and Hill, N. S. (2005) 'Understanding the human side of mergers and acquisitions: An integrative framework', *Journal of Applied Behavioral Science*, 41: 422–443.

Shrivastava, P. (1986) 'Postmerger integration', *Journal of Business Strategy*, 7: 65–76.

Smidts, A., Pruyn, A. T. H. and Van Riel, C. B. M. (2001) 'The impact of employee communication and perceived external prestige on organizational identification', *Academy of Management Journal*, 44: 1051–1062.

Sonenshein, S. (2010) 'We're changing or are we? Untangling the role of progressive, regressive and stability narratives during strategic change implementation', *Academy of Management Journal*, 53: 477–512.

Spector, P. E. (2006) 'Method variance in organizational research: Truth or urban legend?', *Organizational Research Methods*, 9: 221–232.

Tajfel, H. and Turner, J. C. (1986) 'The social identity theory of intergroup behaviour'. In S. Worchel and W. G. Austin (eds), *Psychology of intergroup relations* (pp. 7–24). Chicago, IL: Nelson-Hall.

Teerikangas, S. (2007) 'A comparative overview of the impact of cultural diversity on inter-organizational encounters'. In C. L. Cooper and S. Finkelstein (eds), *Advances in mergers and acquisitions* (pp. 37–76). Amsterdam: JAI Press.

Terry, D. J. and Callan, V. J. (1998) 'In-group bias in response to an organizational merger', *Group Dynamics: Theory, Research and Practice*, 2: 67–81.

Terry, D. J., Carey, C. J. and Callan, V. J. (2001) 'Employee adjustment to an organizational merger: An intergroup perspective', *Personality and Social Psychology Bulletin*, 27: 267–280.

Turner, J. C., Hogg, M. A., Oakes, P. J., Reicher, S. D. and Wetherell, M. (1987) *Rediscovering the social group: A self-categorization theory*. London: Harvester Wheatsheaf.

Ullrich, J. and Van Dick, R. (2007) 'The group psychology of mergers and acquisitions: Lessons from the social identity approach'. In C. L. Cooper and S. Finkelstein (eds), *Advances in mergers and acquisitions* (pp. 1–15). Amsterdam: JAI Press.

Vaara, E. (1999) 'Cultural differences in post-merger problems: Misconceptions and cognitive simplifications', *Nordic Organization Studies*, 1: 59–88.

Vaara, E. (2003) 'Post-acquisition integration as sensemaking: Glimpses of ambiguity, confusion, hypocrisy, and politicization', *Journal of Management Studies*, 40: 859–894.

Van Dick, R., Ullrich, J. and Tissington, P. A. (2006) 'Working under a black cloud: How to sustain organizational identification after a merger', *British Journal of Management*, 17: S69–S79.

Van Knippenberg, D., Van Knippenberg, B., Monden, L. and De Lima, F. (2002) 'Organizational identification after a merger: A social identity perspective', *British Journal of Social Psychology*, 41: 233–252.

Zaheer, S., Schomaker, M. and Genc, M. (2003) 'Identity versus culture in mergers of equals', *European Management Journal*, 21: 185–191.

10

MULTIPLE SHARED IDENTITIES IN CROSS-BORDER M&As

Anna Lupina-Wegener and Rolf van Dick

Introduction

The recent academic literature reveals that constructing a shared identity is crucial to the success of mergers and acquisitions (Lupina-Wegener, Schneider, and van Dick, 2011; Marks and Mirvis, 2011). Shared identity has been typically conceptualized as both *content* (Gaertner *et al.*, 1993)—that is, the perception of a common ingroup identity—and *process* (van Dick, Ullrich, and Tissington, 2006)—that is, the degree of identification with the new organization (see Haslam, 2001, and Haslam, Postmes, and Ellemers, 2003, for conceptualization of shared identity in terms of content and process). While past research has focused on M&As of freestanding organizations, cross-border deals remain underexplored. In cross-border M&As, one organization becomes nested in a new, larger organizational and cultural context. In such conditions, shared identity might need to account for both internal and external foci. This is in line with a qualitative study conducted by Lupina-Wegener, Schneider, and van Dick (2015), who show that in cross-border M&As, shared identity moves beyond a post-merger organization in efforts to differentiate the new organization from reference others, such as the head office or other subsidiaries as new "outgroups." Thus, it might not be enough to operationalize shared identity on the level of the post-merger organization only, as the concept of shared identity may account for the multiple memberships of organizational members, such as function, division, holding, head office, or country.

In this chapter, we extend the current operationalization of a shared identity in M&As. Building on literature on multiple identities and identity complexity (Roccas and Brewer, 2002), we introduce a more nuanced concept of multiple shared identities (MSIs). This accounts for multiple group memberships that are shared by organizational members. Specifically, it refers to a smaller or larger group-level overlap in memberships across pairs of ingroups, with a larger overlap reflecting high

MSI. Thus, to address a research gap in multiple identities in M&As we present a framework that helps understand how MSIs are constructed from a perspective of an acquired organization—that is, the one nested in a larger, acquiring organization, based in a different national culture. The framework depicts that MSIs in the post-merger organizations develop in interactions of relevant stakeholders—that is, members from the merging organizations, or from the outside, such as head office and other subsidiaries. The larger the cultural distance, the more challenging these interactions might be for the stakeholders, but cultural distance can be bridged if organizational members share multiple identities (Reade, 2001; Vora and Kostova, 2007) and cross-vergence facilitating "best-of-both" cultures occurs (Sarala and Vaara, 2009).

The chapter is structured as follows. First, we will present the social identity approach to M&As. Second, we will discuss the concept of multiple shared identities as applied to cross-cultural ventures. Third, we will develop and present a conceptual framework of multiple shared identities as constructed in an acquired organization. Finally, we will illustrate our framework with the case of Chinese acquisition in Europe.

Social identity theory: implications for cross-border mergers and acquisitions

Social identity theory (Tajfel and Turner, 1986) and self-categorization theory (Turner, Hogg, Oakes, Reicher, and Wetherell, 1987) help explain social behavior wherein individuals are not acting on the basis of their personal identities but as members of their group(s) in relation to members of other groups. As such, personal identity—"How am I different from him/her?"—might become less salient in some circumstances, such as during contact with other groups, or when facing external threats. Individuals tend to define themselves in terms of their organizational identity based on attributes shared with ingroup members in terms of characteristics collectively understood by the members to be central, distinctive and enduring (Albert and Whetten, 1985b). Self-categorization theory provides a complementary perspective to social identity theory (Turner *et al.*, 1987; Turner, 1985). Various social identities for self-categorization are available to group members at a particular time (Brewer, 1991) and individuals may choose to identify with a collective, which provides them with distinctiveness and self-esteem. And while identification is referred to as "the perception of oneness or belongingness to some human aggregate" (Ashforth and Mael, 1989: 21), organizational identity is a relatively enduring state that reflects an individual's willingness to define him- or herself as a member of a particular organization (Haslam, 2001). Previous research has demonstrated that employees who identify strongly with their organization show positive work outcomes, including lower turnover intentions and higher job satisfaction, work motivation, cooperative behavior (Riketta, 2005) as well as readiness for change (Rousseau, 1998).

Similar outcomes have been found in M&A research (Bartels, Pruyn, and de Jong, 2009; van Dick *et al.*, 2006), wherein shared identity has been typically conceptualized as both content (Gaertner *et al.*, 1993)—that is, perception of a common ingroup identity—and process (Hogg and Terry, 2000)—that is, degree of identification with the new organization. Overall, this research discloses that group members need to perceive belonging to a superordinate social category, such as an organization or a team, despite intergroup boundaries. When there is a lack of shared identity, conflict might prevail in terms of competing claims on who we are as an organization, and group members might seek privilege for their pre-merger, ingroup identities (Lupina-Wegener *et al.*, 2011).

Despite important insights and extensive research on M&As in general, it remains underexplored how shared identities develop in cross-border M&As. In cross-border M&As, the acquired organization becomes a new subsidiary or a local head office as nested in a new, larger structure of the acquiring organization, its new global head office. Gioia *et al.* (2010: 41) point to specific challenges to shared identity development in such larger structures: "a new nested organization might take longer to attain optimal distinctiveness because its members need to work more intensively to figure out how it is different from the larger organization." Moreover, cultural differences may constitute a specific context for cross-border M&As. In cross-border M&As, it might not be enough to look at a shared identity on an organizational level as a shared identity might also account for differentiation from reference others, such as the global or regional head office and other subsidiaries (Lupina-Wegener,Schneider, and van Dick, 2015).

Summing up, building on existing social identity theory applied to M&As, we argue that understanding how shared identities of multiple foci develops in cross-border M&As can help ensure success, despite cultural differences at the organizational or country level.

Multiple identities in cross-cultural ventures

Organizations constitute a *multiple number of identities* (Mael and Ashforth, 1992; van Knippenberg and van Schie, 2000) in function of employees' collective memberships (Pratt, 2001). These memberships play an important role as individuals tend to act on behalf of the groups with which they identify (van Knippenberg and van Schie, 2000). Thus, awareness of which identities are salient helps explain individual and collective behaviors. More specifically, research has shown that multiple foci of identification may be related to specific work-related attitudes or behaviors. For example, a quantitative study conducted in cross-validated samples of 233 school teachers and 358 bank accountants reveals that while team climate was best predicted by team identification, withdrawal intentions and job satisfaction chiefly related to organizational and occupational identification (van Dick, Wagner, Stellmacher, and Christ, 2004).

In the same vein, the international business literature provides insights into subsidiary managers' belongingness to multiple identities with a focus on dual identities on a single focus, such as nation—i.e., host versus local country (Lee, 2010)—or organization—i.e. head office versus local operations (Vora, Kostova, and Roth, 2007). Dual identities have been related to performance and work-related outcomes of a subsidiary and the head office. Dual identities in subsidiaries enhance subsidiary–parent cooperation (Lee, 2010) and play a key role in ensuring a sustainable economic success of a subsidiary through transfer of management skills and practices (Vora and Kostova, 2007; Vora *et al.*, 2007). Indeed, there is evidence that if dual identities do not emerge, multinational corporations' (MNCs') international expansion is likely to be reduced (Hutzschenreuter, Voll, and Verbeke, 2011; Rugman, Verbeke, and Yuan, 2011). Moreover, if dual identities are not embraced by local employees, problems in communication flows with the head office emerge, decision-making processes can be jeopardized (Sanchez-Burks, Lee, Richard, and Incheol, 2003), role ambiguity prevails (Distefano and Maznevski, 2000), and a lack of cross-cultural leadership is reported (Petrick, Scherer, Brodzinski, Quinn, and Ainina, 1999; Russette, Scully, and Preziosi, 2008).

Quantitative investigations restricted to dual identities so far have prevented further understanding of multiple identities in organizations nested in larger structures. To date, shared belonging of subsidiary members to multiple foci of identities—both "inside" (e.g. organization, department, function, work group, team) and "outside" related (e.g. regional, national, or head office)—has not been investigated. Moreover, it remains to be revealed how specific identities may relate to M&A successes. To address this research gap, we will present a framework of multiple shared identities in cross-border acquisitions. First, we build on past M&A findings to emphasize the importance of shared identities in freestanding organizations. Second, we refer to the cross-culture management literature, studying multiple identities in cross-cultural ventures. This framework may help uncover how multiple identities shared by organizational members may develop in cross-border M&As when there are cultural differences on national and organizational levels.

Conceptual framework: multiple shared identities in cross-border acquisitions

Building on the M&A, cross-border ventures and multiple identities literature, we argue that understanding how multiple shared identities develop might provide important insights into cross-border M&As. MSI refers to group-level overlap in memberships across pairs of ingroups with a certain overlap reflecting high MSI. The framework depicts that MSIs in post-merger organizations develop in interactions among relevant stakeholders both inside (pre-merger groups: employees, managers) and outside the organization (head office and other subsidiaries). These interactions take place in a context of cultural differences, and the larger the cultural distance, the more challenging it might be for organizational members to determine: "Who are we going to become after the acquisition?"—identity; and "How are we going to do business after the acquisition?"—culture. Cultural distance can be bridged if organizational members share multiple identities (Reade, 2001; Vora and Kostova, 2007) and "best-of-both" management is enabled in a cultural cross-vergence (Sarala and Vaara, 2010). In the framework, a particular focus is given to the members of an acquired organization as: for them, it tends to be more difficult to transfer identification from the pre-merger to the post-merger one; and the acquired organization becomes nested in a larger, acquiring organization and rarely vice versa.

Cultural distance

In cross-border M&As, a freestanding organization becomes nested in a new superordinate structure of its acquirer, located in a different country: for example, German-based Wella at the US Procter and Gamble holding or British-based Jaguar at the Indian TATA group. In such deals, cultural differences might be apparent and pose challenges to M&A success.

Following Hofstede (1980: 13), we define culture as a collective "programming of the mind that distinguishes the members of one human group from another." The concept of culture attempts to capture values and beliefs of a typical individual in a society and allows differentiation from other countries' nationals. Research reveals that people from different countries might differ on some dimensions, such as individualism, power distance, uncertainly avoidance, masculinity (Hofstede, 1980), long-term orientation (Hofstede, 2001), performance orientation, assertiveness, future orientation, human orientation, ingroup and institutional collectivism and gender egalitarianism (House, Hanges, Javidan, Dorfman, and Gupta, 2004). In the international business literature, cultural differences are referred to as cultural distance (CD). This has been measured on a macro level as a cumulative difference in cultural norms between two countries (Kogut and Singh, 1988). On a micro level, cultural distance is operationalized as differences in national cultural values of managers in the home office and the local operation (Tihanyi, Griffith, and Russell, 2005). Recently, cultural distance was extended to account for differences not only in national culture but also in language, degree of industrialization, economic development, and political system (Blomkvist and Drogendijk, 2013).

While high CD may have disruptive effects on the performance of cross-border ventures (Brown, Rugman, and Verbeke, 1989), it may also have a positive impact on financial performance (Morosini, Shane, and Singh, 1998), organizational learning, and flexibility (Barkema and Vermeulen, 1998). CD may also be inversely related to turnover in organizational changes (Krishnan, Miller, and Judge, 1997; Lubatkin, Schweiger, and Weber, 1999). Summing up, past research suggests that cultural differences may have a limited direct effect on work-related and organizational performance (Tihanyi *et al.*, 2005). Instead, CD provides a context for managing organizational culture (Rugman, Verbeke, and Nguyen, 2011) and constructing identities (Vora and Kostova, 2007).

Multiple shared identities

In the context of a larger cultural distance and frequent intergroup interactions (Fiol, Hatch, and Golden-Biddle, 1998), members from the acquired organization inquire about their new membership(s): "Who are we?" and "Who are we to become"? Specifically, post-merger identity can be shared by ingroup members both as *identity content*—"Who are we?"—and *strength*—"To what extent do we identify?" (Haslam *et al.*, 2003). Social identity theory suggests that identity process and content result from self-categorization with respect to others (Dutton, Dukerich, and Harquail, 1994). Consequently, ingroup shared meaning about the post-merger identity develops in interactions between members from merging organizations. However, how multiple identities as shared by ingroup members may develop in cross-border acquisitions remains under-researched. We address this research gap by introducing a concept of multiple shared identities, building on existing operationalizations of shared identity in M&As and social identity theory, namely social identity complexity and multiple identities.

First, social identity complexity by Roccas and Brewer (2002) provides important insights on multiple group memberships. They developed social identity complexity referring to individual differences in perception of prototypes of the groups to which they belong and they theorize that an individual's identity structure can be presented in a continuum of multiple membership complexity, with high complexity with differentiation between identities and low complexity with inclusiveness of identities. We extend their work on individual to collective multiple group memberships. Specifically, we coin the concept of multiple shared identities, which refers to group-level overlap in memberships across pairs of ingroups, with an overlap reflecting high MSI, and being spaced out reflecting low MSI. MSI refers to shared attributes both within a subsidiary and beyond its boundaries as relevant in nested organizations. In other words, high MSI requires fit between memberships of ingroup members as perceived to correlate with own group membership (for the salience of social categorization, see Blanz, 1999; Oakes, Turner, and Haslam, 1991).

Moreover, MSI encompasses both the nature of multiple identities and the relationships between multiple identities.

Nature of multiple identities

Multiple identities in a post-merger organization may have internal (group, division, organization) or external (head office, country), foci—that is, they may exist at different levels of abstraction, ranging from higher- (organization, division) to lower-order (job, workgroup) identities or the employees' personal identity (e.g. their career) (Ashforth and Johnson, 2001). Such multiple memberships might be particularly prevalent in cross-border M&As as different stakeholder groups jointly construct identities; besides merging partners, head office and other subsidiaries might be important stakeholders informing the construction of a shared identity after a merger (Lupina-Wegener, Schneider, and van Dick, 2015). Thus, individuals may also embrace identities beyond the organization, such as nation or region (Lee, 2010; Vora and Kostova, 2007), which also resonates with the stakeholder approach that views organizational identity as "emerging from complex, dynamic, and reciprocal interactions among managers, organizational members, and other stakeholders" (Scott and Lane, 2000: 43).

Relationships between multiple identities

Identities may have various, dichotomous relationships. These relationships may include the following identities: utilitarian versus normative (Albert and Whetten, 1985a); competing versus collaborative (Alvesson, Ashcraft, and Thomas, 2008); and prestigious versus stigmatized (Pratt and Rafaeli, 1997). Thus, embracing multiple identities may help to reduce competing demands on organizational members. However, synergies might need to be looked for if identities are compatible and group interdependence is high (Foreman and Whetten, 2002). However, challenges in cross-border acquisitions particularly emerge if identities are competing or stigmatized, such as in ventures led by multinationals from emerging economies in Western markets (Zhang and Edwards, 2007; Zhang, George, and Chan, 2006). In such conditions, developing identity synergy might be difficult and risks posing competing demands on members from merging organizations.

Summing up, MSI accounts for an ingroup overlap across salient memberships, which may vary in both their nature and their relationships.

Cross-cultural convergence

In case of high cultural distance, differences need to be bridged, and ingroup members strive to determine: "How will we do business after the acquisition?" This question is particularly relevant as management is part of culture (Hofstede, 2007) and thus might result in different managerial practices (Kogut and Singh, 1988; Sirmon and Lane, 2004; Weber, 1996).

While in a separation or assimilation M&A mode one party adopts all or part of the acquirer's culture, in a blending or integration M&A mode the aim is to take the best of both parties in order to develop a new culture (Schweiger, Csiszar, and Napier, 1993). Such a two-way transfer of organizational culture, referred to as cultural cross-vergence (Sarala and Vaara, 2009), may be possible if organizational members embrace dual identities on both internal and external foci (Reade, 2001; Vora and Kostova, 2007). Indeed, while organizational culture is an important source of identity for organizational members, identity defines "who we are" in relation to culture (Fiol *et al.*, 1998). Specifically, we argue that a high MSI enables working, with the strength coming from cultural differences on the organizational level. In other words, differences are not suppressed; on the contrary, they are made available to organizational members. Otherwise, if MSI is low, any attempts to transfer managerial practices might be considered as an identity threat (see Lupina-Wegener, Karamustafa, and Schneider, 2015).

First, we propose that a high MSI allows members from the merging organizations to embrace a mindset of the partner and consequently facilitates openness to learning from one another. Second, understanding partners' management practices may inform MSI. Indeed, sharing management practices allows the acquired and acquiring organizations to develop more common aspects, and to feel belonging to the same entity. Thus, members from the acquired group can understand the acquisition from the acquirer's perspective. Otherwise, if cross-vergence is low, organizational members may experience a threat to their ingroup identities if affected by integration decisions.

Summing up, the conceptual framework presented in this chapter facilitates understanding of how MSIs may develop in cross-border acquisitions characterized by a high cultural distance. We shed light on how MSIs may both inform and result from cultural cross-vergence. In the next section, we will illustrate the model with the case of Chinese acquisitions in Europe.

Model illustration: Chinese subsidiaries in Europe

Past research on dual identities in cross-border ventures has mainly been conducted in the context of subsidiaries of Western HQs. Foreign direct investment (FDI) of emerging companies has received little attention (Bruton and Lau, 2008; Lau and Bruton, 2008) with regard to their subsidiaries in Western economies (Tanure, Penido Barcellos, and Leme Fleury, 2009; Zhang and Dodgson, 2007). We consider Chinese acquisitions in Europe of particular relevance in terms of cultural differences and the search for cultural cross-vergence. Qualitative research conducted on UK subsidiaries of Chinese MNCs reveals two-way managerial transfer under conditions of autonomy of local executives (Zhang and Edwards, 2007). Such a limited functional integration and focus on "business stability" aims to preserve core competencies of the acquired Western company (Cogman and Tan, 2010; Kale, Singh, and Raman, 2009). Interestingly, managerial transfer may also go from Chinese acquirers to the European targets. This can be explained by poor financial situations in Western organizations, which find themselves on the brink of bankruptcy. Thus, Chinese acquirers aim to improve management efficiency in their European subsidiaries.

Despite the need for cross-vergence in Sino-Western acquisitions, a two-way managerial transfer might be particularly difficult between national cultures that are opposed in terms of independence from the ingroup and legitimacy of inequality between individuals (Bhagat, Kedia, Harveston, and Triandis, 2002). Indeed, the Chinese business management style is largely shaped by Confucianism and modern socialism, which may not easily match Western managerial practices (Fan, 1998). Interestingly, Chen and Miller (2010) proposed a conceptual framework of ambicultural management to reconcile the Eastern and Western approaches to management, wherein opposites are viewed as complementary and allow weaknesses in leadership (e.g. East: over-reliance on the leader; West: selfish, opportunistic CEOs), strategy (e.g. East: insular relationships with "rivals"; West: short-sighted competitive initiatives), and organization (e.g. East: lack of independent thought; West: opportunistic individualism) to be overcome.

Objectives of the acquisition

We will illustrate the framework by looking at a Chinese acquisition of a European high-technology manufacturer, which faced financial problems triggered by the global crisis in 2008. The main motive for the Chinese acquirer—Alpha—was to access knowledge in manufacturing for its own local production. Alpha also intended to generate profitability by selling high-end European products to a growing population of wealthy Chinese consumers. On the other hand, the acquired organization—Beta—sought Chinese investment in its brand and wished to gain access into the fast-growing Chinese market. Thus, the European manufacturer hoped for increased profitability. It is also important to mention that this acquisition was the second for the European manufacturer: Beta had previously been acquired by Gamma, another MNC.

The integration decision aimed at a gradual increase of strategic interdependence, on the one hand, and a decrease of autonomy, on the other. Beta's strategy was focused on profitability through growth in the Chinese market. Thus, at the acquisition announcement, the subsidiary Beta-Europe was created in order to implement Beta's expansion into China. In the first phase, Beta's manufacturing facilities were constructed in China and based on European development and component sourcing, with medium strategic interdependence between Alpha and Beta. This project was led by Beta-Europe and executed by Beta-China, and the decrease in autonomy at Beta was low. At Beta-China, European expatriates were "pair matched" with their Chinese homologues in order to foster a two-way transfer of managerial practices.

In the second phase, and in addition to China-based manufacturing, Chinese sourcing was introduced in order to reduce production costs at Beta. Sourcing for Chinese manufacturing was led by Beta-China and sourcing for European manufacturing by Beta-Europe. Thus, decentralization took place as strategic interdependence between Beta-Europe and Beta-China increased. Although the two organizations cooperated closely, decisions were taken by the leaders of the respective organizations for their markets. Thus, Beta-Europe's autonomy decreased in favor of the Chinese operations.

In the third, current phase, focus has been devoted to launch joint production. An Alpha–Beta research center was created in Europe—financed and led by the Chinese in order to prepare this R&D project. While strategic interdependence increased between Alpha and Beta, members of Beta-Europe experienced a further reduction in autonomy and faced pressure to reduce costs in the manufacturing process.

Multiple shared identities

In this studied case, three pairs of identities were particularly salient among members of the acquired organization: pre- versus post-Gamma (comparisons with the previous owner; past to present); Alpha versus Beta (comparisons of pre-merger identities); and China versus Europe (differentiations based on national identity).

Pre- versus post-Gamma identities (comparisons between past and present)

The acquisition by Alpha was welcomed by Beta members, who appreciated the fact that they were no longer owned by Gamma—an MNC with multiple businesses. During the Gamma ownership, Beta was: *small*, as it was part of a large structure with imposed centralized processes; and *dependent*, as Beta did not receive necessary investment, growth potential was limited and ultimately led to financial problems. After the acquisition by Alpha, Beta became: *important*, in terms of increased business relevance; and *independent*, due to the autonomy that Alpha granted. Thus, the acquisition facilitated an increase in Beta's identity *self-esteem* (from small to important and independent). The opportunity to regain face after years of humiliation was appreciated by organizational members.

Alpha versus Beta research and manufacturing (comparisons of the pre-merger identities on a functional level)

Complementarities between Alpha and Beta were high, and while the acquisition was crucial for Beta's survival, it was also an important step into Alpha's internationalization. Thus, Alpha's engineering and Beta's cost-driven identities complemented one another. Beta was a *traditional, high-quality* manufacturer whose expertise and experience developed through decades of steady growth. By contrast, Alpha was funded in an early phase of China's entry into the World Trade Organization. Its successes resulted from outstanding cost management, volume growth, and political contacts. Alpha is a *young, fast-growing, and cost-driven* enterprise. Overall, Beta's identity was distinct from Alpha's on *a functional* level, which allowed members from Beta to aspire to Alpha's speed, cost control, and volume growth. Thus, Beta members were both proud of their own organization and strongly admired Alpha for its rapid development.

Chinese versus European manufacturing industry (making sense of conflicting identities on a normative level)

In Alpha's acquisition of Beta, national-level identities were salient. First, *cheap Chinese* was salient among members of the acquired organization—that is, low-end manufacturer. Such low quality was viewed to result from a lack of expertise in manufacturing, an excessive focus on cost, and thus the use of cheap components in manufacturing. Second, *high European quality* was embedded in the national values and resulted from high-quality components and technological innovation. These dual identities—"Made in China" versus "Made in Europe"—were considered not to fit well together. Thus, calls to keep the identities separate came from the Chinese top management, which received immediate support from the European organization. Beta particularly feared stigma due to an association with China's reputation for cheapness.

MSI and cultural cross-vergence

The search for cultural cross-vergence was apparent at Alpha and Beta, with a particular focus on the three managerial practices: strategy, leadership, and organization (for an ambicultural approach to management, see Chen and Miller, 2010). In the early phase of integration, European expatriates were in charge of building a Chinese organization. Each was paired with a Chinese homologue in order to facilitate a two-way knowledge transfer. In the second phase, the "matched pair" system ceased, and Chinese and Europeans either worked together in multicultural teams in China or interacted virtually. In the third phase, Beta-Europe's autonomy decreased and the Alpha–Beta joint research center was established in Europe, with many Chinese engineers relocated there.

Strategy

Taking the best of both Alpha and Beta at the strategic level focused on: improving the bottom line through investment in future products at both organizations; reducing manufacturing costs at Beta; and increasing sales of Beta products in China and sales of Alpha products in Europe. Consequently, production sites were constructed for Beta in China and a joint manufacturing project for Beta and Alpha products was launched. Moreover, in order to ensure an appropriate cost structure, local sourcing was encouraged—that is, Beta-Europe would purchase components only for European manufacturing, while Beta-China was in charge of China-based manufacturing. Quality was supervised by the Beta-Europe team. Members of Beta supported this strategy, aligned with utilitarian identities of Alpha versus Beta (comparisons of the pre-merger identities), which were in a cooperative relationship: Beta's high quality but low volume versus Alpha's high volume but low quality. As Beta members identified strongly with their organization and were committed to its survival, they hoped to benefit from Alpha's rapid growth. Summing up, high dual identity distinctiveness allowed for Beta's support for a change in strategy.

Leadership

Important differences existed with regard to leadership at the European and Chinese operations. First, high power distance was evident at Alpha, wherein one-person-based, fast decisions were predominantly taken. By contrast, at Beta low power distance implied a team-based and time-consuming decision-making process involving a large number of relevant stakeholders. Second, at Alpha and Beta-China there was high reliance on a single leader and, thus, Chinese employees paid close attention to status and seniority and rarely dared to challenge their leaders. By contrast, at Beta-Europe, employees were empowered to take decisions and could rely on support from the hierarchy in complex situations. Third, at the Chinese organizations, employees executed their supervisors' orders and focused strictly on their narrow job descriptions. As a result, they were engaged in an aggressive search for lower component costs, challenging existing suppliers and searching for new, cheaper sources. Less concern was given to quality and technical aspects. At Beta, employees were expected to challenge their supervisors, and they were more empowered in decision-making to ensure quality based on multiple perspectives. Such a decision-making process was time-consuming and the execution was slower than at Alpha as leaders had limited possibilities to push their subordinates. As a result, the Europeans were much slower to find new suppliers and push down costs.

Taking the best of both cultures at the leadership level implied increasing the speed of decision-making at Beta and allowing Chinese employees to express their opinions. Members of Beta supported this strategy, aligned with emotional identities of Gamma versus Beta (comparisons between past and present on an emotional level). Beta's increase in self-esteem (important and independent) supported calls for it to become agile.

At the same time, Beta insisted on maintaining the system whereby its employees were encouraged to challenge their managers and proactively develop alternative solutions; indeed it wished to promote this in the Chinese organizations, too. These calls were aligned with Beta identity in terms of *high quality*. Although Beta appreciated Alpha's speed, it was concerned about the quality of the Chinese firm's decision-making due to blind obedience to superiors.

Summing up, high dual identity distinctiveness facilitated Beta's support for a change in leadership in terms of becoming "faster and agile" but there was still an insistence on maintaining egalitarian "follower–leader" relations.

Organization

Both Europeans and Chinese faced significant challenges in their attempts to achieve cross-vergence at the organizational level. First, important differences existed in the corporate culture, which was engineering-driven at Beta and cost-driven at Alpha. In Europe, work in cross-functional teams was embedded in cohesive corporate cultures that allowed flat structures and broad job definitions. Cultural values at Beta centered on quality and product development in cross-functional teams. An important role was attached to processes coordinating this cross-functional work from product development, sourcing materials that met engineering specifications and manufacturing. In China, job definitions were narrower and work was dominantly carried out in silos. Cultural values at Alpha centered on volume—that is, fast and cheap production. Second, there was a difference in industry culture in Europe and China. While the focus in Europe was on pure facts, in China fast decisions were often based on intuitive assumptions, which in turn were based on informal exchange of information between employees, suppliers, and government. In Europe, the boundaries between key stakeholders were clearly defined and interactions were strictly business driven.

Beta employees felt that the efforts of their Chinese counterparts to implement a cost-driven culture imperiled their European quality. Beta-Europe insisted on maintaining an engineering-driven culture, and thus called for both Beta-China and

Alpha to adopt the processes that were considered necessary to ensure high quality and good brand reputation. After gaining self-esteem and distinctiveness after the acquisition, the Chinese decision not to adopt these processes posed a threat to Beta members and was perceived as an attempt to remove European quality and bring cheapness to Beta.

Summing up, dual identities at the national level were not embraced by Beta; indeed, they were viewed as conflicting. Thus, any attempts by the Chinese top management to adjust Beta's products for the Chinese market or associate Beta with China were viewed as threatening and were resisted.

Work-related outcomes after the acquisition

Collaboration was often difficult and attempts to bring European and Chinese managers closer together often proved problematic. First, Beta employees particularly pointed to the lack of experience of their Chinese counterparts and a lack of business acumen. Due to their relatively young age and low seniority in the industry, it was believed that the Chinese managers were unable to assess risk or envision potential problems and solutions, and that they needed constant supervision to ensure quality in the production process. Second, communication between Europeans and Chinese proved difficult due to language problems. Moreover, while direct communication was dominant in Europe, it was very difficult for Beta employees to understand Chinese communication, particularly with respect to "confirmatory" responses when there was disagreement. Overall, trust between the Chinese and the Europeans proved hard to establish as the European managers felt their Chinese counterparts had a double agenda, and sometimes they doubted their good intentions.

Discussion

Multiple identities were shared by ingroup members on internal and external foci with low-order identities (functional, organizational) embedded in higher-order identities (industry, national). Strategic cross-vergence was encouraged by identities as shared on organizational foci: post-Gamma and Beta. Leadership cross-vergence was encouraged by identities as shared on the functional foci (Alpha versus Beta research and manufacturing). Cross-vergence on an organizational level was impeded by identities on the industry and national foci (China versus Europe).

The present case illustrates the importance of MSI in cultural cross-vergence as applied to M&As which are characterized by strategic interdependence and decreasing autonomy of the acquired organization. In the case of low autonomy decrease but high interdependence, a reverse takeover would have occurred, and MSI would have played an important role to transfer European management practices into Chinese operations. On the other hand, in an acquisition of low strategic interdependence and low autonomy decrease, there is less necessity for MSI as only a few management practices would need to be transferred between Europe and China. Finally, in an acquisition of low strategic interdependence and high autonomy decrease, success of the acquisition would have been difficult to achieve. As such, European managers would tend to perceive any Chinese head office attempts to implement change or decrease autonomy as identity threat.

Practical implications

Unless dual identities develop on both high- and low-order levels, Beta risks a further decline in autonomy due to the efforts of Alpha to maintain its control over organizational processes. Thus, developing multiple shared identities is a priority in this acquisition. Particularly, MSI on national and industry foci requires increased exchange between Chinese and Europeans who work predominantly on a virtual basis. However, the three-month exchange program was recently stopped for financial reasons. Such exchange programs should be encouraged, and anyone working in Sino-European teams should acquire professional experience in the partner's country. Such exchange, however, should focus on assignments that do not imply competition and do not encourage a fight for scarce resources. Global talent management should be established at both Beta and Alpha to ensure a systematic two-way transfer of managerial practices.

References

Albert, S., and Whetten, D. A. 1985a. Organizational identity. In L. L. Cummings, and B. M. Staw (Eds.), *Research in organizational behavior*, Vol. 7: 263–295. Greenwich, CT, and London: JAI Press.

Albert, S., and Whetten, D. A. 1985b. Organizational identity. *Research in Organizational Behavior*, 7: 263–295.

Alvesson, M., Ashcraft, K. L., and Thomas, R. 2008. Identity matters: Reflections on the construction of identity scholarship in organization studies. *Organization*, 15(1): 5–28.

Ashforth, B. E., and Johnson, S. A. 2001. Which hat to wear? The relative salience of multiple identities in organizational contexts. *Social Identity Processes in Organizational Contexts*, 31: 48.

Ashforth, B. E., and Mael, F. 1989. Social identity theory and the organization. *Academy of management review*, 14(1): 20–39.

Barkema, H. G., and Vermeulen, F. 1998. International expansion through start-up or acquisition: A learning perspective. *Academy of Management Journal*, 41(1): 7–26.

Bartels, J., Pruyn, A., and de Jong, M. 2009. Employee identification before and after an internal merger: A longitudinal analysis. *Journal of Occupational and Organizational Psychology*, 82(1): 113–128.

Bhagat, R. S., Kedia, B. L., Harveston, P. D., and Triandis, H. C. 2002. Cultural variations in the cross-border transfer of organizational knowledge: An integrative framework. *Academy of Management Review*, 27(2): 204–221.

Blanz, M. 1999. Accessibility and fit as determinants of the salience of social categorizations. *European Journal of Social Psychology*, 29(1): 43–74.

Blomkvist, K., and Drogendijk, R. 2013. The impact of psychic distance on Chinese outward foreign direct investments. *Management International Review*, 53(5): 659–686.

Brewer, M. B. 1991. The social self: On being the same and different at the same time. *Personality and Social Psychology Bulletin*, 17(5): 475–482.

Brown, L. T., Rugman, A. M., and Verbeke, A. 1989. Japanese joint ventures with Western multinationals: Synthesising the economic and cultural explanations of failure. *Asia Pacific Journal of Management*, 6(2): 225–242.

Bruton, G. D., and Lau, C.-M. 2008. Asian management research: Status today and future outlook. *Journal of Management Studies*, 45(3): 636–659.

Chen, M.-J., and Miller, D. 2010. West meets East: Toward an ambicultural approach to management. *Academy of Management Perspectives*, 24(4): 17.

Cogman, D., and Tan, J. 2010. A lighter touch for postmerger integration. *McKinsey Quarterly*, January: 8–12.

Distefano, J. J., and Maznevski, M. L. 2000. Creating value with diverse teams in global management. *Organizational Dynamics*, 29(1): 45–63.

Dutton, J. E., Dukerich, J. M., and Harquail, C. V. 1994. Organizational images and member identification. *Administrative Science Quarterly*, 39(2): 239–263.

Fan, Y. 1998. The transfer of Western management to China: Context, content and constraints. *Management Learning*, 29(2): 201–221.

Fiol, C. M., Hatch, M. J., and Golden-Biddle, K. 1998. Organizational culture and identity: What's the difference anyway? In D. Whetten, and P. Godfrey (Eds.), *Identity in organizations:: Building theory through conversations*: 56–62. Thousands Oaks, CA: Sage.

Foreman, P., and Whetten, D. A. 2002. Members' identification with multiple-identity organizations. *Organization Science*, 13(6): 618–635.

Gaertner, S. L., Dovidio, J. F., Anastasio, P. A., Bachman, B. A., and Rust, M. C. 1993. The common ingroup identity model: Recategroization and the reduction of intergroup bias. *European Review of Social Psychology*, 4: 1–25.

Gioia, D. A., Price, K. N., Hamilton, A. L., and Thomas, J. B. 2010. Forging an identity: An insider-outsider study of processes involved in the formation of organizational identity. *Administrative Science Quarterly*, 55(1): 1–46.

Haslam, A. 2001. *Psychology in organisations: The social identity approach*. London: Sage.

Haslam, S. A., Postmes, T., and Ellemers, N. 2003. More than a metaphor: Organizational identity makes organizational life possible. *British Journal of Management*, 14(4): 357–369.

Hofstede, G. 1980. *Culture's consequences*. Beverly Hills, CA: Sage.

Hofstede, G. H. 2001. *Culture's consequences: Comparing values, behaviors, institutions and organizations across nations*. Beverly Hills, CA: Sage.

Hofstede, G. 2007. Asian management in the 21st century. *Asia Pacific Journal of Management*, 24(4): 411–420.

Hogg, M. A., and Terry, D. I. 2000. Social identity and self-categorization processes in organizational contexts. *Academy of Management Review*, 25(1): 121–140.

House, R. J., Hanges, P. J., Javidan, M., Dorfman, P. W., and Gupta, V. 2004. *Leadership, culture, and organizations: The GLOBE study of 62 societies*. Beverly Hills, CA: Sage.

Hutzschenreuter, T., Voll, J. C., and Verbeke, A. 2011. The impact of added cultural distance and cultural diversity on international expansion patterns: A Penrosean perspective. *Journal of Management Studies*, 48(2): 305–329.

Kale, P., Singh, H., and Raman, A. P. 2009. Don't integrate your acquisitions, partner with them. *Harvard Business Review*, 87(12): 101–115.

Kogut, B., and Singh, H. 1988. The effect of national culture on the choice of entry mode. *Journal of International Business Studies*, 19(3): 411–432.

Krishnan, H. A., Miller, A., and Judge, W. Q. 1997. Diversification and top management team complementarity: Is performance improved by merging similar or dissimilar teams? *Strategic Management Journal*, 18(5): 361–374.

Lau, C. M., and Bruton, G. D. 2008. FDI in China: What we know and what we need to study next. *Academy of Management Perspectives*, 22(4): 30–44.

Lee, Y.-T. 2010. Home versus host: Identifying with either, both, or neither? The relationship between dual cultural identities and intercultural effectiveness. *International Journal of Cross Cultural Management*, 10(1): 55–76.

Lubatkin, M., Schweiger, D., and Weber, Y. 1999. Top management turnover M related M&As: An additional test of the theory of relative standing. *Journal of Management*, 25(1): 55–73.

Lupina-Wegener, A., Karamustafa, G., and Schneider, S. C. 2015. Causes and consequences of different types of identity threat: Perceived legitimacy of decisions in M&As. In A. Risberg, D. King, and O. Meglio (Eds.), *M&A companion*: 354–366. Abingdon: Routledge.

Lupina-Wegener, A. A., Schneider, S. C., and van Dick, R. 2011. Different experiences of socio-cultural integration: A European merger in Mexico. *Journal of Organizational Change Management*, 24(1): 65–89.

Lupina-Wegener, A., Schneider, S. C., and van Dick, R. 2015. The role of outgroups in constructing a shared identity: A longitudinal study of a subsidiary merger in Mexico. *Management International Review*, 55(5): 677–705.

Mael, F., and Ashforth, B. E. 1992. Alumni and their alma mater: A partial test of the reformulated model of organizational identification. *Journal of Organizational Behavior*, 13(2): 103–123.

Marks, M. L., and Mirvis, P. H. 2011. Merge ahead: A research agenda to increase merger and acquisition success. *Journal of Business and Psychology*, 26(2): 161–168.

Morosini, P., Shane, S., and Singh, H. 1998. National cultural distance and cross-border acquisition performance. *Journal of International Business Studies*, 29(1): 137–158.

Oakes, P. J., Turner, J. C., and Haslam, S. A. 1991. Perceiving people as group members: The role of fit in the salience of social categorizations. *British Journal of Social Psychology*, 30(2): 125–144.

Petrick, J. A., Scherer, R. F., Brodzinski, J. D., Quinn, J. F., and Ainina, M. F. 1999. Global leadership skills and reputational capital: Intangible resources for sustainable competitive advantage. *Academy of Management Executive*, 13(1): 58–69.

Pratt, M. G. 2001. Social identity dynamics in modern organizations: An organizational psychology/organizational behavior perspective. *Social identity processes in organizational contexts*: 13–30.

Pratt, M. G., and Rafaeli, A. 1997. Organizational dress as a symbol of multilayered social identities. *Academy of Management Journal*, 40(4): 862–898.

Reade, C. 2001. Dual identification in multinational corporations: Local managers and their psychological attachment to the subsidiary versus the global organization. *International Journal of Human Resource Management*, 12(3): 405–424.

Riketta, M. 2005. Organizational identification: A meta-analysis. *Journal of Vocational Behavior*, 66(2): 358–384.

Roccas, S., and Brewer, M. B. 2002. Social identity complexity. *Personality and Social Psychology Review*, 6(2): 88–106.

Rousseau, D. 1998. Why workers still identify with organizations. *Journal of Organizational Behavior*, 19(3): 217–233.

Rugman, A. M., Verbeke, A., and Nguyen, P. C. Q. T. 2011. Fifty years of international business theory and beyond. *Management International Review*, 51(6): 755–786.

Rugman, A., Verbeke, A., and Yuan, W. 2011. Re-conceptualizing Bartlett and Ghoshal's classification of national subsidiary roles in the multinational enterprise. *Journal of Management Studies*, 48(2): 253–277.

Russette, J. W., Scully, R. E., and Preziosi, R. 2008. Leadership across cultures: A comparative study. *Academy of Strategic Management Journal*, 7(1): 47–61.

Sanchez-Burks, J., Lee, F., Richard, N., and Incheol, C. 2003. Coversing across cultures: East–West communication styles in work and nonwork contexts. *Journal of Personality and Social Psychology*, 85(2): 363–372.

Sarala, R. M., and Vaara, E. 2010. Cultural differences, convergence, and crossvergence as explanations of knowledge transfer in international acquisitions. *Journal of International Business Studies*, 41(8): 1365–1390.

Schweiger, D. M., Csiszar, E. N., and Napier, N. K. 1993. Implementing international mergers and acquisitions. *Human Resource Planning*, 16: 53–53.

Scott, S. G., and Lane, V. R. 2000. A stakeholder approach to organizational identity. *Academy of Management Review*, 25(1): 43–62.

Sirmon, D. G., and Lane, P. J. 2004. A model of cultural differences and international alliance performance. *Journal of International Business Studies*, 35(4): 306–319.

Tajfel, H., and Turner, J. C. 1986. The social identity theory of intergroup behaviour. In S. Worchel and W. G. Austin (Eds.), *Psychology of intergroup relations*: 7–24. Chicago: Nelson-Hall.

Tanure, B., Penido Barcellos, E., and Leme Fleury, M. T. 2009. Psychic distance and the challenges of expatriation from Brazil. *International Journal of Human Resource Management*, 20(5): 1039–1055.

Tihanyi, L., Griffith, D. A., and Russell, C. J. 2005. The effect of cultural distance on entry mode choice, international diversification, and MNE performance: A meta-analysis. *Journal of International Business Studies*, 36(3): 270–283.

Turner, J. C. I.. 1985. Social categorization and the self-concept: A social cognitive theory of group behavior. In E. J. Lawler (Ed.), *Advances in group processes*: 77–121. Greenwich, CT: JAI Press.

Turner, J. C., Hogg, M. A., Oakes, P. J., Reicher, S. D., and Wetherell, M. S. 1987. *Rediscovering the social group: A self-categorization theory*. Oxford: Basil Blackwell.

van Dick, R., Ullrich, J., and Tissington, P. A. 2006. Working under a black cloud: How to sustain organizational identification after a merger. *British Journal of Management*, 17(Special): 69–79.

van Dick, R., Wagner, U., Stellmacher, J., and Christ, O. 2004. The utility of a broader conceptualization of organizational identification: Which aspects really matter? *Journal of Occupational and Organizational Psychology*, 77(2): 171–191.

van Knippenberg, D., and van Schie, E. 2000. Foci and correlates of organizational identification. *Journal of Occupational and Organizational Psychology*, 73(2): 137–147.

Vora, D., and Kostova, T. 2007. A model of dual organizational identification in the context of the multinational enterprise. *Journal of Organizational Behavior*, 28(3): 327.

Vora, D., Kostova, T., and Roth, K. 2007. Roles of subsidiary managers in multinational corporations: The effect of dual organizational identification. *Management International Review*, 47(4): 595–620.

Weber, Y. 1996. Corporate cultural fit and performance in mergers and acquisitions. *Human Relations*, 49(9): 1181–1202.

Zhang, M. Y., and Dodgson, M. 2007. "A roasted duck can still fly away": A case study of technology, nationality, culture and the rapid and early internationalization of the firm. *Journal of World Business*, 42(3): 336–349.

Zhang, M., and Edwards, C. 2007. Diffusing "best practice" in Chinese multinationals: The motivation, facilitation and limitations. *International Journal of Human Resource Management*, 18(12): 2147–2165.

Zhang, Y., George, J. M., and Chan, T.-S. 2006. The paradox of dueling identities: The case of local senior executives in MNC subsidiaries. *Journal of Management*, 32(3): 400–425.

11

THE LINK BETWEEN CULTURAL DUE DILIGENCE AND SOCIOCULTURAL POST-MERGER INTEGRATION MANAGEMENT AS A CRITICAL SUCCESS FACTOR IN M&As

Natalie Witzmann and Christoph Dörrenbächer

Introduction

Mergers and acquisitions (M&As) are today's main vehicle for corporate growth. This is the case even though 66–75 per cent of M&As fail to create any shareholder value (McKinsey, 2010: 1). Some studies even stress that 40 per cent of M&As among large firms end in what is called a 'total failure', in which the acquiring companies are far from recovering their capital investments (Carleton and Lineberry, 2004: 9). The high failure rate and the immense costs related to the failure of M&As are growing concerns not only for shareholders but also for stakeholders, such as employees, suppliers and community residents. Hence, there is rising interest in finding the reasons for the numerous failures. While traditional research has attempted to explain M&A success and failure by focusing on strategic and financial factors, a growing number of studies focus on cultural aspects. Here, the research suggests that corporate and national cultures of the involved firms should be adequately identified during due diligence and integrated in the post-M&A phase (Stahl, Chua and Pablo, 2012). However, in reality, cultural fit between the acquiring and the target firm seems to be one of the most neglected areas of analysis prior to closing a deal (Chakravorty, 2012). In 2007, Robert Carleton, CEO of Vector Group, stated that 'Cultural Due Diligence will rarely be a critical factor in whether to "do the deal" or not, but rather a significant factor in making the deal work' (cited in Garbade, 2009: 14). Likewise, many researchers argue that the right post-merger integration (PMI) management is the decisive factor in M&A success (e.g. Pablo, 1994; Birkinshaw *et al.*, 2000).

This all leads to the questions of when and by what means cultural issues should be addressed in the M&A process – a complex procedure that encompasses pre-deal planning, deal completion as well as post-deal integration and the creation of value (KPMG, 2002). As indicated above, there is abundant literature on successful post-M&A integration (PMI) management, basically arguing that culture should be integrated carefully. Much less research has been done on cultural due diligence (CDD), with research on the interrelation between CDD and PMI management in its infancy. To address this gap, this chapter will look at the entire process of cultural integration, from pre-deal planning to post-deal implementation, placing particular emphasis on the interrelationship between CDD and PMI. Thereby, we aim to clarify the extent to which CDD is a prerequisite for a successful PMI process. This aim fits neatly into a gap in the M&A literature that has been described succinctly in the following extract from a recent overview article:

> The existing body of knowledge [on M&A] is characterized by several independent streams of management research that have studied discrete variables in either the *pre*acquisition or *post*acquisition stage. From the review of the literature in this article, it can be concluded that despite the considerable amount of research carried out into M&A over the past half century, *there is limited and compartmentalized understanding of the complex acquisition process, since the various streams of research on acquisition activity are only marginally informed by one another.*
>
> *(Gomes* et al., *2013: 30; emphasis added)*

The chapter starts with a short review of the literature on CDD and PMI. Then a conceptual model on the interrelation between CDD and PMI is developed and applied to a single-case: the Hewlett-Packard–Compaq merger. Following an analysis and discussion section, the chapter closes with some recommendations for further research.

Literature review

There is a far-reaching consensus in the literature that bringing together two different organisational cultures in a merger or acquisition is a great challenge. Following Schein (2003), incompatible cultures in M&As do not pose any less risk of failure than incompatibilities of the firms' finances, products or markets. In line with that, Cartwright and Cooper (1993) identify cultural incompatibility as one of the primary reasons for the immense failure rate of M&As. Cultural incompatibility typically unfolds in the sociocultural integration process, 'an interactive and gradual process in which individuals from two organizations learn to work together and cooperate in the transfer of strategic capabilities' (Haspeslagh and Jemison, 1991: 106). Within this process different levels of acculturation can be achieved: assimilation, integration, deculturation and separation (Nahavandi and Malekzadeh, 1988). Another well-known taxonomy by Haspeslagh and Jemison (1991: 138–154) differentiates between absorption (acquired firm adjusts itself to acquirer's culture), preservation (acquired organisation retains its cultural autonomy), symbiosis (best practices of both firms are combined, leading to cultural integration) and holding (firm does not seek any integration or value creation). Despite different levels of integration and acculturation that can be followed by firms involved in M&A, culture clash continues to be stated as the main reason for the failure of many M&As: 'culture is more often a source of conflict than of synergy. Cultural differences are a nuisance at best and often a disaster' (Hofstede quoted in *The Economist*, 2008).

What puzzles, however, given this and similar accounts (e.g. Carleton and Lineberry, 2004), is the fact that there has been little research into culture in the pre-merger phase – that is, the due diligence process. This is even more striking as a more forceful recognition of cultural aspects in the pre-deal phase is considered a prerequisite for a successful post-merger integration phase: 'A culture audit of a potential or recently acquired organization is a valuable source of information, with implications not only for partner selection but also for long-term management' (Cartwright and Cooper, 1993: 68).

Cultural due diligence

CDD aims to investigate the culture of the other party in an M&A in order 'to gather information that will assist in decision making and risk analysis' (Carleton and Lineberry, 2004: 51). Table 11.1 provides a few definitions from the literature.

Three basic insights emanate from these definitions: First, CDD is more than just a simple culture analysis but rather an instrument for a thorough examination and evaluation of the corporate cultures of partners engaged in a merger or an acquisition. Second, CDD serves as an early identification of potential cultural risks (Blöcher, 2004), which should decisively influence the PMI strategy (Carleton and Lineberry, 2004) or foreclose the deal in case of irreconcilable cultural differences and barriers (Schneck, 2007). Third, for these reasons, CDD should by no means play a subordinate role in comparison to the traditional due diligence areas (Schneck, 2007).

Carleton and Lineberry (2004: 69) emphasise that, as with 'any sound organisational research, a CDD process [should] employ both qualitative and quantitative data collection'. They distinguish between 'off-the-shelf' and 'customised' CDD

TABLE 11.1 Definition of the term 'cultural due diligence'

Author	*Definition*
Marks (1999: 14)	'Culture due diligence helps buyers spot likely people problems at a target and determine whether potential clashes might sink the deal.'
Galpin and Herndon (2007: 47)	'The primary value of cultural due diligence is that is raises sensitivity to and awareness of issues that should be proactively managed during integration.'
Carleton and Lineberry (2004: 54)	'Cultural Due Diligence is a systemic and research-based methodology for significantly increasing the odds of success of mergers, acquisitions, and alliances.'

processes. 'Off-the-shelf' assessment models are generally based on quantitative data only. They do not differentiate between value-based and non-value-based differences, lack attention to detail and hence assume a 'one size fits all' (Carleton and Lineberry, 2004: 56). 'Customised' CDD processes, on the other hand, are seen to combine a qualitative research design, including interviews, focus groups and workplace observations, with a customised quantitative survey (Carleton and Lineberry, 2004).

Even though the design of a CDD is, as Blöcher (2004) maintains, little standardised (but determined by the specific needs of the involved companies), Carleton and Lineberry (2004) and Schneck (2007) provide a reasonably simplified CDD process model that draws on both qualitative and quantitative data (see Figure 11.1).

The first step in a CDD process is an acquirer self-assessment (1). This is to detect prevailing problems within the acquiring firm and to provide a solid basis for a comparison with the cultures of potential target firms (2–3). If a potential target is selected, a high-level CDD assessment of the target firm is undertaken (4). Given the access problems in the pre-deal phase, a high-level CDD assessment remains more of an *estimate* rather than the scientific mapping of the target culture. What follows is an assessment of the executive team's compatibility (5) and of the ability to retain key people (6). In the 'post-letter of intent/acceptance' phase, steps 3–6 are typically repeated in order to prepare a detailed cultural profile of the target organisation and to identify potential cultural risks and conflict areas (Zimmer, 2001). Risks and conflict areas, in turn, indicate the cultural difficulties the sociocultural PMI process is expecting.

Sociocultural post-merger integration management

A large number of theoretical and empirical studies stress the importance an effective sociocultural PMI has for the success of M&As (Cartwright and Cooper, 1993; Pablo, 1994; Quah and Young, 2005). Building on the distinction between task and human integration, Birkinshaw *et al.* (2000) argue that the higher the level of human integration in the early stages of the PMI, the easier and more effective the integration of tasks later. Homing in on this finding, Stahl and Voigt (2008) argue that the impact cultural differences have on the integration process, especially on human integration, should be thoroughly analysed and used in order to realise M&A synergies successfully. Despite some slight differences in definitions, these authors all agree that the lower the level of cultural integration, the higher the likelihood of post-M&A problems due to an insufficient or slow-paced task integration.

The difficulty of integrating different corporate cultures after deal is often attributed to a strong resistance to change that organisations face in general and in particular after M&As. Kotter and Schlesinger (2008) identify four common reasons for resistance to change based on their analysis of numerous successful and unsuccessful organisational changes. *Parochial self-interest* relates to people's fear that the change will cause them to lose something of value. Another extremely important reason for resistance to change is *misunderstanding and lack of trust*. In this case,

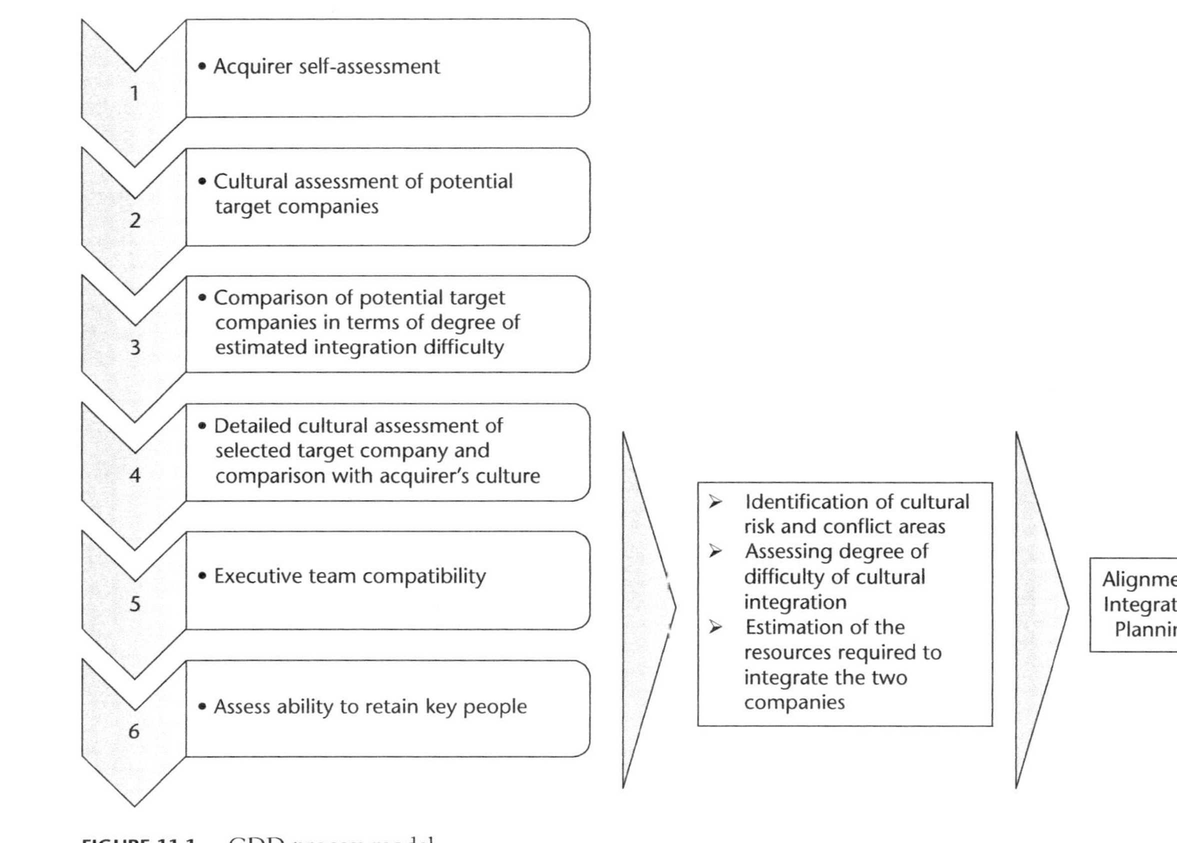

FIGURE 11.1 CDD process model

employees do not comprehend the impact of the change and think that it might cost them more than they will benefit from it. People might also resist change when they *assess the situation differently* from their supervisors and perceive the costs involved as higher than the benefits, not only for themselves but for the entire organisation. The fourth reason – *low tolerance for change* – emerges when people fear they will fail to meet new expectations in terms of skills and behaviour initiated by the change.

Given the overarching importance of overcoming such resistance to change, the last three decades have seen a growing body of research on key success factors that positively influence post-merger human integration. The majority of authors argue that the following interdependent factors require particular attention.

Speed of integration

The optimal speed of PMI has been well debated in the literature. Some researchers argue that firms should take time in fully implementing the changes and gradually prepare the employees for the change, while other authors suggest that people are open for change right after the M&A announcement. There is often talk of the 'first 100 days' as a critical timeframe for post-deal success (Angwin, 2004). Feldmann and Spratt (1999: 2) argue that 'if your transition is not progressing along a hundred-day critical path, you are behind the power curve'. Relating this statement to a human integration perspective, faster integration takes advantage of the employees' initial enthusiasm and reduces the timeframe for employees to experience uncertainty feelings that mostly result from rumours going around the firm, which in turn exponentially increase with time if not actively addressed (Angwin, 2004). Vester (2002) points out the significance of speed during the post-merger integration process, particularly for M&As of technology firms, leading to the assumption that the business environment in which the merging organisations operate may determine the adequate speed of the integration process.

Trust

As Kotter and Schlesinger (2008) pointed out, one source of resistance to change is a lack of trust between the acquiring firm and the employees, as the latter do not understand the consequences of the change and might perceive it as harmful for themselves. The term 'trust' is defined as 'a psychological state comprising the intention to accept vulnerability based upon positive expectations of the intentions or behaviour of another' (Rousseau *et al.*, 1998: 395). Since the situation following the merger or acquisition announcement is highly unpredictable, especially for employees, people feel vulnerable and therefore initially tend to distrust the new organisational form (Stahl *et al.*, 2012). The dynamic nature of trust, however, allows the acquirer to further target employees' trust proactively through communicating shared norms, knowledge and goals among all employees (Bijlsma-Frankema, 2001).

Communication

According to Kotter and Schlesinger (2008), one of best ways to deal with resistance to change is 'education and communication', meaning that the people affected by the change should be educated about it beforehand, and the impacts of the change should be clearly communicated. Also, Haspeslagh and Jemison (1991: 180) advocate alleviating 'concerns by carefully communicating and confirming what will not change to the managers and employees of the acquired firm' before combining the two firms. Bastien's (1987) study of behaviour and communication during M&As found that extensive formal and informal communication was crucial in order to reduce employees' uncertainty feelings, which involve sudden switches from very positive to very negative future scenarios. In periods in which no or poor efforts for communication where made, uncertainty feelings among employees grew immediately, productivity decreased and employee turnover increased. Bastien (1987) concludes that the acquiring firm needs to understand its own and the target firm's corporate cultures so that differing norms and practices do not evolve as sources of conflict and rejection. As Hubbard and Purcell (2001) posit, adequate expectations levels are set through effective acquirer communication, resulting in decreased uncertainty and less loss of confidence among key stakeholders.

Retaining key people

During a merger or acquisition the internal and external environments of the involved firms inevitably become unstable and precarious, making key performers either lose their commitment to the firm or even switch to competitors. For headhunters and competitors, M&As are among the best opportunities to recruit top performers (Galpin and Herndon, 2007). Galpin and Herndon (2007: 127) put it in a nutshell: 'Your best players will find a new team first.' It does not seem surprising, then, that a study measuring top management turnover rates in M&As found that for at least a decade following the acquisition, target firms lose 21 per cent of their executives each year – more than double the turnover rate of non-merged firms (Krug and Shill, 2008: 17). Therefore, 'organisations should give the retention and "rerecruitment" of top performers one of the highest priorities during a merger or acquisition' (Galpin and Herndon, 2007: 128). The term 'rerecruitment' implies not only that key people should be given incentives for staying in the firm but also that actions should be taken to keep these key people motivated (Galpin and Herndon, 2007). A more recent study by Ahammad *et al.* (2012) identified post-acquisition autonomy granted to the acquired company as well as the acquiring firm's engagement to the acquired firm as critical success factors in retaining key executives.

The link between cultural due diligence and sociocultural post-merger integration management

While a few studies focus on pre-deal CDD (Blöcher, 2004; Zimmer, 2001; Schneck, 2007), most studies that show an interest in cultural integration issues exclusively look at PMI management (Pablo, 1994; Stahl and Voigt, 2008; Quah and Young, 2005; Birkinshaw *et al.*, 2000), essentially following Haspeslagh and Jemison's (1991: 132) assertion that 'all value creation takes place after the acquisition'. Thereby, these latter studies more or less all neglect to mention that value creation might start long before the merger or acquisition contract is signed. There are a few exceptions, such as Kotter and Schlesinger's (2008) proposition that communication should start prior to the deal in order to prepare the people for the change. However, even these studies ignore the fact that this requires a solid understanding of the prevailing corporate cultures at both the target and the acquirer firms, which can be attained only through an in-depth cultural analysis before any attempt is made to combine the two organisations. Although still widely neglected in practice as well as in theory, recent findings indicate that attentively connecting pre- and post-merger phases may improve M&A performance in general (Weber *et al.*, 2011). Gomes *et al.* (2013) see the source of the overall negligence of a holistic process approach (e.g. Jemison and Sitkin, 1986; Haspeslagh and Jemison, 1991) in the fact that advocates of this process approach have tended to focus on either one of the stages, rather than connecting the critical success factors of the pre- and post-merger stages.

Summing up, it turns out that the link between pre-deal CDD and PMI management has been largely ignored by researchers. Hence, it is the aim of this chapter to fill this gap by examining the value a CDD entails for sociocultural PMI management in depth.

Concept and methodology

The conceptual model on which this chapter draws is shown in Figure 11.2. It posits that there is a strong interrelation between CDD and PMI and from that a significant value creation for M&As. As Lewin's force-field theory (1963) points out, there are 'driving' and 'restraining' forces in every change process. Change, however, occurs only if the restraining forces are minimised while the driving forces are enhanced. This leads to the assumption that CDD is an indispensable step in identifying restraining forces so as to formulate a strategy of how to minimise them and as such ease the change process. Facilitators for the minimisation of the restraining forces that have been identified previously are communication, trust, speed and the retention of key people, all of which are key success factors for the PMI phase.

Hence, there are two basic propositions of the model. First, pre-deal CDD is able to identify restraining forces that potentially burden the sociocultural PMI integration process. Second, these insights allow for an enhanced fulfilment of key success factors in the sociocultural PMI process.

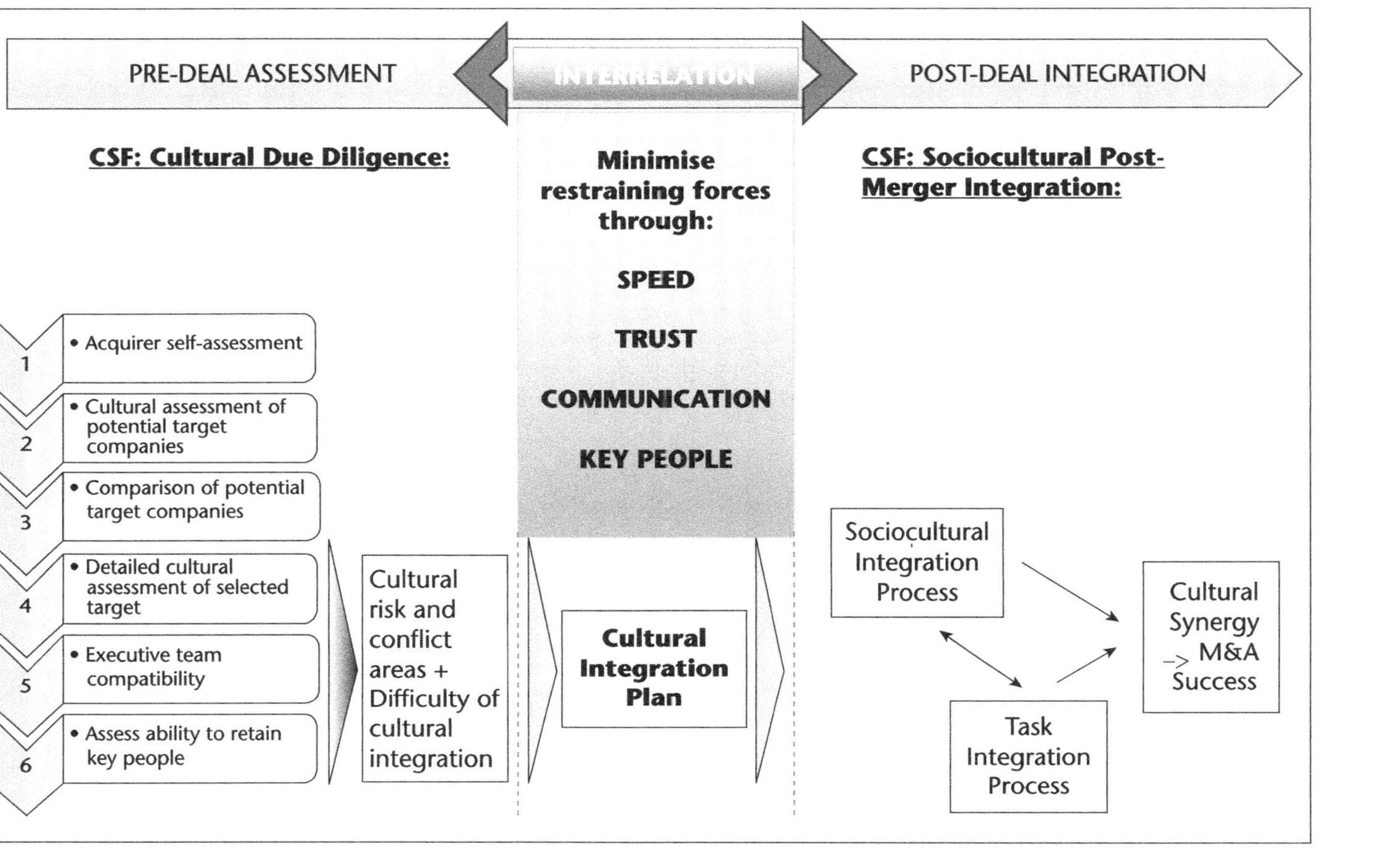

FIGURE 11.2 Conceptual model

Given the rather piecemeal research on the subject and the need for basic theory building, this chapter follows an explorative approach that aims to elucidate and understand the interrelation between CDD and PMI by studying one case in depth – the Hewlett-Packard–Compaq merger of 2002 (Dyer and Wilkins, 1991). Following Yin (2009), single case studies hold great potential for the critical testing of a well-formulated theory proposition. A single case study then enables the researcher to determine whether the proposed theory or hypothesis can bc confirmed or extended, or in contrast entirely disproved. Hence, the single case study can provide a considerable contribution to knowledge and new theory construction.

To this end, in the following sections we examine the different CDD activities of the case merger in the pre-deal phase and anaylse their value for the post-merger phase. The merger of Hewlett-Packard (HP) and Compaq (CPQ) was chosen since HP revealed detailed information about its CDD activities in this merger, which is rare. Moreover, even today it remains one of the biggest mergers in the computer industry, which led to considerable public attention, allowing use to build this study on secondary sources from business journals, academic books and newspaper articles. In addition, relevant material from the home pages of HP and Compaq was studied.

Since there is no direct knowledge on what impact HP's CDD activities had on the rather successful sociocultural PMI, the remainder of the chapter is dedicated to study the integration management processes throughout the pre- and post-deal phases and to examine their interrelation in view of the conceptual model. In other words, we will study whether the CDD facilitated an enhanced fulfilment of key success factors of the PMI, such as speed, trust, communication and the retention of key people.

The case study: cultural integration at the HP–Compaq merger

The HP–Compaq deal is known as the biggest IT merger in history (Smith, 2002), involving 150,000 people in 160 countries (*Business Week*, 2001). The two companies were not in favourable market positions and there was no way for them to compete with major rivals, such as IBM and Dell, aside from this merger (Beer, 2002). Despite some strong opposition from one major shareholder (the son of HP's co-founder, Walter Hewlett), the merger was agreed in March 2002. The new HPQ (HP–Compaq) reached a combined revenue of $87 billion based on the numbers of the last four quarters at that time, putting it neck and neck with IBM for the title of largest technology company in the world (*Business Week*, 2001). HP and Compaq further expected to reach cost synergies of about $2.5 billion by 2004 through the merger (Lohr and Gaither, 2001), which would be achieved through the laying off of 15,000 employees (Kinsman, 2002), among other things.

Looking back at the HP–Compaq merger ten years later, Carly Fiorina, former CEO of HPQ, regards it as definitely successful. In an interview on Bloomberg TV in 2011, she said:

> If you look at the numbers there is no question [that this merger was the right move]. We went from a lagging PC business to the leader in the world in terms of revenue, market share and profitability . . . And we improved the growth rate and the profitability of our already-leading printing business. So, yes, it was a huge success.

This assessment still holds true today. Even though the company has experienced some trouble in recent years, it is still number two (behind Apple) in the highly competitive computer hardware business (*Bloomberg Business Week*, 2014). Referring back to McKinsey's estimate that 66–75 per cent of M&As fail to achieve the anticipated synergies (McKinsey, 2010: 1), it seems that HP and Compaq have done a good job in merging and integrating two large technology companies with strongly established and quite different cultures.

Figure 11.3 provides a timeline of the merger and the main cultural integration activities that took place first in what has been labelled the 'Clean Room', then in the cultural integration team and finally in the so-called fast-start programme.

The Clean Room

In August 2001, one month before the merger was announced, the companies' CEOs Carly Fiorina (HP) and Michael Capellas (Compaq) decided each selected a senior executive from their respective companies to be in charge of the integration effort (Burgelman and Meza, 2004). Fiorina chose executive vice-president Webb McKinney, while Capellas appointed Jeff Clarke, Compaq's chief financial officer (Burgelman and McKinney, 2006). Together, McKinney and Clarke headed the 'Clean Room', in which a Clean Team was able to concentrate exclusively on the merger integration, away from the day-to-day distractions of the still operating – and competing – companies (Burgelman and Meza, 2004). The term 'Clean Room' originated in the health and computer chip industry, where work is done in separate, spotlessly clean environments in order to avoid contamination. In the M&A context, 'contamination' means the flow of confidential information merging companies are not allowed to exchange due to competition rules (Koob, 2006). Hence Clean Room members were permitted to ask their non-Clean Room colleagues for information, but they were forbidden to discuss any integration matters with them (Allen, 2012).

The Clean Room model enabled the merging companies to work on integration plans even though the deal still lay ahead (Koob, 2006). With an initially small, dedicated thirty-person team of project managers, OD experts, consultants and analysts (Burgelman and Meza, 2004), Clarke and McKinney began the integration work (Allen, 2012). During the following six months, the Clean Team ultimately grew to about 2,500 people (Allen, 2012), who all ceased working on daily business operations and instead focused exclusively on the immense integration workload (Burgelman and Meza, 2004). The key objective of the Clean Team's work was to enable the merged company to 'open its doors and hit the ground running on day

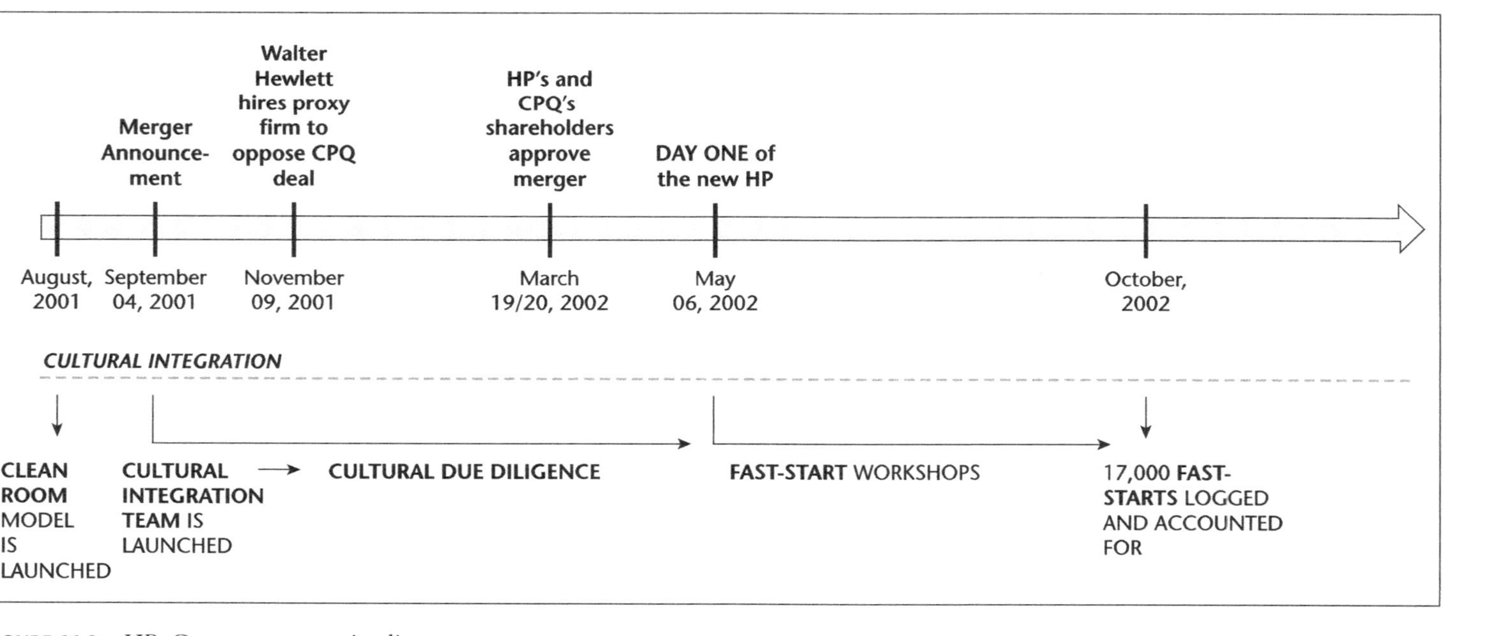

FIGURE 11.3 HP–Compaq merger timeline

one' (Allen, 2012: 51). By March 2002, the Clean Team had already worked an estimated 1.3 million hours on creating a road map for how to mesh the two long-term competitors into a single firm (Lohr, 2002).

Within the Clean Room environment, small, discrete post-merger integration teams were formed according to a 'Noah's Ark' model – a buddy system that was designed to avoid a potential us-versus-them mentality (Burgelman and Meza, 2004). The underlying idea was to match each HP manager with a Compaq counterpart, with these pairs working under the central Post-Merger Integration Office (Central Programme Management Office; CPMO), as illustrated in Figure 11.4 (Allen, 2012). In order to discuss and review their integration plans and proceedings, the Clean Teams met every week in person. Within the Clean Room, an 'adopt-and-go' approach was applied. This essentially meant identifying and selecting the best practices among both firms throughout the merged company (Tam, 2002). This encompassed business models, processes, products, as well as cultural cornerstones, such as corporate values and objectives. Anything that was not identified as best practice was to be eliminated (Harvey, 2002; Allen, 2012; Burgelman and Meza, 2004). Technically, the adopt-and-go approach operated a traffic light system for the 10,000-plus adopt-and-go decisions that had to be made: completed or ahead-of-schedule projects were marked green; projects that were on track were yellow; and those that were behind schedule were red. This approach allowed the combined firms to move fast once the merger received clearance (Allen, 2012). Clarke argued that the adopt-and-go strategy later prevented 'politicking' among employees, as they were aware that the Clean Room decisions were not up for discussion, only for execution (Burgelman and McKinney, 2006: 24). In order to supplement the adopt-and-go approach, Susan D. Bowick, HP's executive vice-president of human resources and workforce development, introduced the 'launch-and-learn' approach, which legitimised fast decision-making to achieve good – but not necessarily perfect – decisions (Burgelman and McKinney, 2006: 25). Finally, this fast decision-making was supported by the principle of 'getting the dead moose on the table', which entailed frank discussions among the teams in order to solve emerging conflicts before the integration of the merging firms took place (Burgelman and Meza, 2004; Burgelman and McKinney, 2006; Allen, 2012).

The Clean Team was closely linked to the Steering Committee, which consisted of a small group of high-ranking senior executives (as illustrated in Figure 11.4) who made quick decisions and had the authority to insist on their execution (without running into lengthy discussions).

Cultural integration team

Within the Clean Team and as a sub-PMI team, the Cultural Integration Team (CIT; see Figure 11.4) was established to ensure an effective and fast cultural integration of the two companies (Burgelman and Meza, 2004; Allen, 2012). The CIT, consisting of HP and Compaq employees as well as some external consultants from Mercer Delta, was introduced immediately after the merger announcement

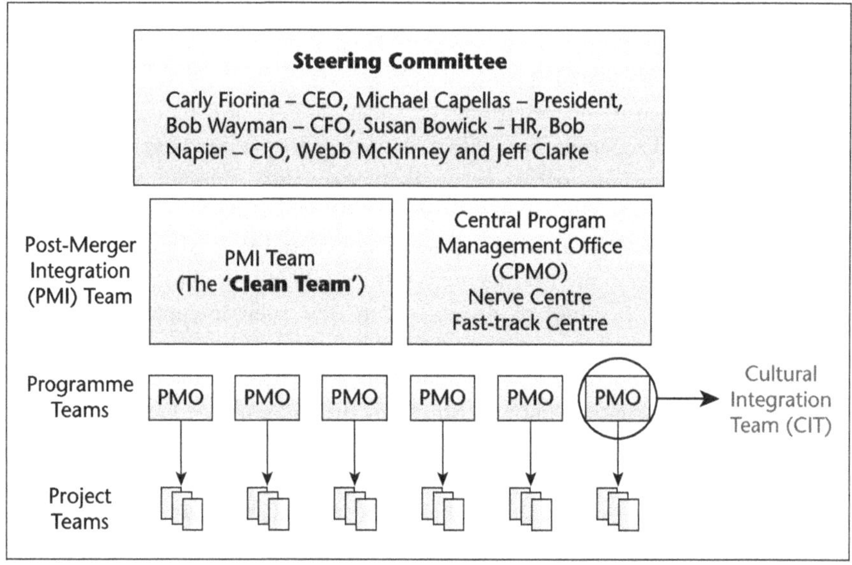

FIGURE 11.4 Merger integration team organisation chart

(Tam, 2002). While the Clean Room itself was developing a new corporate culture through jointly planning the 'new HP way', the CIT was launched solely to examine the cultural differences between the two firms. It did this by conducting an extensive CDD throughout both companies (Allen, 2012). The CDD consisted of 127 individual executive interviews and 138 focus groups that in turn assembled 1,500 managers and individual contributors in 22 countries (Stachowicz-Stanusch, 2009). A large-scale survey was rejected after due consideration as this might have confused employees and could have created uncertainty feelings among the personnel (Allen, 2012). In line with that, Elise Walton, then senior partner at Mercer Delta and a CIT consultant, explained that 'qualitative data was much more valuable [as] we were able to do a content analysis of all comments and the output was immediately useful' (quoted in Allen, 2012: 52).

The CDD assessment revealed many differences between the two strongly established corporate cultures. The major cultural differences are summarised in Table 11.2.

The CDD data was then included in Clean Room decisions, especially concerning human resources, organisational design and structure, staffing of key positions, reward and compensation plans, as well as executive selection (Allen, 2012). Hence, by April 2002, HP announced the names of 150 senior managers who would be in charge of key positions in the new HP's four business lines and international corporate functions. In order to ensure a strong integration effort, pre-merger HP and Compaq both offered retention bonuses to about 8,200 key people, of which only 10 per cent were in executive positions (Burgelman and Meza, 2004). These retention bonuses amounted to 50 per cent of the recipients'

TABLE 11.2 Differences in HP's and Compaq's corporate cultures

Hewlett-Packard's corporate culture	*Compaq's corporate culture*
• Culture of consideration, thoughtfulness, and planning	• Culture of ready, shoot and aim
• More careful culture	• Quicker to act due to fewer discussions
• Voicemail culture	• Email culture
• Impulsive managers	• Bureaucratic managers
• More internally focused	• More externally focused
• Rather systematic	• Rather spontaneous
• Relies on organisation's rich history as a source of knowledge	• Focuses on future possibilities and learn as they go
• Review of events so as to find best practices	• Trial and error; forges ahead without looking back

Sources: Based on DePamphilis (2010: 210–211); Burgelman and Meza (2004: 11); Tam (2002); and Stachowicz-Stanusch (2009: 71–72).

salaries plus 'target bonuses' and were paid in two rates, one upon deal closure and the second after the first year (Fried, 2002).

For the design and launch of the new HPQ culture, the CIT implemented a so-called 'living systems' approach that preferred a communicative and participative form over a top-down method of change (Maturana and Varela, 1980). In line with that, questions such as 'Which values and objectives of the two companies should be preserved?' and 'What should be created?' were asked in order to generate an evolutionary set of cultural cornerstones (Allen, 2012). Then the adopt-and-go approach was applied to pick the best of what existed between the two corporate cultures (see Figure 11.5). Paul Brandling, a long-standing HPQ employee, noted that the underlying bedrock values were teamwork, trust and respect, speed and agility. He further argued that, given that the two corporate cultures would accept those, 'they will start to shape attitudes and behaviours which eventually flesh out into culture' (quoted in Boyd, 2002: 2).

Once the new cultural cornerstones were agreed, the CIT started to share them in interactive sessions with the various Clean Teams (marketing, HR, etc.) (Allen, 2012). These sessions included a 'mirror exchange' exercise in which HP and former Compaq employees had to describe one another, for instance through the use of sports analogies (Tam, 2002). Along with this exercise, the CIT created an employee website that featured a monthly 'culture-in-action' story, illustrating the pre-merger cultures while at the same time highlighting the preserved cultural values. These activities were designed to foster employee engagement and create a mutual cultural awareness and understanding among the two workforces (Allen, 2012).

The Fast-Start programme

The CIT also introduced a 'Fast-Start' programme, an integration workshop programme that aimed to accelerate the work of the newly integrated teams.

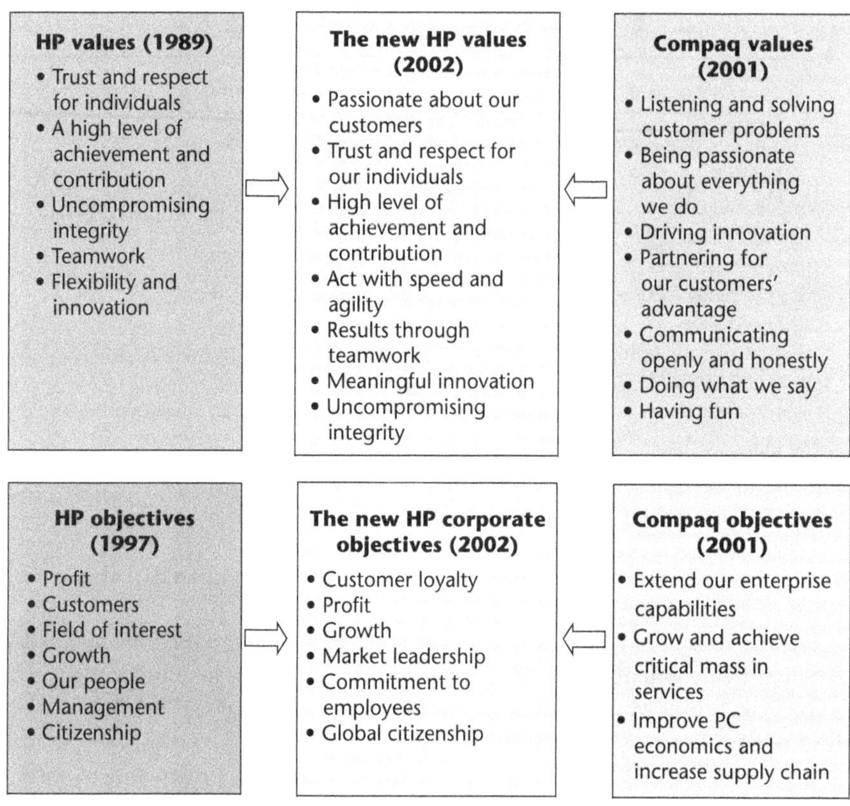

FIGURE 11.5 The values and objectives of the new HP – integrating the best of both cultures

In April 2002, before the Fast-Start programme was initiated and before merger day one, HP held a two-day 'Leadership Readiness Summit' with 300 Compaq and HP leaders to launch the new approach (Tam, 2002). The leaders were supplied with all of the necessary material and knowledge to share within their respective offices (Allen, 2012). Fast-Start consisted of ten modules that newly assigned managers had to walk through in their teams' kick-off meetings, which were attended by HP and former Compaq employees (Stachowicz-Stanusch, 2009). These modules could be completed either in two consecutive full days or split into two-hour sessions over one or two weeks (Allen, 2012), but they had to be completed within the teams' first thirty days (Stachowicz-Stanusch, 2009). The completion of the Fast-Start programme was mandatory for all levels of the firm and its results were tied to the new HPQ balanced scorecard and manager compensation (Tam, 2002). The major objectives of these Fast-Start sessions were to accelerate HPQ's cultural integration and to establish the team cohesion that would drive execution and bring forth the newly combined corporate culture (Stachowicz-Stanusch, 2009). By October 2002, more than 17,000 Fast-Start sessions had taken place (Allen, 2012).

Analysis and discussion

HPs cultural integration strategy

According to Nahavandi and Malekzadeh's (1988) acculturation model, HP's and Compaq's acculturation mode could be identified as 'integration'. This implies that HP as well as Compaq cherished and wished to preserve their own cultures while at the same time perceiving the other firm's corporate culture as very attractive. In the HPQ merger this degree of congruence regarding acculturation preferences led to low acculturative stress and hence to a higher likelihood of achieving cultural synergy. The acculturation congruence in the HPQ merger was a given as both companies were willing to adopt some cultural values and objectives from the other firm while also giving up some of their own, as required by the adopt-and-go approach. Further, HP's extensive efforts concerning its CDD activities and the associated integration mode were in line with Blöcher's (2004) empirical study, which revealed that a CDD is typically applied by acquirers who strive for a high degree of integration.

Likewise, the type of cultural integration strategy adopted by HP and Compaq strongly matches Haspeslagh's and Jemison's (1991) cultural integration model. More specifically, the integration strategy can be identified as a 'symbiosis merger' in which the best practices of both firms are combined, leading to cultural integration. According to Haspeslagh and Jemison (1991), a truly symbiotic merger can be achieved only when both organisations adopt the original characteristics of the partner firm. The intention to achieve symbiosis is recognisable, for instance, in HP's adopt-and-go approach and in the Noah's Ark model. The intention was to retain an optimal interaction between the merging organisations through an evolutionary change process. The key here is that the change process was evolutionary rather than revolutionary. Following O'Toole (cited in Carleton and Lineberry, 2004: 19), 'anthropology indicates that culture changes in one of two basic ways, revolution and evolution, and attempts at revolutionary culture change always fail; it is the shared experience and common history of a group over time that changes the culture'. In line with this, HP's new cultural cornerstones were designed according to an evolutionary set of cultural values and objectives, also influenced by its adopt-and-go approach.

As already indicated, the remarkable effort HP put into its CDD procedure shows a high desire for cultural integration. The various CDD activities within the Clean Room laid the perfect foundation to ensure timely cultural integration, while the Clean Teams developed a new culture, particularly the CIT, which focused exclusively on examining the various cultural factors and helped to create the necessary cultural awareness and understanding between the two corporate cultures.

The link between CDD and PMI

In order to examine the actual value of the CDD for the PMI in the HP–Compaq case, we will now analyse the extent to which the CDD facilitated an enhanced fulfilment of the PMI key success factors: communication, trust, speed and retention of key people.

Communication

Following Kotter and Schlesinger (2008), communication is one of the best ways to deal with resistance to change. HP's early integration efforts and the Clean Room itself were indicators for a timely communication between the merging companies. The launch of the Clean Room and its Clean Teams, consisting of both Compaq and HP employees, allowed the firms to communicate ten months before the deal was finalised. This resolved the many feelings of uncertainty among the two workforces, which were due to the merger's public discussion following a fierce proxy battle launched by a major shareholder (the son of HP's co-founder, Walter Hewlett). In particular, the Clean Room's dialogic approach largely averted dangerous communication holes in that situation, which can instantly lead to increased uncertainty, employee turnover and lower productivity (Bastien, 1987). Remaining uncertainty was tamed by introducing the principle of 'getting the dead moose on the table'. This principle turned implicit communication into a transparent, two-way communication that engendered trust and mutual understanding among the employees. The same effect was provoked by the CIT's 'mirror exchange' exercise. Through an informal and reflective communication exercise, crucial insights for the operations of the new HPQ teams in the post-merger phase could be gained. Finally, the Fast-Start programme clearly communicated the new cultural model that resulted from the Clean Room's work to all levels of the newly combined workforce.

Trust

Another key success factor in the PMI that potentially reduces employees' resistance to change is trust (Stahl *et al.*, 2012). As just discussed, HP's integration efforts displayed a high degree of communication that fought initial distrust resulting from the public debate about the merger. Moreover, the Noah's Ark model contributed to the creation of trust between members of the integration teams within the Clean Room. Also, decisions taken by the Clean Teams were trusted in the two organisations as they were co-decided by colleagues. Finally, the launch-and-learn approach created trust in that it foresaw that decisions that turn out to have too many negative effects might be changed as part of the learning process (Kotter and Schlesinger, 2008). Overall, trust among the partners was generated in the pre-deal phase with considerable positive effects for an accelerated integration process in the PMI phase.

Speed

For the HP–Compaq merger, which occurred within the extremely fast-moving high-technology industry, the speed of integration was even more important than usual (Burgelman and Meza, 2004). The adopt-and-go approach substantially accelerated the decision-making process among the various integration teams. This strategy stopped politicking and contentious debate and as such facilitated high execution speed. Especially, the traffic light system simplified the 10,000-plus adopt-and-go decisions and was a critical success factor for achieving high integration speed. Similarly, the launch-and-learn approach encouraged the Clean Teams to make decisions that were 'fast and good enough' (Burgelman and McKinney, 2006: 25). Hence, employees did not waste time trying to achieve perfect solutions. Moreover, the Clean Room's operating principle of 'getting the dead moose on the table' reduced conflict and the time needed to resolve such conflicts. Taken together, all of these pre-deal integration activities contributed to 'the fact that the new HP was ready to operate as one from the first day the merger took effect' (Burgelman and Meza, 2004: 20). Given HP's extensive pre-deal integration efforts and the Fast-Start programme, HP was able to take full advantage of the famous first hundred days and initial employee enthusiasm.

Retention of key people

Although HP was initially able to retain key people through bonuses and financial rewards, about two years after the merger many key executives who were involved in the integration work had resigned or retired. Just six months after the merger, Michael Capellas, former CEO of Compaq and HPQ's COO, left the newly merged company; he was not replaced by another president (DiCarlo, 2002). Soon afterwards, in November 2003, Jeff Clarke, one of the leaders of the Clean Room and former CFO of Compaq, unexpectedly resigned from HPQ. Susan Bowick, executive vice-president of HR, resigned at around the same time, and Webb McKinney also announced his early retirement (Lohr, 2003b). In 2005, following some harsh criticism, HP's CEO Carly Fiorina was forced out by the company's board of directors (La Monica, 2005). The reasons for these and other key resignations were manifold. Some executives apparently lost interest once most of the work was accomplished (Allen, 2012). Others seized opportunities to accept more attractive job offers at other companies (Lohr, 2003a). Unsurprisingly, the departures of key people who had steered the integration work led to a fading of the integration effort. Nevertheless, the cultural integration that had been achieved by that time was already rather high.

Summing up, even though the final key success factor (the retention of key people) was not enhanced through CDD, it can still be concluded that the CDD created substantial value for the PMI. During the CDD, restraining forces to the PMI could be identified and the enhanced attainment of key success factors such as communication, speed and trust significantly promoted the subsequent integration activities. As a result, the CDD can be seen as a prerequisite for a successful PMI leading to cultural synergy and in turn increasing the potential success of the merger.

Conclusion

Given the large number of M&As and their persistently high failure rate (McKinsey, 2010), researchers and M&A experts have devoted considerable effort to trying explain the recurring failures. Most of these studies, however, have neglected the fact that value creation in M&As is a dynamic process ranging from extensive pre-merger planning to a well-organised post-merger implementation of the cultural integration plan. To fill that gap, this chapter has examined the interrelationship of the pre-deal CDD and the sociocultural PMI through an in-depth literature review and a case study. To the best of our knowledge, this study is the first to address this relationship. It therefore fills an important gap in the body of research on cultural aspects of mergers and acquisitions. At the same time it proposes a variable to be tested in research on cultural aspects of post-merger integration problems (Weber *et al.*, 2009, 2011). In addition, this chapter adds to the more general literature on the link between pre-acquisition and post-acquisition stages in M&As, a field of research that is still in its infancy (Gomes *et al.*, 2013). Here, our proposition that the CDD is a prerequisite for the sociocultural PMI and hence for the successful creation of cultural synergy can be confirmed, in that the case study showed that the attainment of almost all key success factors was enhanced through a pre-deal CDD.

The first limitation of our study relates to the well-known problem of statistical generalisation of single case studies. Second, our findings are limited because we draw on secondary data. Even though the size and the overall importance of the merger in the industry provided a solid amount of authentic, reliable and representative textual data that allowed for a triangulation of content, original data might have provided further interesting explanations on issues that have been barely or not at all reported. Given these limitations, further research should build on this chapter and seek to confirm the positive relationship between cultural CDD and a successful PMI that we found for a larger number of cases, applying either a case comparison or a survey approach. This would also facilitate examination of the research question with a broader set of data sources, including primary sources gained through participant observation or interviews.

Finally, in addition to some general recommendations that have been mentioned by other studies (e.g. on maintaining leadership attention on cultural matters throughout the whole process), two important practical lessons can be learned from our case study. First, managers concerned with integration processes should be aware that cultural integration facilitates and accelerates the operational integration. Therefore, especially if the business environment is a fast-changing one, integration speed is essential and cultural integration should by no means play a subordinate role. Second, managers should ensure a timely cultural integration through a 'clean room' environment, foster employee engagement throughout the integration work and invest in a thorough CDD to reveal critical cultural gaps that may lead to conflict.

References

Ahammad, F. M., Glaister K. W., Weber, Y. and Tarba, S. Y. (2012) 'Top management retention on cross-border acquisitions: The roles of financial incentives, acquirer's commitment and autonomy', *European Journal of International Management*, Vol. 6, No. 4, pp. 458–480.

Allen, A. M. (2012) 'Culture Integration in a "clean room": Reflections about the HP–Compaq merger 10 years later', *OD Practitioner*, Vol. 44, No. 3, pp. 50–54.

Angwin, D. (2004) 'Speed in M&A integration: The first 100 days', *European Management Journal*, Vol. 22, No. 4, pp. 418–430.

Bastien, D. T. (1987) 'Common patterns of behavior and communication in corporate mergers and acquisitions', *Human Resource Management*, Vol. 26, No. 1, pp. 17–33.

Beer, M. (2002) 'HP readies layoffs during Compaq merger', *Agence France Press*, 8 May.

Bijlsma-Frankema, K. (2001) 'On managing cultural integration and cultural change processes in mergers and acquisitions', *Journal of European Industrial Training*, Vol. 25, No. 2, pp. 192–207.

Birkinshaw, J., Bresman, H. and Håkanson, L. (2000) 'Managing the post-acquisition integration process: How the human integration and task integration processes interact to foster value creation', *Journal of Management Studies*, Vol. 37, No. 3, pp. 395–425.

Blöcher, A. (2004) *Cultural Due Diligence: Möglichkeiten und Grenzen der Erfassung und Bewertung von Unternehmenskulturen bei Unternehmenszusammenschlüssen*, Aachen: Shaker Verlag.

Bloomberg Business Week (2014) 'Computer hardware industry leaders', March 2014. Available at: http://investing.businessweek.com/research/stocks/financials/ratios.asp?ticker=HPQ (ccessed 6 March 2014).

Bloomberg TV (2011) 'Carly Fiorina, former chairman and CEO, Hewlett Packard', 22 August.

Boyd, T. (2002) 'HP contemplates cultural divide', *Australian Financial Review*, 11 May.

Burgelman, R. A. and McKinney, W. (2006) 'Managing the strategic dynamics of acquisition integration: Lessons from HP and Compaq', *California Management Review*, Vol. 48, No. 3, pp. 6–27.

Burgelman, R. A. and Meza, P. (2004) 'HP and Compaq combined: In search of scale and scope', *Stanford Graduate School of Business*, 15 July.

Business Week (2001) 'The key players in the HP–Compaq merger', 24 December.

Carleton, J. R. and Lineberry, C. S. (2004) *Achieving Post-Merger Success: A Stakeholder's Guide to Cultural Due Diligence, Assessment, and Integration*, San Francisco, CA: Pfeiffer.

Cartwright, S. and Cooper, C. L. (1993) 'The role of culture compatibility in successful organisational marriage', *Academy of Management Executive*, Vol. 7, No. 2, pp. 57–70.

Chakravorty, J. N. (2012) 'Why do mergers and acquisitions quite often fail?', *Advances in Management*, Vol. 5, No. 5, pp. 21–28.

DePamphilis, D. M. (2010) *Mergers, Acquisitions, and Other Restructuring Activities: An Integrated Approach to Process, Tools, Cases, and Solutions*, 5th edition, London: Elsevier.

DiCarlo, L. (2002) 'Michael Capellas's Next Move', *Forbes*, 11 November.

Dyer, W. G. and Wilkins, A. L. (1991) 'Better stories, not better constructs, to generate better theory: A rejoinder to Eisenhardt', *Academy of Management Review*, Vol. 16, No. 3, pp. 613–619.

Economist, The (2008) 'Guru Geert Hofstede', 28 November. Available at: www.economist.com/node/12669307 (accessed 26 August 2016).

Feldmann, M. L. and Spratt, M. F. (1999) *A Summary of Five Frogs on a Log: A CEO's Field Guide to Accelerating the Transition in Mergers, Acquisitions, and Gut-Wrenching Change*, New York: HarperCollins

Fried, I. (2002) 'Global 2000: HP deal: Some get layoffs, others bonuses', *CNET News*, 14 January.

Galpin, T. J. and Herndon, M. (2007) *The Complete Guide to Mergers and Acquisitions: Process Tools to Support M&A Integration at Every Level*, 2nd edition, San Francisco, CA: John Wiley & Sons, Inc.

Garbade, M. J. (2009) *International Mergers & Acquisitions, Cooperations and Networks in the E-Business Industry*, München: GRIN Verlag.

Gomes, E., Angwin, D., Weber, Y. and Tarba, S. Y. (2013) 'Critical success factors through the mergers and acquisitions process: Revealing pre- and post-M&A connections for improved performance', *Thunderbird International Business Review*, Vol. 55, pp. 13–36.

Harvey, F. (2002) 'No culture clash seen for HP: "Adapt and go" system', *National Post (Canada)*, 28 May.

Haspeslagh, P. C. and Jemison, D. B. (1991) *Managing Acquisition: Creating Value through Company Renewal*, New York: The Free Press.

Hubbard, N. and Purcell, L. (2001) 'Managing employee expectations during acquisitions', *Human Resource Management Journal*, Vol. 11, pp. 17–33.

Jemison, D. and Sitkin, S. B. (1986) 'Corporate acquisitions: A process perspective', *Academy of Management Review*, Vol. 11, pp. 145–163.

Kinsman, M. (2002) 'Merger imperils "HP Way"', *Copley News Service*, 8 April.

Koob, J. (2006) 'Clean teams: The fast track to M&A integration and value', Marsh & McLennan Companies. Available at: www.mmc.com/views/viewpoint/Koob2006.php (accessed 27 December 2012).

Kotter, J. P. and Schlesinger, L. A. (2008) 'Choosing strategies for change', *Harvard Business Review*, Vol. 86, Nos. 7/8, pp. 130–139.

KPMG (2002) 'Unlocking shareholder value: The keys to success', Institute of Mergers, Acquisitions and Alliances. Available at: www.imaa-institute.org/docs/m&a/kpmg_01_Unlocking%20Shareholder%20Value%20-%20The%20Keys%20to%20Success.pdf (accessed 27 August 2012).

Krug, J. A. and Shill, W. (2008) 'The big exit: Executive churn in the wake of M&As', *Journal of Business Strategy*, Vol. 29. No. 4, pp. 15–21.

La Monica, P. R. (2005) 'Fiorina out, HP stock soars', *CNN Money,* 10 February.

Lewin, K. (1963) *Feldtheorie in den Sozialwissenschaften*, Wabern-Bern: Verlag Hans Huber Bern.

Lohr, S. (2002) 'Assembling a big merger: Hewlett's Man For the Details', *New York Times*, 25 March.

Lohr, S. (2003a) 'Force in Hewlett–Compaq merger resigns', *New York Times*, 26 November.

Lohr, S. (2003b) 'Key executive in HP– Compaq deal resigns', *International Herald Tribune*, 26 November.

Lohr, S. and Gaither, C. (2001) 'A family struggle, a company's fate', *New York Times*, 2 December.

Marks, M. L. (1999) 'Adding cultural fit to your diligence checklist', *Mergers & Acquisitions: The Dealermaker's Journal*, Vol. 34, No. 3, pp. 14–20.

Maturana, H. R. and Varela, F. J. (1980) *Autopoiesis and Cognition: The Realization of the Living*, Dordrecht: D. Reidel.

McKinsey (2010) 'A new generation of M&A: A McKinsey perspective on the opportunities and challenges'. Available at: http://bit.ly/VP7bXF (ccessed 16 September 2012).

Nahavandi, A. and Malekzadeh, A. R. (1988) 'Acculturation in mergers and acquisitions', *Academy of Management Review*, Vol. 13, No. 1, pp. 79–90.

Pablo, A. L. (1994) 'Determinants of acquisition integration level: A decision-making perspective', *Academy of Management Journal*, Vol. 37, No. 4, pp. 803–836.

Quah, P. and Young, S. (2005) 'Post-acquisition management: A phases approach for cross-border M&As', *European Management Journal*, Vol. 23. No. 1, pp. 65–75.

Rousseau, D. M., Sitkin, S. B., Burt, R. S. and Camerer, C. (1998) 'Not so different after all: A cross-discipline view of trust', *Academy of Management Review*, Vol. 23, No. 3, pp. 393–404.

Schein, E. H. (2003) *Organisationskultur: The Ed Schein Corporate Culture Survival Guide*, Bergisch Gladbach: Edition Humanistische Psychologie.

Schneck, O. (2007) 'Cultural Due Diligence: Warum Unternehmensübernahmen scheitern', *Kredit & Rating Praxis*, Vol. 4, pp. 23–29.

Smith, M. (2002) 'Erskine workers await fate in wake of HP merger', *The Herald*, 8 May.

Stachowicz-Stanusch, A. (2009) 'Culture due diligence based on HP/Compaq Merger case study', *Journal of Intercultural Management*, Vol. 1, No. 1, pp. 64–81.

Stahl, G. K. and Voigt, A. (2008) 'Do cultural differences matter in mergers and acquisitions? A tentative model and examination', *Organization Science*, Vol. 19, No. 1, pp. 160–176.

Stahl, G. K., Chua, C. H. and Pablo, A. L. (2012) 'Does national context affect target firm employees' trust in acquisitions?', *Management International Review*, Vol. 52, No. 3, pp. 395–423.

Tam, P. (2002) 'HP designs workshops to break postmerger ice', *Wall Street Journal*, 11 July.

Vester, J. (2002) 'Lessons learned about integration acquisitions', *Research Technology Management*, Vol. 45, pp. 33–41.

Weber, Y., Tarba, S.Y. and Reichel, A. (2009) 'International mergers and acquisitions performance revisited: The role of cultural distance and post-acquisition integration approach implementation', *Advances in Mergers and Acquisitions*, Vol. 8, pp. 1–18.

Weber, Y., Tarba, S.Y. and Reichel, A. (2011) 'A model of the influence of culture on integration approaches and international mergers and acquisitions performance', *International Studies of Management and Organization*, Vol. 41, No.3, pp. 9–24.

Weber, Y., Tarba, S.Y. and Rozen Bachar, Z. (2011) 'Mergers and acquisitions performance paradox: The mediating role of integration approach', *European Journal of International Management*, Vol. 5, pp. 373–393.

Yin, R. K. (2009) *Case Study Research: Design and Methods*, 4th edition, Thousand Oaks, CA: Sage.

Zimmer, A. (2001) *Unternehmenskultur und Cultural Due Diligence bei Mergers & Acquisitions*, Aachen: Shaker Verlag.

12

ACQUISITION IN THE BANKING SECTOR IN THE TRANSITION PROCESS TO THE MARKET ECONOMY

Ruth Alas, Tiit Elenurm, Tiiu Allikmäe, and Riina Varts

Introduction

Globalization of businesses has intensified cross-border mergers and acquisitions. More than decade ago mergers and acquisitions became the dominant mode of growth (Adler, 1997). East European transition economies were exposed to cross-border acquisitions after the collapse of the command economy. The financial sector was one of the fields of radical change as in the Soviet command economy there was no role for commercial banking. During the first years of the economic transition many new commercial banks were created but when commercial banking became more mature, concentration processes in this sector began.

This chapter analyses an example of the cross-border acquisition and merger of commercial banks in one of the Baltic countries by a commercial bank from another country at a time when all of the banks involved were quite new institutions. Studies of managers in Estonian companies in the 1990s have pointed out market-driven changes in strategy, organizational culture, leadership style and the mission of their organizations that can be interpreted as the impact of radical transformation factors in that decade (Alas and Sharifi, 2002: 313–331). As a result of its liberal economic policy and rapid privatization, to some extent Estonia was ahead of other two Baltic countries, Latvia and Lithuania, in the second half of the 1990s in developing commercial banking and other market economy institutions. The rapid transition towards a market economy served as a driver of pan-Baltic expansion for the leading Estonian commercial banks. It was for the young managers of these organizations their first experience of cross-border organizational change and human resource management challenges. At the same time the largest new commercial banks in Estonia themselves became acquisition targets for established commercial banks from the Nordic countries.

Human resource management issues surrounding M&As have been the focus of several studies (Aguilera and Dencker, 2004; Zhang *et al.*, 2014). HRM has the potential to play an important role in M&A integration, for example, by reinforcing the new 8HRM system and corporate culture and providing leadership and communication to reduce turnover depending on the chosen integration approach. Weber *et al.* (2011b, 2012) highlight the links between HRM practices that take into consideration cultural differences, knowledge-based theory of M&A integration and international management.

The aim of this chapter is to explore the possibilities and challenges of using human resource management practices in the implementation of organizational changes, specifically during the cross-border acquisition and merger of banks from two transition economies. We start with an overview of change management and human resources management literature in the context of cross-cultural acquisition and merger processes, then present an analysis of the case of Hansabank, which acquired two banks in Lithuania and then merged these banks into an integrated cross-border corporate structure.

Theoretical framework

Change management and mergers of organizations

Dopson and Neumann (1998) have perceived change as a necessary evil for survival in the context of uncertainty. Organizational change has been often seen as an individual-level phenomenon because it occurs only when the majority of individuals change their behaviour or attitudes (Whelan-Berry *et al.*, 2003). Multiple-interacting changes in a global environment have led to a highly complex, confusing and unpredictable state. At the end of the twentieth century this shifted the focus of the change process from product innovation and technological change to behavioural aspects of change and to attitudes about change in organizations (Bergquist, 1993). Recent decades of globalization and institutional and structural changes in economies have increased the role of cross-border and inter-organizational change management.

Usually scholars analyse such features of organizational change as content, type, structure and process. Armenakis and Bedeian (1999) have divided the research on organizational change into: content research; contextual research; process research; and criterion research. Nutt (2003) combines structure and process. His structural research is similar to content research (Armenakis and Bedeian, 1999), and process research is presented in both typologies.

Although the type of change and the process of change are both important building blocks in any model for dealing with change, there is also a third crucial factor – the readiness to change in the particular organization. The readiness factors act like a bridge between identifying what needs to happen and the activity of implementing the change. Struckman and Yammarino (2003) combine types of change with readiness to change, but they do not take process into account. Therefore, Alas (2007) has developed a model connecting types of change, process of change, readiness to change and the institutional environment as the context of change. When studying change readiness in the context of acquisition and merger, it is important to understand the nature of cooperation and conflict between the organization that is leading the process and the organization that has to adapt to the new situation. Conflict can reflect differences of interests but also stereotypes based on earlier organizational practices. Organizational learning capabilities are essential for organizational change. Disciplines of the learning organization, such as building shared vision and mental models, team learning and system thinking (Senge, 2001), can be adjusted to acquisition and merger processes.

More advanced change management processes that are focused on integration in mergers and acquisitions could improve economic results of such organizational changes. Weber *et al.* (2009, 2011c) have created the conceptual framework of four main integration approaches: absorption; symbiosis; preservation; and holding. Choices among these integration approaches are influenced by synergy potentials of organizations, by cultural differences and by cultural-specific dimensions that can be either national or organizational. Absorption as an integration approach implies a high level of integration and the lowest autonomy for the local management of the acquired organization. Weber *et al.* (2009) assume that such an approach can be operational for achieving a high level of synergy only if the level of cultural difference is low. Cultural clash and employee resistance emerge from the desire to keep autonomy rather than impose practices that reflect a very different culture. In this framework preservation is the approach that implies the lowest level of integration and the highest autonomy for the management team of the acquired company. Weber *et al.* (2011c) conclude that when there is a high level of synergy potential but also a high level of cultural difference, the symbiotic approach to the integration process is selected and the effectiveness of the integration depends on integration activities focused on human resources at the post-merger stage.

Ellis *et al.* (2012) discuss a framework of four integration approaches – preservation; absorption; symbiotic; and transformation – and stress that the transformation approach requires significant changes in both previously independent firms as the new merged firm seeks to reinvent itself by discarding old procedures and developing a new culture and routines. Their research is especially focused on large interrelated mergers and acquisitions. Although banks in the Baltic countries are small compared to global corporations, in the banking sector the alignment of structures and processes in order to transform business activities as part of the general transition to a market economy is an important priority.

Advanced human resource management practices are instrumental for dealing with post-merger conflicts. The potential for conflict stems from the tension between both organizational cultures and different national cultures. A knowledge-based view helps to address the post-merger cross-cultural conflict. Knowledge integration capability refers to the ability to handle acquisition by exploiting synergy through resource sharing and the deployment and transfer of resources and capabilities from one organization to another (Weber *et al.*, 2011b).

Creating harmony, synergy and knowledge transfer between partners is therefore an important focus of human resource management in the post-merger context.

Losing values and identity can be seen as a threat (Van Dick *et al.*, 2006), especially among groups that have previously had influential roles in the organization that is being acquired. Changing the power structure is inevitable in many acquisitions in order to create new synergies and to increase the efficiency of operations. There is, however, a need to persuade different professional groups that their legitimate interests will be taken into consideration and fair selection and promotion practices will be applied. Curall and Inpeken (2002) and Weber and Diori (2012) have demonstrated that trust is crucial for the formation of cooperative alliances, such as marketing partnerships and joint ventures. It is even more important in situations where independent organizations are merged and the fair selection of managers and employees is a challenge. Buono and Bowditch (1989) argue that a merger or acquisition is ultimately a human process. Therefore, involvement of the HRM function in the M&A process is a matter of humanitarian concern to mitigate grief among those people who have been acquired (Hunt and Downing, 1990). Weber *et al.* (2012) explain that in the context of mergers and acquisitions, for employees of the acquired firm or the subordinate partner, the period after the announcement of the takeover is a time of intense personal risk analysis, in which they decide whether to leave or stay in the organization. The top management of the acquiring firm may risk opportunistic behaviour if it allows members of the acquired organization a high degree of autonomy without building mutual trust relations.

One important change readiness factor is the leadership and communication strategy of the change leaders. The top management team has an impact on post-acquisition performance of the company and effectively influences the organizational culture (Kiessling and Harvey, 2006). During an acquisition, the position of the former top management team is often challenged. Appropriate communication modes at the right time and in the right place as well as personal examples are among the most important leadership tools in such situation. Weber *et al.* (2011d), in a cross-cultural comparative study, present evidence that acquirers from Germany, Japan and Belgium have different post-merger communication intensity. In Japan post-merger communication contributes more to the stock market value than it does in Germany because average acquirers from Japan increase post-merger communication more than German acquirers do. Different post-merger communication patterns reflect cultural differences and human resource management practices.

Human resource management and culture in mergers and acquisitions

The term human resource management (HRM) refers to the design and applications of a formal system in an organization to ensure effective and efficient use of human talent to achieve the organization's goals (Mathis and Jackson, 2002). The concept of HRM gained importance when it became clear that strategic decisions are increasingly related to human resource considerations (Daft, 2006) and HRM has impact on an organization's strategic capabilities (Fombrun *et al.*, 1984; Wright *et al.*, 1994).

The Michigan model of HRM emphasizes that people are resources, and the utilization of these resources must be closely linked with the strategic objectives of the company (Fombrun *et al.*, 1984). According to the Harvard model, the workforce is the most valuable, specific and critical resource in an organization. Both models connect human resources with business strategy (Beer *et al.*, 1985).

The authors of this chapter define HRM as a set of practices in an organization to ensure the effective and efficient use of human capital to achieve the organization's goals. Thus, managing human resources has become one of the critical success factors in most organizations. Both the existence of proper personnel and the ways in which people are managed are crucial for achieving competitive advantage. In the current study, the authors analyse how HRM practices could be used in the merger process of two banking organizations in Lithuania, taking into consideration that one of these organizations is already integrated to the group-level corporate structure and the new owners wish to change the organizational culture of the new and larger organization that has been acquired. This provides a good opportunity to understand the role of HRM practices in dealing with cultural differences between organizations in the same country but also with cross-border cultural differences and knowledge transfer challenges between more and less market-oriented organizational cultures.

Ahammad *et al.* (2014) have suggested a conceptual framework that explains the influence of the knowledge transfer on acquisition. This influence is mediated by national cultural differences, organizational cultural differences and employee retention. A knowledge-based view of human resource management activities that enhance M&A performance has also been developed by Weber and Tarba (2010: 205). Zhang *et al.* (2014) stress the effect of leadership style on talent retention during post-merger integration and use evidence from China when proposing that an authoritative, coaching, task- and relationship-focused approach has a positive influence on talent retention and on effective post-merger integration in the Chinese context. In other cultures the effect of such a leadership style may be different, however.

In his cross-border research, Hofstede (1980, 2001) defined culture as a set of shared values and beliefs as well as expected behaviours. The Hofstede framework for cross-cultural studies includes cultural dimensions of individualism–collectivism, uncertainty avoidance, power distance and masculinity–femininity (Hofstede, 1980). Power distance reflects inequality in the social hierarchy and the relationship with authority. The individualism–collectivism dimension reflects relationships between the individual and the group. Masculinity–femininity is related to distinct versus overlapping gender roles. Uncertainty avoidance relates to the extent to which the members of a culture feel threatened in unknown situations. Research evidence concerning two more cultural dimensions – long-term versus short-term orientation and indulgence versus restraint – has been collected over recent decades (Hofstede *et al.*, 2010). The evolution of Hofstede's approach from IBM-based research around 1970 to the comprehensive framework that focuses on dimensions at the national level has been described by Minkov and Hofstede (2011). Hofstede *et al.*'s (2010) research evidence can be used to interpret some differences and similarities between Lithuanian and Estonian management cultures that are relevant for M&A processes. Estonia and other Baltic countries have the lowest power distance in Eastern Europe. The Estonian ranking in this index (global rank 59–61) is the same as the USA's ranking and one place lower than the Lithuanian ranking. Estonia and Lithuania have equal rankings in the individualism index (global rank 23–26). Lithuania (global rank 43–44) is slightly higher in the uncertainty avoidance index than Estonia (47–49). Estonia is a little higher in the masculinity index (global rank 66) than Lithuania (global rank 70–71).

Weber *et al.* (2009) point out that the performance of a particular post-acquisition integration strategy should be related to Hofstede's uncertainty avoidance and individualism/collectivism scores. Successful acquirers from high-level uncertainty avoidance countries try to avoid conflicts and prefer formal procedures. Weber *et al.* (2009) also refer to earlier research results that show higher power distance tends to lead to an absorption integration approach. In their analysis of mergers and acquisitions Weber *et al.* (2011d) differentiate between the following dimensions of corporate culture: approach to innovation and activity; approach to risk; horizontal relationship; vertical–hierarchical contact; autonomy and decision-making; approach to performance; and approach to rewards.

Culture is critical in the preparation of organizational change programmes and when anticipating readiness for change. Weber *et al* (2011a) highlight the role of cultural differences and negotiations in mergers and acquisitions and stress that research efforts should be directed towards the proper selection and training of managers who will be in contact with the members of the foreign negotiating team when planning the acquisition and post-merger integration processes. Corporate culture analysis can serve as a tool for better assessment of cultural differences and enhance the effectiveness of interventions during various stages of the post-merger integration process (Weber and Tarba, 2012). The impact of cultural differences on change readiness in organizations that are involved in M&A activities depends on the partners' integration efforts. Calipha *et al.* (2010) present an overview of M&A motives, including external motives, such as growth and globalization, and more internal motives, such as changing business models and achieving synergies. Regional cross-border acquisitions are less ambitious than new acquisitions by banks that already have a global presence, but taking into consideration the short history of commercial banking in the Baltic countries even acquisitions inside the region assume that the acquiring organization will learn new change practices.

Earlier research does not provide enough case-based evidence about M&A-related change management and integration efforts, where all organizations that have direct roles in the change process represent the banking sector of transition economies. We use the case study in order to fill this research gap and reflect both the specific context of cross-border acquisition in the rapidly changing banking sector and the influence of post-merger efforts to overcome cultural, communication and trust barriers by changing human resource management practices.

Hansabank privatizes the Lithuanian Savings Bank

The history of Hansabank (Hansapank in Estonian) dates back to 1 July 1991, when it started operating as a branch of the Tartu Commercial Bank. Hansabank started operations as an independent bank on 10 January 1992. Soviet roubles were still used in Estonia during the first few months of its operation, but in June 1992 a new national currency – the Estonian crown – was introduced. This was an important step in the country's macro-economic stabilization and in overcoming hyperinflation. However, several commercial banks, including the Tartu Commercial Bank, were unable to adapt to the new macro-economic environment and faced bankruptcy.

From the very beginning, Hansabank employed only young people, excluding those with Soviet banking experience. It became the norm to fill vacancies through internal competition, which offered very good career opportunities for bank employees. An emphasis was placed on integrity and openness. The chairman of the board, Hannes Tamjärv stated: that the bank had 'managed to bring together decent and honest people guided by pure common sense'. By 1994, Hansabank had become the biggest bank in Estonia; and by 1995, the biggest in the Baltic states. By the end of 2004, the net annual profit of Hansabank Group was €182.8 million.

In 1996, Hansabank shocked the Estonian public by acquiring the eighth-largest bank in Latvia, Deutsche Lettische Bank (DLB). Then, in January 1998, Hansabank (1,200 employees) announced its plan to merge with another Estonian bank, Hoiupank (2,000 employees). Hoiupank had operated in the Soviet command economy as a savings bank but had gone through restructuring to become a commercial bank after its privatization in the early 1990s. The merger would result in the creation of the biggest banking group in the Baltic states. Yet it would be some time before the merger could be finalized because Hoiupank wanted to choose the new bank's president – a condition that was unacceptable to Hansabank. Hoiupank officially ceased operations in July 1998, but the merger of the two banks was not completed until June 1999, when their databases were combined. The merger was carried out on the basis of a plan devised by the international consultancy company McKinsey. All positions in the new bank were disclosed for open competition and employees from both banks were invited to apply. Hansabank's management viewed this as best practice and continued to use the approach in their later cross-border acquisitions.

On 17 October 1998, Sweden's Swedbank acquired €93.9 million of shares in Hansabank, which at that time was the biggest foreign investment in the Estonian economy. Acquisitions and business expansion processes were therefore taking place on three levels: as Hoiupank was merging with Hansabank, and Hansabank was expanding its operations to the other Baltic countries, Nordic banks started to acquire significant stakes in Hansabank and other leading Estonian banks.

At the end of 1999, by which time preparations to expand activities into Lithuania had already been under discussion for a year and a half, Hansabank finally received a banking operation licence from the Bank of Lithuania and became the first bank to offer banking services in all three Baltic states.

The new bank in Lithuania was named Hansabankas. Hansabank employed a Lithuanian citizen as CEO, whose first task was to form a team to start the new bank from scratch. He was assisted by a Hansabank employee from Estonia, who helped him to implement the 'Hansa best practice' strategy and launch a major recruitment campaign. Hansabankas was founded in July 1999 and by the end of 2000 it had achieved 3 per cent market share of savings and loans in Lithuania. It had four branch offices, nine cash dispensers (ATMs) and 12,000 clients, with 1,800 using the firm's internet bank, hanza.net. The headquarters was on the main street of Vilnius – Gedimino Street. The bank was integrated into the internal communication system of Hansabank Group and the corporate culture of its employees was comparable to that of Hansabank. Most of Hansabankas's employees were under thirty years of age and almost all of them had already obtained or were still studying for a degree. However, Hansabankas was viewed as an Estonian bank in Lithuania, and its presence in the Lithuanian banking landscape was quite limited when compared with Hansabank's profile in Estonia.

These acquisitions led to the foundation of the Hansabank Group, which included the commercial banks in Estonia, Latvia and Lithuania, and the Hansa Capital Group, which had subsidiaries that offered leasing and factoring services in Estonia, Latvia, Lithuania and Russia, as well as Hansabank Markets. Hansabank Group had its own intranet-based internal communication system and the working language of the group was English. Furthermore, in each country the group had its own communication system in the local language, which enabled knowledge sharing about the group, local affairs and work information. The information technology in the enterprises of the Hansabank Group was among the most advanced in Eastern Europe. The group had a facilitating corporate culture, where relations between superiors and subordinates were more like those of partners. Hierarchical barriers were also lowered by the adoption of a personal approach among managers to their subordinates.

To become equally strong in all three Baltic countries, on 1 June 2001 Hansabank privatized the Lithuanian Savings Bank (Lietuvos Taupomasis Bankas; LTB). On 2 October 2000, Hansabank had presented its takeover bid to privatize the Lithuanian Savings Bank, and on 29 December 2000 the Lithuanian State Property Fund started privatization negotiations with Hansabank. A survey showed that Lithuanians had not expected Estonians to privatize their savings bank (a cultural issue), but had rather been looking for a 'strong foreign investor' from Western Europe.

AS Hansapank and the Lithuanian State Property Fund signed a purchasing contract on 23 April 2001 for the purchase of 90.73 per cent of AB Lietuvos Taupomasis Bankas shares from the Republic of Lithuania. On 15 May, the Bank of Estonia confirmed the purchase of LTB, which was followed by a corresponding confirmation on 24 May by the Board of Competition in Lithuania. The contract became effective on 1 June, which was also the first day, according to the privatization contract, that the managers and employees of Hansabank were allowed to enter LTB and become acquainted with the actual situation in the bank. Up till then, Hansabank had relied on the privatization documents. On 5 June 2001, there was an extraordinary meeting of LTB shareholders and they elected a new council for the bank. On the same day, the new council appointed a new board. Hansabank set the ambitious goal of integrating LTB into the Hansabank Group in just one year. By then, the new Hansabank Group member was expected to be showing a profit.

LTB had been prepared for privatization for several years, but for various reasons all of the previous attempts had failed. The management had been replaced several times. Although the last management of LTB had taken significant steps to reorganize the bank into a modern financial institution, it was still trading at a loss. At the end of 2000, LTB had about 150,000 clients, with the majority of them private; 402 branch offices; and 70 cash dispensers. It had also issued approximately 100,000 bank cards. Its offices were not integrated into a unified network and the level of information technology was poor – even the exchange rates on the boards were changed twice a day by hand. The bank did not have any marketing strategy; every region and office provided information about its own activity independently. The interiors of some branch offices looked like savings banks from the Soviet period. However, although the use of graphics and the bank logo were ineffective and did not follow any rules, the spontaneous recognition of the bank in the Lithuanian market was almost 100 per cent. The bank had not formulated any values that would have enhanced brand equity. The employees felt that the key to its wide recognition lay in the fact that LTB was the largest and oldest bank in the Lithuanian market and that its branch offices, which were in almost every town and village, were easily accessible. Another factor could have been that all transactions in LTB were carried out without any service fee and all deposits were guaranteed by the state.

At the moment of the merger, Hansabankas in Lithuania employed 150 employees who were loyal to their employer, Hansabank Group. They were young and had a very strong team spirit. The values of the Hansabank brand – quality, innovation and vitality – were often quoted. LTB at that time employed 3,500 people across 15 regions, with the majority of them long-term employees from the former Soviet period. At the beginning of the privatization process, one teller celebrated her fortieth anniversary of working in the same office. When Hansabank's plan to privatize LTB became known, the personnel manager of the bank called all of the branch office human resource managers into his office. He told them that the young, English-speaking, well-educated Hansabank would immediately lay off every LTB employee who was over forty-five, did not speak English and did not have a degree. The only people in LTB who met all of these criteria worked at headquarters, so the personnel manager's assessment generated considerable fear and opposition towards the new owner.

The management practices in LTB were rather bureaucratic. There were rumours that documents were considered valid only if they had seven signatures and were sealed. All decisions were made by the board of the bank, so it took weeks to reach one. All tasks had to be passed down the hierarchical structure. If somebody needed to see a manager, they often had to wait for hours in the presence of the secretary, behind the manager's closed office door. The bank had established its own code of practice, which guaranteed some managers and employees more rights than others. The higher management had a twenty-four-hour service of personal drivers and security personnel, and they could use prestigious Lithuanian holiday resorts owned by LTB on preferential terms and conditions. These status symbols were important. The bank organized sports days twice a year, but only a selected circle of people were invited to these events, even though they were ostensibly organized for all personnel at the local regional level. The office of the chairman of the board was a three-room apartment – including a bathroom – furnished with antique furniture. In the opinion of the new owners, this office could have accommodated at least three families. Meanwhile, the offices of ordinary personnel had not been refurbished for years, the ventilation was insufficient and there were no air-conditioners. The offices of the management, on the other hand, were in much better condition and were sufficiently equipped. The corridors of the offices were painted in dark colours and the offices sealed with massive dark wooden doors.

Although LTB had been prepared for privatization for years and had been restructured several times, there was little internal distribution of information. People had to put the picture together on their own from bits and pieces they could gather. Word-of-mouth was the most common means for the dissemination of information. The channels of internal communication included: faxes for disseminating managerial decisions and other official documentation; an internal postal system; and an unofficial intranet page. The intranet was accessible only to head office employees and was mainly used for exchanging personal messages, such as purchase, sale or exchange notices, birthday congratulations and photos of events. Only one person could upload such information. Email was accessible in the headquarters and in the head offices of some regions, but it was practically unused and not considered an official channel of communication.

When the board of Hansabank Group decided to merge Hansabankas and LTB, they decided to use the merger of Hansabank and Hoiupank in Estonia in 1998 as a template to follow.

The local Hansabankas staff did not have sufficient resources to merge the two banks, so a new team of managers, trainers, communicators and personnel staff was formed and sent to Lithuania to carry out the process of integration. They expected to be on site in Lithuania for three or four months. This 'Estonian task force' of specialists and managers was given training prior to their mission. The training sessions had to shape the attitudes of the integration team so they would not feel like integrators but rather as part of a cooperative international team in which the majority of members were Lithuanian. The sessions also focused on the topic of cultural differences – how to communicate with the Lithuanians, which ice-breaking topics would be best, and so on. For instance, asking about family and children and showing a genuine interest in the private life of the communication partner can be a very good technique for bringing people together. The training sessions therefore emphasized the importance of approaching counterparts from a human rather than a rational perspective. Managers learned to differentiate between active and passive resistance, mitigate the straightforward approach of Estonian business culture, double-check that the tasks they had to implement had been understood, and assess the importance of recognition and feedback. It was considered crucial to use face-to-face communication in such a complicated situation involving different cultures. In order to integrate LTB, Hansabank created executive committees in key areas, such as IT, human resources, public relations and communication, retail banking, risk management, leasing, factoring and e-banking.

Challenges of the post-merger integration process

One critical area in the preliminary integration plan was the development of Lithuanian managers in such a way that they would be able to implement the Hansabank Group culture in the new merged bank. Therefore, the key question was how to support the management of change by using human resource management. At the same time more advanced internal communication was needed to inform people about the desired culture. The aim of the internal communication was to create in the minds of the employees of Hansa–LTB an image of the new owner as an open-minded, trustworthy and honest employer that was ready to help the employees manage the process of change. All communication had to correspond to the core values of Hansabank Group and express respect for people from different cultural backgrounds.

A major challenge during the merger of Hansabankas and LTB was explaining one of the basic principles of communication – first pass information to your own personnel and only later to the public. This principle had to be apporved at management level. It was essential that nobody was in a preferential position when it came to accessing information (e.g. from Hansabankas or from any enterprise in the Hansabank Group) and the same information would reach all the employees at the same time. The role of internal communication was to help the managers to set up a comprehensive communication plan and specify their management function. The new owner, Hansabank Group, and its values were introduced via all channels of internal communication, mainly using real-life situations as examples. Representatives of Hansabank Group also followed the principle 'walk the talk': they socialized with employees and worked hard when necessary. Personal chats between employees, managers and personnel staff were also extremely valuable. At the same time it was emphasized through the sophisticated information technology of the Hansabank Group that the employees of LTB would benefit from training opportunities, open communication and the transparency of personnel and payment policies as essential elements of the new human resource management practices.

According to the code of practice in Hansabank Group, everybody in the organization should address each other with the personal, informal 'you', which reduces barriers between management levels and makes communication more open. However, this informal form of address might be problematic in an organization with a more traditional culture. Indeed, in Catholic Lithuania, and especially in LTB, which had previously been dominated by an autocratic culture, the principle was strongly resisted at first. There were no communication problems at the level of top management, but other employees and managers found it difficult to practise the new form of address in their day-to-day communication with colleagues and subordinates. Such informality was interpreted as disrespectful, so it was agreed that it would be introduced gradually, depending on the readiness of the staff.

Human resource management and internal communication functions worked as the sources and transmitters of information that supported organizational changes. The Personnel Department, as the source of information, identified problems, then the Internal Communication Department started to look for and propose solutions. For instance, the Personnel Department found that the Lithuanian employees felt uncomfortable because of uncertainty over merger-related changes, so the Communication Department commissioned a psychologist to write an article for the internal newspaper about people's reactions to change. Similarly, the Personnel Department discovered a need to disseminate more information about the next steps in the post-acquisition merger process and the Communication Department offered ways to satisfy this need. For instance, the Personnel Department wanted to let people know how job vacancies would be filled, so the Communication Department issued a special newsletter which gave an overview of all the vacancies and the terms and conditions for competition for these positions. A special information telephone line was also introduced to answer employees' questions, and the internal newspaper and intranet published the contact details of important members of the Personnel Department. Frequently asked questions and answers were published in the intranet's hotline directory.

The task was to introduce the Lithuanians to the personnel and management culture of Hansabank Group and the practice of job evaluation interviews and competency patterns with the aim of implementing the group's management culture within LTB. This was not easy because the differences between the cultures of Hansabank and LTB were substantial. On the other hand, it was advantageous that Hansabankas, athough a smaller organization than LTB, already enjoyed a positive working culture and the Lithuanians could see that it was successful.

The creation of the new structure

In order to inculcate the new culture, a new structure was created and all personnel had to apply for the new positions. The employees of Hansabankas and LTB applied for jobs in the newly merged bank under the same terms and with the same requirements. The fair selection of employees was monitored by a committee comprising representatives from both banks. This committee approved all decisions and checked that the candidates from both banks had been duly considered, scrutinized the reasons for each successful candidate's selection, and ensured that inter-bank politics had not been involved. They had to fill in a form on these points for every selection that was made.

The top manager of the Lithuanian bank was appointed by Estonians. He then selected the members of the executive board. The remaining positions within the bank were available through open competition, overseen by the fair selection committee. At first, the committee was chaired by an Estonian, but later she was replaced by the Lithuanian head of the local Personnel Department.

The management of the merged Lithuanian bank was ostensibly assembled on the basis of LTB and Hansabankas. However, in practice most of the positions were filled by employees of Hansabankas, with only a handful going to (younger and achievement-oriented) LTB managers. The new management was seconded by the integration team in all fields of activity. Every member of the new board had a 'shadow' in the person of an integration team member. In practice, the inner circle at the table during a meeting would consist of Lithuanians, with another circle of Estonian 'shadows' – consultants from the integration team – sitting behind them. Prior to each meeting, the Lithuanian manager would discuss all of the issues on the agenda with his/her 'shadow'. During the meeting, the Lithuanians would discuss these matters among themselves, but the consultants were constantly ready to offer advice, if necessary. The entire process of training the management and Personnel Department took place in the form of a consultancy.

Developments in the field of human resources management

The integration plan dictated that the personnel manager should be found within Lithuania, although the Estonian human resources team also had an essential role to play because it was its job to join the two staffs together, select the best candidates and ensure fairness. However, no suitable candidate for the position of personnel manager could be found in either of the two Lithuanian banks. Hansabank Group representatives were looking for a person with experience in commercial banking and extensive knowledge of contemporary human resource management. Therefore, it was necessary to send a team from Tallinn to handle the situation during the critical initial stage of the post-merger integration. It remained in Lithuania for the whole summer and consisted of the personnel manager, the personnel development manager, a personnel development specialist and a personnel information technology specialist. Its first task was to fill the position of personnel manager. The successful (external) candidate was a personnel consultant from a consultancy company. Meanwhile, the existing employees of the Personnel Department remained in their positions. Once again, a 'shadow' system was employed, with the new personnel manager overseen by a member of the integration team. This practice could be compared to mentoring, although it was rather more subtle than that. Besides offering guidance to the Lithuanians, it aimed to make them feel as if they were managing the whole system themselves. This was one reason why the Estonian Hansabank integration team remained in Lithuania for only a few months – they did not want to undermine the authority of the local management in the eyes of the Lithuanian employees.

On the first day, the four personnel experts from the integration team arranged a meeting with the employees of the local Personnel Department. None of the Lithuanians spoke English, so all of the material they had prepared in English had to be translated into Russian. However, the Estonians had already forgotten most of the Russian they had learned at school because they had been used to working in English at Hansabank for several years. They just about managed to make themselves understood in their broken Russian during the meeting, but emphasized that the working language of the new bank would have to be English.

No members of staff lost their jobs due to their poor grasp of English. On the contrary, language courses were initiated and everybody who needed to use English in his or her work was encouraged to enrol. A compromise could always be found. In the other enterprises in Hansabank Group, only management was required to have a working knowledge of English. All the channels of internal communication continued to use Lithuanian. Only the common lines of group communication (internal newspaper and intranet) were accessible to the Lithuanians in English. Therefore, knowledge of English was an advantage, whereas information about 'how things are done in the group' was presented solely in English.

The Estonian personnel experts stressed to the Lithuanian Personnel Department staff that they had come to help and have a look at how the integration should be carried out. To aid trust building, the Estonians went bowling with the local personnel employees in order to get better acquainted with them. Unfortunately, though, the local personnel employees exhibited old Soviet attitudes, so it was felt they could not be appointed to key positions in the new organization if it were to survive at a time of rapid transformation in the increasingly competitive commercial banking environment. On the other hand, the integration team did not want to replace the whole department, so the employees had to be motivated to adopt new ways of thinking and working practices. The Estonians wrote an article for the internal newspaper, which was edited by members of the internal communication team. In this they highlighted the work of the local Personnel Department, praised them and encouraged them to try even harder.

The new personnel manager, who had been recruited as part of the integration process, employed a new training manager and emphasized the importance of training. All of the Personnel Department staff were engaged in the process of recruiting new employees, which turned out to be a new experience for them and therefore called for special training. The training sessions were not carried out by the Estonians, but subcontracted to a Lithuanian company, which was chosen by the new Lithuanian personnel manager. He also introduced a new vision of personnel management and encouraged workers with outdated views to learn new methods and see things in a new light. In addition, the Hansabank competency model was introduced.

Employees attended many meetings that aimed to introduce the values and goals of the new bank, and highlight integrity and trust. In order to stress the importance of transparency, the Lithuanian managers' old oak doors were replaced with glass doors.

Conclusions

The current chapter has discussed human resource management and leadership during a merger process. The largest Estonian bank, Hansabank, purchased a large

Lithuanian bank, LTB, and started to integrate it into the Hansabank Group. Transformational change was required within LTB once the purchase was finalized. The main focus of the chapter has been on the changes that were made to the organizational culture of LTB. The activities of the Personnel Department were key success factors that helped to improve the management of the Lithuanian bank and achieve the desired organizational culture. The post-merger integration type in this case was a combination of absorption and symbiosis, when using Weber *et al.*'s (2009) framework. Symbiosis elements were present in the attempts to facilitate participation of LTB staff through transparent recruitment and open communication channels. Absorption elements were apparent in the implementation of quite rapid cultural changes reflecting Hansabank Group core values and in the transformation of business and communication practices in the acquired organization. Transformation features discussed in Ellis *et al.* (2012) were in this case driven by the strategic goals of the Hansabank Group to change existing processes and culture in a newly acquired subsidiary in order to improve its competitive position in the rapidly changing Baltic banking environment, where Hansbank itself was acquired by the more established Swedbank.

Hofstede *et al.* (2010) pointed out some cultural differences between Estonians and Lithuanians that were taken into account during the post-merger integration process. Differences between Hansabank Group's and LTB's respective corporate cultures were, however, more important than differences between the Estonian and Lithuanian national cultures. Hansabank Group represented a new organization that was founded in the market economy. By contrast, LTB to a large extent represented the organizational culture of a command economy.

As the Hansabank Group had previously acquired Hansabankas, the Lithuanian employees of LTB had greater trust in the process of integration than might otherwise have been the case. The new corporate culture was accepted much more readily because it was introduced and spread primarily by Hansabankas's Lithuanian staff, rather than by Estonians from Hansabank Group. However, the integration team from the Estonian headquarters also played an important role in this process.

There was no opportunity for a systematic pre-merger assessment of change readiness in the acquired Lithuanian bank. While it is generally rather complicated to acquire internal information during pre-acquisition negotiations, preliminary information was available only from interviews with top managers and from public surveys that were unrelated to the bank itself. It was therefore impossible to make a detailed integration plan before the privatization deal was signed. When the merger process began in earnest, it was crucial to reduce the psychological stress of the employees at both of the banks and the leasing company. This stress was due to the decision to privatize and the news that had filtered out about the merger. In order to provide the employees with the information they needed, it was first essential to create effective channels of internal communication.

The acceptance of change and participation in the actual process of change starts within the staff themselves. It is possible to learn how to cope with change and the likelihood of success is greater if people appreciate the need for flexibility and have the ability to act fast. Nothing changes for the better until people develop a positive attitude. Therefore, in any process of change, it is essential to know what is going on in people's minds and what emotions they are experiencing. Successful management of change is based on taking action according to uniform principles – everyone involved must move in the same direction. Internal communication can help managers to establish a uniform plan of communication and allow them to monitor the process from a distance. The different phases of change require different approaches and emphasis. If the people involved in the process of change are able to contribute to the process, they will accept the new situation more readily. In any case, it is better to have the necessary information and direction instead of suggestions and to make the process as transparent as possible.

To conclude, the activities of the local Personnel Department, such as transparent recruitment and top management team development, were key success factors that helped to improve the management of the Lithuanian bank and achieve the desired organizational culture.

Limitations of the present case study are related to the impact of a specific historical context of transition to the market economy and specific features of the banking sector. It is difficult to differentiate in such a case between the influence of personal priorities or competencies in the change team and general practices in such post-integration programmes. At the same time, the case demonstrates a successful integration programme between organizations that were involved in the rapid transition towards a market economy. The banking sector is still partly state-owned and heavily regulated by state authorities in many countries, and the global financial crisis has increased state involvement in the banking sectors of even advanced market economies. This case study can be used for further international research into mergers and acquisitions that are influenced by privatization and deregulation of the banking sector.

References

Adler, N. 1997. *International Dimensions of Organizational Behavior.* Cincinnati, OH: South-Western College Publishing.

Aguilera, R.V. and Dencker, J.C. 2004. 'The role of human resource management in cross-border mergers and acquisitions.' *International Journal of Human Resource Management,* 15(8): 1355–1370.

Ahammad, M.F., Tarba, S.Y., Liu, Y. and Glaister, K.W. 2014. 'Knowledge transfer and cross-border acquisition performance: The impact of cultural distance and employee retention.' *International Business Review,* 25(1): 66–75.

Alas, R. 2007. 'The triangular model for dealing with organizational change.' *Journal of Change Management,* 7(3–4): 255–271.

Alas, R. and Sharifi, S. 2002. 'Organizational learning and resistance to change in Estonian companies.' *Human Resource Development International,* 5: 313–331.

Armenakis, A.A. and Bedeian, A., G. 1999. 'Organizational change: A review of theory and research in the 1990s.' *Journal of Management,* 25: 293–315

Beer, M., Spector, B., Lawrence, P., Mills, D. and Walton, R. 1985. *Human Resources Management: A General Manager's Perspective.* New York: The Free Press.

Bergquist, W. 1993. *The Postmodern Organization: Mastering the Art of Irreversible Change.* San Francisco, CA: Jossey-Bass.

Buono, A.F. and Bowditch, J.L. 1989. *The Human Side of Mergers and Acquisitions: Managing Collisions between People, Cultures and Organizations.* San Francisco, CA: Jossey-Bass.

Calipha, R., Tarba, S. and Brock, D. 2010. 'Mergers and acquisitions: A review of phases, motive and success factors.' *Advances in Mergers and Acquisitions*, 9: 1–24.

Curall, S.C. and Inpeken, A. 2002. 'A multilevel approach to trust in joint ventures.' *Journal of International Business Studies*, 33(3): 479–495.

Daft, R.L. 2006. *The New Era of Management.* Mason, OH: Thomson South-Western.

Dopson, S. and Neumann, J.E. 1998. 'Uncertainty, contrariness and the double-find: Middle managers' reactions to changing contracts.' *British Journal of Management*, 9: 53–70.

Ellis, K.M., Weber, Y., Raveh, A. and Tarba, S.Y. 2012. 'Integration in large, related M&As: Linkages between contextual factors, integration approaches and process dimensions.' *European Journal of International Management*, 6(4): 368–394.

Fombrun, C. J., Tichy, N.M. and Devanna, M.A. 1984. *Strategic Human Resource Management.* New York: Wiley.

Hofstede, G. 1980. *Culture's Consequences: International Differences in Work-related Values.* Beverly Hill, CA: Sage.

Hoftstede, G. 2001. *Culture's Consequences: International Differences in Work-related Values.* 2nd edition. Thousand Oaks, CA: Sage.

Hofstede, G., Hofstede, G.J. and Minkov, M. 2010. *Cultures and Organizations: Software of the Mind: Intercultural Cooperation and its Importance for Survival.* New York: McGraw-Hill.

Hunt, J.W. and Downing, S. 1990. 'Mergers, acquisitions and human resource management.' *International Journal of Human Resource Management*, 1(2): 195–209.

Kiessling, T. and Harvey, M. 2006. 'The human resource management issues during an acquisition: The target firm's top management team and key managers.' *International Journal of Human Resource Management*, 17(7): 1307–1320.

Mathis, R.L. and Jackson, J. H. 2002. *Human Resource Management: Essential Perspectives.* 2nd edition. Cincinnati, OH: South-Western Publishing.

Minkov, M. and Hofstede, G. 2011. 'The evolution of Hofstede's doctrine.' *Cross Cultural Management: An International Journal*, 18(1): 10–20.

Nutt, P.C. 2003. 'Implications for organizational change in the structure process duality.' In R.W. Woodman and W.A. Pasmore (eds), *Research in Organizational Change and Development.* Greenwich, CT: JAI Press, Vol. 14: 147–193.

Senge, P. 2001. *The Dance of Change.* London: Nicholas Brealey.

Struckman, C.H. and Yammarino, F. J. 2003. 'Organizational change: A categorization scheme and response model with readiness factors.' In R.W. Woodman and W.A. Pasmore (eds), *Research in Organizational Change and Development.* Greenwich, CT: JAI Press, Vol. 14: 1–50.

Van Dick, R., Ullrich, J. and Tissington, P.A. 2006. 'Working under a black cloud: How to sustain organizational identification after a merger.' *British Journal of Management*, 17(S1): 69–79.

Weber, Y., Belkin, T. and Tarba, S.Y. 2011a. 'Negotiations, cultural differences, and planning in mergers and acquisitions.' *Journal of Transnational Management*, 16: 107–115.

Weber, Y. and Drori, I. 2012. 'Culture–performance relationship in mergers and acquisition: The role of trust.' *European Journal of Cross-Cultural Competence and Management*, 2(3/4): 252–274.

Weber,Y., Rachman-Moore, D. and Tarba, S.Y. 2011b. 'HR practices during post-merger conflict and merger performance.' *International Journal of Cross Cultural Management*, 12(1): 73–99.

Weber, Y. and Tarba, S.Y. 2010. 'Human resource practices and performance of mergers and acquisitions in Israel.' *Human Resource Management Review*, 20: 203–211.

Weber, Y. and Tarba, S.Y. 2012. 'Mergers and acquisitions process: The use of corporate culture analysis.' *Cross Cultural Management: An International Journal*, 19(3): 288–303.

Weber, Y., Tarba, S.Y. and Bachar, Z.R. 2011c. 'Mergers and acquisitions performance paradox: The mediating role of integration approach.' *European Journal of International Management*, 5(4): 373–393.

Weber, Y., Tarba S.H. and Reichel, A. 2009. 'International mergers and acquisitions performance revisited: The role of cultural distance and post-acquisition integration approach.' *Advances in Mergers and Acquisitions*, 6: 1–17.

Weber, Y., Tarba, S.Y. and Reichel, A. 2011d. 'A model of the influence of culture on integration approaches and international mergers and acquisitions performance.' *International Studies of Management and Organization*, 41(3): 9–24.

Whelan-Berry, K.S., Gordon, J.R. and Hinings, C.R. 2003. 'The relative effect of change drivers in large-scale organizational change: An empirical study.' In R.W. Woodman and W.A. Pasmore (eds), *Research in Organizational Change and Development*. Greenwich, CT: JAI Press, Vol. 14: 99–146.

Wright, P.M., McMahan, G.C. and McWilliams, A. 1994. 'Human resources and sustained competitive advantage: A resource based perspective.' *International Journal of Human Resource Management*, 5(2): 301–326.

Zhang, J., Ahammad, M.F., Tarba, S., Cooper, C.L., Glaister, K.W. and Wang, J. 2014. 'The effect of leadership style on talent retention during merger and acquisition integration: Evidence from China.' *International Journal of Human Resource Management*, 27(7): 1021–1050.

13

DOES ACQUISITION EXPERIENCE MATTER?

From yes or no to why, when, and how

Florian Bauer, Andreas Strobl, and Kurt Matzler

Introduction

Mergers and acquisitions (M&A) remain an essential strategy for corporate development, enabling many firms to cope with changing environments, markets, and technologies (Bauer and Matzler, 2014; Swaminathan *et al.*, 2008; Weber and Drori, 2011). For example, in 2010 General Electric announced a plan to invest about US$30 billion over the next three years on acquisitions in order to cope with market developments. Like GE, other global players as well as medium-sized firms have spent billions of dollars on non-organic growth strategies (Jansen, 2008). This overall importance of M&A is demonstrated by the annual global transaction value that approximates the GDPs of large economies, such as Germany's (e.g. GDP of Germany was US$3.8 billion in 2014; transaction volume in 2014 was US$3.6 billion). Even though the market for M&A is strongly cyclical – usually following global economic development – the overall importance of M&A is still increasing and we are currently entering a new boom period (Düsterhoff, 2015). One significant change since the M&A peak in 2000 is that a major part of M&A activity was among small- and medium-sized firms. After the economic downturn in 2007 and the subsequent downturn in the M&A market, M&A activity is now increasing again and cross-border deals are becoming increasingly important (Shimizu *et al.*, 2004).

Due to their popularity, M&A transactions have received a lot of scientific and practical attention. However, despite some thousand studies and perhaps a hundred thousand papers on the topic, our understanding of the phenomenon is still limited and "M&A are still a puzzle for academics and practitioners" (Capasso and Meglio, 2005, p. 219) and their popularity is in contrast to their low success rates (Weber and Drori, 2011). While some research results seem intuitively and logically appealing, others are quite surprising, indicating a greater complexity behind the phenomenon. In a meta-analytic review of commonly analyzed success factors in M&A, namely the acquisition of conglomerates, of related firms, the method of payment, and prior acquisition experience, King and colleagues (2004) reached the conclusion that these variables only explain a minor portion of variance and that other variables influencing acquisition performance remain uncovered. Acquisition experience literature commonly draws a learning curve perspective, indicating that with an increasing amount of acquisitions, the post-merger performance (independent from its definition) increases (Kusewitt, 1985; Muehlfeld *et al.*, 2012). It is argued that experienced acquirers can develop specific routines that make their acquisition processes more effective and thus lead to better performance (Barkema and Schijven, 2008). Even though this makes sense intuitively, the acquisition performance of experienced serial acquirers like Siemens or GE shows great variation, ranging from successful, to neutral, to value-destroying acquisitions. Siemens' acquisition of Nixdorf (US$1,000 million) or Daimler and Chrysler (US$30,000 million) show that even highly experienced companies (so-called serial acquirers) can fail, whereas some acquisition greenhorns can succeed. The results from research reflect this variation (King *et al.*, 2004). Some studies indicate a positive relationship between acquisition experience and performance (Barkema *et al.*, 1996), whereas others suggest a negative (Kusewitt, 1985), a U-shaped (Haleblian and Finkelstein, 1999), an inverted U-shaped (Hayward, 2002), or a non-significant (Zollo and Singh, 2004) relationship. In the above-mentioned meta-analysis, King and colleagues (2004) conclude that there is no evidence for a significant relationship on a cumulative level. In this paper we draw a more fine-grained and nuanced perspective on acquisition experience, as we try to investigate why, when, and how acquisition experience can have beneficial or detrimental effects (see Table 13.1).

With empirical evidence from survey data of 115 acquisitions, several personal interviews with M&A managers, and acquisition consulting experience, we develop possible approaches for firms to benefit from prior experience. Further details on our research activity can be found in the box 'About this research'. Due to confidentiality agreements, we are not allowed to give the names of any firms.

TABLE 13.1 Why, when (1), when (2), and how does experience matter?

Why – an experience fit perspective	Why the transfer of experience can have beneficial, neutral, or detrimental effects.
When – a process perspective	When is experience beneficial? In which phases and for which specific tasks can experience be a trigger for value creation or destruction?
When – a structural perspective on non-organic growth	When do growing pains and acute abdominal pain destroy value? When should firms implement counter-measures to avoid value-destroying crisis?
How – an experience knowledge transition perspective	Experience and what then? How should firms use their experience?

ABOUT THIS RESEARCH

Since 2009, we have focused on the topic of M&A from various perspectives, including strategy, organization, and processes. In total we have primary survey data on more than 800 individual acquisitions, several dozen interviews with managers responsible for and affected by M&A activities, and deep insights into acquisition programs as we have observed several acquirers during their acquisitions. For this chapter, we rely on two sources. First, we collected survey data on 115 transactions carried out within the German-speaking part of Europe between 2008 and 2011. The mail and internet survey was conducted in 2014 to ensure that each integration was complete or at least close to its final stage. Second, we gained insights from two acquirers we accompanied over the course of several acquisitions; additionally, we gained insights from interviews with managers in charge of the enterprises. Both data sources give fascinating insights into the so-called 'Champions League' of strategic and organizational management, namely M&A. Our research effort has improved our understanding of this complex phenomenon.

Does experience matter?

Why – an experience fit perspective

M&A-experience research is usually based on a learning curve perspective and the common measurement of experience is the number of transactions. At first glance, it seems logical that firms will gather valuable experience in closing deals and integrating targets and as a consequence will improve their acquisition performance as they increase their number of acquisitions (Ellis *et al.*, 2011). Yet, this assumption has a major weakness. It ignores the *type* of experience that is gained and its usefulness in subsequent acquisitions. Until now there has been little research into the value and transferability of experience from one M&A transaction to the next.

One firm we observed during its first and several subsequent acquisitions, a medium-sized hidden champion from southern Germany, made its first acquisition in China in the course of developing new geographical markets. All executives and middle-management – besides their general respect for such an important strategic move – had a lot of respect for cultural and legal differences. This was maybe due to many cautionary tales of previous investments by well-known German firms in China (e.g. Steiff's quality issues, and violations of intellectual property rights for Stihl).

> We are aware of the situation. China is different. Many firms have failed after entering this exciting, big market. They have a different culture and a different behavior.
>
> *(Sales manager of the acquiring firm)*

However, the acquisition went well and a year later the firm decided to pursue another. Its experience with cultural and institutional aspects of the acquisition, as well as the integration of sales channels and harmonization of marketing and brands, was transferred to the second acquisition, and it was even more successful than the first. As a consequence, a third acquisition was planned in India and the acquirer's experience from the first two transactions proved to be beneficial again. The management team developed fine-grained routines and confidence over their acquisition management capabilities steadily increased.

> We had an acquisition blueprint, a perfect and detailed acquisition project plan, and there was an atmosphere like in Frank Sinatra's song "New York, New York": if we can make it there, we'll make it anywhere.
>
> *(CEO of the acquiring firm)*

A fourth acquisition targeted a domestic firm for technology and resource purposes. Compared to the previous transactions, this promised to be straightforward, given the similar legal systems and cultural backgrounds of the target and the acquirer. However,

> Our domestic deal seemed like a child's play, but, hell, it ended in disaster.
>
> *(CFO of the acquiring firm)*

Figure 13.1 presents the company's acquisition history.

What went wrong? Following the learning curve perspective, drawing from experience in countries (China and India) that were known to be difficult, the fourth acquisition should have been simple. Yet the opposite was the case. The transaction turned out to be a disaster. It would be easy to assume that this failure was rooted in overconfidence triggered by previous successes or due to narcissistic personalities in management seeking recognition (Billet and Qian, 2008). But if we take a closer look at the experience the company gained and then transferred to subsequent transactions, a generalization error can be detected. With its acquisitions in China, it became experienced in dealing with cultural and institutional differences, integrating sales channels, and transferring its marketing and brand reputation (with seals of quality like 'Made in Germany') across borders. This Chinese experience then proved valuable for the subsequent acquisition in India. Again, integrating distribution channels and transferring marketing know-how were core obstacles that had to be overcome. However, the domestic acquisition was different for several reasons. First, national/cultural or institutional differences were not an issue, so the firm's experience in overcoming such obstacles had no value. Second, integrating sales channels and a one-way (from buyer to target) transfer of marketing and brand management practices is different from *exchanging* technological know-how and capabilities, which demands a bi-directional information and resource stream. Thus, during its three transnational transactions, the acquirer acted mainly as a sender, whereas during the domestic transition the acquirer suddenly had to act as *both*

	First M&A experience	**Second M&A experience**	**Third M&A experience**	**Fourth M&A experience**
Acquisition in	China	China	India	Domestic deal
Acquisition motive	Market-seeking motive	Market-seeking motive	Market-seeking motive	Resource/technology-seeking motive
Type and value-sources of experience	Acquirer becomes aware of problems: • With cultural • differences • With institutional differences • In realigning targets • with regards to market purposes	Acquirer is sensitized to: • Cultural and institutional differences • Problems and threats occurring when realigning target firms with regards to market purposes	Acquirer applies its operating experience and routines. Acquirer is an expert in dealing with: • Cultural differences • Institutional differences • The realignment of target with regards to market purposes Acquirer can apply its developed acquisition routines from prior experience	Acquirer applies its operating experience and routines from the previous three transactions in China and India. The gained experience has no use for the fourth acquisition, the fourth acquisition is not comparable to the other ones.
	Transfer of experience	Transfer of experience	Transfer of experience	
Situational fit	=	=	≠	
Acquirer development	"Greenhorn acquirer"	"Versed acquirer"	"Acquisition expert"	"Failed acquisition expert"
Value of experience	**None**	**Positive**	**Positive**	**Disastrous**

FIGURE 13.1 Acquisition history of an acquirer

sender and recipient simultaneously. As a consequence, the well-developed integration approaches that had worked so well in an international context with market-seeking motives now led to confused and unsatisfied employees, resistance, increased employee turnover, and ultimately a loss of know-how. "What was acquired was lost two years later," the CEO commented.

This example demonstrates that a one-by-one transfer of routines developed through experience can be successful, problematic, or without any consequence in subsequent acquisitions, depending on the degree of fit between the initial and the subsequent transactions (Ellis *et al.*, 2011). Thus, experience and knowledge transfer from one acquisition to the next must always take differences into account.

When (1) – a process perspective

When equating acquisition experience to the number of transactions, we count an acquisition – from the initial idea to the accomplished integration (that is, between three to five years after a deal has been finalized) – as one experience "point" without understanding when – in which phases or with regards to which tasks – it matters. Here a more detailed perspective on different phases and corresponding tasks is beneficial. On a meta-level, there is general agreement that M&As consist of three phases: pre-merger; merger; and post-merger. Each of these phases consists of dozens of interrelated tasks that may not necessarily be treated as parallel activities. Each task can contribute to value creation if performed well or to value destruction if performed badly. Figure 13.2 displays the phases and some related tasks during acquisitions.

When talking about the use and the value of acquisition experience, we refer to the experience with specific tasks to be accomplished during the pre-merger,

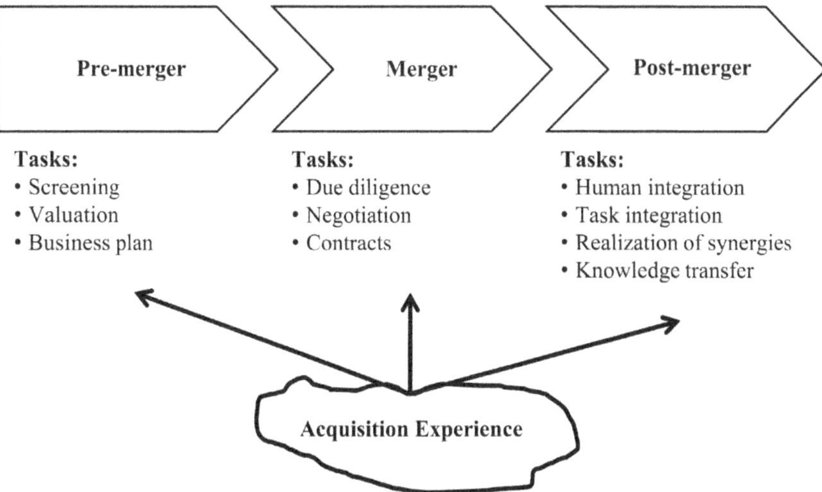

FIGURE 13.2 An experience–process perspective

merger, or post-merger integration phase or specific routines (Barkema and Schijven, 2008). Thus, experienced acquirers perform specific acquisition-related tasks such as target screening, due diligence, or post-merger integration more efficiently and more effectively than others.

While specific tasks can be repeated in a similar way in every acquisition, other tasks require tailored approaches in every acquisition, and thus need to be treated like new, initial processes. While the development of business plans, target valuations (depending on the strategic rationale behind the transaction), or a due diligence request list could follow standardized routines based on prior acquisition experience, this turns out to be almost impossible when it comes to soft issues (e.g. issues related to company culture) or when humans are involved. These are usually the main differentiators between organizations and are often cited as the main obstacles (Blake and Mouton, 1985; Huselid *et al.*, 1997; Weber *et al.*, 2012). Even though the pre-merger and the merger phases require a lot of managerial know-how and resources, the clean-up begins on day two, immediately after the big party, when many firms are suffering from a hangover. The integration phase is decisive, as value creation or destruction takes place after closing the deal (Haspeslagh and Jemison, 1991). Many firms fail during integration or simply underestimate the required realignment efforts (Vester, 2002; Birkinshaw *et al.*, 2000; Pablo, 1994). It is no wonder that Joe Kaeser (CEO of Siemens) aims to increase the performance of already acquired business units, where little attention has previously been paid to this. However, many individual but interrelated tasks must be performed to turn such a statement into an actual increase in performance. Integration is a highly complex, multi-dimensional (Shrivastava, 1986), long-term (e.g. Bauer and Matzler, 2014; Homburg and Bucerius, 2005, 2006) process, continuing for three to five years after the deal has been made (Homburg and Bucerius, 2006). Even though the harmonization of accounting and controlling (which is legally mandatory in most countries) as well as IT issues can be performed with well-developed routines based on experience, a standardized approach to other tasks – like human integration – can have disastrous consequences. Research results indicate that there is no generally applicable blueprint for integration strategies, and integration typologies lack empirical evidence (Angwin and Meadows, 2014). One reason might be that different acquisition motives require different levels of organizational autonomy and strategic interdependence that could occur in parallel in one acquisition (Zaheer *et al.*, 2013). Additionally, targets usually differ from one another with regards to organizational culture, leadership-styles, and/or structures. Thus, the use of integration experience – beyond some specific tasks – is strongly case sensitive and depends on the strategic need for integration.

When (2) – much is too much – a structural perspective on non-organic growth

Firm growth goes hand in hand with structural, managerial, and organizational cultural transitions (Whetten, 1987; Flamholtz and Randle, 2007). And ggressive growth commonly leads to growing pains when non-organic growth strategies are pursued. A major issue here is that a firm's structural growth mostly lags behind the pace of sales growth. When conducting many subsequent acquisitions, managers tend to neglect organizational structures as their focus is to grow without wasting resources on structural realignment, which is time consuming, expensive, and complex (Miles *et al.*, 1978). Thus, structural realignment is perceived as an unaesthetic task. One Austrian firm we observed during its acquisition processes had the aim of achieving a global footprint as quickly as possible. The reasons were twofold: first, they wanted to spread their country market risk; and second, they wanted to grow. To some extent, they followed a bridgehead strategy – first entering a specific country, then starting to export to neighboring countries, and finally investing in the whole region with brownfield developments. They entered the Spanish market with the aim of developing a business division in south-west Europe (France, Spain, Portugal, and Italy) through the acquisition of the number two in the Spanish market. In a second step, headquarters managers screened the regional markets for subsequent brownfield investments. Within three years, eighteen acquisitions had been made and the target firms were mandated to the South-West Europe Division (S-WED), with its regional headquarters in the original bridgehead in Spain. Over the next three years, the division created a strong entrepreneurial spirit due to a high level of autonomy that was tolerated by the corporate headquarters, which was focusing on rapid non-organic growth in other regions at the time. The S-WED became a powerful actor in the firm's network because it contributed a major share of European sales. As a consequence, it strived to maintain its autonomous position in the firm.

> Our vision for the future is to keep autonomy for tying in with past success.
> *(S-WED executive)*

This fairy tale of endless growth and success turned into a nightmare a few years later. The first indication of the upcoming storm came during 2012's annual budget meeting, attended by divisional executives, the CEO, the CFO, and the COO at the firm's headquarters in Austria. As a marginal side-note, the S-WED executive requested €10 million for an acquisition. The board members were blind-sided and demanded more information and some time to make a decision. However, the S-WED executive replied: "A 'no' is not acceptable. We have already signed a non-disclosure agreement, and have agreed on a transaction plan and a non-binding offer. What do you want from us? Shall we grow and develop or not?" Six months later, headquarters was in charge of the transaction process after reevaluating the target and renegotiating the deal. In an interview, the S-WED executive expressed his dismay at this course of events: "I lost face. No partner or employee will trust me in the future. My reputation is busted. The next time I buy a pencil, will the guys from headquarters come and tell me that I do not have their approval to spend ten cents?"

A major problem for this fast-growing firm was that its structures remained the same for a decade. While investing heavily in non-organic growth, headquarters missed the opportunity to establish clear responsibilities and realign and adapt the firm's organizational structures to meet the needs of the emerging organization. What ensued was a painful but necessary restructuring process at the cost of S-WED's autonomy.

How – an experience knowledge transition perspective

When talking about experience and its relationship to performance, the literature tends to oversimplify (Ellis *et al.*, 2011). Acquisition experience can be transferred in either explicit or implicit acquisition knowledge. While explicit acquisition knowledge consists of recorded lessons learned, procedural instructions, and/or standardized management techniques (Dierkes *et al.*, 2001; Nonaka and Takeuchi, 1995; Lam, 2000), tacit acquisition knowledge is rooted in individuals and its is not – or hardly – recordable (Nonaka and Van Krogh, 2009; Lam, 2000). Anyway, explicit and tacit acquisition knowledge are not opposite ends of a spectrum (Lam, 2000), and the interaction between and combination of the two are necessary (Nonaka and Takeuchi, 1995) to increase the likelihood to acquisition success.

Based on the results of a survey of 115 acquisitions, we developed four different types of acquirer with regards to their acquisition knowledge transition behavior (see Figure 13.3). To identify the different types of acquirer, acquisition knowledge

Degree of tacit M&A knowledge at the individual level		
	The implicit knowing • Is an ideal crisis manager, can react fast and flexibly. • Decisions based on implicit knowledge are not always transparent and traceable. Deviation from Ø-Performance: + 5.47%	**The all-rounder** • Makes use of both types of acquisition experience. • Standardizes where possible but keeps the necessary flexibility. Deviation from Ø-Performance: + 6.52%
	The unthoughtful • Acts completely unreflectively • Not interested in lessons • learned from previous acquisitions. Deviation from Ø-Performance: -14.79%	**The codifier** • Reflects on each transaction. • Experience is codified. • Does not understand why an experience - transfer is not always possible. Deviation from Ø-Performance: -4.18%
	Degree of codified and recorded M&A experience	

FIGURE 3.3 The effects of codified and recorded experience and tacit acquisition knowledge on M&A performance

transition was investigated along the dimension of degree of tacit M&A knowledge transition at the individual level and degree of codified and recorded M&A experience. Interestingly, from a statistical standpoint, the four types do not differ significantly in terms of previous M&A activity. The unthoughtful acquirer has never transformed its acquisition experience into either explicit or tacit acquisition knowledge. This unreflected approach causes strong negative effects (14.79 percent lower than other acquirers' M&A performance). While inexperienced acquirers thoroughly analyze, plan, and manage their acquisitions, unthoughtful acquirers do not care and act impulsively.

Anyway, codification is not the ultimate route to success. Transforming acquisition experience only into explicit, codified knowledge limits managerial possibilities and required degrees of freedom in decision-making. As M&A processes are project management to its fullest extent, there is a clear need for flexibility to react quickly when unpredictable events and situations arise, whereas the strict application of rules destroys value, as is indicated by the codifier type's negative deviation from average performance. In contrast to the codifier, the implicit knowing type can react quickly. This makes them ideal crisis managers that should be given sufficient scope for decision-making. However, although the results indicate above-average performance, their decisions lack transparency and could therefore cause organizational resistance. All-rounders achieve the best performance, as they balance codified and tacit acquisition knowledge. They implement transparent and standardized processes where possible, but allow for quick and unconventional decisions and solutions.

Implications

Experience can have a significant impact during acquisitions, but the acquisition experience–performance relationship is more complex than is often assumed. Acquisition experience can be both a blessing and a curse at the same time. In this section, we outline the implications of this for future research and practice.

Research implications

Recent research on acquisition experience has adopted a transfer theory perspective by arguing that not all acquisitions are alike (Ellis *et al.*, 2011; Bower, 2001; Haleblian and Finkelstein, 1999). Our case example shows that transferring experience can have beneficial, neutral, or even detrimental effects. Thus, the situational fit between initial acquisition experience and a subsequent transaction is decisive (Haleblian and Finkelstein, 1999; Hayward, 2002). Our case demonstrated that there is no overall acquisition experience but rather specific experience with regards to specific tasks (Barkema and Schijven, 2008; Hayward, 2002). While task integration-related experiences can be transferable, human-related experiences are often untransferable. Anyway, acquisition experience is not easy to capture (Hayward, 2002); and even when it is captured, this is mostly done through simple proxies (Lord and Ranft,

2000), such as the number of acquisitions in a specific timeframe before the initial observation (Ellis *et al.*, 2011; Haleblian and Finkelstein, 1999). However, secondary data might not provide the necessary richness of information , as acquisitions are not comparable. Thus, an in-depth analysis is needed to understand which routines can be transferred for which specific tasks without modification and which tasks need individual considerations for each acquisition. Consequently, a primary data research approach would be beneficial.

Another issue derives from the fact that we do not know how firms proceed with their experiences. The separation of explicit and tacit M&A knowledge was valuable as it showed diverging effects. Simple codification disregards heterogeneous circumstances, while the application of tacit knowledge leads to less transparency. Firms and managers that apply both types of knowledge have the highest probability of succeeding. Analysis of how firms assess their experience and how they transfer it into explicit and tacit knowledge could be a fruitful stream for improving our understanding of the effect of acquisition experience.

Finally, we believe that a process learning perspective would be useful. Acquisitions are not static events. Many parallel processes must be managed between target screening and final integration. The current research broadly ignores this complexity (Meglio and Risberg, 2010), but it would be valuable to understand the effects of experience during the process.

In addition to these implications for researchers, our work has several implications for managers.

Managerial implications

Managers must be aware of the various effects of acquisition experience. Our research reveals that firms can make use of this experience and avoid traps if it is utilized carefully. First, a situational fit of previous and subsequent acquisitions is a decisive antecedent if experience is transferable in a beneficial way. Next to organizational issues such as target size, age, and structure, managers should concentrate on the strategic rationale of the acquisition. If individual acquisitions are not comparable, managers should treat eahc of them as a discrete process and not in a "we have always done it this way" manner. Second, experience should not be assessed solely in terms of the number of previous acquisitions, as experience is not necessarily relevant to the whole M&A project. Rather, experience matters only with respect to specific tasks, and top performers have well-developed routines for some tasks but display flexibility with respect to others in the M&A process. Managers would be well advised to reflect on their past acquisitions to identify which tasks belong in which category. Third, non-organic growth can be beneficial as it allows for quick growth, market entry, and technology gain, but organizations are complex systems and if specific issues are changed or adapted, other things have to be changed or adapted, too. To avoid growing pains, managers should pay attention to and address the time-consuming, expensive, and unaesthetic task of structural realignment. Growing through acquisitions is merely the qualification for the Champions

League. True champions achieve sustainable advantages as they prepare their organizations for managing growth. Fourth, experience can matter, but firms need to transform their acquisition experience into acquisition knowledge. In doing so, they should be aware that checklists, recorded lessons learned, procedural instructions, and/or standardized management techniques are not always the best options. They can alleviate the organizational pain that is often associated with non-organic growth strategies by providing guidelines during the process. M&A management is the epitome of project management, and unforeseeable events happen on a daily basis. Thus, firms must allow their managers to be flexible in their decision-making. Top-performing acquirers always establish a balance between standardized processes and flexibility.

To conclude, an oversimplistic appraisal of acquisition experience can lead to disastrous results. Firms and managers must be aware of the complex interdependencies of acquisition experience. Additionally, those that rely solely on their experience will fail, as experience must be transformed in acquisition knowledge. Once again, the reality is more complex than is often assumed, and firms should reflect on their past acquisitions to identify those tasks that can be standardized and those that need to be addressed on an individual basis. Careful assessment of each individual acquisition is crucial, too. We trust that our research will help firms and managers to appreciate the complex nature of acquisition experience, and allow them to make the most of that experience.

References

Angwin, D., and Meadows, M. (2014). New integration strategies for post-acquisition management. *Long Range Planning*, 48(4), pp. 235–251.

Barkema, H. G., and Schijven, M. (2008). How do firms learn to make acquisitions? A review of past research and an agenda for the future. *Journal of Management*, 30(4), pp. 594–634.

Barkema, H. G., Bell, J., and Pennings, J. M. (1996). Foreign entry, cultural barriers, and learning. *Strategic Management Journal*, 17, pp. 151–166.

Bauer, F., and Matzler, K. (2014). Antecedents of M&A success: The role of strategic complementarity, cultural fit, and degree and speed of integration. *Strategic Management Journal*, 35(2), pp. 269–291.

Bijlsma-Frankema, K. (2001). On managing cutural integration and cultural change processes in mergers and acquisitions. *Journal of European Industrial Training*, 25, pp. 192–207.

Billet, M., and Qian, Y. (2008). Are overconfident CEOs born or made? Evidence of self-attribution bias from frequent acquirers. *Management Science*, 54(6), pp. 1037–1051.

Birkinshaw, J., Bresman, H., and Hakanson, L. (2000). Managing the post-acquisition integration process: How human integration and task integration processes interact to foster value creation. *Journal of Management Studies*, 37(3), pp. 365–425.

Blake, R., and Mouton, J. (1985). How to achieve integration on the human side of the merger. *Organization Dynamics*, 13(3), pp. 41–56.

Bower, J. (2001). Not all M&As are alike – and that matters. *Harvard Business Review*, 79, pp. 92–102.

Capasso, A., and Meglio, O. (2005). Knowledge transfer in mergers and acquisitions: How frequent acquirers learn to manage the integration process. In A. Capasso, G. B. Dagnino, and A. Lanza (eds.), *Strategic capabilities and knowledge transfer within and between organizations* (pp. 199–225). Northampton: Edward Elgar.

Chakravorty, J. (2012). Why do mergers and acquisitions quite often fail? *Advances in Management*, 5(5), pp. 21–28.

Cording, M., Christman, P., and King, D. (2008). Reducing causal ambiguity in acquisition integration: Intermediate goals as mediators of integration decisions and acquisition performance. *Academy of Management Journal*, 51(4), pp. 744–767.

Dierkes, M., Berthoin Antal, A., Child, J., and Nonaka, I. (2001). *Handbook of organizational learning and knowledge*. New York: Oxford University Press.

Düsterhoff, H. (2015). Wende ja, welle nein: Jahresrückblick auf das deutsche M&A – Geschehen 2014. *M&A Review*, 26(2), pp. 73–81.

Ellis, K., Reus, T., Lamont, B., and Ranft, A. (2011). Transfer effects in large acquisitions: How size specific experience matters. *Academy of Management Journal*, 6, pp. 1261–1276.

Finkelstein, S., and Halebian, J. (2002). Understanding acquisition performance: The role of transfer effects. *Organization Science*, 13(1), pp. 36–47.

Flamholtz, E., and Randle, Y. (2007). *Growing pains: Transitioning from an entrepreneurship to a professionally managed firm*. San Francisco, CA: Jossey-Bass.

Haleblian, J., and Finkelstein, S. (1999). The influence of organizational acquisition experience on acquisition performance: A behavioral learning perspective. *Administrative Science Quarterly*, 44, pp. 29–56.

Haspeslagh, P. C., and Jemison, D. B. (1991). *Managing acquisitions*. New York: The Free Press.

Hayward, M. (2002). When do firms learn from their acauisition experience? Evidence from 1990–1995. *Strategic Management Journal*, 23(1), pp. 21–39.

Homburg, C., and Bucerius, M. (2005). A marketing perspective on mergers and acquisitions: How marketing integration affects postmerger performance. *Journal of Marketing*, 69, pp. 96–113.

Homburg, C., and Bucerius, M. (2006). Is speed of integration really a success factor of mergers and acquisitions? An analysis of the role of internal and external relatedness. *Strategic Management Journal*, 27, pp. 347–367.

Huselid, M., Jackson, S., and Schuler, R. (1997). Technical and strategic human resource management effectivness as determinants of firm performance. *Academy of Management Journal*, 40(1), pp. 171–188.

Jansen, S. A. (2008). *Mergers and acquisitions*. 5th edition. Wiesbaden: Gabler Verlag.

King, D. E., Dalton, D. R., Daily, C. M., and Covin, J. G. (2004). Meta-analyses of post-acquisition performance: Indications of unidentified moderators. *Strategic Management Journal*, 25, pp. 187–200.

Kusewitt, J. J. (1985). An exploratory study of strategic acquisition factors relating to performance. *Strategic Management Journal*, 6, pp. 151–169.

Lam, A. (2000). Tacit knowledge, organizational learnuing and societal institutions: An integrated framework. *Organization Studies*, 21(3), pp. 487–513.

Lord, M., and Ranft, A. (2000). Organizational learning about new international markets: Exploring the internal transfer of local market knowledge. *Journal of International Business Studies*, 31(4), pp. 573–589.

Meglio, O., and Risberg, A. (2010). Mergers and acquisitions: Time for a methodological rejuvenation in the field? *Scandinavian Journal of Management*, 26, pp. 87–95.

Miles, R., Snow, C., Meyer, A., and Coleman Jr., H. (1978). Organizational strategy, structure, and processes. *Academy of Management Review*, 3(3), pp. 546–562.

Muehlfeld, K., Sahib, P., and Van Witteloostuijn, A. (2012). Contextual theory of organizational learning from failures and successes: A study of acquisition completion in the global newspaper industry, 1981–2008. *Strategic Management Journal*, 33, pp. 938–964.

Nonaka, I., and Takeuchi, H. (1995). *The knowledge-creating company: How Japanese companies create the dynamics of innovation*. New York: Oxford University Press.

Nonaka, I., and Von Krogh, G. (2009). Tacit knowledge and knowledge conversion: Controversy and advancement in organizational knowledge creation theory. *Organization Science*, 20(3), pp. 635–652.

Pablo, A. (1994). Determinants of acquisition integration level: A decision making perspective. *Academy of Management Journal*, 37(4), pp. 803–836.

Shimizu, K., Hitt, M., Vaidyanath, D., and Pisano, V. (2004). Theoretical foundations of cross-border mergers and acquisitions: A review of current research and recommendations for the future. *Journal of International Management*, 10, pp. 307–353.

Shrivastava, P. (1986). Postmerger integration. *Journal of Business Strategy*, 7(1), pp. 65–76.

Swaminathan, V., Murshed, F., and Hulland, J. (2008). Value creation following merger and acquisition announcements: The role of strategic emphasis alignment. *Journal of Marketing Research*, 45, pp. 33–47.

Vester, J. (2002). Lessons learned about integrating acquisitions. *Research Technology Management*, 45, pp. 33–41.

Weber, Y. T. (2011). A model of the influence of culture on integration approaches and international mergers and acquisitions performance. *International Studies of Management and Organization*, 41(3), pp. 9–24.

Weber, Y., and Drori, I. (2011). Integrating organizational and human behaviour perspectives in mergers and acquisitions. *International Studies of Management and Organization*, 41 (3), pp. 73–95.

Weber, Y., Rachman-Moore, D., and Tarba, S. (2012). HR practices during post-merger conflict and merger performance. *International Journal of Cross Cultural Management*, 12(1), pp. 73–99.

Whetten, D. (1987). Organizational growth and decline processes. *Annual Review of Sociology*, 13, pp. 335–358.

Zaheer, A., Castaner, X., and Souder, D. (2013). Synergy sources, target autonomy, and integration in acquisitions. *Journal of Management*, 39(3), pp. 604–632.

Zollo, M., and Singh, H. (2004). Deliberate learning in corporate acquisitions: Post-acquisition strategies and integration cpability in US bank mergers. *Strategic Management Journal*, 25, pp. 1233–1256.

14

STRATEGIC ALLIANCES IN THE ORGANIZATIONAL AND FINANCIAL LITERATURES

A review

Ian P. L. Kwan

Introduction

This review identifies relevant theories and methods from the strategy literature on organizational learning and from the finance literature on valuation concerning strategic alliances. It proceeds as follows. The first section reviews answers to preliminary questions about strategic alliances, serving as an introduction to the topic for readers. The next section reviews earlier strategy literature on the market-based view, resource-based view, knowledge-based view, and transaction cost approaches, analyzing strategic alliances in the light of each. It also reviews relevant financial methods of valuation, including the discounted cash flow method, real options method, and event study method, again applying them to the case of alliances. The final section provides a summary of studies on value creation by strategic alliances.

Preliminary questions and answers on strategic alliances

Many researchers on strategic alliances frequently introduce the setting of their academic papers by describing a significant aspect of strategic alliance activity to attract their readers' attention. This is often a definition of what a strategic alliance is or some important or well-known aspect of alliances, such as how often they occur, who engages in them, why they engage in them, when they occur, when they break up, and so on. These preliminary issues provide context for the readers and lead to the papers' main issues. I would like to do the same in this chapter by providing a summary of answers to common preliminary questions on strategic alliances that are often found in the introductory sections of this literature.

What is a strategic alliance?

A strategic alliance is a cooperative agreement made between two or more independent firms to achieve a mutual set of objectives (Kogut, 1988; Gulati, 1998; Ireland, Hitt, and Vaidyanath, 2002). Through an alliance, firms necessarily commit to share a subset of their tangible and intangible resources (Barney, 1991; Grant, 1991). Tangible resources include physical assets such as plant and equipment, or services such as a proprietary distribution network or computer system, while intangible resources include access to intellectual capital tied up in licensed patents and production processes.

An alliance is a hybrid organizational form through which two or more firms can combine their business resources. The alliance organizational form lies in the continuum between a market exchange contract and a merger of firms (Kogut, 1988; Lerner and Rajan, 2006; Villalonga and McGahan, 2005). A firm can access the resources of another through market exchange contracts quickly and without the buyer and seller knowing each other. Market exchange contracts are characterized by their standard terms, standard product or service quality, industry accepted delivery times, common pricing methods, and so on. A firm can also access the resources of another by merging with that firm. Mergers are characterized by their complexity, extended personal negotiations, and information asymmetries (Zollo and Reuer, 2010).

In this chapter, I use *strategic alliance* or simply *alliance* as a collective term to mean licensing agreements, franchise agreements, contractual (non-equity) joint ventures, and equity joint ventures (Inkpen, 1998a; Parkhe, 1991).

Where? How many? How significant?

Alliances are found in almost all industries, in both domestic and international business environments. However, they are most prevalent in high-technology, fast-changing, highly competitive, research-intensive industries, including computers, telecommunications, pharmaceuticals, chemicals, electronics, biotechnology, and services (Kale, Dyer, and Singh, 2002; Rothaermel and Deeds, 2004). Alliances are less common in stable, mature industries (Koza and Lewin, 1998).

The empirical findings of Eisenhardt and Schoonhoven (1996) provide a good answer to the question of where to find alliances from both a strategic and a social point of view.

- More alliances are formed in industries that have more competitors. In competitive markets with many players, greater market power can be achieved through forming an alliance. Alliances with well-known firms also provide legitimacy to less well-known firms, especially in a crowded market.
- There is a greater rate of alliance formation in industries that require greater innovation. As innovative products are costly to create, firms tend to choose alliances to gain access to and share their own innovative know-how to reduce costs.

- Alliances form more often when there are a large number of top management team members. Top management members provide the necessary connections to potential alliance partners.
- The more previous employees the top management team has had, the greater will be the rate of alliance formation.
- The more senior were the previous positions of top management members, the more frequent will be the rate of alliance formation.
- Although the empirical support is not strong, the frequency of alliance formation tends to be highest in emergent-stage markets, lower in growth-stage markets, and lowest in mature-stage markets.

International joint ventures are the usual mode of entry for domestic firms to enter into global markets (Berg, Duncan, and Friedman, 1982; Harrigan, 1985), especially those of emerging economies (Peng, 2003; Fang, 2011) because their structural attributes help firms to reduce risk (Reuer and Leiblein, 2000).

The number of alliances has grown significantly over the past 30 years. There was a huge wave of 57,000 alliances for US firms between 1996 and 2001 (Dyer, Kale, and Singh, 2004). World-wide, 20,000 alliances were formed between 1998 and 2000 (Anand and Khanna, 2000). According to the Securities Data Corporation (SDC) Joint Ventures and Alliances database, in 2005 over 52,000 completed or pending alliances were reported. According to a 2009 study by KPMG International, the number of joint venture strategic alliances continued to grow in spite of the global financial crisis.[1]

The volume of assets and revenue linked with alliances in mainstream business is also very significant. Before the year 2000, many of world's largest firms had over 20 percent of their assets and over 30 percent of their R&D budget tied up with alliances (Ernst, 2004; Kale and Singh, 2009). In the 2007–2008 financial year, more than 80 percent of Fortune 1000 CEOs believed that alliances would account for 26 percent of their companies' revenues (Kale, Singh, and Bell, 2009; Kale and Singh, 2009). In sum, as a way of doing business, alliances seem here to stay for some time into the future.

Why do firms form alliances?

Some commonly cited motives why firms form alliances include:

- strengthening their competitive position through combined market power (Kogut, 1991);
- increasing scale efficiencies through reduced transaction costs (Hennart, 1988; Ahuja, 2000);
- gaining access to new and critical resources and capabilities (Hitt *et al.*, 2000; Rothaermel and Boeker, 2008);
- accessing new technologies and innovative know-how of partners (Hamel, 1991; Vanhaverbeke, Duysters, and Noorderhaven, 2002);

- responding to strategic resource interdependence between partners (Gulati, 1998);
- lowering the risk of entering new markets for the first time (Inkpen and Beamish, 1997; Garcia-Canal, Duarte, Criado, and Llaneza, 2002);
- trust and repeated ties (Gulati, 1995); and
- complementarity of resource bases (Lin, Yang, and Arya, 2009).

Other reasons why firms may form alliances include:

- following the momentum created from successfully forming previous alliances (Dyer, Kale, and Singh, 2004);
- taking advantage of the resources available through the rich industry network (Mitsuhashi and Greve, 2009; Ahuja, Polidoro, and Mitchell, 2009);
- perceptions of fairness of between firms negotiating an alliance (Ariño and Ring, 2010); and
- the relative status of firms within the industry or alliance network (Lin, Yang, and Arya, 2009).

Rothaermel and Boeker (2008) provide a good summary of different motives for alliance formation in the introductory section of their paper with the requisite citations to the literature.

Do alliances create value? How is it shared?

On average, the formation of alliances creates value for the partners' stock holders, albeit in the short term (McConnell and Nantell, 1985; Chan, Kensinger, Keown, and Martin, 1997; Anand and Khanna, 2000). There is a positive correlation between the short-term performance measured by stock market reaction to alliance announcements and the long-term performance measured by alliance managers' assessments of success (Kale, Dyer, and Singh, 2002).

Alliance value creation depends on the experience firms gain from forming alliances and the type of alliance contract that is drafted (Anand and Khanna, 2000). For example, experience in joint ventures creates more value than more experience in licensing agreements. Furthermore, Anand and Khanna (2000) found that more experience in joint ventures that involved research and production showed stronger learning effects than those of marketing joint ventures. However, there are conflicting results about the effect of partner-specific experience on alliance value creation. While Hoang and Rothaermel (2005) find partner-specific experience or repeated alliances with the same partner to have a negative impact on value creation, Zollo, Reuer, and Singh (2002) and Gulati, Lavie, and Singh (2009) argue that it has a significantly positive effect.

Asymmetries in the sharing of value created from alliances depend on the position in the value chain and the resource dependency between partners (Dyer, Singh, and Kale, 2008). Partners of horizontal joint ventures tend to share the synergy gains equally, while suppliers of vertical joint ventures tend to gain significantly more than buyers (Johnson and Houston, 2000). Kumar (2010) found that partners with a strong resource dependency on the other joint venture partner experienced lower gains than the less dependent partner. This finding agrees with other research (Adegbesan and Higgins, 2011; Inkpen and Beamish, 1997), which shows that asymmetries in sharing of value created also depend on the bargaining positions in terms of the partners' mutual resource dependency. Other factors that drive asymmetric gains include differences in the firms' abilities to learn and benefit from that learning (Hamel, 1991) and differences in information access among parent firms (Reuer and Koza, 2000).

Do alliances fail? How often? Why are they unstable?

Although alliances on average create value, more than half of them fail (Kale and Singh, 2009). In fact, various studies have estimated the failure rate to be anywhere between 30 and 70 percent, where "failure" is defined as either not meeting the goals set by the parent firm or not delivering the operational or strategic benefits they were designed to achieve (Bamford, Gomes-Casseres, and Robinson, 2004). Alliances are particularly prone to failure in the first few years after formation (Kogut, 1989; Bleeke and Ernst, 1993).

International alliances are more unstable because of the significant coordination costs, cultural and language differences, difficulties reconciling conflicting goals between independently owned partners, and always the threat of creating a competitor (Porter, 1990; Inkpen and Beamish, 1997; Peng and Shenkar, 2002; Fang, 2011). They are also notorious for their 50 percent failure rates (Bleeke and Ernst, 1993; Kogut, 1988).

Alliances, both domestic and international, often fail because of poor partner selection, which later results in a mismatch of resources and insignificant synergy gains (Hitt *et al.*, 2000). Failure can also be due to poor management of the alliance, which fails to build social capital that maximizes the trust between the partners and to develop adequate learning systems within the alliance (Ireland, Hitt, and Vaidyanath, 2002). Competitive rivalry between partners may also cause alliance failure (Kogut, 1989; Dussauge, Garrette, and Mitchell, 2000). While reducing competitive rivalry may have been an initial reason behind allying firms' decision to cooperate, the same competitive forces may later drive them to take advantage of each other.

In general, failures to form alliances or challenges in managing alliances can be understood in terms of the internal tensions between the partners. Specifically, the three key dimensions are: cooperation versus competition; rigidity versus flexibility; and short-term versus long-term orientation (Das and Teng, 2000a). These internal tensions are feedback mechanisms that force the partners to engage in the renegotiation of the alliance contract or to modify their behavior to restore balance to the relationship (Ariño and de la Torre, 1998). Coupled with the tensions caused by the simultaneous changes in the external business environment, the alliance relationship co-evolves in tandem, adding to the instability (Doz, 1996; Das and Teng, 2002).

Which one? Alliance or acquisition?

Combining resources through alliances and acquisitions are similar but not identical processes (Yin and Shanley, 2008). Acquisitions are competitive processes and involve the displacement of the target firm's management. Alliances, on the other hand, are cooperative and require ongoing dealings with the partner's management (Dyer, Kale, and Singh, 2004). Choosing between engaging in one or the other requires firms to analyze at least three factors: the desired resources and synergies; the market place in which they are competing; and their ability to collaborate with the partner firm (Dyer, Kale, and Singh, 2004: 110). However, firms may have a pre-specified preference to engage in one form of governance over the other because of certain characteristics of the firm itself, rather than the characteristics of the deal or the partner/target (Villalonga and McGahan, 2005).

Firms that are more likely to engage in an acquisition have similar resource bases to the target and more prior acquisition experience, while firms that are more likely to engage in an alliance tend to have complementary resource bases with the target and more prior alliance experience (Wang and Zajac, 2007). Furthermore, the decision a firm makes to ally or acquire is taken in view of its overall position in the network of firms with which it has relationships, rather than as if it were independent of these influences (Yang, Lin, and Lin, 2010).

Firms may also engage in an alliance with the intention of investing in an option to acquire the partner later (Kogut, 1991; Chi, 2000). Gaining partner-specific alliance experience with a target before acquiring it is one way in which firms reduce information asymmetries before engaging in an acquisition (Agarwal, Anand, and Croson, 2006; Zaheer, Hernandez, and Banerjee, 2010; Porrini, 2004). However, the most recent literature that looks at the relationship between alliances and acquisitions (Ragozzino and Moschieri, 2014) finds that less than 1.3 percent of 25,000 global acquisitions occurring between 1995 and 2012 involved a prior alliance between acquirer and target before the acquisition, suggesting that the practice of acquiring an alliance partner is not as widespread as the theory would suggest.

A review of the strategy and financial valuation literatures

Theories from the strategy literature

The following sub-sections provide brief summaries of various theoretical views of the firm that are found in the strategy literature. The idea is to highlight relevant parts of these theories that provide insights into strategic alliances from the organizational learning and financial valuation perspectives. The four sub-sections cover: the market-based view; resource-based view; knowledge-based view; and transaction cost approach.

Market-based view

The market-based view (MBV) is an outside perspective of the firm and concerns how companies position themselves in the market or industry in order to compete profitably (Makhija, 2003). Originating from early industrial organization theory (see Bain, 1950, 1956; Mason, 1964), MBV describes how firms effect long-term profitability by erecting entry barriers to increase monopoly power over customers and bargaining power over suppliers (Grant, 1991). These barriers, which may prevent new industry entrants, are formed by developing: greater economies of scale; finer product market differentiation; higher capital resource requirements; lower cost advantages; more complex proprietary knowledge; more exclusive access to distribution channels; and lobbying for government policy that discriminates against competitors that do not meet certain standards (Bain, 1956; Porter, 1979a). MBV is based on two assumptions: that entry barriers provide *common and equal* protection to all incumbent firms, conferring some degree of monopoly or oligopoly power; and that firm resources are homogeneous and hence relatively transferrable between incumbent firms (i.e. *mobile resources*). This version of MBV, however, cannot explain why over the long term in the same industry different firms or groups of firms can coexist, with each pursuing different strategies while at same time earning different profit margins.

Explaining this mutual but differential coexistence requires extending MBV to include concepts such as strategic groups and mobility barriers (see Porter, 1979b; Caves and Porter, 1978). It is worth summarizing these concepts in more detail because of the similarities and relevance in respect to strategic alliances and valuation. As Porter (1979b) and Caves and Porter (1977) explain, an industry consists of multiple *strategic groups* – collections of firms that are defined by their member firms' adherence to a particular strategy. Each strategic group erects its own set of entry barriers *to prevent the mobility* of new rival groups entering the industry (inter-industry mobility) and *to deter the mobility* of other strategic groups within the industry entering their territory (inter-group mobility). Strategic groups with high mobility entry barriers are relatively more insulated from competitive rivalry within the industry, have superior bargaining power over other strategic groups both within and outside the industry, and experience less threat from rivals. Thus, the distribution of profitability rates enjoyed by individual firms will depend on two structural influences:

- *the structural nature of the firm's industry relative to other industries* – the greater the bargaining power the firm's industry has over its buyer or supplier industries, the more profitable will be the industry as a whole; and
- *the structural nature of the firm's strategic group relative to other strategic groups* – the higher the mobility barriers of the strategic group, the greater will be that group's share of the industry profits.

Mobility barriers include investments in advertising, R&D, or building an in-house service capability (Porter, 1979b: 217), which, while costly in the short run, protect long-run profits.

The presence of multiple strategic groups in an industry, Porter (1979b: 217–218) goes on to explain, affects the nature of inter-firm rivalry and hence the average level and dispersion of profits enjoyed by industry participants under the basic rule that *the greater rivalry, the lower the profits*. Three factors affect the competitive rivalry between strategic groups:

- *number and size distribution* – the more groups and the more they are equal in size, the greater will be the rivalry;
- *strategic distance* – the more similar they are in strategy, the more will be the rivalry (this can be described in terms of advertising, cost structure, R&D, etc.); and
- *market interdependence* – the more they share the same customers from the same market segment, the greater the rivalry.

Porter (1979a, 1985) summarizes the principal concepts of MBV in his celebrated five-forces model, which includes:

- threats of new entrants;
- threats from substitutes;
- bargaining power of suppliers;
- bargaining power of customers; and
- industry rivalry.

The model can be applied at either the firm or the industry level (i.e. inter-firm and inter-group rivalry). Under MBV, the role of management is therefore to assess the industry environment and to position the firm in attractive market segments according to three generic competitive strategies:

- low-cost strategy in which it can take high market share;
- differentiation strategy in which it tries to dominate in a certain number of segments; or
- niche strategy in which it aims for high margins in selected segments.

(Porter, 1985)

While MBV is an external view of the firm from the industry or market level, Porter recognizes the importance of the structure and organization within firms. His widely celebrated *value chain* (Porter, 1985) divides the firm into primary or line activities and secondary or support activities. The ability for the firm to manage the linkages between these activities effectively is a source of competitive advantage that positively affects the profit margins the firm is able to achieve from customers above its competitors.

Application to alliances

MBV would therefore argue that strategic alliances of same-industry firms are motivated to cooperate (i.e. collude) in order to achieve at least one of three main objectives (Grant, 1991; Makhija, 2003):

- to increase market power or strengthen market position against other competing firms or alliances;
- to raise higher entry barriers to prevent new rival firms or alliances from entering the market segment; or
- to increase bargaining power against common suppliers and customers of the alliance partners.

MBV would further argue that the formation of strategic alliances dynamically changes the structure of market power of the industry as competing alliances (i.e. strategic groups) change their mobility barriers with respect to each other. If the formation of alliances consolidates the industry into a smaller number of alliances, industry rivalry should decrease, positively affecting profit margins. If the number of alliances increases, the opposite effect would be observed. Furthermore, Porter (1979b: 217) would argue that the strength of monopoly or oligopoly power enjoyed by alliance firms is a function of the unity of strategy amongst the allying firms. However, divergent strategies amongst allying firms reduces this power, with a concomitant decrease in margins, because of increased difficulty in tacit coordination between partnering firms and decreased information flow through common customers.

But not all alliances which may seem to be motivated by collusion are contrary to public welfare, even amongst firms in a concentrated industry. As Kogut (1988: 322) points out,

> Where there are strong network externalities, such as in technological compatibility of communication services, joint R&D of standards can result in lower prices and improved quality in the final market. Research joint ventures which avoid costly duplication among firms but still preserve downstream competition can similarly be shown to be welfare-improving.

Other studies do show that alliances are motivated by market-positioning motives, however. Vickers (1985) shows that firms may sometimes use joint ventures to patent small technological innovations pre-emptively as deterrents against new market entrants. Using a simple model of Cournot competition, Mathews (2006) shows how an incumbent deters an entrepreneurial firm from market entry by selling equity in its firm.

Resource-based view

In contrast to MBV, the resource-based view (RBV) is an inside perspective of the firm and concerns how a firm combines its strategically important resources using the capabilities it has developed to compete profitably against other firms (see Barney, 1991; Grant, 1991; Peteraf, 1993; Prahalad and Hamel, 1990). The origins of RBV stem from the work of Penrose (1959), who observed that strategic resource heterogeneity between firms was a source of earning sustainable Ricardian rents – that is, firms with superior resources have lower average costs than other firms (Peteraf, 1993) and the asymmetry of resource positions leads to the sustainability of above-average rents (Amit and Schoemaker, 1993). Following Penrose's work, RBV arose from a certain "dissatisfaction with the static, equilibrium framework industrial organization economics that [had] dominated much of contemporary thinking about business strategy" (Grant, 1991: 114). It began to emerge in the 1980s as an alternative explanation for the competitive strategies of firms (Wernerfelt, 1984; Barney, 1986). Rather than focusing on the competitive position of a firm in the market, "managers should instead [focus] their analysis on their unique skills and resources" (Dierickx and Cool, 1989: 1504).

Unlike MBV, which views strategic firm resources as homogeneous and mobile between firms of the same strategic group (i.e. easily transferrable), RBV conceptualizes each firm as a bundle of heterogeneous strategic resources that are generally not easily transferrable between firms (Barney, 1991) and therefore are not usually traded in strategic factor markets (Barney, 1986). Firms can develop a sustained competitive advantage and achieve superior profitability if they have access to strategic resources that possess four important attributes:

- valuable;
- rare;
- non-imitable; and
- non-substitutable.

(Barney, 1991)

However, competitive advantage is not achieved merely by combining strategic resources, but requires a careful system of coordination and control across an entire firm, which in turn fits the firm's corporate strategy (Collis and Montgomery, 1998).

Scholars have put forward various classifications of a firm's strategic resources. Grant (1991) provides six major categories of resources: financial; physical, human; technological; reputational; and organizational. Barney (1991) groups resources into just three categories: physical capital; human capital; and organizational capital.

As strategic resources are generally not traded in strategic factor markets, to access new ones, firms need to either develop them internally or combine theirs with those of other firms (Wernerfelt, 1984; Dierickx and Cool, 1989). The internal accumulation of a strategic resource, however, requires choosing appropriate time paths of flow variables to build the resource stocks (Dierickx and Cool, 1989) – that is, a firm builds a strategic resource through a deliberate and consistent policy of acting, which requires time and constant effort. Dierickx and Cool (1989: 1507–1509) distinguish between stocks and flows of assets or strategic resources. The term "stock" refers to the level of asset accumulation, while flow refers to the rate of accumulation. These authors also identify several characteristics of the process of accumulating stocks of strategic resources:

- *time decompression economies* – certain resources need a minimum amount of time to build and shortening the process leads to diseconomies or lower-quality stock;
- *asset mass efficiencies* – a minimum stock of existing resources is required to build new ones efficiently ("success is needed to breed success");
- *asset interconnectedness* – the growth in stock of one asset may depend on the level of stock of other assets (growth interdependencies);
- *asset erosion* – the strategic value of resource stocks decreases over time and certain "maintenance costs" need to be paid to keep them from decaying excessively;
- *causal ambiguity* – the direction of resource accumulation is not linear, and depends on current levels of stock and on factors that are beyond the firm's control or simply random; and
- *asset substitution* – stocks of strategic resources can be substituted by other resources.

These characteristics do not apply to all resources, but to those of a strategic nature.

Application to alliances

If a firm cannot overcome the stock and flow process limitations to build its own strategic resources, it will need to resort to strategic alliances and acquisitions in order to remain competitive. While these forms of business combinations may help the firm to catch up with or even overtake its competitors by "leap-frogging" certain requirements of the resource-building process – for example, jumping over the time diseconomies to build a minimum asset base – it may still be limited by the other requirements, such as managing the interdependencies between its existing asset base and the assets to be combined. Firms that have developed a capability to combine resources accessed through a strategic alliance or acquired through an acquisition are therefore at a distinct advantage (Kogut and Zander, 1992; Bresman, Birkinshaw, and Nobel, 1999; Hamel, 1991). The ability to learn as an organization is itself a strategic firm resource (Grant, 1991; Kogut and Zander, 1993).

Knowledge-based view: organizational learning and capabilities

The study of organizational learning and how firms develop organizational capabilities has emerged from the knowledge-based view (KBV) of firms, an important extension of RBV. Under KBV, the firm is conceived as an organizational structure through which knowledge is created (Nonaka, 1991, 1994).

Knowledge is a special type of firm resource that has been categorized into two types: *tacit knowledge* and *explicit knowledge* (Nonaka, 1994; Grant, 1996a). The categories can be further analyzed according to three important characteristics (Grant, 1996a):

- *Transferability*. Explicit knowledge is transferred as soon as it is revealed because it can be codified in a common format or language that others can read and interpret, such as: statistics, lists, tables, descriptions, and so on. Tacit knowledge, in contrast, is "sticky" because it stays with the knowledge owner and is transferred to the learner only if it is constantly practiced with use and experience. It is not easily codified or expressed in a standard language.
- *Aggregability*. While explicit knowledge, because of its common format, can be easily stored and transferred in limitless quantities, tacit knowledge resides with the knowledge owner and is not easily duplicated or imitated.
- *Appropriability*. This refers to the resource owner's ability to receive a return equal to the value created by the resource (Teece, 1987). While explicit knowledge becomes a public good (i.e. has low marginal cost) and loses its appropriability as soon as it is revealed, tacit knowledge increases in appropriability because its non-transferability and non-aggregability make it a rare and valuable good. In sum, tacit knowledge is a strategic resource, while explicit knowledge is not and quickly loses value.

Tacit knowledge is more easily transferred if the learner already has a base of similar knowledge – that is, absorptive capacity (Cohen and Levinthal, 1990). *Absorptive capacity* is firm's ability to value, assimilate, and utilize new external knowledge, and it is critical to its innovative capability and sustainable competitive advantage (Zahra and George, 2002). The development of absorptive capacity is history- or path-dependent and the failure of a firm to continue to invest in its development, especially in fast-pace and research-intensive industries, may foreclose future opportunities for absorptive capacity development (Cohen and Levinthal, 1990; Dierickx and Cool, 1989). While absorptive capacity is a firm-level resource, it can also be conceptualized as an inter-firm-level resource called *relative absorptive capacity* (Lane and Lubatkin, 1998). Relative absorptive capacity is based on the dyadic relationship between two firms, for example in a strategic alliance, and depends on the similarity between the firms' knowledge bases, organizational structures and policies, and business strategies.

Application to alliances

Firms are able to access each other's tacit knowledge resources through strategic alliances (Inkpen, 1998b; Stuart, 2000; Gomes-Casseres, Hagedoorn, and Jaffe, 2006). Value creation through strategic alliances is enhanced because the tacit knowledge resources of each allying firm are imperfectly mobile (not easily transferred), imperfectly imitable, and imperfectly substitutable (Das and Teng, 2000b; Grant and Baden-Fuller, 2004). Furthermore, as firms share their tacit knowledge resources, they tend to become more specialized in their area of knowledge expertise (Mowery, Oxley, and Silverman, 1996). Specialization in knowledge creation allows allying firms to prosper in competitive environments by allowing each one, on the one hand, to focus efforts on creation of its specialized knowledge while, on the other, to access its alliance partners' specialized knowledge and integrate it with their own (Grant and Baden-Fuller, 1995, 2004).[2]

Firms also learn how to learn as they gain experience in strategic alliances (Anand and Khanna, 2000). They internalize this ability by setting up intra- and inter-organizational routines to increase the efficiency and effectiveness with which the knowledge is accessed and transferred, positively affecting the performance of the alliance (Inkpen, 2000; Zollo, Reuer, and Singh, 2002). Firms also learn from their repeated alliances with the same partner (Gulati, 1995), as well as from their alliance failures (Ariño and de la Torre, 1998). Repeated alliances with the same partner, however, in general lead to deterioration in the value created (Goerzen, 2007). Experience from prior alliances reduces the time needed to complete the negotiation of subsequent alliances (Ariño, Reuer, Mayer, and Jané, 2014)

Organizational routines are patterns of behavior that are followed repeatedly, but change if conditions change (Nelson and Winter, 1982; Dyer and Singh, 1998). In markets that are moderately stable, organizational routines are internal firm processes that are complex, detailed, and analytic, and they produce predictable outcomes (Eisenhardt and Martin, 2000: 1106; Cyert and March, 1963; Nelson and Winter, 1982). Because of their tacit nature, organizational routines can become a source of competitive advantage (Grant, 1996b; Dyer and Singh, 1998). For example, Dyer and Hatch (2006) found a significant performance difference between auto manufacturers that used the same supplier network. Whereas Toyota established greater knowledge-sharing routines with the common supplier network, resulting in faster learning and lower defect rates, US auto manufacturers shared much less knowledge with this same supplier network, resulting in slower learning and a higher rate of defects, *ceteris paribus*.

However, in high-velocity markets, where industry structure is blurred and emergent, firms learn how to adapt their organizational routines agilely into flexible modes of operating, converting them into *dynamic capabilities* (Teece, Pisano, and Shuen, 1997; Eisenhardt and Martin, 2000; Helfat *et al.*, 2007). Under these market conditions, dynamic capabilities are simple, experimental, and unstable processes that produce unpredictable outcomes. Dynamic capabilities are a subset of organizational routines that include product innovation, strategic decision-making, and alliancing, and they are a further source of sustainable competitive advantage (Eisenhardt and Martin, 2000: 1111). Operating routines are another subset of organizational routines that are geared to the normal or stable operation of the firm. While operating routines are directed at the firm's operations, dynamic capabilities are directed at the *modification* of operating routines (Zollo and Winter, 2002: 340).

As firms learn to learn from their alliance experience, they develop *alliance capability* (Kale and Singh, 2007; Kale, Dyer, and Singh, 2002; Simonin, 1997). Alliance capability consists of how a firm is able to coordinate, communicate with, and integrate or bond an individual alliance into its network of alliances (Schreiner,

Kale, and Corsten, 2009). One of the key success factors for firms to build alliance capability is setting up a dedicated alliance function. The alliance function plays the role of articulating, codifying, sharing, and internalizing the organizational routines of alliance management that make up the firm's alliance capability (Kale and Singh, 2007; Heimeriks and Duysters, 2007).

Transaction cost approach

The transaction cost approach has its origins in a classic paper on "The nature of the firm" by Coase (1937), who observed that goods and services produced by firms are the product of early stage processing and assembly of activities (Williamson, 1981: 550). The basic idea of the approach is that firms purchase production inputs based on minimizing the sum of the production and transaction costs. Transaction costs include "the costs of negotiation, drawing up contracts, managing the necessary logistics, and monitoring the accounts receivables" (Child and Faulkner, 1998: 20). Furthermore, firms will choose an organizational form that enables them to access or purchase their production inputs at the lowest transaction cost (Williamson, 1979). These forms include market exchange contracts (at one extreme), mergers or acquisitions of suppliers (at the other extreme), or a middle-ground hybrid form, such as alliances, including licensing contracts to joint ventures.

Three critical dimensions of the transaction to acquire inputs determine a firm's preferred organizational form: frequency of transactions; uncertainty of acquiring inputs; and asset specificity involved in input production and supply (Williamson, 1975, 1979, 1985). The second and third are the two most critical dimensions (Williamson, 1991; Hennart, 1988; Dyer and Singh, 1998; Amit and Schoemaker, 1993). Market uncertainty incurs transaction costs involved with performance monitoring, while asset specificity incurs transaction costs relating to acquiring inputs at stable prices (Kogut, 1988; Hennart, 1988).

Application to alliances

Kogut (1988: 321) explains how uncertainty makes equity joint ventures (alliances) the preferred organizational form: two or more firms that are vertically contiguous in the supply chain will choose an alliance over other organizational forms when uncertainties exist over downstream demand or upstream supply. The supplier's transaction cost involves monitoring the quality of the buyer's market information about downstream conditions; the buyer's cost is monitoring the quality and timely delivery of the supplier's inputs; and both will incur price negotiation costs. The uncertainties over the general market conditions amplify the monitoring costs for both firms. Under these uncertain conditions, a market exchange contract would not be the preferred organizational form. A merger of firms, on the other hand, would also be excluded because uncertainty over market conditions demands flexibility in the organizational relationship. An alliance provides this flexibility in conditions of uncertainty and at the same time introduces a *mutual hostage* situation through the joint commitment of financial and real assets that aligns the firms' incentives and reduces the associated transaction costs of monitoring and negotiating the transaction of inputs and market information.

Hennart (1988: 371) explains in a different way why an equity joint venture (alliance) would be preferred when resources with high asset specificity are involved. Such resources require large investments over an extended period of time and include tacit knowledge assets that are not readily marketable or physical assets with high operating leverage.[3] Again, take two firms in vertically contiguous positions in the supply chain. The downstream firm needs inputs from the upstream firm, but a market exchange contract for the inputs it needs does not exist; developing its own source of inputs is prohibitively expensive in terms of development costs and time; and acquiring the upstream firm for the sake of accessing its inputs introduces other transaction costs that complicate its problems, such as managing a new business and displacing the old management. For the upstream firm, acquiring the downstream firm to ensure a buyer again incurs management transaction costs; and the downstream firm's required input volume may not match its current output. An alliance such as an equity joint venture between the two firms will avoid many of these transaction costs, however. The upstream alliance partner can produce the inputs at low or negligible marginal cost, while the downstream partner can obtain the inputs at a lower total cost, compared to producing the inputs itself. The incentives of the alliances align their cost structures.

In sum, the transaction cost approach provides insights into the economic incentives that drive firms to choose certain organizational forms over others by focusing on the level of the transaction between firms. The approach is not an alternative to MBV, RBV, or KBV. In fact all these theoretical views should be seen as complementary explanations (Kogut, 1988: 322).

Theories from the financial valuation literature

"A valuation is just an opinion" (Fernández, 2009: 8). Value should not be confused with price, which is the quantity of money agreed between a buyer and seller to exchange goods or services (Fernández, 2002). Value, on the other hand, is a subjective judgment that depends on how important the good in question is to the buyer or seller. A good may be more valuable to one buyer than another. Thus, the *valuation* made by a single investor on a firm's traded stock is contingent on his or her expectations of the future and on the risk assessment of the firm (Fernández and Bilan, 2007). The traded *price* for that stock, however, is the consensus of valuations made by market participants who publicly manifest their opinion by buying or selling that stock.

The assessment and measurement of synergies are of fundamental importance to valuation for any form of business resource combination, such as an alliance or M&A. In finance, there are two main sets of synergies, especially in the case of mergers: operating synergies and financial synergies (Damodaran, 2005, 2012). *Operating synergies* include:

- greater economies of scale because of larger size with the same fixed costs;
- increased pricing power because of reduced competition and the ability to earn higher margins;
- complementary functional strength brought by combining the best practices of firms; and
- increased sales in new or existing markets because of extended sales network and complementary brand recognition.

Financial synergies from the merger of two firms include:

- increased debt capacity and hence lower cost of debt capital because combining uncorrelated operating cash flows reduces their overall volatility;
- increased tax benefits, especially if one of the firms has accumulated tax losses that can be used to reduce the combined firm's tax burden;
- diversification, which reduces the overall cash flow volatility of the portfolio of firms, although this synergy is usually valid only for privately held firms; and
- cheaper access to project capital, especially when a capital constrained firm with good projects is acquired by another with excess cash, thus avoiding the need to go to the capital markets.

Both types of synergies, if they are realized, show up in the valuation as increased cash flows or lower discount rates (Damodaran, 2005).

While the valuation of synergies generated by M&As depends to a great extent on the assumptions upon which they are based, valuing alliances has the additional difficulty of defining the limits to firm boundaries. As alliance partners commit to share both tangible and intangible resources without legally merging as one entity, the boundary between them is blurred, making it difficult to accrue value created to one party or the other. A firm's bargaining power against its alliance partner will determine to a great extent the portion of the total value pie created (Adegbesan and Higgins, 2011; Adegbesan, 2009).

This section provides a summary of theories and methods that could be used to value the wealth creation of strategic alliances. However, the purpose of the summary is not to provide an exhaustive account of all the theories or methods in the financial literature, but rather to highlight certain issues that could be related to valuing strategic alliances within the context of this paper. For proper treatment of the methods mentioned, please refer to the references provided.

Discounted cash flow method

The discounted cash flow (DCF) method of valuation is the financial "gold standard" for both firm and project valuation. The basic economic intuition is that the present value of a stream of cash flows (PV_0) is the sum of the discounted value of those cash flows (CF) each discounted by a rate (k), as shown in Equation (1). The term "cash flow" refers to the "future net cash in-flow" – that is, the difference between cash received and cash paid out within each time period in the future. The discount rate is usually simplified so that $k_1 = k_2 = \ldots = k$ and depends on the risk of receiving the cash flows: if the risk is low, then the cash flows are discounted at a lower rate; if the risk is high, then the discount rate is higher. The net present value (NPV) is the remaining economic value after making the investment (I_0) today in order to receive the cash flows, as shown in Equation (2).

$$PV_0 = \frac{CF_1}{1+k_1} + \frac{CF_2}{(1+k_2)^2} + \frac{CF_3}{(1+k_3)} + \ldots$$
$$= \frac{CF_1}{1+k} + \frac{CF_2}{(1+k)^2} + \frac{CF_3}{(1+k)^3} + \ldots \quad (1)$$

$$NPV_0 = PV_0 - I_0 \quad (2)$$

DCF is easy to apply once the cash flows and discount rate have been determined. However, the differences in the assumptions used to calculate these values can be problematic. Determining the value of cash flows requires assessing and measuring the operational and financial synergies outlined above, tasks that depend to a great degree on the assumptions made. Calculating the discount rate also requires tacit know-how on forecasting market interest rates, industry risks, and the systematic risk of the firm. Understandably, these are all non-trivial tasks.

There are many "flavors" of DCF, depending on whether one is valuing a firm or project, a firm that is stable, growing, or in decline, a high-technology or standard-technology firm, whether the firm has debt or is all equity funded, and so on. Fernández (2002: 38) proposes three basic methods of DCF:[4]

- *FCF method*: Free cash flows (FCF) discounted by the weighted average cost of capital (WACC) of the firm. Free cash flows are defined as the after-tax surplus cash generated by a firm's operations (or project) regardless of any financing costs, and is a measure of that firm's ability to make money regardless of the origins of its capital.
- *CFe method*: Equity cash flows discounted by the required return to equity holders, k_e.
- *CFd method*: Debt cash flows discounted by the required return to debt holders, k_d.

Fernández (2005a) gives a more comprehensive account of the three methods of DCF.

The FCF method (see Brealey, Myers, and Allen, 2008) enables the calculation of the total value of the firm or project (V_{FCF}). Theoretically (i.e. in the absence of market inefficiencies and financial distress costs), the total value of the firm[5] (or project) equals the market value of the equity (E) and the market value of debt (D) issued by the firm, as in Equation (3).

$$V_{FCF} = E + D = PV(FCF, WACC) \quad (3)$$

where PV(FCF, k) is the DCF operator given by Equation (1) and

$$NPV_{FCF} = V_{FCF} - I_0 \quad (3a)$$

where

$$WACC = [Ek_e + (1-T)Dk_d] / [E+D] \quad (3b)$$

and T is the firm's marginal tax rate.

The FCF method, however, assumes that the capital structure of the firm (debt to equity ratio) remains constant, which may not always be the case unless the firm continuously rebalances its financing structure.[6]

A useful extension of the DCF method is the adjusted present value (APV) method, which does not assume a constant capital structure. The intuition to APV is that the value of the firm or project (V_{APV}) is equal to the sum of the value generated by the unlevered firm or project (V_u)[7] and the value generated by the tax benefits due to debt,[8] as in Equation (4). APV is a particularly useful method for project valuation as project value should not depend on the source of financing for the project, but rather only on the cash flows it generates and the risk of the project with respect to the firm's risk.

$$V_{APV} = V_u + \text{Value of tax benefits due to debt} = V_{FCF} \quad (4)$$

where $V_u = PV(FCF, k_u)$ = Unlevered value of firm or project and

$$NPV_{APV} = V_{APV} - I_0 \quad (4a)$$

and where

$$k_u = r_A = [Ek_e + Dk_d] / [E+D] \quad (4b)$$

where r_A is the expected return to assets,[9] k_u is the unlevered expected return to equity, k_e is the levered expected return to equity and

$$k_e = R_f + \beta(R_m - R_f) \rightarrow \text{Capital Asset Pricing Model} \quad (4c)$$

where R_f is the risk free rate, R_m is the market risk premium, and β is the systematic risk of the firm's stock.

Application to alliances

Strategic alliances can be considered joint projects between allying firms who share a subset of their resources. Equations (3) and (4) can be combined to give equations (5a) and (5b), one for each firm in the alliance (say, Firm A and Firm B):

$$E_A + D_A = V_{uA} + V_{TDA} \quad (5a)$$

$$E_B + D_B = V_{uB} + V_{TDB} \quad (5b)$$

where V_{TD} is the value of the tax benefits due to debt of Firm A or Firm B.

If the risk of the alliance project is no different from the risk of the respective parent firms' risk and no new debt is issued, then there should be no change in the market value of debt and all the benefits of the project should go to the equity holders. However, if the project risk is different from the respective partner firms' risks, there may be a change in the market value of debt.

Research has shown that firms tend to choose alliances as the organizational form through which to undertake projects that are more risky than their normal business risk (Contractor and Lorange, 1988; Robinson, 2008). Given this, questions arise as to what the appropriate discount rate should be to value the expected cash flows from the alliance and the commensurate effect on capital structure of each allying firm.

Real options methods

One disadvantage of the discounted cash flow method is that it assumes that once the decision has been made to accept or reject a project it will not be changed later. In practice, managers do change their decisions as new information arrives that gives them a better indication of the future performance of the project. If the news is good, they may decide to go ahead or even expand the project's scope; if it is bad, they may scale it back or even abandon it altogether. The option to choose based on future market conditions is therefore valuable. DCF methods, however, do not account for this strategic managerial flexibility. The real options methods do.

Myers (1977) first used the term *real option* to refer to the present value of the future assets in which a firm has the *discretion to invest* depending on the market conditions in later periods. He observed that

> [M]ost firms are valued as going concerns, and this value reflects and expectation of continued future investment by the firm. However, the investment is discretionary. The amount invested depends on the net present values of opportunities as they arrive in the future. In unfavorable future states of nature, the firm will invest nothing.
>
> *(Myers, 1977: 148)*

Some types of investment decisions are more suitable for using the real options methods (Amram and Kulatilaka, 1999: 25–27), such as:

- *irreversible investments* – large investments in fixed assets can be built in flexible stages or delayed until more favorable times;
- *flexibility investments* – designing manufacturing processes so that they can switch between several different products or uses;
- *insurance investments* – when exposed to risk, paying an insurance premium provides protection in the event of a loss;
- *modular investments* – stages of product design that can be upgraded or changed independently of other modules allows flexibility to meet future requirements;

- *platform investments* – a technology platform, such as Apple's iOs operating system, allows many different yet-to-be-designed products to be sold through the same platform; and
- *learning investments* – exploration of oil or minerals allows for future investments in oil production based on initial finding.

There are three main types of real options embedded in the investments made by firms (Damodaran, 2008: 235):

- *option to expand* an investment;
- *option to delay* an investment; and
- *option to abandon* an investment.

Real options methods incorporate the flexibility of strategic managerial decision-making into the valuation process using the theories of financial options (Black and Scholes, 1973).

In financial options, the buyer of a call option pays a premium for the right but not the obligation to buy the underlying asset at a preset exercise price before the option expiry date. If the price of the underlying asset is below the exercise price at the time of expiry, the call option owner will obviously not exercise the option. Thus, the option owner has downside *protection* from loss as well as upside *opportunity* for gain. In an analogous manner, the buyer of a put option buys the right but not the obligation to sell the underlying asset at a preset exercise price if the price of the underlying asset falls below the exercise price before the option expires. Regardless of the type of option, an option always has positive value as long as it has not expired. The underlying asset can be any asset, including stocks, bonds, real estate, commodities, and so on.

Table 14.1 presents the analogy between a financial American-style call option and a real option to expand a project (see Hull, 2000; Damodaran, 2008).

TABLE 14.1 A comparison of a financial call and real option to expand

Financial call cption	*Symbol*	*Real option to expand*
Value of underlying asset, e.g. a stock price	S	Estimated present value of project cash flows
Exercise price of call option	K	Cost of investment in expansion if option is exercised
Volatility of underlying asset e.g. standard deviation of stock price returns	σ	Standard deviation in project value, usually obtained by simulations
Time remaining to option expiry	T	Time remaining to decide before expiry of option to expand
Dividends of underlying asset	δ	Other income from the project
Risk-free rate	r	Risk-free rate taken from government Treasury bills

Application to alliances

Alliances can be understood as joint investments by the partnering firms in real options (Kogut, 1991; Chi, 2000; Folta and Miller, 2002). Although they are started as a joint project, changes in the market conditions may make it favorable for one partner to buy out the other's share and expand the project under its own management. Alliance contracts may be designed with this buyout option included (see Reuer and Ariño, 2007). In a similar vein, in order to increase the number and value of their growth options, Reuer and Tong (2010) show that cash-rich firms will often use investments in alliances with new publicly listed technology firms as a way of discovering new technologies and market opportunities to which they would otherwise not have access. However, despite the theory of the option approach, in practice very few acquisitions involve a prior alliance between acquirer and target (Ragozzino and Moschieri, 2014).

Alliance capability or capabilities in general can also be understood as a real option. Firms that have invested in strengthening their alliance learning routines by simplifying and making them more flexible, especially in times of high market volatility, will be more able to respond and take advantage of market upswings (Kogut and Kulatilaka, 2001).

Valuation of projects using real options methodsis not without difficulties, however. Once touted as a way of unifying strategic thinking with financial option methods (Kester, 1984; Bowman and Hurry, 1993), difficulties in customizing the reality to the financial models has limited its wider use (Bowman and Moskowitz, 2001). Nevertheless, as a way of thinking about projects, real options methods continue to provide a way forward for research (see Krychowski and Quélin, 2010).

Event study method

The discounted cash flow and real options methods require information inputs that come from within the firm to evaluate expected performance of the firm or a project. However, event study methods of evaluating firm performance rely solely on publicly available sources, namely corporate security prices. The purpose of an event study is to examine the market reaction, reflected in corporate security prices, to news of firm-specific events, such as earnings announcements or mergers (Brown and Warner, 1980, 1985). The methods assume that the market is efficient and that investors react quickly in consonance with the publicly available information about the event.

According to Kothari and Warner (2005), in the period 1974–2000 the five major finance journals published 565 studies that used the event study method, and this number has continued to grow. The vast majority of these studies examine corporate stock prices. They further note that many other studies look specifically at the statistical properties of event studies. Much fewer studies, however, examine corporate bond prices, mainly due to the lack of transparency in corporate bond markets until recently (Bessembinder and Maxwell, 2008).

TABLE 14.2 Basic methods of calculating abnormal returns for stocks and bonds

	Stocks	*Bonds*
Mean adjusted	$AR_{it} = SR_{it} - E(SR_{it})$	$AR_{it} = (SR_{it} - TR_{it}) - E(SR_{it} - TR_{it})$
Market adjusted	$AR_{it} = SR_{it} - E(R_{mt})$	$AR_{it} = SR_{it} - MPR_{it}$
Factor model adjusted	$AR_{it} = SR_{it} - FMR_{it}$	$AR_{it} = SR_{it} - FFFMR_{it}$

Notes: I = security; t = event time; AR_{it} = abnormal return of security of i at time t; SR = security return; E(.) = mean or expected return in estimation period; R_{mt} = return on market portfolio at time t; TR = return of treasury security of matching maturity; MPR = matching portfolio return for a portfolio of bonds with similar in credit rating and time to maturity; FMR = factor model return, where the factor model can be one of the CAPM models; FFFMR = Fama French factor model return, where Fama and French (1993) factor model is used as the benchmark.

The basic approach is similar in all event studies methods, which is to calculate the abnormal returns,[10] where "abnormal" is defined as the security return compared with some benchmark return. Three methods – summarized briefly in Table 14.2 – are used to calculate benchmark return. (For stocks, see Brown and Warner, 1980; for bonds, see Bessembinder, Kahle, Maxwell, and Xu, 2009.)

The main disadvantage of the event study method is that it is valid only for short-term security performance. Improvements have been made to the event study method for long-term horizons, but serious limitations still exist (see Kothari and Warner, 2005). A more thorough review of the event study method used in the financial and accounting literature can be found in Corrado (2011).

A review of studies of strategic alliance value creation

There are many studies in both the financial and strategy literatures that examine the value creation effects of strategic alliance formation. The vast majority use the event study methodology to measure the short-term market reaction of announcements of alliances. In fact, in my review of the empirical literature, the use of any other method was the exception rather than the rule.

Tables 14.3a and 14.3b provide summaries of a partial list of this empirical literature. As mentioned earlier, Kothari and Warner (2005) noted that more than 500 papers in the top five financial journals have employed the event study method. Some conclusions can be drawn from analyzing Tables 14.3a and 14.3b:

- The most prevalent method for studying value creation from strategic alliance formation has been the event study method.
- Strategic alliances in general create value for their stock holders in the short term.
- There are studies that show strong negative effects on value creation, although they are in the minority. These studies are of international joint ventures (Reuer, Park, and Zollo, 2002; Chung, Koford, and Lee, 1993)
- No event studies examine the effect of strategic alliance formation on corporate bonds.

TABLE 14.3a Selected key studies on the value creation of strategic alliances

Researchers	*Sample period*	*Sample*	*Event window*	* = *AR (day 0)*/ ** = *CAR (over event window)*
McConnell and Nantell (1985)	1972–1979	136 domestic US joint ventures (in various industries: real estate development, nuclear power, coal mining, petrochemical, satellite communication, others)	2 days (–1/0)	*0.73% all joint ventures *1.10% smaller partner *0.63% larger partner Dollar value gains smaller/larger partner were $4.5m/$6.6m
Chan, Kensinger, Keown, and Martin (1997)	1983–1992	345 alliances: 114 all public partners 231 only one public partner (involving 460 firms, with 394 in hi-tech industries and 66 in low-tech industries)	26 days (–20/+5)	*0.64% all alliances *2.22% smaller partner *0.19% larger partner Dollar value gains: smaller/larger partner were $8.9m/$8.1m
Das, Sen, and Sengupta (1998)	1987–1991	119 US–Japanese alliances: 49 technology alliances 70 marketing alliances	7 days (–3/+3)	**0.20% all alliances **1.6% technology alliances **–0.8% marketing alliances
Anand and Khanna (2000)	1990–1993	1,576 alliances: 870 joint ventures 1,106 licensing agreements	12 days (–10/+1)	*0.67%/**1.82% JVs *1.42%/**3.06% Licensing Dollar value gains: JV/licensing deals were $44.1m/$20.4m
Kale, Dyer, and Singh (2002) Kale, Dyer, and Singh (2001)	1993–1997	1,572 alliances reported by 78 companies with more than $500 million in 1997 in whose industries alliances are generally considered an important part of firm strategy (e.g. computers, telecoms, pharmaceuticals, chemicals, electronics, and services)	14 days (–10/+3)	*0.84% all alliances *1.35% with alliance function *0.18% without alliance function Dollar value gains: all/with alliance function/without alliance function were $58.3m/$75.1m/$20.2m
Reuer, Park, and Zollo (2002)	1995–1997	1,318 international joint ventures	3 days (–1/+1)	**–1.83% all joint ventures

TABLE 14.3b Other studies on the value creation of strategic alliances

- Koh and Venkatraman (1991) – study joint venture announcements and find they are in general value creating
- Chung, Koford, and Lee (1993) – study international joint ventures and find a strong *negative* effect on value creation
- Mohanram and Nanda (1996) – find value creation at the parent-level but not at the firm-level
- Johnson and Houston (2000) – study the motives of joint ventures and find asymmetries in partners' value creation
- Gupta and Misra (2000) – study the effect of experience in international joint ventures and find it value creating for partners
- Brooke and Oliver (2005) – study the source of gains for strategic alliances
- Mantecon and Chatfield (2007) – compare value creation in short-term market reaction with assets sales of terminating joint ventures
- Kumar (2007; 2010) – find asymmetrical gains for the shareholders of parents of joint venture partners
- Bösecke and Pfaffenberger (2009) – study value creation in small European utilities and find significantly positive returns
- Keasler and Denning (2009) – large sample study confirms that strategic alliances on average create value
- Gulati, Lavie, and Singh (2009) – study the effect of partner-specific experience on repeated alliances and find it significant
- Sánchez-Lorda and García-Canal (2012) – study how equity investors value prior experience in alliances and acquisitions
- Amici *et al.* (2013) – study US and European banking sector alliances and find they create value for non-bank partners

Conclusion

In this chapter, I reviewed relevant theories and methods in the strategy and financial literature and applied them to develop an understanding of strategic alliances from organizational learning and valuation perspectives. I began by answering preliminary questions about strategic alliances to serve as an introduction for readers who may be unfamiliar with the strategic alliance literature. I then reviewed the strategy literature theories of the firm from a market-based view, resource-based view, knowledge-based view, and transaction cost approach, and applied them to further readers' understanding of strategic alliances. From the financial valuation literature, I reviewed the discounted cash flow, real options, and event study methods and explored how these could be applied to understanding strategic alliances. Finally, I summarized the results of many prior studies on the value creation of strategic alliances.

Notes

1 This may be due to the sample of executives surveyed. In my own research, conducted using SDC Platinum data, there was a significant drop in the number of alliances from 2008 onwards.

2 While transfer of tacit knowledge through an alliance is more efficient than market exchange contracts, transfer of tacit knowledge within a (multinational) firm itself is still more efficient than across an alliance (Almeida, Song, and Grant, 2002).

3 Operating leverage can be thought of as the ratio of fixed costs to variable costs. Firms with high operating leverage make large upfront investments and need large sales volumes to break even. Each dollar of sales contains a high percentage of profit because the variable or marginal costs of production are relatively small or almost negligible. For example, an airline operator would have high operating leverage compared with a supermarket chain.

4 There are, of course, many more. See, for example, Copeland, Koller, and Murrin (2000) and Brealey, Myers, and Allen (2008).

5 Another name for the value of the firm is *enterprise value*.

6 This assumption is required to ensure no change in k_u or k_d such that WACC also remains constant.

7 V_u means the value of the firm or project *as if it were* entirely funded by equity, i.e. no debt or unlevered.

8 The equation states "value" of tax benefits due to debt, *not* "present value" as it does in Brealey, Myers, and Allen (2008: 546). This point is argued in Fernández (2004, 2005b) and Fieten *et al.* (2005).

9 This is also called the *opportunity cost of capital* and is the "simplest" formula to find k_u, the unlevered expected return to equity (Brealey, Myers, and Allen, 2008: 543). Note that, in this formula, k_e and k_d are observable values, where k_e is the levered return to equity, the return to equity when the firm also has debt financing.

10 The term *abnormal return* is used synonymously with *excess returns* or *excess residuals*.

References

Adegbesan, J.A. 2009, "On the origins of competitive advantage: strategic factor markets and heterogeneous resource complementarity," *Academy of Management Review*, vol. 34, no. 3, pp. 463–475.

Adegbesan, J.A. and Higgins, M.J. 2011, "The intra-alliance division of value created through collaboration," *Strategic Management Journal*, vol. 32, no. 2, pp. 187–211.

Agarwal, R., Anand, J. and Croson, R. 2006, "Are there benefits from engaging in an alliance with a firm prior to its acquisition?" in *Strategic Alliances: Governance and Contracts*, ed. A. Ariño and J.J. Reuer, New York: Palgrave Macmillan Press, pp. 88–97.

Ahuja, G. 2000, "Collaboration networks, structural holes, and innovation: a longitudinal study," *Administrative Science Quarterly*, vol. 45, no. 3, pp. 425–455.

Ahuja, G., Polidoro Jr., F. and Mitchell, W. 2009, "Structural homophily or social asymmetry? The formation of alliances by poorly embedded firms," *Strategic Management Journal*, vol. 30, no. 9, pp. 941–958.

Almeida, P., Song, J. and Grant, R.M. 2002, "Are firms superior to alliances and markets? An empirical test of cross-border knowledge building," *Organization Science*, vol. 13, no. 2, pp. 147–161.

Amici, A., Fiordelisi, F., Masala, F., Ricci, O. and Sist, F. 2013, "Value creation in banking through strategic alliances and joint ventures," *Journal of Banking and Finance*, vol. 37, no. 5, pp. 1386–1396.

Amit, R. and Schoemaker, P.J.H. 1993, "Strategic assets and organizational rent," *Strategic Management Journal*, vol. 14, no. 1, pp. 33–46.

Amram, M. and Kulatilaka, N. 1999, *Real options: managing strategic investment in an uncertain world*, Boston, MA: Harvard Business School Press.

Anand, B.N. and Khanna, T. 2000, "Do firms learn to create value? The case of alliances," *Strategic Management Journal*, vol. 21, no. 3 (Special Issue: Strategic Networks), pp. 295–315.

Ariño, A. and de la Torre, J. 1998, "Learning from failure: towards an evolutionary model of collaborative ventures," *Organization Science*, vol. 9, no. 3 (Special Issue: Managing Partnerships and Strategic Alliances), pp. 306–325.

Ariño, A., Reuer, J.J., Mayer, K.J. and Jané, J. 2014, "Contracts, negotiation, and learning: an examination of termination provisions," *Journal of Management Studies*, vol. 51, no. 3, pp. 379–405.

Ariño, A. and Ring, P.S. 2010, "The role of fairness in alliance formation," *Strategic Management Journal*, vol. 31, no. 10, pp. 1054–1087.

Bain, J.S. 1956, *Barriers to new competition*, Cambridge, MA: Harvard University Press.

Bain, J.S. 1950, "Workable competition in oligopoly: theoretical considerations and some empirical evidence," *American Economic Review*, vol. 40, no. 2, pp. 35–47.

Bamford, J., Gomes-Casseres, B. and Robinson, M. 2004, *Mastering alliance strategies*, San Francisco, CA: Jossey-Bass.

Barney, J. 1991, "Firm resources and sustained competitive advantage," *Journal of Management*, vol. 17, no. 1, p. 99.

Barney, J.B. 1986, "Strategic factor markets: expectations, luck, and business strategy," *Management Science*, vol. 32, no. 10, pp. 1231–1241.

Berg, S.V., Duncan, J. and Friedman, P. 1982, *Joint venture strategies and corporate innovation*, Cambridge: Oelgeschlager, Gunn and Hain.

Bessembinder, H., Kahle, K.M., Maxwell, W.F. and Xu, D. 2009, "Measuring abnormal bond performance," *Review of Financial Studies*, vol. 22, no. 10, pp. 4219–4258.

Bessembinder, H. and Maxwell, W. 2008, "Markets: transparency and the corporate bond market," *Journal of Economic Perspectives*, vol. 22, no. 2, pp. 217–234.

Black, F. and Scholes, M. 1973, "The pricing of options and corporate liabilities," *Journal of Political Economy*, vol. 81, no. 3, pp. 637–654.

Bleeke, J. and Ernst, D. 1993, *Collaborating to compete: using strategic alliances and acquisitions in the global marketplace*, New York: John Wiley and Sons Inc.

Bösecke, K. and Pfaffenberger, W. 2009, *Value creation in mergers, acquisitions, and alliances*, Wiesbaden: Gabler.

Bowman, E.H. and Hurry, D. 1993, "Strategy through the option lens: an integrated view of resource investments and the incremental-choice process," *Academy of Management Review*, vol. 18, no. 4, pp. 760–782.

Bowman, E.H. and Moskowitz, G.T. 2001, "Real options analysis and strategic decision making," *Organization Science*, vol. 12, no. 6, pp. 772–777.

Brealey, R., Myers, S. and Allen, F. 2008, *Principles of corporate finance*, 9th edition, Boston: McGraw-Hill/Irwin.

Bresman, H., Birkinshaw, J. and Nobel, R. 1999, "Knowledge transfer in international acquisitions," *Journal of International Business Studies*, vol. 30, no. 3, pp. 439–462.

Brooke, J. and Oliver, B. 2005, "The source of abnormal returns from strategic alliance announcements," *Pacific-Basin Finance Journal*, vol. 13, no. 2, pp. 145–161.

Brown, S.J. and Warner, J.B. 1985, "Using daily stock returns: the case of event studies," *Journal of Financial Economics*, vol. 14, no. 1, pp. 3–31.

Brown, S.J. and Warner, J.B. 1980, "Measuring security price performance," *Journal of Financial Economics*, vol. 8, no. 3, pp. 205–258.

Caves, R.E. and Porter, M.E. 1978, "Market structure, oligopoly, and stability of market shares," *Journal of Industrial Economics*, vol. 26, no. 4, pp. 289–313.

Caves, R.E. and Porter, M.E. 1977, "From entry barriers to mobility barriers: conjectural decisions and contrived deterrence to new competition," *Quarterly Journal of Economics*, vol. 19, no. 2, pp. 241–261.

Chan, S.H., Kensinger, J.W., Keown, A.J. and Martin, J.D. 1997, "Do strategic alliances create value?" *Journal of Financial Economics*, vol. 46, no. 2, pp. 199–221.

Chi, T. 2000, "Option to acquire or divest a joint venture," *Strategic Management Journal*, vol. 21, no. 6, pp. 665–687.

Child, J. and Faulkner, D. 1998, *Strategies of cooperation: managing alliances, networks, and joint ventures*, Oxford: Oxford University Press.

Chung, I.Y., Koford, K.J. and Lee, I. 1993, "Stock market views of corporate multinationalism: some evidence from announcements of international joint ventures," *Quarterly Review of Economics and Finance*, vol. 33, no. 3, pp. 275–293.

Coase, R.H. 1952 [1937], "The nature of the firm," in *Readings in price theory*, ed. G.J. Stigler and K.E. Boulding, Homewood, IL: Irwin, pp. 386–405.

Cohen, W.M. and Levinthal, D.A. 1990, "Absorptive capacity: a new perspective on learning and innovation," *Administrative Science Quarterly*, vol. 35, no. 1 (Special Issue: Technology, Organizations, and Innovation), pp. 128–152.

Collis, D.J. and Montgomery, C.A. 1998, "Creating corporate advantage," *Harvard Business Review*, vol. 76, no. 3, pp. 70–83.

Contractor, F.J. and Lorange, P. 1988, *Cooperative strategies in international business: joint ventures and technology, partnerships between firms*, Lexington, MA: Lexington Books.

Copeland, T., Koller, T. and Murrin, J. 2000, *Valuation, measuring and managing the value of companies*, 3rd edition, New Jersey: John Wiley and Sons Inc.

Corrado, C.J. 2011, "Event studies: a methodology review," *Accounting and Finance*, vol. 51, no. 1, pp. 207–234.

Cyert, R.M. and March, J.G. 1963, *A behavioral theory of the firm*, Englewood Cliffs, NJ: Prentice-Hall.

Damodaran, A. 2012, *Investment valuation: tools and techniques for determining the value of any asset*, New York: Wiley.

Damodaran, A. 2008, *Strategic risk taking: a framework for risk management*, Upper Saddle River, NJ: Prentice-Hall.

Damodaran, A. 2005, *The value of synergy*, working paper edition, New York: Stern Business School.

Das, S., Sen, P.K. and Sengupta, S. 1998, "Impact of strategic alliances on firm valuation," *Academy of Management Journal*, vol. 41, no. 1, pp. 27–41.

Das, T.K. and Teng, B. 2002, "The dynamics of alliance conditions in the alliance development process," *Journal of Management Studies*, vol. 39, no. 5, pp. 725–746.

Das, T.K. and Teng, B. 2000a, "Instabilities of strategic alliances: an internal tensions perspective," *Organization Science*, vol. 11, no. 1, pp. 77–101.

Das, T.K. and Teng, B. 2000b, "A resource-based theory of strategic alliances," *Journal of Management*, vol. 26, no. 1, pp. 31–61.

Dierickx, I. and Cool, K. 1989, "Asset stock accumulation and sustainability of competitive advantage," *Management Science*, vol. 35, no. 12, pp. 1504–1511.

Doz, Y.L. 1996, "The evolution of cooperation in strategic alliances: initial conditions or learning processes?" *Strategic Management Journal*, vol. 17, no. S1 (Special Issue: Evolutionary Perspectives on Strategy), pp. 55–83.

Dussauge, P., Garrette, B. and Mitchell, W. 2000, "Learning from competing partners: outcomes and durations of scale and link alliances in Europe, North America and Asia," *Strategic Management Journal*, vol. 21, no. 2, pp. 99–126.

Dyer, J.H. and Hatch, N.W. 2006, "Relation-specific capabilities and barriers to knowledge transfers: creating advantage through network relationships," *Strategic Management Journal*, vol. 27, no. 8, pp. 701–719.

Dyer, J.H., Kale, P. and Singh, H. 2004, "When to ally and when to acquire (cover story)," *Harvard Business Review*, vol. 82, no. 7, pp. 108–115.

Dyer, J.H. and Singh, H. 1998, "The relational view: cooperative strategy and sources of interorganizational competitive advantage," *Academy of Management Review*, vol. 23, no. 4, pp. 660–679.

Dyer, J.H., Singh, H. and Kale, P. 2008, "Splitting the pie: rent distribution in alliances and networks," *Managerial and Decision Economics*, vol. 29, no. 2, pp. 137–148.

Eisenhardt, K.M. and Martin, J.A. 2000, "Dynamic capabilities: what are they?" *Strategic Management Journal*, vol. 21, nos. 10/11 (Special Issue: The Evolution of Firm Capabilities), pp. 1105–1121.

Eisenhardt, K.M. and Schoonhoven, C.B. 1996, "Resource-based view of strategic alliance formation: strategic and social effects in entrepreneurial firms," *Organization Science*, vol. 7, no. 2, pp. 136–150.

Ernst, D. 2004, "Envisioning collaboration," in *Mastering Alliance Strategies*, ed. J. Bamford, B. Gomes-Casseres and M. Robinson, San Francisco: Jossey-Bass, pp. 19–29.

Fama, E.F. and French, K.R. 1993, "Common risk factors in the returns on stocks and bonds," *Journal of Financial Economics*, vol. 33, no. 1, pp. 3–56.

Fang, E. 2011, "The effect of strategic alliance knowledge complementarity on new product innovativeness in China," *Organization Science*, vol. 22, no. 1, pp. 158–172.

Fernández, P. 2009, *100 questions in finance*, Working Paper WP-817, IESE Business School, Spain.

Fernández, P. 2005a, *Financial literature about discoutned cash flow valuation*, Working Paper No. 606, IESE Business School, Spain.

Fernández, P. 2005b, "Reply to comment on 'The value of tax shields is NOT equal to the present value of tax shields,'" *Quarterly Review of Economics and Finance*, vol. 45, no. 1, pp. 188–192.

Fernández, P. 2004, "The value of tax shields is NOT equal to the present value of tax shields," *Journal of Financial Economics*, vol. 73, no. 1, pp. 145–165.

Fernández, P. 2002, *Valuation methods and shareholder value creation*, California: Academic Press.

Fernández, P. and Bilan, A. 2007, *110 common errors in company valuations*, Working Paper No. 714, IESE Business School, Spain.

Fieten, P., Kruschwitz, L., Laitenberger, J., Löffler, A., Tham, J., Vélez-Pareja, I. and Wonder, N. 2005, "Comment on 'The value of tax shields is NOT equal to the present value of tax shields,'" *Quarterly Review of Economics and Finance*, vol. 45, no. 1, pp. 184–187.

Folta, T.B. and Miller, K.D. 2002, "Real options in equity partnerships," *Strategic Management Journal*, vol. 23, no. 1, pp. 77–88.

García-Canal, E., Duarte, C.L., Criado, J.R. and Llaneza, A.V. 2002, "Accelerating international expansion through global alliances: a typology of cooperative strategies," *Journal of World Business*, vol. 37, no. 2, pp. 91–107.

Goerzen, A. 2007, "Alliance networks and firm performance: the impact of repeated partnerships," *Strategic Management Journal*, vol. 28, no. 5, pp. 487–509.

Gomes-Casseres, B., Hagedoorn, J. and Jaffe, A.B. 2006, "Do alliances promote knowledge flows?," *Journal of Financial Economics*, vol. 80, no. 1, pp. 5–33.

Grant, R.M. 1996a, "Toward a knowledge-based theory of the firm," *Strategic Management Journal*, vol. 17, no. S2 (Special Issue: Knowledge and the Firm), pp. 109–122.

Grant, R.M. 1996b, "Prospering in dynamically-competitive environments: organizational capability as knowledge integration," *Organization Science*, vol. 7, no. 4, pp. 375–387.

Grant, R.M. 1991, "The resource-based perspective of competitive advantage," *California Management Review*, vol. 33, pp. 114–135.

Grant, R.M. and Baden-Fuller, C. 2004, "A knowledge accessing theory of strategic alliances," *Journal of Management Studies*, vol. 41, no. 1, pp. 61–84.

Grant, R.M. and Baden-Fuller, C. 1995, "A knowledge-based theory of inter-firm collaboration," *Academy of Management Best Papers Proceedings*, no. 1, pp. 17–21.

Gulati, R. 1998, "Alliances and networks," *Strategic Management Journal*, vol. 19, no. 4 (Special Issue: Editor's Choice), pp. 293–317.

Gulati, R. 1995, "Does familiarity breed trust? The implications of repeated ties for contractual choice in alliances," *Academy of Management Journal*, vol. 38, no. 1, pp. 85–112.

Gulati, R., Lavie, D. and Singh, H. 2009, "The nature of partnering experience and the gains from alliances," *Strategic Management Journal*, vol. 30, no. 11, pp. 1213–1233.

Gupta, A. and Misra, L. 2000, "The value of experiential learning by organizations: evidence from international joint ventures," *Journal of Financial Research*, vol. 23, no. 1, pp. 77–102.

Hamel, G. 1991, "Competition for competence and inter-partner learning within international strategic alliances," *Strategic Management Journal*, vol. 12, no. S1 (Special Issue: Global Strategy), pp. 83–103.

Harrigan, K.R. 1985, *Strategies for joint ventures*, Lexington, MA; Lexington Books.

Heimeriks, K.H. and Vanhaverbeke, W. 2007, "Alliance capability as a mediator between experience and alliance performance: an empirical investigation into the alliance capability development process," *Journal of Management Studies*, vol. 44, no. 1, pp. 25–49.

Helfat, C.E., Finkelstein, S., Mitchell, W., Peteraf, M.A., Singh, H., Teece, D.J. and Winter, S.G. 2007, *Dynamic capabilities: understanding strategic change in organizations*, Malden, MA, and Oxford: Blackwell.

Hennart, J. 1988, "A transaction costs theory of equity joint ventures," *Strategic Management Journal*, vol. 9, no. 4, pp. 361–374.

Hitt, M.A., Dacin, M.T., Levitas, E., Arregle, J. and Borza, A. 2000, "Partner selection in emerging and developed market contexts: resource-based and organizational learning perspectives," *Academy of Management Journal*, vol. 43, no. 3, pp. 449–467.

Hoang, H. and Rothaermel, F.T. 2005, "The effect of general and partner-specific alliance experience on joint R&D project performance," *Academy of Management Journal*, vol. 48, no. 2, pp. 332–345.

Hull, J. 2000, *Options, futures, and other derivatives*, 4th edition, Upper Saddle River, NJ, and London: Prentice-Hall International.

Inkpen, A.C. 2000, "Learning through joint ventures: a framework of knowledge acquisition," *Journal of Management Studies*, vol. 37, no. 7, pp. 1019–1043.

Inkpen, A. 1998a, "Learning, knowledge acquisition, and strategic alliances," *European Management Journal*, vol. 16, no. 2, pp. 223–229.

Inkpen, A.C. 1998b, "Learning and knowledge acquisition through international strategic alliances," *Academy of Management Executive*, vol. 12, no. 4 (Special Issue: Competitiveness and Global Leadership in the 21st Century), pp. 69–80.

Inkpen, A.C. and Beamish, P.W. 1997, "Knowledge, bargaining power, and the instability of international joint ventures," *Academy of Management Review*, vol. 22, no. 1, pp. 177–202.

Ireland, R.D., Hitt, M.A. and Vaidyanath, D. 2002, "Alliance management as a source of competitive advantage," *Journal of Management*, vol. 28, no. 3, pp. 413–446.

Johnson, S.A. and Houston, M.B. 2000, "A reexamination of the motives and gains in joint ventures," *Journal of Financial and Quantitative Analysis*, vol. 35, no. 1, pp. 67–85.

Kale, P., Dyer, J.H. and Singh, H. 2002, "Alliance capability, stock market response, and long-term alliance success: the role of the alliance function," *Strategic Management Journal*, vol. 23, no. 8, pp. 747–767.

Kale, P., Dyer, J. and Singh, H. 2001, "Value creation and success in strategic alliances: alliancing skills and the role of alliance structure and systems," *European Management Journal*, vol. 19, no. 5, pp. 463–471.

Kale, P. and Singh, H. 2009, "Managing strategic alliances: what do we know now, and where do we go from here?" *Academy of Management Perspectives*, vol. 23, no. 3, pp. 45–62.

Kale, P. and Singh, H. 2007, "Building firm capabilities through learning: the role of the alliance learning process in alliance capability and firm-level alliance success," *Strategic Management Journal*, vol. 28, no. 10, pp. 981–1000.

Kale, P., Singh, H. and Bell, J. 2009, "Relating well: building capabilities for sustaining alliance networks," in *The network challenge: strategies for managing the new interlinked enterprise*, ed. P. Kleindorfer and Y. Wind, London: Pearson Press, pp. 353–363.

Keasler, T.R. and Denning, K.C. 2009, "A re-examination of corporate strategic alliances: new market responses," *Quarterly Journal of Finance and Accounting*, vol. 48, no. 1, pp. 21–47.

Kester, W.C. 1984, "Today options for tomorrow's growth," *Harvard Business Review*, vol. 62, no. 2, pp. 153–160.

Kogut, B. 1991, "Joint ventures and the option to expand and acquire," *Management Science*, vol. 37, no. 1, pp. 19–33.

Kogut, B. 1989, "The stability of joint ventures: reciprocity and competitive rivalry," *Journal of Industrial Economics*, vol. 38, no. 2, pp. 183–198.

Kogut, B. 1988, "Joint ventures: theoretical and empirical perspectives," *Strategic Management Journal*, vol. 9, no. 4, pp. 319–332.

Kogut, B. and Kulatilaka, N. 2001, "Capabilities as real options," *Organization Science*, vol. 12, no. 6, pp. 744–758.

Kogut, B. and Zander, U. 1993, "Knowledge of the firm and the evolutionary theory of the multinational corporation," *Journal of International Business Studies*, vol. 24, no. 4, pp. 625–645.

Kogut, B. and Zander, U. 1992, "Knowledge of the firm, combinative capabilities, and the replication of technology," *Organization Science*, vol. 3, no. 3 (Focused Issue: Management of Technology), pp. 383–397.

Koh, J. and Venkatraman, N. 1991, "Joint venture formations and stock market reactions: an assessment in the information technology sector," *Academy of Management Journal*, vol. 34, no. 4, pp. 869–892.

Kothari, S.P. and Warner, J.B. 2005, "The econometrics of event studies" in *Handbook of corporate finance: empirical corporate finance*, ed. B. EckboEspen, North-Holland: Elsevier, pp. 3–36.

Koza, M.P. and Lewin, A.Y. 1998, "The co-evolution of strategic alliances," *Organization Science*, vol. 9, no. 3 (Special Issue: Managing Partnerships and Strategic Alliances), pp. 255–264.

Krychowski, C. and Quélin, B.V. 2010, "Real options and strategic investment decisions: can they be of use to scholars?" *Academy of Management Perspectives*, vol. 24, no. 2, pp. 65–78.

Kumar, M.V.S. 2010, "Differential gains between partners in joint ventures: role of resource appropriation and private benefits," *Organization Science*, vol. 21, no. 1, pp. 232–248.

Kumar, M.V.S. 2007, "Asymmetric wealth gains in joint ventures: theory and evidence," *Finance Research Letters*, vol. 4, no. 1, pp. 19–27.

Lane, P.J. and Lubatkin, M. 1998, "Relative absorptive capacity and interorganizational learning," *Strategic Management Journal*, vol. 19, no. 5, pp. 461–477.

Lavie, D. 2007, "Alliance portfolios and firm performance: a study of value creation and appropriation in the US software industry ," *Strategic Management Journal*, vol. 28, no. 12, pp. 1187–1212.

Lavie, D. 2006, "The competitive advantage of interconnected firms: an extension of the resource-based view," *Academy of Management Review*, vol. 31, no. 3, pp. 638–658.

Lerner, J. and Rajan, R. 2006, "NBER Conference on corporate alliances," *Journal of Financial Economics*, vol. 80, no. 1, pp. 1–3.

Lin, Z, Yang, H. and Arya, B. 2009, "Alliance partners and firm performance: resource complementarity and status association," *Strategic Management Journal*, vol. 30, no. 9, pp. 921–940.

Makhija, M. 2003, "Comparing the resource-based and market-based views of the firm: empirical evidence from Czech privatization," *Strategic Management Journal*, vol. 24, no. 5, pp. 433–451.

Mantecon, T. and Chatfield, R.E. 2007, "An analysis of the disposition of assets in a joint venture," *Journal of Banking and Finance*, vol. 31, no. 9, pp. 2591–2611.

Mason, E.S. 1964, *Economic concentration and the monopoly problem*, New York: Atheneum.

Mathews, R.D. 2006, "Strategic alliances, equity stakes, and entry deterrence," *Journal of Financial Economics*, vol. 80, no. 1, pp. 35–79.

McConnell, J.J. and Nantell, T.J. 1985, "Corporate combinations and common stock returns: the case of joint ventures," *Journal of Finance*, vol. 40, no. 2, pp. 519–536.

Mitsuhashi, H. and Greve, H.R. 2009, "A matching theory of alliance formation and organizational success: complementarity and compatibility," *Academy of Management Journal*, vol. 52, no. 5, pp. 975–995.

Mohanram, P. and Nanda, A. 1996, "When do joint ventures create value?" *Academy of Management Best Papers Proceedings*, no. 1, pp. 36–40.

Mowery, D.C., Oxley, J.E. and Silverman, B.S. 1996, "Strategic alliances and interfirm knowledge transfer," *Strategic Management Journal*, vol. 17, no. S2 (Special Issue: Knowledge and the Firm), pp. 77–91.

Myers, S.C. 1977, "Determinants of corporate borrowing," *Journal of Financial Economics*, vol. 5, no. 2, pp. 147–175.

Nelson, R.R. and Winter, S.G. 1982, *An evolutionary theory of economic change*, Cambridge, MA: Harvard University Press.

Nonaka, I. 1994, "A dynamic theory of organizational knowledge creation," *Organization Science*, vol. 5, no. 1, pp. 14–37.

Nonaka, I. 1991, "The knowledge-creating company," *Harvard Business Review*, vol. 69, no. 6, pp. 96–104.

Parkhe, A. 1991, "Interfirm diversity, organizational learning, and longevity in global strategic alliances," *Journal of International Business Studies*, vol. 22, no. 4, pp. 579–601.

Peng, M.W. 2003, "Institutional transitions and strategic choices," *Academy of Management Review*, vol. 28, no. 2, pp. 275–296.

Peng, M.W. and Shenkar, O. 2002, "Joint venture dissolution as corporate divorce," *Academy of Management Executive*, vol. 16, no. 2, pp. 92–105.

Penrose, E.T. 1959, *The theory of the growth of the firm*, London: Basil Blackwell.

Peteraf, M.A. 1993, "The cornerstones of competitive advantage: a resource-based view," *Strategic Management Journal*, vol. 14, no. 3, pp. 179–191.

Porrini, P. 2004, "Can a previous alliance between an acquirer and a target affect acquisition performance?" *Journal of Management*, vol. 30, no. 4, pp. 545–562.

Porter, M.E. 1990, *Competitive advantage of nations*, New York: The Free Press.

Porter, M.E. 1985, *Competitive advantage: creating and sustaining superior performance*, New York: The Free Press.

Porter, M.E. 1979a, "How competitive forces shape strategy," *Harvard Business Review*, vol. 57, no. 2, pp. 137–145.

Porter, M.E. 1979b, "The structure within industries and companies' performance," *Review of Economics and Statistics*, vol. 61, no. 2, pp. 214–227.

Prahalad, C.K. and Hamel, G. 1990, "The core competence of the corporation," *Harvard Business Review*, vol. 68, no. 3, pp. 79–91.

Ragozzino, R. and Moschieri, C. 2014, "When theory doesn't meet practice: do firms really stage their investments?" *Academy of Management Perspectives*, vol. 28, no. 1, pp. 22–37.

Reuer, J.J. and Ariño, A. 2007, "Strategic alliance contracts: dimensions and determinants of contractual complexity," *Strategic Management Journal*, vol. 28, no. 3, pp. 313–330.

Reuer, J.J. and Koza, M.P. 2000, "Asymmetric information and joint venture performance: theory and evidence for domestic and international joint ventures," *Strategic Management Journal*, vol. 21, no. 1, pp. 81–88.

Reuer, J.J. and Leiblein, M.J. 2000, "Downside risk implications of multinationality and international joint ventures," *Academy of Management Journal*, vol. 43, no. 2, pp. 203–214.

Reuer, J.J., Park, K.M. and Zollo, M. 2002, "Experimental learning in international joint ventures: the role of experience heterogeneity and venture novelty," in *Cooperative strategies and alliances*, ed. F.J. Contractor and P. Lorange, Amsterdam: Elsevier Science, pp. 321–346.

Reuer, J.J. and Tong, T.W. 2010, "Discovering valuable growth opportunities: an analysis of equity alliances with IPO firms," *Organization Science*, vol. 21, no. 1, pp. 202–215.

Robinson, D.T. 2008, "Strategic alliances and the boundaries of the firm," *Review of Financial Studies*, vol. 21, no. 2, pp. 649–681.

Rothaermel, F.T. and Boeker, W. 2008, "Old technology meets new technology: complementarities, similarities, and alliance formation," *Strategic Management Journal*, vol. 29, no. 1, pp. 47–77.

Rothaermel, F.T. and Deeds, D.L. 2004, "Exploration and exploitation alliances in biotechnology: a system of new product development," *Strategic Management Journal*, vol. 25, no. 3, pp. 201–221.

Sánchez-Lorda, P. and García-Canal, E. 2012, "When and how previous experience affects the stock market reaction to business combinations," *European Journal of Cross-Cultural Competence and Management*, vol. 2, no. 3, pp. 319–343.

Schreiner, M., Kale, P. and Corsten, D. 2009, "What really is alliance management capability and how does it impact alliance outcomes and success?" *Strategic Management Journal*, vol. 30, no. 13, pp. 1395–1419.

Shi, W., Sun, J. and Prescott, J.E. 2012, "A temporal perspective of merger and acquisition and strategic alliance initiatives: review and future direction," *Journal of Management*, vol. 38, no. 1, pp. 164–209.

Simonin, B.L. 1997, "The importance of collaborative know-how: an empirical test of the learning organization," *Academy of Management Journal*, vol. 40, no. 5, pp. 1150–1174.

Stuart, T.E. 2000, "Interorganizational alliances and the performance of firms: a study of growth and innovation rates in a high-technology industry," *Strategic Management Journal*, vol. 21, no. 8, pp. 791–811.

Teece, D.J. 1987, "The competitive challenge," in *Profiting from technological innovation: implications for integration collaboration, licensing and public policy*, ed. D.J. Teece, Cambridge, MA: Ballinger, pp. 185–219.

Teece, D.J., Pisano, G. and Shuen, A. 1997, "Dynamic capabilities and strategic management," *Strategic Management Journal*, vol. 18, no. 7, pp. 509–533.

Vanhaverbeke, W., Duysters, G. and Noorderhaven, N. 2002, "External technology sourcing through alliances or acquisitions: an analysis of the application-specific integrated circuits industry," *Organization Science*, vol. 13, no. 6, pp. 714–733.

Vickers, J. 1985, "Pre-emptive patenting, joint ventures, and the persistence of oligopoly," *International Journal of Industrial Organization*, vol. 3, no. 3, pp. 261–273.

Villalonga, B. and McGahan, A.M. 2005, "The choice among acquisitions, alliances, and divestitures," *Strategic Management Journal*, vol. 26, no. 13, pp. 1183–1208.

Wang, L. and Zajac, E.J. 2007, "Alliance or acquisition? A dyadic perspective on interfirm resource combinations," *Strategic Management Journal*, vol. 28, no. 13, pp. 1291–1317.

Wassmer, U. and Dussauge, P. 2012, "Network resource stocks and flows: how do alliance portfolios affect the value of new alliance formations?" *Strategic Management Journal*, vol. 33, no. 7, pp. 871–883.

Wernerfelt, B. 1984, "A resource-based view of the firm," *Strategic Management Journal*, vol. 5, no. 2, pp. 171–180.

Williamson, O.E. 1991, "Comparative economic organization: the analysis of discrete structural alternatives," *Administrative Science Quarterly*, vol. 36, no. 2, pp. 269–296.

Williamson, O.E. 1985, *The economic institutions of capitalism*, New York: The Free Press.

Williamson, O.E. 1981, "The economics of organization: the transaction cost approach," *American Journal of Sociology*, vol. 18, no. 3, pp. 548–577.

Williamson, O.E. 1979, "Transaction-cost economics: the governance of contractual relations," *Journal of Law and Economics*, vol. 22, no. 2, pp. 233–261.

Williamson, O.E. 1975, *Markets and hierarchies*, New York: The Free Press.

Yang, H., Lin, Z. and Lin, Y. 2010, "A multilevel framework of firm boundaries: firm characteristics, dyadic differences, and network attributes," *Strategic Management Journal*, vol. 31, no. 3, pp. 237–261.

Yin, X. and Shanley, M. 2008, "Industry determinants of the "merger versus alliance" decision," *Academy of Management Review*, vol. 33, no. 2, pp. 473–491.

Zahra, S.A. and George, G. 2002, "Absorptive capacity: a review, reconceptualization, and extension," *Academy of Management Review*, vol. 27, no. 2, pp. 185–203.

Zaheer, A., Hernandez, E. and Banerjee, S. 2010, "Prior alliances with targets and acquisition performance in knowledge-intensive industries," *Organization Science*, vol. 21, no. 5, pp. 1072–1091.

Zollo, M. and Reuer, J.J. 2010, "Experience spillovers across corporate development activities," *Organization Science*, vol. 21, no. 6, pp. 1195–1212.

Zollo, M., Reuer, J.J. and Singh, H. 2002, "Interorganizational routines and performance in strategic alliances," *Organization Science*, vol. 13, no. 6, pp. 701–713.

Zollo, M. and Winter, S.G. 2002, "Deliberate learning and the evolution of dynamic capabilities," *Organization Science*, vol. 13, no. 3, pp. 339–351.

INDEX

Page numbers in *italics* denotes a table/figure